HARDPRESS.NET
HOME OF HARD-TO-FIND BOOKS

The Life of Horace Greeley, Editor of the New York Tribune
by James Parton

Address:
HardPress
8345 NW 66TH ST #2561
MIAMI FL 33166-2626
USA
Email: info@hardpress.net

YOUNG GREELEY'S ARRIVAL IN NEW-YORK.

THE LIFE

OF

HORACE GREELEY,

EDITOR OF THE NEW YORK TRIBUNE

BY J. PARTON.

"If, on a full and final review, my life and practice shall be found unworthy my principles, let due infamy be heaped on my memory ; but let none be thereby led to distrust the principles to which I proved recreant, nor yet the ability of some to adorn them by a suitable life
and conversation. To unerring time be all this committed."

Horace Greeley in 1846.

NEW YORK:
PUBLISHED BY MASON BROTHERS.
1855.

STEREOTYPED BY

THOMAS B. SMITH,

216 William St., N. Y.

PRINTED BY

JOHN A. GRAY

95 & 97 Cliff St.

TO

THE YOUNG MEN OF THE FREE STATES,

𝕿𝖍𝖎𝖘 𝖁𝖔𝖑𝖚𝖒𝖊

IS RESPECTFULLY DEDICATED

BY ONE OF THEIR NUMBER.

THE JOURNALISTS ARE NOW THE TRUE KINGS AND CLERGY: HENCE-
FORTH HISTORIANS, UNLESS THEY ARE FOOLS, MUST WRITE NOT OF BOUR-
BON DYNASTIES, AND TUDORS, AND HAPSBURGS; BUT OF STAMPED, BROAD-
SHEET DYNASTIES, AND QUITE NEW SUCCESSIVE NAMES, ACCORDING AS
THIS OR THE OTHER ABLE EDITOR, OR COMBINATION OF ABLE EDITORS,
GAINS THE WORLD'S EAR.

Sartor Resartus.

Preface.

JUSTICE, alike to the author and to his subject, demands the explicit statement of a fact.

Horace Greeley is wholly innocent of this book. Until I had determined to write it, I had no acquaintance with him of a personal nature, and no connection except that which exists between every subscriber to the Tribune and its editor. Since that time, I have had a few short interviews with him—heard and overheard a few facts of his career from his own lips —had two or three of my best stories spoiled by his telling me that that part of them which redounded most to his credit was untrue. He has had nothing whatever to do with the composition of the volume, nor has he seen a page of it in manuscript or proof, nor does he know one word of its contents.

I undertook the task simply and solely because I liked the man, because I gloried in his career, because I thought the story of his life ought to be told.

The writings of an editor usually pass away with the occasions that called them forth. They may have aroused, amused,

instructed and advanced a nation—many nations. They may
have saved or overturned systems and dynasties; provoked or
prevented wars, revolutions and disasters; thrown around
Prejudice and Bigotry the decent mantle of Respectability, or
torn it off; made great truths familiar and fruitful in the public mind, or given a semblance of dignity to the vulgar hue
and cry which assails such truths always when they are new.
These things, and others equally important, an editor may do,
editors have done. But he rarely has leisure to produce a
WORK which shall perpetuate his name and personal influence.
A collection of his editorial writings will not do it, for he is
compelled to write hastily, diffusely, and on the topics of the
hour. The story of his life *may*. It is the simple narratives
in Franklin's autobiography that have perpetuated, not the
name of that eminent man, the thunder and lightning have his
name in charge, but the influence of his personality in forming
the characters of his countrymen.

The reader has a right to know the manner in which the facts
and incidents of this work were obtained. I procured, first of
all, from various sources, a list of Mr. Greeley's early friends,
partners and relations; also, a list of the places at which he
has resided. All of those places I visited; with as many of
those persons as I could find I conversed, and endeavored to
extract from them all they knew of the early life of my hero.
From their narratives, and from the letters of others to whom
I wrote, the account of his early life was compiled. To all of
them, for the readiness with which they made their communications, to many of them for their generous and confiding hos-

pitality to a stranger, I again offer the poor return of my sincere thanks.

For the rest, I am indebted to the following works : E. L. Parker's History of Londonderry; the Bedford Centennial; the New Hampshire Book; the Rose of Sharon; the Life of Margaret Fuller; Horace Greeley's Hints towards Reforms, and Glances at Europe; also, to files of the New Yorker, Log Cabin, Jeffersonian, American Laborer, Whig Almanac, and Tribune. Nearly every number—there are more than five thousand numbers in all—of each of those periodicals, I have examined, and taken from them what they contain respecting the life and fortunes of their editor.

This book is as true as I could make it; nothing has been inserted or suppressed for the sake of making out a case. Errors of detail in a work containing so many details as this can scarcely be avoided; but upon the correctness of every important statement, and upon the general fidelity of the picture presented, the reader may rely. Horace Greeley, as the reader will discover, has been a marked person from his earliest childhood, and he is remembered by his early friends with a vividness and affection very extraordinary. Moreover, in the political and personal contentions of his public life, he has frequently been compelled to become autobiographical; therefore, in this volume he often tells his own story. That he tells it truly, that he is incapable of insincerity, every one with truth enough in his heart to recognize truth in others will perceive.

The opinion has been recently expressed that the life of a man ought not to be written in his lifetime. To which, among

many other things, this might be replied : If the lives of pol
iticians like Tyler, Pierce, and others, may be written in
their lifetime, with a view to subserve the interests of party,
why may not the life of Horace Greeley, in the hope of sub-
serving the interests of the country ?   Besides, those who think
this work ought not to have been written are at liberty not to
read it.

There are those who *will* read it ; and, imperfect as it is, with
pleasure.   They are those who have taken an interest in Horace Greeley's career, and would like to know how he came to
be the man he is.   J. P.

New York, December, 1854

CONTENTS.

CHAPTER I.

THE SCOTCH-IRISH OF NEW HAMPSHIRE.

CHAPTER II.

ANCESTORS.—PARENTAGE.—BIRTH.

CHAPTER III.

EARLY CHILDHOOD.

CHAPTER VII.

HE WANDERS.

CHAPTER VIII.

ARRIVAL IN NEW YORK.

CHAPTER IX.

FROM OFFICE TO OFFICE.

CHAPTER X.

THE FIRST PENNY PAPER—AND WHO THOUGHT OF IT

CHAPTER XVI.

THE TRIBUNE AND FOURIERISM.

CHAPTER XVII.

THE TRIBUNE'S SECOND YEAR.

CHAPTER XVIII.

THE TRIBUNE AND J. FENIMORE COOPER.

CHAPTER XIX.

THE TRIBUNE CONTINUES.

CHAPTER XX.

MARGARET FULLER.

CHAPTER XXIX.

POSITION AND INFLUENCE OF HORACE GREELEY.

CHAPTER XXX.

APPEARANCE—MANNERS—HABITS.

CHAPTER XXXI.

THE LIFE OF HORACE GREELEY.

CHAPTER I.

THE SCOTCH-IRISH OF NEW HAMPSHIRE.

Londonderry in Ireland—The Siege—Emigration to New England—Settlement of Londonderry, New Hampshire—The Scotch-Irish introduce the culture of the potato and the manufacture of linen—Character of the Scotch-Irish—Their simplicity—Love of fun—Stories of the early clergymen—Traits in the Scotch-Irish character—Zeal of the Londonderrians in the Revolution—Horace Greeley's allusion to his Scotch-Irish ancestry.

NEW HAMPSHIRE, the native State of Horace Greeley, was settled in part by colonists from Massachusetts and Connecticut, and in part by emigrants from the north of Ireland. The latter were called Scotch-Irish, for a reason which a glance at their history will show.

Ulster, the most northern of the four provinces of Ireland, has been, during the last two hundred and fifty years, superior to the rest in wealth and civilization. The cause of its superiority is known. About the year 1612, when James I. was king, there was a rebellion of the Catholics in the north of Ireland. Upon its suppression, Ulster, embracing the six northern counties, and containing half a million acres of land, fell to the king by the attainder of the rebels. Under royal encouragement and furtherance, a company was formed in London for the purpose of planting colonies in that fertile province, which lay waste from the ravages of the recent war. The land was divided into shares, the largest of which did not exceed two thousand acres. Colonists were invited over from England and Scotland. The natives were expelled from their fastnesses in the hills, and forced to settle upon the plains. Some efforts, it appears, were made to teach them arts and agriculture. Robbery and assassination were punished. And, thus, by the infusion of new blood, and the partial improvement of the ancient race, Ulster, which had been the most savage and turbulent of the Irish provinces, became, and remains to this day, the best cultivated, the richest, and the most civilized.

One of the six counties was Londonderry, the capital of which, called by the same name, had been sacked and razed during the rebellion. The city was now rebuilt by a company of adventurers from London, and the county was settled by a colony from Argyleshire in Scotland, who were thenceforth called Scotch-Irish. Of what stuff these Scottish colonists were made, their after-history amply and gloriously shows. The colony took root and flourished in Londonderry. In 1689, the year of the immortal siege, the city was an important fortified town of twenty-seven thousand inhabitants, and the county was proportionally populous and productive. William of Orange had reached the British throne. James II. returning from France had landed in Ireland, and was making an effort to recover his lost inheritance. The Irish Catholics were still loyal to him, and hastened to rally round his banner. But Ulster was Protestant and Presbyterian; the city of Londonderry was Ulster's stronghold, and it was the chief impediment in the way of James' proposed descent upon Scotland. With what resolution and daring the people of Londonderry, during the ever-memorable siege of that city, fought and endured for Protestantism and freedom, the world well knows. For seven months they held out against a besieging army, so numerous that its slain numbered nine thousand. The besieged lost three thousand men. To such extremities were they reduced, that among the market quotations of the times, we find items like these:—a quarter of a dog, five shillings and six-pence; a dog's head, two and six-pence; horse-flesh, one and six-pence per pound; horse-blood, one shilling per quart; a cat, four and six-pence; a rat, one shilling; a mouse, six-pence. When all the food that remained in the city was nine half-starved horses and a pint of meal per man, the people were still resolute. At the very last extremity, they were relieved by a provisioned fleet, and the army of James retired in despair.

On the settlement of the kingdom under William and Mary, the

Presbyterians of Londonderry did not find themselves in the enjoyment of the freedom to which they conceived themselves entitled. They were dissenters from the established church. Their pastors were not recognized by the law as clergymen, nor their places of worship as churches. Tithes were exacted for the support of the Episcopal clergy. They were not proprietors of the soil, but held their lands as tenants of the crown. They were hated alike, and equally, by the Irish Catholics and the English Episcopalians. When, therefore, in 1617, a son of one of the leading clergyman returned from New England with glowing accounts of that 'plantation,' a furor of emigration arose in the town and county of Londonderry, and portions of four Presbyterian congregations, with their four pastors, united in a scheme for a simultaneous removal across the seas. One of the clergymen was first despatched to Boston to make the needful inquiries and arrangements. He was the bearer of an address to " His Excellency, the Right Honorable Colonel Samuel Smith, Governor of New England," which assured his Excellency of " our sincère and hearty inclination to transport ourselves to that very excellent and renowned plantation, upon our obtaining from his Excellency suitable encouragement." To this address, the original of which still exists, two hundred and seven names were appended, and all but seven in the hand-writing of the individuals signing—a fact which proves the superiority of the emigrants to the majority of their countrymen, both in position and intelligence. One of the subscribers was a baronet, nine were clergymen, and three others were graduates of the University of Edinburgh.

On the fourth of August, 1718, the advance party of Scotch-Irish emigrants arrived in five ships at Boston. Some of them remained in that city and founded the church in Federal street, of which Dr. Channing was afterwards pastor. Others attempted to settle in Worcester ; but as they were Irish *and* Presbyterians, such a storm of prejudice against them arose among the enlightened Congregationalists of that place, that they were obliged to flee before it, and seek refuge in the less populous places of Massachusetts. Sixteen families, after many months of tribulation and wandering, selected for their permanent abode a tract twelve miles square, called Nutfield, which now embraces the townships of London derry, Derry and Winham, in Rockingham county, New Hamp shire. The land was a free gift from the king, in consideration of the services rendered his throne by the people of Londonderry in the defense of their city. To each settler was assigned a farm of one hundred and twenty acres, a house lot, and an out lot of sixty acres. The lands of the men who had personally served during the siege, were exempted from taxation, and were known down to the period of the revolution as the *Exempt Farms*. The settlement of Londonderry attracted new emigrants, and it soon became one of the most prosperous and famous in the colony.

It was there that the potato was first cultivated, and there that linen was first made in New England. The English colonists at that day appear to have been unacquainted with the culture of the potato, and the familiar story of the Andover farmer who mistook the balls which grow on the potato vine for the genuine fruit of the plant, is mentioned by a highly respectable historian of New Hampshire as " a well-authenticated fact."

With regard to the linen manufacture, it may be mentioned as a proof of the thrift and skill of the Scotch-Irish settlers, that, as early as the year 1748, the linens of Londonderry had so high a reputation in the colonies, that it was found necessary to take measures to prevent the linens made in other towns from being fraudulently sold for those of Londonderry manufacture. A town meeting was held in that year for the purpose of appointing " fit and proper persons to survey and inspect linens and hollands made in the town for sale, so that the credit of our manufactory be kept up, and the purchaser of our linens may not be imposed upon with foreign and outlandish linens in the name of ours." Inspectors and sealers were accordingly appointed, who were to examine and stamp " all the hollands made and to be made in our town, whether brown, white, speckled, or checked, that are to be exposed for sale ;" for which service they were empowered to demand from the owner of said linen " sixpence, old tenor, for each piece." And this occurred within thirty years from the erection of the first log-hut in the township of Londonderry. However, the people had brought their spinning and weaving implements with them from Ireland, and their industry was not once interrupted by an attack of Indians.

These Scotch-Irish of Londonderry were a very peculiar people.

They were *Scotch-Irish* in character and in name; of Irish vivacity, generosity, and daring; Scotch in frugality, industry, and resolution; a race in whose composition nature seems, for once, to have kindly blended the qualities that render men interesting with those that render them prosperous. Their habits and their minds were simple. They lived, for many years after the settlement began to thrive, upon the fish which they caught at the falls of Amoskeag, upon game, and upon such products of the soil as beans, potatoes, samp, and barley. It is only since the year 1800 that tea and coffee, those ridiculous and effeminating drinks, came into anything like general use among them. It was not till some time after the Revolution that a chaise was seen in Londonderry, and even then it excited great wonder, and was deemed an unjustifiable extravagance. Shoes, we are told, were little worn in the summer, except on Sundays and holidays; and then they were *carried in the hand to within a short distance of the church, where they were put on !* There was little buying and selling among them, but much borrowing and lending. "If a neighbor killed a calf," says one writer, "no part of it was sold; but it was distributed among relatives and friends, the poor widow always having a piece; and the minister, if he did not get the shoulder, got a portion as good." The women were robust, worked on the farms in the busy seasons, reaping, mowing, and even ploughing on occasion; and the hum of the spinning-wheel was heard in every house. An athletic, active, indomitable, prolific, long-lived race. For a couple to have a dozen children, and for *all* the twelve to reach maturity, to marry, to have large families, and die at a good old age, seems to have been no uncommon case among the original Londonderrians.

Love of fun was one of their marked characteristics. One of their descendants, the Rev. J. H. Morrison, has written—"A prominent trait in the character of the Scotch-Irish was their ready wit. No subject was kept sacred from it; the thoughtless, the grave, the old, and the young, alike enjoyed it. Our fathers were serious, thoughtful men, but they lost no occasion which might promise sport. Weddings, huskings, log-rollings and raisings—what a host of queer stories is connected with them! Our ancestors dearly loved fun. There was a grotesque humor, and yet a seriousness, pathos and *strangeness* about them, which in its way has, perhaps, never been equaled.   It was the sternness of the Scotch Covenanter, softened by a century's residence abroad, amid persecution and trial, wedded to the comic humor and pathos of the Irish, and then grown wild in the woods among their own New England mountains."

There never existed a people at once so jovial and so religious. This volume could be filled with a collection of their religious repartees and pious jokes.   It was Pat. Larkin, a Scotch-Irishman, near Londonderry, who, when he was accused of being a Catholic, because his parents were Catholics, replied: "If a man happened to be born in a stable, would that make him a horse?" and he won his bride by that timely spark.

Quaint, bold, and witty were the old Scotch-Irish clergymen, the men of the siege, as mighty with carnal weapons as with spiritual.   There was no taint of the sanctimonious in *their* rough, honest, and healthy natures.   During the old French war, it is related, a British officer, in a peculiarly "stunning" uniform, came one Sunday morning to the Londonderry Meeting House.   Deeply conscious was this individual that he was exceedingly well dressed, and he took pains to display his finery and his figure by standing in an attitude, during the delivery of the sermon, which had the effect of withdrawing the minds of the young ladies from the same. At length, the minister, who had both fought and preached in Londonderry 'at home,' and feared neither man, beast, devil, nor red-coat, addressed the officer thus : " Ye are a braw lad ; ye ha'e a braw suit of claithes, and we ha'e a' seen them ; *ye may sit doun.*"   The officer subsided instantly, and old Dreadnought went on with his sermon as though nothing had happened.   The same clergyman once began a sermon on the vain self-confidence of St. Peter, with the following energetic remarks : " Just like Peter, aye mair forrit than wise, ganging swaggering about wi' a sword at his side; an' a puir hand he made of it when he came to the trial; for he only cut off a chiel's lug, an' he *ought to ha' split down his head.*"   On another occasion, he is said to have opened on a well-known text in this fashion : " ' I can do all things ;' ay, *can* ye Paul ?   I'll bet ye a dollar o' *that* (placing a dollar on the desk). But stop ! let 's see what else Paul says : ' I can do all things through Christ, which strengtheneth me ;' ay, sae can I, Paul.   I draw my bet," and he returned the dollar to his pocket.   They *prayed* a joke sometimes, those Scotch-Irish clergymen. One pastor, dining with a new settler, who had no table, and served up his dinner in a basket, implored Heaven to bless the man " in his *basket*, and in his store;" which Heaven did, for the man afterwards grew rich. "What is the difference," asked a youth, "between the Congregationalists and Presbyterians?" "The difference is," replied the pastor, with becoming gravity, "that the Congregationalist goes home between the services and eats a regular dinner; but the Presbyterian puts off his till after meeting."

And how pious they were! For many years after the settlement, the omission of the daily act of devotion in a single household would have excited general alarm. It is related as a *fact*, that the first pastor of Londonderry, being informed one evening that an individual was becoming neglectful of family worship, immediately repaired to his dwelling. The family had retired; he called up the master of the house, inquired if the report was true, and asked him whether he had omitted family prayer that evening. The man confessed that he had; and the pastor, having admonished him of his fault, refused to leave the house until the delinquent had called up his wife, and performed with her the omitted observance. The first settlers of some of the towns near Londonderry walked every Sunday eight, ten, twelve miles to church, taking their children with them, and crossing the Merrimac in a canoe or on a raft. The first public enterprises of every settlement were the building of a church, the construction of a block-house for defense against the Indians, and the establishment of a school. In the early times, of course, every man went to church with his gun, and the minister preached peace and good-will with a loaded musket peering above the sides of the pulpit.

The Scotch-Irish were a singularly *honest* people. There is an entry in the town-record for 1734, of a complaint against John Morrison, that, having found an axe on the road, he did not leave it at the next tavern, 'as the laws of the country doth require.' John acknowledged the fact, but pleaded in extenuation, that the axe was of so small value, that it would not have paid the cost of proclaiming. The session, however, censured him severely, and exhorted him to repent of the evil. The following is a curious extract from the records of a Scotch-Irish settlement for 1756: " *Voted*, to give Mr. John Houston equal to forty pounds sterling, in old tenor, as the law shall find the rate in dollars or sterling money, for his yearly stipend, if he is our ordained minister. And what number of Sabbath days, annually, we shall think ourselves not able to pay him, he shall have at his own use and disposal, deducted out of the aforesaid sum in proportion." The early records of those settlements abound in evidence, that the people had an habitual and most scrupulous regard for the rights of one another.

Kind, generous, and compassionate, too, they were. Far back in 1725, when the little colony was but seven years old, and the people were struggling with their first difficulties, we find the session ordering two collections in the church, one to assist James Clark to ransom his son from the Indians, which produced five pounds, and another for the relief of William Moore, whose two cows had been killed by the falling of a tree, which produced three pounds, seventeen shillings. These were great sums in those early days. We read, also, in the History of Londonderry, of MacGregor, its first pastor, becoming the champion and defender of a personal enemy who was accused of arson, but whom the magnanimous pastor believed innocent. He volunteered his defense in court. The man was condemned and imprisoned, but MacGregor continued his exertions in behalf of the prisoner until his innocence was established and the judgment was reversed.

That they were a brave people need scarcely be asserted. Of that very MacGregor the story is told, that when he went out at the head of a committee, to remonstrate with a belligerent party, who were unlawfully cutting hay from the out-lands of Londonderry, and one of the hay-stealers, in the heat of dispute, shook his fist in the minister's face, saying, "Nothing saves you, sir, but your black coat," MacGregor instantly exclaimed, "Well, it shan't save *you*, sir," and pulling off his coat, was about to suit the action to the word, when the enemy beat a sudden retreat, and troubled the Londonderrians no more. The Scotch-Irish of New Hampshire were among the first to catch the spirit of the Revolution. They confronted British troops, and successfully too, *before* the battle of Lexington. Four English soldiers had deserted from their quarters in Boston, and taken refuge in Londonderry. A party of troops, dispatched for their arrest, discovered, secured, and conveyed them part of the way to Boston. A band of young men assembled and pursued them ; and so overawed the British officer by the boldness of their demeanor, that he gave up his prisoners, who were escorted back to Londonderry in triumph. There were remarkably few tories in Londonderry. The town was united almost as one man on the side of Independence, and sent, it is believed, more men to the war, and contributed more money to the cause, than any other town of equal resources in New England. Here are a few of the town-meeting " votes" of the first months of the war : " *Voted*, to give our men that have gone to the Massachusetts government seven dollars a month, until it be known what Congress will do in that affair, and that the officers shall have as much pay as those in the Bay government."—" *Voted*, that a committee of nine men be chosen to inquire into the conduct of those men that are thought not to be friends of their country."—" *Voted*, that the aforesaid committee have no pay."—" *Voted*, that twenty more men be raised immediately, to be ready upon the first emergency, as minute men."— " *Voted*, that twenty more men be enlisted in Capt. Aiken's company, as minute men."—" *Voted*, that the remainder of the stock of powder shall be divided out to every one that hath not already received of the same, as far as it will go ; provided he produces a gun of his own, in good order, and is willing to go against the enemy, and promises not to waste any of the powder, only in self-defense ; and provided, also, that he show twenty good bullets to suit his gun, and six good flints." In 1777 the town gave a bounty of thirty pounds for every man who enlisted for three years. All the records and traditions of the revolutionary period breathe unity and determination Stark, the hero of Bennington, was a Londonderrian.

Such were the Scotch-Irish of New Hampshire ; of such material were the maternal ancestors of Horace Greeley composed ; and from his maternal ancestors he derived much that distinguishes him from men in general.

In the " New Yorker" for August 28, 1841, he alluded to his Scotch-Irish origin in a characteristic way. Noticing Charlotte Elizabeth's " Siege of Derry," he wrote :

" We do not like this work, and we choose to say so frankly. What is the use of reviving and aggravating these old stories (alas !

how true!) of scenes in which Christians of diverse creeds have tortured and butchered each other for the glory of God? We had ancestors in that same Siege of Derry,—on the Protestant side, of course,—and our sympathies are all on that side; but we cannot forget that intolerance and persecution—especially in Ireland—are by no means exclusively *Catholic* errors and crimes. Who persecutes in Ireland *now?* On what principle of Christian toleration are the poor man's pig and potatoes wrested from him to pay tithes to a church he abhors? We do hope the time is soon coming when man will no more persecute his brother for a difference of faith; but that time will never be hastened by the publication of such books as the Siege of Derry."

CHAPTER II.

ANCESTORS.——PARENTAGE.——BIRTH.

Origin of the Family—Old Captain Ezekiel Greeley—Zaccheus Greeley—Zaccheus the Second—Roughness and Tenacity of the Greeley race—Maternal Ancestors of Horace Greeley—John Woodburn—Character of Horace Greeley's Great-grandmother—His Grandmother—Romantic Incident—Horace Greeley is born " as black as a chimney"—Comes to his color—Succeeds to the name of Horace.

THE name of Greeley is an old and not uncommon one in New England. It is spelt Greeley, Greely, Greale, and Greele, but all who bear the name in this country trace their origin to the same source.

The tradition is, that very early in the history of New England— probably as early as 1650—three brothers, named Greeley, emigrated from the neighborhood of Nottingham, England. One of them is supposed to have settled finally in Maine, another in Rhode Island, the third in Massachusetts. All the Greeleys in New England have descended from these three brothers, and the branch of the family with which we have to do, from him who settled in Massachusetts. Respecting the condition and social rank of these brothers, their occupation and character, tradition is silent. But from

the fact that no coat-of-arms has been preserved or ever head of by any member of the family, and from the occupation of the majority of their descendants; it is plausibly conjectured that they were farmers of moderate means and of the middle class.

Tradition further hints that the name of the brother who found a home in Massachusetts was Benjamin, that he was a farmer, that he lived in Haverhill, a township bordering on the south-eastern corner of New Hampshire, that he prospered there, and died respected by all who knew him at a good old age. So far, tradition. We now draw from the memory of individuals still living.

The son of Benjamin Greeley was Ezekiel, "old Captain Ezekiel," who lived and greatly flourished at Hudson, New Hampshire, (then known as Nottingham West,) and is well remembered there, and in all the region round about. The captain was not a military man. He was half lawyer, half farmer. He was a sharp, cunning, scheming, cool-headed, cold-hearted man, one who lived by his wits, who always got his cases, always succeeded in his plans, always prospered in his speculations, and grew rich without ever doing a day's work in his life. He is remembered by his grandsons, who saw him in their childhood, as a black-eyed, black-haired, heavy-browed, stern-looking man, of complexion almost as dark as that of an Indian, and not unlike an Indian in temper. "A cross old dog," "a hard old knot," "as cunning as Lucifer," are among the complimentary expressions bestowed upon him by his descendants. "All he had," says one, "was at the service of the rich, but he was hard upon the poor." "His religion was nominally Baptist," says another, "but really to get money." "He got all he could, and saved all he got," chimes in a third. He died, at the age of sixty-five, with "all his teeth sound, and worth three hundred acres of good land. He is spoken of with that sincere respect which, in New England, seems never to be denied to a very *smart* man, who succeeds by strictly legal means in acquiring property, however wanting in principle, however destitute of feeling, that man may be. Happily, the wife of old Captain Ezekiel was a gentler and better being than her husband.

And, therefore, Zaccheus, the son of old Captain Ezekiel, was a gentler and better man than his father. Zaccheus inherited part of his father's land, and was a farmer all the days of his life. He was not, it appears, "*too* fond of work," though far more industrious

than his father; a man who took life easily, of strict integrity,
kind-hearted, gentle-mannered, not ill to do in the world, but not
what is called in New England "'fore-handed." He is remembered
in the neighborhood where he lived chiefly for his extraordinary
knowledge of the Bible. He could quote texts more readily, correctly, and profusely than any of his neighbors, laymen or clergymen. He had the reputation of knowing the whole Bible by heart.
He was a Baptist; and all who knew him unite in declaring that a
worthier man never lived than Zaccheus Greeley. He had a large
family, and lived to the age of ninety-five.

His second son was named Zaccheus also, and he is the father of
Horace Greeley. He is still living, and cultivates an ample domain
in Erie County, Pennsylvania, acquired in part by his own arduous
labors, in part by the labors of his second son, and in part by the
liberality of his eldest son Horace. At this time, in the seventy-
third year of his age, his form is as straight, his step as decided,
his constitution nearly as firm, and his look nearly as young, as
though he were in the prime of life.

All the Greeleys that I have seen or heard described, are persons
of marked and peculiar characters. Many of them are "characters." The word which perhaps best describes the quality fo
which they are distinguished is *tenacity*. They are, as a race, tenacious of life, tenacious of opinions and preferences, of tenacious
memory, and tenacious of their purposes. One member of the
family died at the age of one hundred and twenty years; and a
large proportion of the early generations lived more than three
score years and ten. Few of the name have been rich, but most
have been persons of substance and respectability, acquiring their
property, generally, by the cultivation of the soil, and a soil, too,
which does not yield its favors to the sluggard. It is the boast
of those members of the family who have attended to its geneal-
ogy, that no Greeley was ever a prisoner, a pauper, or, worse than
either, a tory! Two of Horace Greeley's great uncles perished at
Bennington, and he was fully justified in his assertion, made in the
heat of the Roman controversy a few years ago, that he was "born
of republican parentage, of an ancestry which participated vividly
in the hopes and fears, the convictions and efforts of the American
Revolution." And he added: "We cannot disavow nor prove rec-

reant to the principles on which that Revolution was justified—on which only it *can* be justified. If adherence to these principles makes us 'the unmitigated enemy of Pius IX.,' we regret the enmity, but cannot abjure our principles."

The maiden name of Horace Greeley's mother was Woodburn, Mary Woodburn, of Londonderry.

The founder of the Woodburn family in this country was John Woodburn, who emigrated from Londonderry in Ireland, to Londonderry in New Hampshire, about the year 1725, seven years after the settlement of the original sixteen families. He came over with his brother David, who was drowned a few years after, leaving a family. Neither of the brothers actually served in the siege of Londonderry; they were too young for that; but they were both men of the true Londonderry stamp, men with a good stroke in their arms, a merry twinkle in their eyes, indomitable workers, and not more brave in fight than indefatigable in frolic; fair-haired men like all their brethren, and gall-less.

John Woodburn obtained the usual grant of one hundred and twenty acres of land, besides the " out-lot and home-lot " before alluded to, and he took root in Londonderry and flourished. He was twice married, and was the father of two sons and nine daughters, all of whom (as children did in those healthy times) lived to maturity, and all but one married. John Woodburn's second wife, from whom Horace Greeley is descended, was a remarkable woman. Mr. Greeley has borne this testimony to her worth and influence, in a letter to a friend which some years ago escaped into print: " I think I am indebted for my first impulse toward intellectual acquirement and exertion to my mother's grandmother, who came out from Ireland among the first settlers in Londonderry. She must have been well versed in Irish and Scotch traditions, pretty well informed and strong minded; and my mother being left motherless when quite young, her grandmother exerted great influence over her mental development. I was a third child, the two preceding having died young, and I presume my mother was the more attached to me on that ground, and the extreme feebleness of my constitution. My mind was early filled by her with the traditions, ballads, and snatches of history she had learned from her grandmother, which, though conveying very distorted and incorrect ideas of history, yet served to awaken in me a thirst for knowledge and a lively interest in learning and history." John Woodburn died in 1780. Mrs. Woodburn, the subject of the passage just quoted, survived her husband many years, lived to see her children's grand-children, and to acquire throughout the neighborhood the familiar title of "Granny Woodburn."

David Woodburn, the grandfather of Horace Greeley, was the eldest son of John Woodburn, and the inheritor of his estate. He married Margaret Clark, a granddaughter of that Mrs. Wilson, the touching story of whose deliverance from pirates was long a favor-ite tale at the firesides of the early settlers of New Hampshire. In 1720, a ship containing a company of Irish emigrants bound to New England was captured by pirates, and while the ship was in their possession, and the fate of the passengers still undecided, Mrs. Wilson, one of the company, gave birth to her first child. The cir-cumstance so moved the pirate captain, who was himself a husband and a father, that he permitted the emigrants to pursue their voyage unharmed. He bestowed upon Mrs. Wilson some valuable pres-ents, among others a silk dress, pieces of which are still preserved among her descendants; and he obtained from her a promise that she would call the infant by the name of his wife. The ship reached its destination in safety, and the day of its deliverance from the hands of the pirates was annually observed as a day of thanks-giving by the passengers for many years. Mrs. Wilson, after the death of her first husband, became the wife of James Clark, whose son John was the father of Mrs. David Woodburn, whose daugh-ter Mary was the mother of Horace Greeley.

The descendants of John Woodburn are exceedingly numerous, and contribute largely, says Mr. Parker, the historian of London-derry, to the hundred thousand who are supposed to have de-scended from the early settlers of the town. The grandson of John Woodburn, a very genial and jovial gentleman, still owns and tills the land originally granted to the family. At the old homestead, about the year 1807, Zaccheus Greeley and Mary Woodburn were married.

Zaccheus Greeley inherited nothing from his father, and Mary Woodburn received no more than the usual household portion from hers. Zaccheus, as the sons of New England farmers usually do, or did in those days, went out to work as soon as he wa* old enough to do a day's work. He saved his earnings, and in his twenty-fifth year was the owner of a farm in the town of Amherst, Hillsborough county, New Hampshire.

There, on the third of February, 1811, Horace Greeley was born. He is the third of seven children, of whom the two elder died before he was born, and the four younger are still living.

The mode of his entrance upon the stage of the world was, to say the least of it, unusual. The effort was almost too much for him, and, to use the language of one who was present, " he came into the world as black as a chimney." There were no signs of life. He uttered no cry; he made no motion; he did not breathe. But the little discolored stranger had articles to write, and was not permitted to escape his destiny. In this alarming crisis of his existence, a kind-hearted and experienced aunt came to his rescue, and by arts, which to kind-hearted and experienced aunts are well known, but of which the present chronicler remains in ignorance, the boy was brought to life. He soon began to breathe; then he began to blush; and by the time he had attained the age of twenty minutes, lay on his mother's arm, a red and smiling infant.

In due time, the boy received the name of Horace. There had been another little Horace Greeley before him, but he had died in infancy, and his parents wished to preserve in their second son a living memento of their first. The name was not introduced into the family from any partiality on the part of his parents for the Roman poet, but because his father had a relative so named, and because the mother had read the name in a book and liked the sound of it. The sound of it, however, did not often regale the maternal ear; for, in New England, where the name of the courtly satirist is frequently given, its household diminutive is "Hod;" and by that elegant monosyllable the boy was commonly called among his juvenile friends.

2*

CHAPTER III.

EARLY CHILDHOOD.

The Village of Amherst—Character of the adjacent country—The Greeley farm
The Tribune in the room in which its Editor was born—Horace learns to read—
Book up-side down—Goes to school in Londonderry—A district school forty
years ago—Horace as a young orator—Has a mania for spelling hard words—Gets
great glory at the spelling school—Recollections of his surviving schoolfellows—
His future eminence foretold—Delicacy of ear—Early choice of a trade—His
courage and timidity—Goes to school in Bedford—A favorite among his schoolfellows—His early fondness for the village newspaper—Lies in ambush for the
post-rider who brought it—Scours the country for books—Project of sending him
to an academy—The old sea-captain—Horace as a farmer's boy—Let us do our
stint first—His way of fishing.

AMHERST is the county town of Hillsborough, one of the three
counties of New Hampshire which are bounded on the South by
the State of Massachusetts. It is forty-two miles north-west of
Boston.

The village of Amherst is a pleasant place. Seen from the summit
of a distant hill, it is a white dot in the middle of a level plain, en-
circled by cultivated and gently-sloping hills. On a nearer approach the traveler perceives that it is a cluster of white houses,
looking as if they had alighted among the trees and might take to
wing again. On entering it he finds himself in a very pretty village, built round an ample green and shaded by lofty trees. It contains three churches, a printing-office, a court-house, a jail, a
tavern, half a dozen stores, an exceedingly minute watchmaker's
shop, and a hundred private houses. There is not a human being
to be seen, nor a sound to be heard, except the twittering of birds
overhead, and the distant whistle of a locomotive, which in those
remote regions seems to make the silence audible. The utter
silence and the deserted aspect of the older villages in New England are remarkable. In the morning and evening there is
some appearance of life in Amherst; but in the hours of the day
when the men are at work, the women busy with their household
affairs, and the children at school, the visitor may sit at the win-

The farm owned by Zaccheus Greeley when his son Horace was born, was four or five miles from the village of Amherst. It consisted of fifty acres of land—heavy land to till—rocky, moist, and uneven, worth then eight hundred dollars, now two thousand. The house, a small, unpainted, but substantial and well-built farmhouse, stood, and still stands, upon a ledge or platform, half way up a high, steep, and rocky hill, commanding an extensive and almost panoramic view of the surrounding country. In whatever direction the boy may have looked, he saw *rock*. Rock is the feature of the landscape. There is rock in the old orchard behind the house ; rocks peep out from the grass in the pastures; there is rock along the road ; rock on the sides of the hills ; rock on their summits ; rock in the valleys ; rock in the woods ;—rock, rock, everywhere rock. And yet the country has not a barren look. I should call it a *serious* looking country ; one that would be congenial to grim covenanters and exiled round-heads. The prevailing colors are dark, even in the brightest month of the year. The pine woods, the rock, the shade of the hill, the color of the soil, are all dark and serious. It is a still, unfrequented region. One may ride along the road upon which the house stands, for many a mile, without passing a single vehicle. The turtles hobble across the road fearless of the crushing wheel. If any one wished to know the full meaning of the word *country*, as distinguished from the word *town*, he need do no more than ascend the hill on which Horace Greeley saw the light, and look around.

Yet, the voice of the city is heard even there ; the opinions of the city influence there ; for, observe, in the very room in which our hero was born, on a table which stands where, in other days, a bed stood, we recognize, among the heap of newspapers, the well-known heading of the WEEKLY TRIBUNE.

Such was the character of the region in which Horace Greeley passed the greater part of the first seven years of his life. His father's neighbors were all hard-working farmers—men who worked their own farms—who were nearly equal in wealth, and to whom the idea of social inequality, founded upon an inequality in possessions, did not exist, even as an idea. Wealth and want were alike unknown. It was a community of plain people, who had derived all their book-knowledge from the district school, and depended upon the village newspaper for their knowledge of the world without. There were no heretics among them. All the people either cordially embraced or undoubtingly assented to the faith called Orthodox, and all of them attended, more or less regularly, the churches in which that faith was expounded.

The first great peril of his existence escaped, the boy grew apace, and passed through the minor and ordinary dangers of infancy without having his equanimity seriously disturbed. He was a "quiet and peaceable child," reports his father, and, though far from robust, suffered little from actual sickness.

To say that Horace Greeley, from the earliest months of his existence, manifested signs of extraordinary intelligence, is only to repeat what every biographer asserts of his hero, and every mother of her child. Yet, common-place as it is, the truth must be told. Horace Greeley *did*, as a very young child, manifest signs of extraordinary intelligence. He took to learning with the promptitude and instinctive, irrepressible love, with which a duck is said to take to the water. His first instructor was his mother; and never was there a mother better calculated to awaken the mind of a child, and keep it awake, than Mrs. Greeley.

Tall, muscular, well-formed, with the strength of a man without his coarseness, active in her habits, not only capable of hard work, but delighting in it, with a perpetual overflow of animal spirits, an exhaustless store of songs, ballads and stories, and a boundless, exuberant good will toward all living things, Mrs. Greeley was the life of the house, the favorite of the neighborhood, the natural friend and ally of children; whatever she did she did "with a will." She was a great reader, and remembered all she read. "She worked," says one of my informants, "in doors and out of doors, could out-rake any man in the town, and could *load* the hay-wagons as fast and as well as her husband. She hoed in the garden; she labored in the field; and, while doing more than the work of an ordinary man and an ordinary woman combined, would laugh and sing all day long, and tell stories all the evening."

To these *stories* the boy listened greedily, as he sat on the floor at her feet, while she spun and talked with equal energy. They "served," says Mr. Greeley, in a passage already quoted, "to awaken in me a *thirst* for knowledge, and a lively *interest* in learning and history." Think of it, you word-mongering, gerund-grinding teachers who delight in signs and symbols, and figures and "facts," and feed little children's souls on the dry, innutr'tious husks of knowledge; and think of it, you play-abhorring, fiction-forbidding parents! Awaken the *interest* in learning, and the *thirst* for knowledge, and there is no predicting what may or what may not result from it. Scarcely a man, distinguished for the supremacy or the beauty of his immortal part, has written the history of his childhood without recording the fact that the celestial fire was first kindled in his soul by means similar to those which awakened an "interest in learning" and a "thirst for knowledge" in the mind of Horace Greeley.

Horace learned to read before he had learned to talk; that is, before he could pronounce the longer words. No one regularly taught him. When he was little more than two years old, he began to pore over the Bible, opened for his entertainment on the floor, and examine with curiosity the newspaper given him to play with. He cannot remember a time when he could not read, nor can any one give an account of the process by which he learned, except that he asked questions incessantly, first about the pictures in the newspaper, then about the capital letters, then about the smaller ones, and finally about the words and sentences. At three years of age he could read easily and correctly any of the books prepared for children; and at four, any book whatever. But he was not satisfied with overcoming the ordinary difficulties of reading. Allowing that nature gives to every child a certain amount of mental force to be used in acquiring the art of reading, Horace had an overplus of that force, which he employed in learning to read with his book in positions which increased the difficulty of the feat. All the friends and neighbors of his early childhood, in reporting him a prodigy unexampled, adduce as the unanswerable and clinching proof of the fact, that, at the age of four years, he could read any book in whatever position it might be placed,—right-side up, up-side down, or sidewise.

His third winter Horace spent at the house of his grandfather, David Woodburn, in Londonderry, attended the district school there, and distinguished himself greatly. He had no right to attend the Londonderry school, and the people of the rural districts are apt to be strenuous upon the point of not admitting to their school pupils from other towns; but Horace was an engaging child; "every one liked the little, white-headed fellow," says a surviving member of the school committee, "and so we favored him."

A district school—and what was a district school forty years ago? Horace Greeley never attended any but a district school, and it concerns us to know what manner of place it was, and what was its routine of exercises.

The school-house stood in an open place, formed (usually) by the crossing of roads. It was very small, and of one story; contained one apartment, had two windows on each side, a small door in the gable end that faced the road, and a low door-step before it. It was the thing called HOUSE, in its simplest form. But for its roof, windows, and door, it had been a BOX, large, rough, and unpainted. Within and without, it was destitute of anything ornamental. It was not enclosed by a fence; it was not shaded by a tree. The sun in summer, the winds in winter, had their will of it: there was nothing to avert the fury of either. The log school-houses of the previous generation were picturesque and comfortable; those of the present time are as prim, neat, and orderly (and as elegant sometimes) as the cottage of an old maid who enjoys an annuity; but the school-house of forty years ago had an aspect singularly forlorn and uninviting. It was built for an average of thirty pupils, but it frequently contained fifty; and then the little school-room was a compact mass of young humanity: the teacher had to dispense with his table, and was lucky if he could find room for his chair. The side of the apartment opposite the door was occupied, chiefly, by a vast fireplace, four or five feet wide, where a carman's load of wood could burn in one prodigious fire. Along the sides of the room was a low, slanting shelf, which served for a desk to those who wrote, and against the sharp edge of which the elder pupils leaned when they were not writing. The seats were made of "slabs," inverted, supported on sticks, and without backs. The elder pupils sat along the sides of the room,—the girls on one side, the boys on the other; the youngest sat nearest the fire, where they were as much too warm as those who sat near the door were too cold. In a school of forty pupils, there would be a dozen who were grown up, marriageable young men and women. Not unfrequently married men, and occasionally married women, attended school in the winter. Among the younger pupils, there were usually a dozen who could not read, and half as many who did not know the alphabet. The teacher was, perhaps, one of the farmer's sons of the district, who knew a little more than his elder pupils, and only a little; or he was a student who was working his way through college. His wages were those of a farm-laborer, ten or twelve dollars a month and his board. He boarded "*round*," *i. e.* he lived a few days at each of the houses of the district, stopping longest at the most agreeable place. The grand qualification of a teacher was the ability "to do" any sum in the arithmetic. To know arithmetic was to be a learned man. Generally, the teacher was very young, sometimes not more than sixteen years old; but, if he possessed the due expertness at figures, if he could read the Bible without stumbling over the long words, and without mispronouncing more than two thirds of the proper names, if he could write well enough to set a decent copy, if he could mend a pen, if he had vigor enough of character to assert his authority, and strength enough of arm to maintain it, he would do. The school began at nine in the morning, and the arrival of that hour was announced by the teacher's rapping upon the window frame with a ruler. The boys, and the girls too, came tumbling in, rosy and glowing, from their snowballing and sledding. The first thing done in school was reading. The "first class," consisting of that third of the pupils who could read best, stood on the floor and read round once, each individual reading about half a page of the English Reader. Then the second class. Then the third. Last of all, the youngest children said their letters. By that time, a third of the morning was over; and then the reading began again; for public opinion demanded of the teacher that he should hear every pupil read four times a day, twice in the morning and twice in the afternoon. Those who were not in the class reading, were employed, or were supposed to be employed, in ciphering or writing. When they wanted to write, they went to the teacher with their writing-book and pen, and he set a copy,— "Procrastination is the thief of time," "Contentment is a virtue," or some other wise saw,—and mended the pen. When they were puzzled with a "sum," they went to the teacher to have it elucidated. They seem to have written and ciphered as much or as little as they chose, at what time they chose, and in what manner. In some schools there were classes in arithmetic and regular instruction in writing, and one class in grammar; but such schools, forty years ago, were rare. The exercises of the morning were concluded with a general *spell*, the teacher giving out the words from a spelling-book, and the pupils spelling them at the top of their voices. At noon the school was dismissed; at one it was summoned again, to go through, for the next three hours, precisely the same routine as that of the morning. In this rude way the last generation of children learned to read, write, and cipher. But they learned something more in those rude school-houses. They learned obedience. They were tamed and disciplined. The means employed were extremely unscientific, but the thing was *done!* The means, in fact, were merely a ruler, and what was called, in contradistinction to that milder weapon, " the heavy gad ;" by which expression was designated five feet of elastic sapling of one year's growth. These two implements were plied vigorously and often. Girls got their full share of them. Girls old enough to be wives were no more exempt than the young men old enough to marry them, who sat on the other side of the schoolroom. It was thought, that if a youth of either sex was not too old to do wrong, neither he nor she was too old to suffer the consequences. In some districts, a teacher was valued in proportion to his severity ; and if he were backward in applying the ferule and the " gad," the parents soon began to be uneasy. They thought he had no energy, and inferred that the children could not be learning much. In the district schools, then, of forty years ago, all the pupils learned to read and to obey ; most of them learned to write ; many acquired a competent knowledge of figures ; a few learned the rudiments of grammar; and if any learned more than these, it was generally due to their unassisted and unencouraged exertions. There were no school-libraries at that time. The teachers usually possessed little general information, and the little they did possess was not often made to contribute to the mental nourishment of their pupils.

On one of the first benches of the Londonderry school-house, near the fire, we may imagine the little white-headed fellow, whom everybody liked, to be seated during the winters of 1813–14 and '14–'15. He was eager to go to school. When the snow lay on the ground in drifts too deep for him to wade through, one of his aunts, who still lives to tell the story, would take him up on her shoulders and carry him to the door. He was the possessor that winter, of three books, the "Columbian Orator," Morse's Geography, and a spelling book. From the Columbian Orator, he learned many pieces by heart, and among others, that very celebrated oration which probably the majority of the inhabitants of this nation have at some period of their lives been able to repeat, beginning,

> "You'd scarce expect one of my age
> To speak in public on the stage."

One of his schoolfellows has a vivid remembrance of Horace's reciting this piece before the whole school in Londonderry, before he was old enough to utter the words plainly. He had a lisping, whining little voice, says my informant, but spoke with the utmost confidence, and greatly to the amusement of the school. He spoke the piece so often in public and private, as to become, as it were, identified with it, as a man who knows one song suggests that song by his presence, and is called upon to sing it wherever he goes.

It is a pity that no one thinks of the vast importance of those "Orators" and reading books which the children read and wear out in reading, learning parts of them by heart, and repeating them over and over, till they become fixed in the memory and embedded in the character forever. And it is a pity that those books should contain so much false sentiment, inflated language, Buncombe oratory, and other trash, as they generally do! To compile a series of Reading Books for the common schools of this country, were a task for a conclave of the wisest and best men and women that ever lived; a task worthy of them, both from its difficulty and the incalculable extent of its possible results.

Spelling was the passion of the little orator during the first winters of his attendance at school. He spelt incessantly in school and out of school. He would lie on the floor at his grandfather's house, for hours at a time, spelling hard words, all that he could find in the Bible and the few other books within his reach. It was the standing amusement of the family to try and puzzle the boy with words, and no one remembers succeeding. Spelling, moreover, was one of the great points of the district schools in those days, and he who could out-spell, or, as the phrase was, "spell down" the whole school, ranked second only to him who surpassed the rest in arithmetic. Those were the palmy days of the spelling-school. The pupils assembled once a week, voluntarily, at the school-house, chose "sides," and contended with one another long and earnestly for the victory. Horace, young as he was, was eager to attend the spelling school, and was never known to injure the "side" on which he was chosen by missing a word, and it soon became a prime object at the spelling-school to get the first choice, because that enabled the lucky side to secure the powerful aid of Horace Greeley. He is well remembered by his companions in orthography. They delight still to tell of the little fellow, in the long evenings, falling asleep in his place, and when it came his turn, his neighbors gave him an anxious nudge, and he would wake instantly, spell off his word, and drop asleep again in a moment.

Horace went to school three terms in Londonderry, spending part of each year at home. I will state as nearly as possible in their own words, what his school-fellows there remember of him.

One of them can just recall him as a very small boy with a head as white as snow, who "was almost always up head in his class, and took it so much to heart when he did happen to lose his place, that he would cry bitterly; so that some boys when they had gained the right to get above him, declined the honor, because it hurt Horace's feelings so." He was the pet of the school. Those whom he used to excel most signally liked him as well as the rest. He was an active, bright, eager boy, but not fond of play, and seldom took part in the sports of the other boys. One muster day, this informant remembers, the clergyman of Londonderry, who had heard glowing accounts of Horace's feats at school, took him on his lap in the field, questioned him a long time, tried to puzzle him with hard words, and concluded by saying with strong emphasis to one of the boy's relatives, "Mark my words, Mr. Woodburn, that boy was *not* made for nothing."

Another, besides confirming the above, adds that Horace was in some respects exceedingly brave, and in others exceedingly tim

orous. He was never afraid of the dark, could not be frightened
by ghost-stories, never was abashed in speaking or reciting, was
not to be overawed by supposed superiority of knowledge or rank,
would talk up to the teacher and question his decision with perfect
freedom, though never in a spirit of impertinence. Yet he could
not stand up to a boy and fight. When attacked, he would neither fight nor run away, but "stand still and take it." His ear
was so delicately constructed that any loud noise, like the report of
a gun, would almost throw him into convulsions. If a gun were
about to be discharged, he would either run away as fast as his
legs could carry him, or else would throw himself upon the
ground and stuff grass into his ears to deaden the dreadful noise.
On the fourth of July, when the people of Londonderry inflamed
their patriotism by a copious consumption of gunpowder, Horace
would run into the woods to get beyond the sound of the cannons
and pistols. It was at Londonderry, and about his fourth year, that
Horace began the habit of reading or book-devouring, which he
never lost during all the years of his boyhood, youth, and apprenticeship, and relinquished only when he entered that most exacting
of all professions, the editorial. The gentleman whose reminiscences I am now recording, tells me that Horace in his fifth and
sixth years, would lie under a tree on his face, reading hour after
hour, completely absorbed in his book; and "if no one stumbled
over him or stirred him up," would read on, unmindful of dinner
time and sun-set, as long as he could see. It was his delight in
books that made him, when little more than an infant, determine
to be a printer, as printers, he supposed, were they who made books
"One day," says this gentleman, "Horace and I went to a black
smith's shop, and Horace watched the process of horse-shoeing with
much interest. The blacksmith, observing how intently he looked
on, said, 'You'd better come with me and learn the trade.' 'No.'
said Horace in his prompt, decided way, 'I'm going to be a printer.'
He was then six years old, and very small for his age; and this positive choice of a career by so diminutive a piece of humanity
mightily amused the by-standers. The blacksmith used to tell the
story with great glee when Horace *was* a printer, and one of some
note."

Another gentleman, who went to school with Horace at Londonderry, writes :—" I think I attended school with Horace Greeley two summers and two winters, but have no recollection of seeing him except at the school-house. He was an exceedingly mild, quiet and inoffensive child, entirely devoted to his books at school. It used to be said in the neighborhood, that he was the same out of school, and that his parents were obliged to secrete his books to prevent his injuring himself by over study. His devotion to his books, together with the fact of his great advancement beyond others of his age in the few studies then pursued in the district school, rendered him notorious in that part of the town. He was regarded as a prodigy, and his name was a household world. He was looked upon as standing alone, and entirely unapproachable by any of the little mortals around him. Reading, parsing, and spelling are the only branches of learning which I remember him in, or in connection with which his name was at that time mentioned, though he might have given some attention to writing and arithmetic, which completed the circle of studies in the district school at that time; but in the three branches first named he excelled all, even in the winter school, which was attended by several young men and women, some of whom became teachers soon after. Though mild and quiet, he was ambitious in the school ; to be at the head of his class, and be accounted the best scholar in school, seemed to be prominent objects with him, and to furnish strong motives to effort. I can recall but one instance of his missing a word in the spelling class. The classes went on to the floor to spell, and he al-most invariably stood at the head of the 'first class,' embracing the most advanced scholars. He stood there at the time referred to, and by missing a word, lost his place, which so grieved him that he wept like a punished child. While I knew him he did not engage with other children in the usual recreations and amusements of the school grounds ; as soon as the school was dismissed at noon, he would start for home, a distance of half a mile, with all his books under his arm, including the New Testament, Webster's Spelling Book, English Reader, &c., and would not return till the last moment of intermission ; at least such was his practice in the summer time. With regard to his aptness in spelling, it used to be said that the minister of the town, Rev. Mr. McGregor, once attempted to find a word or name in the Bible which he could not spell correctly, but failed to do so. I always supposed, however, that this was an exaggeration, for he could not have been more than seven years old at the time this was told. My father soon after removed to another town thirty miles distant, and I lost sight of the family entirely, Horace and all, though I always remembered the gentle, flaxen-haired schoolmate with much interest, and often wondered what became of him ; and when the ' Log Cabin ' appeared, I took much pains to assure myself whether this Horace Greeley was the same little Horace grown up, and found it was."

From his sixth year, Horace resided chiefly at his father's house. He was now old enough to walk to the nearest school-house, a mile and a half from his home. He could read fluently, spell any word in the language ; had some knowledge of geography, and a little of arithmetic ; had read the Bible through from Genesis to Revelations ; had read the Pilgrim's Progress with intense interest, and dipped into every other book he could lay his hands on. From his sixth to his tenth year, he lived, worked, read and went to school, in Amherst and the adjoining town of Bedford. Those who were then his neighbors and schoolmates there, have a lively recollection of the boy and his ways.

Henceforth, he went to school only in the winter. Again he attended a school which he had no right to attend, that of Bedford, and his attendance was not merely permitted, but sought. The school-committee expressly voted, that no pupils from other towns should be received at their school, *except Horace Greeley alone ;* and, on entering the school, he took his place, young as he was, at the head of it, as it were, by acclamation. Nor did his superiority ever excite envy or enmity. He bore his honors meekly. Every one liked the boy, and took pride in his superiority to themselves. All his schoolmates agree in this, that Horace never had an enemy at school.

The snow lies deep on those New Hampshire hills in the winter, and presents a serious obstacle to the younger children in their way to the school-house ; nor is it the rarest of disasters, even now, for children to be lost in a drift, and frozen to death. (Such a calamity happened two years ago, within a mile or two of the old Greeley homestead.) "Many a morning," says one of the neighbors— ther. a stout schoolboy, now a sturdy farmer—"many a morning I have carried Horace-on my back through the drifts to school, and put my own mittens over his, to keep his little hands from freezing." He adds, "I lived at the next house, and I and my brothers often went down in the evening to play with him; but he never would play with us till he had got his lessons. We could neither coax nor force him to." He remembers Horace as a boy of a bright and active nature, but neither playful nor merry; one who would utter acute and "old-fashioned" remarks, and make more fun for others than he seemed to enjoy himself.

His fondness for reading grew with the growth of his mind, till it amounted to a passion. His father's stock of books was small indeed. It consisted of a Bible, a "Confession of Faith," and perhaps all told, twenty volumes beside; and they by no means of a kind calculated to foster a love of reading in the mind of a little boy. But a *weekly newspaper* came to the house from the village of Amherst; and, except his mother's tales, that newspaper probably had more to do with the opening of the boy's mind and the tendency of his opinions, than anything else. The family well remember the eagerness with which he anticipated its coming. Paper-day was the brightest of the week. An hour before the post-rider was expected, Horace would walk down the road to meet him, bent on having the first *read;* and when he had got possession of the precious sheet, he would hurry with it to some secluded place, lie down on the grass, and greedily devour its contents. The paper was called (and is still) the *Farmer's Cabinet.* It was mildly Whig in politics. The selections were religious, agricultural, and miscellaneous; the editorials few, brief, and amiable; its summary of news scanty in the extreme. But it was the *only* bearer of tidings from the Great World. It connected the little brown house on the rocky hill of Amherst with the general life of mankind. The boy, before he could read himself, and before he could understand the meaning of war and bloodshed, doubtless heard his father read in it of the triumphs and disasters of the Second War with Great Britain, and of the rejoicings at the conclusion of peace. He himself may have read of Decatur's gallantry in the war with Algiers, of Wellington's victory at Waterloo, of Napoleon's fretting away his life on the rock of St. Helena, of Monroe's inauguration, of the dismantling of the fleets on the great lakes, of the progress of the

Erie Canal project, of Jackson's inroads into Florida, and the subsequent cession of that province to the United States, of the first meeting of Congress in the Capitol, of the passage of the Missouri Compromise. During the progress of the various commercial treaties with the States of Europe, which were negotiated after the conclusion of the general peace, the whole theory, practice, and history of commercial intercourse, were amply discussed in Congress and the newspapers; and the mind of Horace, even in his ninth year, was mature enough to take some interest in the subject, and derive some impressions from its discussion. The *Farmer's Cabinet*, which brought all these and countless other ideas and events to bear on the education of the boy, is now one of the thousand papers with which the *Tribune* exchanges.

Horace scoured the country for books. Books were books in that remote and secluded region; and when he had exhausted the collections of the neighbors, he carried the search into the neighboring towns. I am assured that there was not one readable book within seven miles of his father's house, which Horace did not borrow and read during his residence in Amherst. He was never without a book. As soon, says one of his sisters, as he was dressed in the morning, he flew to his book. He read every minute of the day which he could snatch from his studies at school, and on the farm. He would be so absorbed in his reading, that when his parents required his services, it was like rousing a heavy sleeper from his deepest sleep, to awaken Horace to a sense of things around him and an apprehension of the duty required of him. And even then he clung to his book. He would go reading to the cellar and the cider-barrel, reading to the wood-pile, reading to the garden, reading to the neighbors; and pocketing his book only long enough to perform his errand, he would fall to reading again the instant his mind and his hands were at liberty.

He kept in a secure place an ample supply of pine knots, and as soon as it was dark he would light one of these cheap and brilliant illuminators, put it on the back-log in the spacious fire-place, pile up his school books and his reading books on the floor, lie down on his back on the hearth, with his head to the fire and his feet coiled away out of the reach of stumblers; and there he would lie and read all through the long winter evenings, silent, motionless, dead to the world around him, alive only to the world to which he was transported by his book. Visitors would come in, chat a while, and go away, without knowing he was present, and without his being aware of their coming and going. It was a nightly struggle to get him to bed. His father required his services early in the morning, and was therefore desirous that he should go to bed early in the evening. He feared, also, for the eye-sight of the boy, reading so many hours with his head in the fire and by the flaring, flickering light of a pine knot. And so, by nine o'clock, his father would *begin* the task of recalling the absent mind from its roving, and rousing the prostrate and dormant body. And when Horace at length had been forced to beat a retreat, he kept his younger brother awake by telling over to him in bed what he had read, and by reciting the school lessons of the next day. His brother was by no means of a literary turn, and was prone—much to the chagrin of Horace—to fall asleep long before the lessons were all said and the tales all told.

So entire and passionate a devotion to the acquisition of knowledge in one so young, would be remarkable in any circumstances. But when the situation of the boy is considered—living in a remote and *very* rural district—few books accessible—few literary persons residing near—the school contributing scarcely anything to his mental nourishment—no other boy in the neighborhood manifesting any particular interest in learning—the people about him all engaged in a rude and hard struggle to extract the means of subsistence from a rough and rocky soil—such an intense, absorbing, and persistent love of knowledge as that exhibited by Horace Greeley, must be accounted very extraordinary.

That his neighbors so accounted it, they are still eager to attest. Continually the wonder grew, that one small head should carry all he knew.

There were not wanting those who thought that superior means of instruction ought to be placed within the reach of so superior a child. I have a somewhat vague, but very positive, and fully confirmed story, of a young man just returned from college to his father's house in Bedford, who fell in with Horace, and was so struck with his capacity and attainments that he offered to send him to an academy in a neighboring town, and bear all the expenses of his maintenance and tuition. But his mother could not let him go, his father needed his assistance at home, and the boy himself is said not to have favored the scheme. A wise, a fortunate choice, I cannot help believing. That academy *may* have been an institution where boys received more good than harm—where real *knowledge* was imparted—where souls were inspired with the love of high and good things, and inflamed with an ambition to run a high and good career—where boys did *not* lose all their modesty and half their sense—where chests were expanded—where cheeks were ruddy—where limbs were active—where stomachs were peptic. It *may* have been. But if it was, it was a different academy from many whose praises are in all the newspapers. It was better not to run the risk. If that young man's offer had been accepted, it is a question whether the world would have ever heard of Horace Greeley. Probably his fragile body would not have sustained the brain-stimulating treatment which a forward and eager boy generally receives at an academy.

A better friend, though not a better meaning one, was a jovial neighbor, a sea-captain, who had taken to farming. The captain had seen the world, possessed the yarn-spinning faculty, and besides being himself a walking traveler's library, had a considerable collection of books, which he freely lent to Horace. His salute, on meeting the boy, was not 'How do you do, Horace?' but 'Well, Horace, what's the capital of Turkey?' or, 'Who fought the battle of Eutaw Springs?' or, 'How do you spell Encyclopedia, or Kamtschatka, or Nebuchadnezzar?' The old gentleman used to question the boy upon the contents of the books he had lent him, and was again and again surprised at the fluency, the accuracy, and the fullness of his replies. The captain was of service to Horace in various ways, and he is remembered by the family with gratitude. To Horace's brother he once gave a sheep and a load of hay to keep it on during the winter, thus adapting his benefactions to the various tastes of his juvenile friends.

A clergyman, too, is spoken of, who took great interest in Horace, and gave him instruction in grammar, often giving the boy erroneous information to test his knowledge. Horace, he used to say, could never be shaken on a point which he had once clearly understood, but would stand to his opinion, and defend it against anybody and everybody—teacher, pastor, or public opinion.

In New England, the sons of farmers begin to make themselves useful almost as soon as they can walk. They feed the chickens, they drive the cows, they bring in wood and water, and soon come to perform all those offices which come under the denomination of "*chores*." By the time they are eight or nine years old, they frequently have tasks assigned them, which are called "stints," and not till they have done their stint are they at liberty to play. The reader may think that Horace's devotion to literature would naturally enough render the farm work distasteful to him; and if he had gone to the academy, it might. I am bound, however, to say that all who knew him in boyhood, agree that he was not more devoted to study in his leisure hours, than he was faithful and assiduous in performing his duty to his father during the hours of work. *Faithful* is the word. He could be *trusted* any where, and to do anything within the compass of his strength and years. It was hard, sometimes, to rouse him from his books; but when he had been roused, and was entrusted with an errand or a piece of work, he would set about it vigorously, and lose no time till it was done. "Come," his brother would say sometimes, when the father had set the boys a task and had gone from home; "come, Hod, let's go fishing." "No," Horace would reply, in his whining voice, "let us do our stint first." "He was *always* in school, though," says his brother, "and as we hoed down the rows, or chopped at the woodpile, he was perpetually talking about his lessons, asking questions, and narrating what he had read."

Fishing, it appears, was the only sport in which Horace took much pleasure, during the first ten years of his life. But his love of fishing did not originate in what the Germans call the "sport impulse." Other boys fished for sport; Horace fished for *fish*. He fished *industriously*, keeping his eyes unceasingly on the float, and never distracting his own attention, or that of the fish, by conversing with his companions. The consequence was that he would often catch more than all the rest of the party put together. Shooting was the favorite amusement of the boys of the neighborhood, but Horace could rarely be persuaded to take part in it. When he did accompany a shooting-party, he would never carry or discharge a gun, and when the game was found he would lie down and stop his ears till the murder had been done.

CHAPTER IV.

HIS FATHER RUINED—REMOVAL TO VERMONT.

New Hampshire before the era of manufactures—Causes of his father's failure—Rum in the olden time—An execution in the house—Flight of the father—Horace and the Rum Jug—Compromise with the creditors—Removal to another farm—Final ruin—Removal to Vermont—The winter journey—Poverty of the family—Scene at their new home—Cheerfulness in misfortune.

But while thus Horace was growing up to meet his destiny, pressing forward on the rural road to learning, and *secreting* character in that secluded home, a cloud, undiscerned by him, had come over his father's prospects. It began to gather when the boy was little more than six years old. In his seventh year it broke, and drove the family, for a time, from house and land. In his tenth, it had completed its work—his father was a ruined man, an exile, a fugitive from his native State.

In those days, before the great manufacturing towns which now afford the farmer a market for his produce had sprung into existence along the shores of the Merrimac, before a net-work of railroads regulated the price of grain in the barns of New Hampshire by the standard of Mark Lane, a farmer of New Hampshire was not, in his best estate, *very* far from ruin. Some articles which forty years ago were quite destitute of pecuniary value, now afford an ample profit. Fire-wood, for example, when Horace Greeley was a boy, could seldom be sold at any price. It was usually burned up on the land on which it grew, as a worthless incumbrance. Fire-wood now, in the city of Manchester, sells for six dollars a cord, and at any point within ten miles of Manchester for four dollars. Forty years ago, farmers had little surplus produce, and that little had to be carried far, and it brought little money home. In short, before the manufacturing system was introduced into New Hampshire, affording employment to her daughters in the factory, to her sons on the land, New Hampshire was a poverty-stricken State.

It is one of the wonders of party infatuation, that the two States which if they have not gained most, have certainly most to gain from the "American system," should have always been, and should still be its most rooted opponents. But man the partisan, like man the sectarian, is, always was, and will ever be, a poor creature.

The way to thrive in New Hampshire was to work very hard, keep the store-bill small, stick to the farm, and be no man's security. Of these four things, Horace's father did only one—he worked hard. He was a good workman, methodical, skillful, and persevering. But he speculated in lumber, and lost money by it. He was 'bound,' as they say in the country, for another man, and had to pay the money which that other man failed to pay. He had a free and generous nature, lived well, treated the men whom he employed liberally, and in various ways swelled his account with the store-keeper.

Those, too, were the jolly, bad days, when everybody drank strong drinks, and no one supposed that the affairs of life could possibly be transacted without its agency, any more than a machine could *go* without the lubricating oil. A field could not be 'logged,' hay could not be got in, a harvest could not be gathered, unless the jug of liquor stood by the spring, and unless the spring was visited many times in the day by all hands. No visitor could be sent unmoistened away. No holiday could be celebrated without drinking-booths. At weddings, at christenings, at funerals, rum seemed to be the inducement that brought, and the tie that bound, the company together. It was rum that cemented friendship, and rum that clinched bargains; rum that kept out the cold of winter, and rum that moderated the summer's heat. Men drank it, women drank it, children drank it. There were families in which the first duty of every morning was to serve around to all its members, even to the youngest child, a certain portion of alcoholic liquor. Rum had to be bought with money, and money was hard to get in New Hampshire. Zaccheus Greeley was not the man to stint his workmen. At his house and on his farm the jug was never empty. In his cellar the cider never was out. And so, by losses which he could not help, by practices which had not yet been discovered to be unnecessary, his affairs became disordered, and he began to descend the easy steep that leads to the abyss of bankruptcy. He *arrived*—lingered a few years on the edge—was pushed in—and scrambled out on the other side.

It was on a Monday morning. There had been a long, fierce rain, and the clouds still hung heavy and dark over the hills. Horace, then only nine years old, on coming down stairs in the morning, saw several men about the house; neighbors, some of them; others were strangers; others he had seen in the village. He was too young to know the nature of an *Execution*, and by what right the sheriff and a party of men laid hands upon his father's property. His father had walked quietly off into the woods; for, at that period, a man's person was not exempt from seizure. Horace had a vague idea that the men had come to rob them of all they possessed; and wild stories are afloat in the neighborhood, of the boy's conduct on the occasion. Some say, that he seized a hatchet, ran to the neighboring field, and began furiously to cut down a favorite pear-tree, saying, "They shall not have *that*, anyhow." But his mother called him off, and the pear-tree still stands. Another story is, that he went to one of his mother's closets, and taking as many of her dresses as he could grasp in his arms, ran away with them into the woods, hid them behind a rock, and then came back to the house for more. Others assert, that the article carried off by the indignant boy was not dresses, but a gallon of rum. But whatever the boy did, or left undone, the reader may imagine that it was to all the family a day of confusion, anguish, and horror. Both of Horace's parents were persons of incorruptible honesty; they had striven hard to place such a calamity as this far from their house; they had never experienced themselves, nor witnessed at their earlier homes, a similar scene; the blow was unexpected; and mingled with their sense of shame at being publicly degraded, was a feeling of honest rage at the supposed injustice of so summary a proceeding. It was a dark day; but it passed, as the darkest day will.

An "arrangement" was made with the creditors. Mr. Greeley gave up his own farm, temporarily, and removed to another in the adjoining town of Bedford, which he cultivated on shares, and devoted principally to the raising of hops. Misfortune still pursued him. His two years' experience of hop-growing was not satisfactory. The hop-market was depressed. His own farm in Amherst was either ill managed or else the seasons were unfavorable. He gave up the hop-farm, poorer than ever. He removed back to his old home in Amherst. A little legal maneuvering or rascality on the part of a creditor, gave the finishing blow to his fortunes; and, in the winter of 1821, he gave up the effort to recover himself, became a bankrupt, was sold out of house, land, and household goods by the sheriff, and fled from the State to avoid arrest, leaving his family behind. Horace was nearly ten years old. Some of the debts then left unpaid, he discharged in part thirty years after.

Mr. Greeley had to begin the world anew, and the world was all before him, where to choose, excepting only that portion of it which is included within the boundaries of New Hampshire. He made his way, after some wandering, to the town of Westhaven, in Rutland county, Vermont, about a hundred and twenty miles northwest of his former residence. There he found a large landed proprietor, who had made one fortune in Boston as a merchant, and married another in Westhaven, the latter consisting of an extensive tract of land. He had now retired from business, had set up for a country gentleman, was clearing his lands, and when they were cleared he rented them out in farms. This attempt to "found an estate," in the European style, signally failed. The "mansion house" has been disseminated over the neighborhood, one wing here, another wing there; the "lawn" is untrimmed; the attempt at a park-gate has lost enough of the paint that made it tawdry once, to look shabby now. But this gentleman was useful to Zaccheus Greeley in the day of his poverty. He gave him work, rented him a small house nearly opposite the park-gate just mentioned, and thus enabled him in a few weeks to transport his family to a new home.

It was in the depth of winter when they made the journey. The teamster that drove them still lives to tell how 'old Zac Greeley came to him, and wanted he should take his sleigh and horses, and go over with him to New Hampshire State, and bring his family back;' and how, when they had got a few miles on the way, he said to Zac, said he, that he (Zac) was a stranger to him, and he did n't feel like going so far without enough to secure him; and so Zac gave him enough to secure him, and away they drove to New Hampshire State. One sleigh was sufficient to convey all the little property the law had left the family, and the load could not have been a heavy one, for the distance was accomplished in a little less than three days. The sleighing, however, was good, and the Connecticut river was crossed on the ice. The teamster remembers well the intelligent, white-headed boy who was so pressing with his questions, as they rode along over the snow, and who soon exhausted the man's knowledge of the geography of the region in which he had lived all his days. "He asked me," says he, "a great dea. about Lake Champlain, and how far it was from Plattsburgh to this, that, and t' other place; but, Lord! he told me a d——d sight more than I could tell *him*." The passengers in the sleigh were Horace, his parents, his brother, and two sisters, and all arrived safely at the little house in Westhaven,—safely, but very, very poor. They possessed the clothes they wore on their journey, a bed or two, a few —very few—domestic utensils, an antique chest, and one or two other small relics of their former state; and they possessed nothing more.

A lady, who was then a little girl, and, as little girls in the country will, used to run in and out of the neighbors' houses at all hours without ceremony, tells me that, many times, during that winter she saw the newly-arrived family taking sustenance in the following manner:—A five-quart milk-pan filled with bean porridge—an hereditary dish among the Scotch-Irish—was placed upon the floor, the children clustering around it. Each child was provided with a spoon, and dipped into the porridge, the spoon going directly from the common dish to the particular mouth, without an intermediate landing upon a plate, the meal consisting of porridge, and porridge only. The parents sat at a table, and enjoyed the dignity of a separate dish. This was a homely way of dining; but, adds my kind informant, "they seemed so happy over their meal, that many a time, as I looked upon the group, I wished our mother would let *us* eat in that way—it seemed *so* much better than sitting at a table and using knives, and forks, and plates." There was no repining in the family over their altered circumstances, nor any attempt to conceal the scantiness of their furniture. To what the world calls "appearances" they seemed *constitutionally* insensible.

CHAPTER V.

AT WESTHAVEN, VERMONT.

THE family were gainers in some important particulars, by their change of residence. The land was better. The settlement was more recent. There was a better chance for a poor man to acquire property. And what is well worth mention for its effect upon the opening mind of Horace, the scenery was grander and more various. That part of Rutland county is in nature's large manner. Long ranges of hills, with bases not too steep for cultivation, but rising into lofty, precipitous and fantastic summits, stretch away in every direction. The low-lands are level and fertile. Brooks and rivers come out from among the hills, where they have been officiating as water-power, and flow down through valleys that open and expand to receive them, fertilizing the soil. Roaming among these hills, the boy must have come frequently upon little lakes locked in on every side, without apparent outlet or inlet, as smooth as a mirror, as silent as the grave. Six miles from his father's house was the great Lake Champlain. He could not see it from his father's door, but he could see the blue mist that rose from its surface every morning and evening, and hung over it, a cloud veiling a Mystery. And he could see the long line of green knoll-like hills that formed its opposite shore. And he could go down on Sundays to the shore itself, and stand in the immediate presence of the lake.

3*

Nor is it a slight thing for a boy to *see* a great natural object which he has been learning about in his school books; nor is it an uninfluential circumstance for him to live where he can see it frequently. It was a superb country for a boy to grow up in, whether his tendencies were industrial, or sportive, or artistic, or poetical. There was rough work enough to do on the land. Fish were abundant in the lakes and streams. Game abounded in the woods. Wild grapes and wild honey were to be had for the search after them. Much of the surrounding scenery is sublime, and what is not sublime is beautiful. Moreover, Lake Champlain is a stage on the route of northern and southern travel, and living upon its shores brought the boy nearer to that world in which he was destined to move, and which he had to know before he could work in it to advantage. At Westhaven, Horace passed the next five years of his life. He was now rather tall for his age; his mind was far in advance of it. Many of the opinions for which he has since done battle, were distinctly formed during that important period of his life to which the present chapter is devoted.

At Westhaven, Mr. Greeley, as they say in the country, 'took jobs;' and the jobs which he took were of various kinds. He would contract to get in a harvest, to prepare the ground for a new one, to 'tend' a saw-mill; but his principal employment was clearing up land; that is, piling up and burning the trees after they had been felled. After a time he kept sheep and cattle. In most of his undertakings he prospered. By incessant labor and by reducing his expenditures to the lowest possible point, he saved money, slowly but continuously.

In whatever he engaged, whether it was haying, harvesting, sawing, or land-clearing, he was assisted by all his family. There was little work to do at home, and after breakfast, the house was left to take care of itself, and away went the family, father, mother, boys, girls, and oxen, to work together. Clearing land offers an excellent field for family labor, as it affords work adapted to all degrees of strength. The father chopped the larger logs, and directed the labor of all the company. Horace drove the oxen, and drove them none too well, say the neighbors, and was gradually supplanted in the office of driver by his younger brother. Both the boys could chop the smaller trees. Their mother and sisters gathered together the light wood into heaps. And when the great logs had to be rolled upon one another, there was scope for the combined skill and strength of the whole party. Many happy and merry days the family spent together in this employment. The mother's spirit never flagged. Her voice rose in song and laughter from the tangled brush-wood in which she was often buried; and no word, discordant or unkind, was ever known to break the perfect harmony, to interrupt the perfect good humor that prevailed in the family. At night, they went home to the most primitive of suppers, and partook of it in the picturesque and labor-saving style in which the dinner before alluded to was consumed. The neighbors still point out a tract of fifty acres which was cleared in this sportive and Swiss-Family-Robinson-like manner. They show the spring on the side of the road where the family used to stop and drink on their way; and they show a hemlock-tree, growing from the rocks above the spring, which used to furnish the brooms, weekly renewed, which swept the little house in which the little family lived. To complete the picture, imagine them all clad in the same material, the coarsest kind of linen or linsey-woolsey, home-spun, dyed with butternut bark, and the different garments made in the roughest and simplest manner by the mother.

More than three garments at the same time, Horace seldom wore in the summer, and these were—a straw hat, generally in a state of dilapidation, a tow-shirt, never buttoned, a pair of trousers made of the family material, and having the peculiarity of being very short in both legs, but shorter in one than the other. In the winter he added a pair of shoes and a jacket. During the five years of his life at Westhaven, probably his clothes did not cost three dollars a year; and, I believe, that during the whole period of his childhood, up to the time when he came of age, not fifty dollars in all were expended upon his dress. He never manifested, on any occasion, in any company, nor at any part of his early life, the *slightest* interest in his attire, nor the *least* care for its effect upon others. That amiable trait in human nature which inclines us to decoration, which make us desirous to present an agreeable figure to others, and to abhor peculiarity in our appearance, is a trait which Horace never gave the smallest evidence of possessing.

He went to school three winters in Westhaven, but not to any great advantage. He had already gone the round of district schoo. studies, and did little more after his tenth year than walk over the course, keeping lengths ahead of all competitors, with little effort. "He was always," says one of his Westhaven schoolmates, "at the top of the school. He seldom had a teacher that could teach him anything. Once, and once only, he missed a word. His fair face was crimsoned in an instant. He was terribly *cut* about it, and I fancied he was not himself for a week after. I see him now, as he sat in class, with his slender body, his large head, his open, ample forehead, his pleasant smile, and his coarse, clean, homespun clothes. His attitude was always the same. He sat with his arms loosely folded, his head bent forward, his legs crossed, and one foot swinging. He did not seem to pay attention, but nothing escaped him. He appeared to attend more from curiosity to hear what sort of work *we* made of the lesson than from any interest he took in the subject for his own sake. Once, I parsed a word egregiously wrong, and Horace was so taken aback by the mistake that he was startled from his propriety, and exclaimed, loud enough for the class to hear him, ' *What* a fool!' The manner of it was so ludicrous that I, and all the class, burst into laughter."

Another schoolmate remembers him chiefly for his gentle manner and obliging disposition. "I never," she says, "knew him to fight, or to be angry, or to have an enemy. He was a peacemaker among us. He played with the boys sometimes, and I think was fonder of snowballing than any other game. For girls, *as* girls, he never manifested any preference. On one occasion he got into a scrape. He had broken some petty rule of the school, and was required, as a punishment, to inflict a certain number of blows upon another boy, who had, I think, been a participator in the offense. The instrument of flagellation was placed in Horace's hand, and he drew off, as though he was going to deal a terrific blow, but it came down so gently on the boy's jacket that every one saw that Horace was shamming. The teacher interfered, and told him to strike harder; and a *little* harder he did strike, but a more harmless flogging was never administered. He seemed not to have the power, any more than the will, to inflict pain."

If Horace got little good himself from his last winters at school he was of great assistance to his schoolfellows in explaining to them the difficulties of their lessons. Few evenings passed in which some strapping fellow did not come to the house with his grammar or his slate, and sit demurely by the side of Horace, while the distracting sum was explained, or the dark place in the parsing lesson illuminated. The boy delighted to render such assistance. However deeply he might be absorbed in his own studies, as soon as he saw a puzzled countenance peering in at the door, he knew his man, knew what was wanted; and would jump up from his recumbent posture in the chimney-corner, and proceed, with a patience that is still gratefully remembered, with a perspicuity that is still mentioned with admiration, to impart the information required of him. Fancy it. It is a pretty picture. The 'little white-headed fellow' generally so abstracted, now all intelligence and animation, by the side of a great hulk of a young man, twice his age and three times his weight, with a countenance expressing perplexity and despair. An apt question, a reminding word, a few figures hastily scratched on the slate, and light flashes on the puzzled mind. He wonders he had not thought of that: he wishes Heaven had given *him* such a 'head-piece.'

To some of his teachers at Westhaven, Horace was a cause of great annoyance. He knew too much. He asked awkward questions. He was not to be put off with common-place solutions of serious difficulties. He wanted things to hang together, and liked to know how, if *this* was true, *that* could be true also. At length, one of his teachers, when Horace was thirteen years old, had the honesty and good sense to go to his father, and say to him, point blank, that Horace knew more than he did, and it was of no use for him to go to school any more. So Horace remained at home, read hard all that winter in a little room by himself, and taught his youngest sister beside. He had attended district school, altogether, about forty-five months.

At Westhaven, the pine-knots blazed on the hearth as brightly and as continuously as they had done at the old home in Amherst. There was a new reason why they should; for a candle was a luxury now, too expensive to be indulged in. Horace's home was a favorite evening resort for the children of the neighborhood—a fact which says much for the kindly spirit of its inmates. They came to hear his mother's songs and stories, to play with his brother and sisters, to get assistance from himself; and they liked to be there, where there was no stiffness, nor ceremony, nor discord. Horace cared nothing for their noise and romping, but he could never be induced to join in an active game. When he was not assisting some bewildered arithmetician, he lay in the old position, on his back in the fireplace, reading, always reading. The boys would hide his book, but he would get another. They would pull him out of his fiery den by the leg; and he would crawl back, without the least show of anger, but without the slightest inclination to yield the point.

There was a game, however, which could sometimes tempt him from his book, and of which he gradually became excessively fond. It was draughts, or 'checkers.' In that game he acquired extraordinary skill, beating everybody in the neighborhood; and before he had reached maturity, there were few draught-players in the country—if any—who could win two games in three of Horace Greeley. His cronies at Westhaven seem to have been those who were fond of draughts. In his passion for books, he was alone among his companions, who attributed his continual reading more to indolence than to his acknowledged superiority of intelligence. It was often predicted that, whoever else might prosper, Horace never would.

And yet, he gave proof, in very early life, that the Yankee element was strong within him. In the first place, he was always *doing* something; and, in the second, he always had something to *sell*. He saved nuts, and exchanged them at the store for the articles he wished to purchase. He would hack away, hours at a time, at a pitch-pine stump, the roots of which are as inflammable as pitch itself, and, tying up the roots in little bundles, and the little bundles into one large one, he would " back" the load to the store, and sell it for kindling wood. His favorite out-door sport, too, at Westhaven, was bee-hunting, which is not only an agreeable and exciting pastime, but occasionally rewards the hunter with a prodigious mass of honey—as much as a hundred and fifty pounds having been frequently obtained from a single tree. This was profitable sport, and Horace liked it amazingly. His share of the honey generally found its way to the store. By these and other expedients, the boy managed always to have a little money, and when a peddler came along with books in his wagon, Horace was pretty sure to be his customer. Yet he was only half a Yankee. He could earn money, but the bargaining faculty he had not.

What did he read? Whatever he could get. But his preference was for history, poetry, and—newspapers. He had read, as I have before mentioned, the whole Bible before he was six years old. He read the Arabian Nights with intense pleasure in his eighth year; Robinson Crusoe in his ninth; Shakspeare in his eleventh; in his twelfth, thirteenth, and fourteenth years, he read a good many of the common, superficial histories—Robertson's, Gold-smith's, and others—and as many tales and romances as he could borrow. At Westhaven, as at Amherst, he roamed far and wide in search of books. He was fortunate, too, in living near the 'mansion-house' before mentioned, the proprietor of which, it appears, took some interest in Horace, freely lent him books, and allowed him to come to the house and read there as often and as long as he chose.

A story is told by one who lived at the 'mansion-house' when Horace used to read there. Horace entered the library one day, when the master of the house happened to be present, in conversation with a stranger. The stranger, struck with the awkwardness and singular appearance of the boy, took him for little better than an idiot, and was inclined to laugh at the idea of lending books to 'such a fellow as *that*.' The owner of the mansion defended his conduct by extolling the intelligence of his protégé, and wound up with the usual climax, that he should "not be surprised, sir, if that boy should come to be President of the United States." People in those days had a high respect for the presidential office, and really believed—many of them did—that to get the highest place it was only necessary to be the greatest man. Hence it was a very common mode of praising a boy, to make the safe assertion that he *might*, one day, if he persevered in well-doing, be the President of the United States. That was before the era of wire-pulling and rotation in office. He must be either a very young or a very old man who can *now* mention the presidential office in connection with the future of any boy not extraordinarily vicious. Wire-pull-ing, happily, has robbed the schoolmasters of one of their bad argu-ments for a virtuous life. But we are wandering from the library.

The end of the story is, that the stranger looked as if he thought Horace's defender half mad himself; and, "to tell the truth," said the lady who told me the story, "we all thought Mr. —— had made a crazy speech." Horace does not appear to have made a favorable impression at the 'mansion-house.'

But he read the books in it, for all that. Perhaps it was there, that he fell in with a copy of Mrs. Hemans' poems, which, wherever he found them, were the first poems that awakened his enthusiasm, the first writings that made him aware of the better impulses of his nature. "I remember," he wrote in the Rose of Sharon for 1841, "as of yesterday, the gradual unfolding of the exceeding truthfulness and beauty, the profound heart-knowledge (to coin a Germanism) which characterizes Mrs. Hemans' poems, upon my own immature, unfolding mind. —'Cassabianca,' 'Things that change,' 'The Voice of Spring,' 'The Traveler at the Source of the Nile,' 'The Wreck,' and many other poems of kindred nature are enshrined in countless hearts—especially of those whose intellectual existence dates its commencement between 1820 and 1830—as gems of priceless value; as spirit-wands, by whose electric touch they were first made conscious of the diviner aspirations, the loftier, holier energies within them."

Such a testimony as this may teach the reader, if he needs the lesson, not to undervalue the authors whom his fastidious taste may place among the Lesser Lights of Literature. To you, fastidious reader, those authors may have little to impart. But among the hills in the country, where the feelings are fresher, and minds are unsated by literary sweets, there may be many a thoughtful boy and earnest man, to whom your Lesser Lights are Suns that warm, illumine, and quicken!

The incidents in Horace's life at Westhaven were few, and of the few that did occur, several have doubtless been forgotten. The people there remember him vividly enough, and are profuse in imparting their general impressions of his character; but the facts which gave rise to those impressions have mostly escaped their memories. They speak of him as an *absorbed* boy, who rarely saluted or saw a passer-by—who would walk miles at the road-side, following the zig-zag of the fences, without once looking up—who was often taken by strangers for a natural fool, but was known by his intimates to be, in the language of one of them—"a darned smart fellow, in spite of his looks"—who was utterly blameless in all his ways, and works, and words—who had not, and could not have had, an enemy, because nature, by leaving out of his composition the diabolic element, had made it impossible for him to *be* one. The few occurrences of the boy's life, which, in addition to these general reminiscences of his character, have chanced to escape oblivion, may as well be narrated here.

As an instance of his nervous timidity, a lady mentions, that when he was about eleven years old, he came to her house one evening on some errand, and staid till after dark. He started for home, at length, but had not been gone many minutes before he burst into the house again, in great agitation, saying he had seen a wolf by the side of the road. There had been rumors of wolves in the neighborhood. Horace declared he had seen the eyes of one glaring upon him as he passed, and he was so overcome with terror, that two of the elder girls of the family accompanied him home. They saw no wolf, nor were there any wolves about at the time; the mistake probably arose from some phosphorescent wood, or some other bright object. A Vermont boy of that period, as a general thing, cared little more for a wolf than a New York boy does for a cat, and could have faced a pack of wolves with far less dread than a company of strangers. Horace was never abashed by an audience; but two glaring eye-balls among the brush-wood sent him flying with terror.

In nothing are mortals more wise than in their fears. That which we stigmatize as cowardice—what is it but nature's kindly warning to her children, not to confront what they cannot master, and not to undertake what their strength is unequal to? Horace was a *match* for a rustic auditory, and he feared it not. He was not a match for a wild beast; so he ran away. Considerate nature!

Horace, all through his boyhood, kept his object of becoming a printer steadily in view; and soon after coming to Vermont, about his eleventh year, he began to think it time for him to take a step towards the fulfillment of his intention. He talked to his father on the subject, but received no encouragement from him. His father said, and very truly, that no one would take an apprentice so young. But the boy was not satisfied; and, one morning, he trudged off to

Whitehall, a town about nine miles distant, where a newspaper was published, to make inquiries. He went to the printing office, saw the printer, and learned that his father was right. He *was* too young, the printer said; and so the boy trudged home again.

A few months after, he went on another and much longer pedestrian expedition. He started, with seventy-five cents in his pocket and a small bundle of provisions on a stick over his shoulder, to walk to Londonderry, a hundred and twenty miles distant, to see his old friends and relatives. He performed the journey, staid several weeks, and came back with a shilling or two more money than he took with him—owing, we may infer, to the amiable way aunts and uncles have of bestowing small coins upon nephews who visit them. His re-appearance in New Hampshire excited unbounded astonishment, his age and dimensions seeming ludicrously out of proportion to the length and manner of his solitary journey. He was made much of during his stay, and his journey is still spoken of there as a wonderful performance, only exceeded, in fact, by Horace's second return to Londonderry a year or two after, when he drove, over the same ground, his aunt and her four children, in a 'one-horse wagon,' and drove back again, without the slightest accident.

As a set-off to these marvels, it must be recorded, that on two other occasions he was taken for an idiot—once, when he entered a store, in one of the brownest of his brown studies, and a stranger inquired, "What darn fool is that?"—and a second time, in the manner following. He was accustomed to call his father "*Sir*," both in speaking to, and speaking of him. One day, while Horace was chopping wood by the side of the road, a man came up on horse-back and inquired the way to a distant town. Horace could not tell him, and, without looking up, said, "ask *Sir*," meaning, ask father. The stranger, puzzled at this reply, repeated his question, and Horace again said, "ask *Sir*." "I *am* asking," shouted the man. "Well, ask *Sir*," said Horace, once more. "*Aint* I asking you—fool?" screamed the man. "But I want you to ask *Sir*," said Horace. It was of no avail, the man rode away in disgust, and inquired at the next tavern "who that tow-headed fool was down the road?"

In a similar absent fit it must have been, that the boy once attempted, in vain, to yoke the oxen that he had yoked a hundred times before without difficulty. To see a small boy yoking a pair of oxen is, O City Reader, to behold an amazing exhibition of the power of Mind over Matter. The huge beasts *need* not come under the yoke—twenty men could not compel them—but they *do* come under it at the beck of a boy that can just stagger under the yoke himself, and whom one of the oxen, with one horn and a shake of the head, could toss over a hay-stack. The boy, with the yoke on his shoulders, and one of the 'bows' in his hand, marches up to the 'off' ox, puts the bow round his neck, thrusts the ends of the bow through the holes of the yoke, fastens them there—and one ox is his. But the other! The boy then removes the other bow, holds up the end of the yoke, and commands the 'near' ox to approach, and 'come under here, sir.' Wonderful to relate! the near ox obeys! He walks slowly up, and takes his place by the side of his brother, as though it were a pleasant thing to pant all day before the plough, and he was only too happy to leave the dull pasture. But the ox is a creature of habit. If you catch the near ox first, and then try to get the off ox to come under the near side of the yoke, you will discover that the off ox has an opinion of his own. He won't come. This was the mistake which Horace, one morning in an absent fit, committed, and the off ox could not be brought to deviate from established usage. After much coaxing, and, possibly, some vituperation, Horace was about to give it up, when his brother chanced to come to the field, who saw at a glance what was the matter, and rectified the mistake. "Ah!" his father used to say, after Horace had made a display of this kind, "that boy will never get along in this world. He'll never know more than enough to come in-when it rains."

Another little story is told of the brothers. The younger was throwing stones at a pig that preferred to go in a direction exactly contrary to that in which the boys wished to drive him—a common case with pigs, *et cetera*. Horace, who never threw stones at pigs, was overheard to say, "Now, you ought n't to throw stones at that hog; he don't *know* anything."

The person who heard these words uttered by the boy, is one of those bibulant individuals who, in the rural districts, are called 'old winkers,' and his face, tobacco-stained, and rubicund with the drinks of forty years, gleamed with the light of other days, as he hicconghed out the little tale. It may serve to show how the boy is remembered in Westhaven, if I add a word or two respecting my interview with this man. I met him on an unfrequented road; his hair was gray, his step was tottering; and thinking it probable he might be able to add to my stock of reminiscences, I asked him whether he remembered Horace Greeley. He mumbled a few words in reply; but I perceived that he was far gone towards intoxication, and soon drove on. A moment after, I heard a voice calling behind me. I looked round, and discovered that the voice was that of the soaker, who was shouting for me to stop. I alighted and went back to him. And now that the idea of my previous questions had had time to imprint itself upon his half-torpid brain, his tongue was loosened, and he entered into the subject with an enthusiasm that seemed for a time to burn up the fumes that had stupefied him. He was full of his theme; and, besides confirming much that I had already heard, added the story related above, from his own recollection. As the tribute of a sot to the champion of the Maine-Law, the old man's harangue was highly interesting.

That part of the town of Westhaven was, thirty years ago, a desperate place for drinking. The hamlet in which the family lived longer than anywhere else in the neighborhood, has ceased to exist, and it decayed principally through the intemperance of its inhabitants. Much of the land about it has not been improved in the least degree, from what it was when Horace Greeley helped to clear it; and drink has absorbed the means and the energy which should have been devoted to its improvement. A boy growing up in such a place would be likely to become either a drunkard or a tee-totaler, according to his organization; and Horace became the latter. It is rather a singular fact, that, though both his parents and all their ancestors were accustomed to the habitual and liberal use of intoxicating liquors and tobacco, neither Horace nor his brother could ever be induced to partake of either. They had a constitutional aversion to the taste of both, long before they understood the nature of the human system well enough to know that stimulants of all kinds are necessarily pernicious. Horace was therefore a tee-totaler before tee-totalism came up, and he took a sort of pledge before the pledge was inverted. It happened one day that a neighbor stopped to take dinner with the family, and, as a matter of course, the bottle of rum was brought out for his entertainment. Horace, it appears, either tasted a little, or else took a disgust at the smell of the stuff, or perhaps was offended at the effects which he saw it produce. An idea struck him. He said, "Father, what will you give me if I do not drink a drop of liquor till I am twenty-one?" His father, who took the question as a joke, answered, "I'll give you a dollar." "It's a bargain," said Horace. And it *was* a bargain, at least on the side of Horace, who kept his pledge inviolate, though I have no reason to believe he ever received his dollar. Many were the attempts made by his friends, then and afterwards, to induce him to break his resolution, and on one occasion they tried to force some liquor into his mouth. But from the day on which the conversation given above occurred, to this day, he has not knowingly taken into his system any alcoholic liquid.

At Westhaven, Horace incurred the second peril of his life. He was nearly strangled in coming into the world; and, in his thirteenth year, he was nearly strangled out of it. The family were then living on the banks of the Hubbarton river, a small stream which supplied power to the old 'Tryon Sawmill,' which the father, assisted by his boys, conducted for a year or two. Across the river, where it was widened by the dam, there was no bridge, and people were accustomed to get over on a floating saw-log, pushing along the log by means of a pole. The boys were floating about in the river one day, when the log on which the younger brother was standing, rolled over, and in went the boy, over head and ears, into water deep enough to drown a giraffe. He rose to the surface and clung to the bark of the log, but was unable to get upon it from the same cause as that which had prevented his standing upon it—it would roll. Horace hastened to his assistance. He got upon the log to which his brother was clinging, lay down upon it, and put down a hand for his brother to grasp. His brother did grasp it, and pulled with so much vigor, that the log made another revolution, and in went Horace. Neither of the boys could swim. They clung to the log and screamed for assistance; but no one happened to be near enough to hear them. At length, the younger of the drowning pair managed, by climbing over Horace, and sousing him completely under the log, to get out. Horace emerged, half-drowned, and again hung for life at the rough bark. But the future hero of ten thousand paragraphs was not to be drowned in a mill-pond; so the log floated into shallower water, when, by making a last, spasmodic effort, he succeeded in springing up high enough to get safely upon its broad back. It was a narrow escape for both; but Horace, with all his reams of articles forming in his head, came as near taking a summary departure to that bourn where no 'RIBUNE could have been set up, as a boy could, and yet not *go*. He went dripping home, and recovered from the effects of his ad-venture in due time.

This was Horace Greeley's *first* experience of 'log-rolling.' It was not calculated to make him like it.

One of the first subjects which the boy seriously considered, and perhaps the first upon which he arrived at a decided opinion, was Religion. And this was the more remarkable from the fact, that his education at home was not of a nature to direct his attention strongly to the subject. Both of his parents assented to the Ortho-dox creed of New England; his father inherited a preference for the Baptist denomination; his mother a leaning to the Presbyter-ian. But neither were members of a church, and neither were par-ticularly devout. The father, however, was somewhat strict in certain observances. He would not allow novels and plays to be read in the house on Sundays, nor an heretical book at any time. The family, when they lived near a church, attended it with con-siderable regularity—Horace among the rest. Sometimes the father would require the children to read a certain number of chapters in the Bible on Sunday. And if the mother—as mothers are apt to be—was a little less scrupulous upon such points, and occasionally winked at Sunday novel-reading, it certainly did not arise from any set disapproval of her husband's strictness. It was merely that she was the mother, he the father, of the family. The religious educa-tion of Horace was, in short, of a nature to leave his mind, not un-biased in favor of orthodoxy—that had been almost impossible in New England thirty years ago—but as nearly in equilibrium on the subject, in a state as favorable to original inquiry, as the place and circumstances of his early life rendered possible.

There was not in Westhaven one individual who was known to

be a dissenter from the established faith; nor was there any dissenting sect or society in the vicinity; nor was any periodical of a heterodox character taken in the neighborhood; nor did any heretical works fall in the boy's way till years after his religious opinions were settled. Yet, from the age of twelve he began to doubt; and at fourteen—to use the pathetic language of one who knew him then—" he was little better than a Universalist."

The theology of the seminary and the theology of the farm-house are two different things. They are as unlike as the discussion of the capital punishment question in a debating society is to the discussion of the same question among a company of criminals accused of murder. The unsophisticated, rural mind meddles not with the metaphysics of divinity; it takes little interest in the Foreknowledge and Free-will difficulty, in the Election and Responsibility problem, and the manifold subtleties connected therewith. It grapples with a simpler question:—'*Am I in danger of being damned?*' 'Is it likely that I shall go to hell, and be tormented with burning sulphur, and the proximity of a serpent, forever, and ever, and ever?' To minds of an ampler and more generous nature, the same question presents itself, but in another form:—Is it a fact that nearly every individual of the human family will forever fail of attaining the WELFARE of which he was created capable, and be ' *lost*,' beyond the hope, beyond the possibility of recovery?' Upon the latter form of the inquiry, Horace meditated much, and talked often during his thirteenth and fourteenth years. When his companions urged the orthodox side, he would rather object, but mildly, and say with a puzzled look, "It don't seem consistent."

While he was in the habit of revolving such thoughts in his mind, a circumstance occurred which accelerated his progress towards a rejection of the damnation dogma. It was nothing more than his chance reading in a school-book of the history of Demetrius Poliorcètes. The part of the story which bore upon the subject of his thoughts may be out-lined thus:—

Demetrius, (B. C. 301,) surnamed Poliorcètes, *besieger of cities*, was the son of Antigonus, one of those generals whom the death of Alexander the Great left masters of the world. Demetrius was one of the ' fast ' princes of antiquity, a handsome, brave, ingenious man, but vain, rash and dissolute. He and his father ruled over Asia Minor and Syria. Greece was under the sway of Cassander and Ptolemy, who had re-established in Athens aristocratic institutions, and held the Athenians in servitude. Demetrius, who aspired to the glory of succoring the distressed, and was not averse to reducing the power of his enemies, Cassander and Ptolemy, sailed to Athens with a fleet of two hundred and fifty ships, expelled the garrison and obtained possession of the city. Antigonus had been advised to retain possession of Athens, the key of Greece; but he replied:—"The best and securest of all keys is the friendship of the people, and Athens was the watch-tower of the world, from whence the torch of his glory would blaze over the earth." Animated by such sentiments, his son, Demetrius, on reaching the city, had proclaimed that "his father, in a happy hour, he hoped, for Athens, had sent him to re-instate them in their liberties, and to restore their laws and ancient form of government." The Athenians received him with acclamations. He performed all that he promised, and more. He gave the people a hundred and fifty thousand measures of meal, and timber enough to build a hundred galleys. The gratitude of the Athenians was boundless. They bestowed upon Demetrius the title of king and god-protector. They erected an altar upon the spot where he had first alighted from his chariot. They created a priest in his honor, and decreed that he should be received in all his future visits as a god. They changed the name of the month *Munychion* to *Demetrion*, called the last day of every month *Demetrius*, and the feasts of Bacchus *Demetria*. "The gods," says the good Plutarch, "soon showed how much offended they were at these things." Demetrius enjoyed these extravagant honors for a time, added an Athenian wife to the number he already possessed, and sailed away to prosecute the war. A second time the Athenians were threatened with the yoke of Cassander; again Demetrius, with a fleet of three hundred and thirty ships, came to their deliverance, and again the citizens taxed their ingenuity to the utmost in devising for their deliverer new honors and more piquant pleasures. At length Demetrius, after a career of victory, fell into misfortune. His domains were invaded, his father was slain, the kingdom was dismembered, and Demetrius, with a remnant of his army, was obliged to fly. Reaching Ephesus in want of money, he spared the temple filled with treasure ; and fearing his soldiers would plunder it, left the place and embarked for Greece. *His dependence was upon the Athenians,* with whom he had left his wife, his ships, and his money. Confidently relying upon their affection and gratitude, he pursued his voyage with all possible expedition as to a secure asylum. *But the fickle Athenians failed him in his day of need!* At the Cyclades, Athenian ambassadors met him, and mocked him with the *entreaty* that he would by no means go to Athens, as the people had declared by an edict, that they would receive no king into the city ; and as for his wife, he could find her at Megare, whither she had been conducted with the respect due to her rank. Demetrius, who up to that moment had borne his reverses with calmness, was cut to the heart, and overcome by mingled disgust and rage. He was not in a condition to avenge the wrong. He expostulated with the Athenians in moderate terms, and waited only to be joined by his galleys, and turned his back upon the ungrateful country. Time passed. Demetrius again became powerful. Athens was rent by factions. Availing himself of the occasion, the injured king sailed with a considerable fleet to Attica, landed his forces and invested the city, which was soon reduced to such extremity of famine that a father and son, it is related, fought for the possession of a dead mouse that happened to fall from the ceiling of the room in which they were sitting. The Athenians were compelled, at length, to open their gates to Demetrius, who marched in with his troops. He commanded all the citizens to assemble in the theater. They obeyed. *Utterly at his mercy, they expected no mercy, felt that they deserved no mercy.* The theater was surrounded with armed men, and on each side of the stage was stationed a body of the king's own guards. Demetrius entered by the tragedian's passage, advanced across the stage, and confronted the assembled citizens, who awaited in terror to hear the signal for their slaughter. But no such signal was heard. He addressed them in a soft and persuasive tone, complained of their conduct in gentle terms, forgave their ingratitude, took them again into favor, gave the city a hundred thousand measures of wheat, and promised the re-establishment of their ancient institutions. The people, relieved from their terror, astonished at their *good* fortune, and filled with enthusiasm at such

4

generous forbearance, overwhelmed Demetrius with acclamations.

Horace was fascinated by the story. He thought the conduct of Demetrius not only magnanimous and humane, but just and politic. Sparing the people, misguided by their leaders, seemed to him the best way to make them ashamed of their ingratitude, and the best way of preventing its recurrence. And he argued, if mercy is best and wisest on a small scale, can it be less so on a large? If a *man* is capable of such lofty magnanimity, may not God be who *made* man capable of it? If, in a human being, revenge and jealousy are despicable, petty and vulgar, what impiety is it to attribute such feelings to the beneficent Father of the Universe? The sin of the Athenians against Demetrius had every element of enormity. Twice he had snatched them from the jaws of ruin. Twice he had supplied their dire necessity. Twice he had refused all reward except the empty honors they paid to his name and person. He had condescended to become one of them by taking a daughter of Athens as his wife. He had entrusted his wife, his ships and his treasure to their care. Yet in the day of his calamity, when for the first time it was in their *power* to render him a service, when he was coming to them with the remnant of his fortune, without a doubt of their fidelity, with every reason to suppose that his misfortunes would render him dearer to them than ever; *then* it was that they determined to refuse him even an admittance within their gates, and sent an embassy to meet him with mockery and subterfuge.

Of the offenses committed by man against man, there is one which man can seldom lift his soul up to the height of forgiving. It is to be slighted in the day of his humiliation by those who showed him honor in the time of his prosperity. Yet man *can* forgive even this. Demetrius forgave it; and the nobler and greater a man is, the less keen is his sense of personal wrong, the less difficult it is for him to forgive. The poodle must show his teeth at every passing dog; the mastiff walks majestic and serene through a pack of snarling curs.

Amid such thoughts as these, the orthodox theory of damnation had little chance; the mind of the boy revolted against it more and more; and the result was, that he became as our pious friend lamented, "little better than a Universalist"—in fact *no* better. From the age of fourteen he was known wherever he lived as a champion of Universalism, though he never entered a Universalist church till he was twenty years old. By what means he managed to 'reconcile' his new belief with the explicit and unmistakable declarations of what he continued to regard as Holy Writ, or how anybody has ever done it, I do not know. The boy appears to have shed his orthodoxy easily. His was not a nature to travail with a new idea for months and years, and arrive at certainty only after a struggle that rends the soul, and leaves it sore and sick for life. He was young; the iron of our theological system had not entered into his soul; he took the matter somewhat lightly; and, having arrived at a theory of the Divine government, which accorded with his own gentle and forgiving nature, he let the rest of the theological science alone, and went on his way rejoicing.

Yet it was no slight thing that had happened to him. A man's Faith is the man. Not to have a Faith is not to be a man. Beyond all comparison, the most important fact of a man's life is the formation of the Faith which he adheres to and lives by. And though Horace Greeley has occupied himself little with things spiritual, confining himself, by a necessity of his nature, chiefly to the promotion of material interests, yet I doubt not that this early change in his religious belief was the event which gave to all his subsequent life its direction and character. Whether that change was a desirable one, or an undesirable, is a question upon which the reader of course has a decided opinion. The following, perhaps, may be taken as the leading consequences of a deliberate and intelligent exchange of a severe creed in which a person has been educated, for a less severe one to which he attains by the operations of his own mind:

It quickens his understanding, and multiplies his ideas to an extent which, it is said, no one who has never experienced it can possibly conceive. It induces in him a habit of original reflection upon subjects of importance. It makes him slow to believe a thing, merely because many believe it—merely because it has long been believed. It renders him open to conviction, for he cannot forget that there was a time when he held opinions which he now clearly sees to be

erroneous. It dissolves the spell of Authority; it makes him dis-
trustful of Great Names. It lessens his terror of Public Opinion;
for he has confronted it—discovered that it shows more teeth than
it uses—that it harms only those who fear it—that it bows at length
in homage to him whom it cannot frighten. It throws him upon
his own *moral* resources. Formerly, Fear came to his assistance in
moments of temptation; hell-fire rolled up its column of lurid smoke
before him in the dreaded distance. But now he sees it not. If he
has the Intelligence to know, the Heart to love, the Will to choose,
the Strength to do, the RIGHT; he does it, and his life is high, and
pure, and noble. If Intelligence, or Heart, or Will, or Strength is
wanting to him, he vacillates; he is not an integer, his life is not.
But, in either case, his Acts are the measure of his Worth.

Moreover, the struggle of a heretic with the practical difficulties
of life, and particularly his early struggle, is apt to be a hard one;
for, *generally*, the Rich, the Respectable, the Talented, and the
Virtuous of a nation are ranged on the side of its Orthodoxy in an
overwhelming majority. They feel themselves allied with it—dependent upon it. Above all, they believe in it, and think they
would be damned if they did not. They are slow to give their
countenance to one who dissents from their creed, even though he
aspire only to make their shoes, or clean them, and though they
more than suspect that the rival shoemaker round the corner keeps
a religious newspaper on his counter solely for the effect of the
thing upon pious consumers of shoe-leather.

To depart from the established Faith, then, must be accounted a
risk, a danger, a thing uncomfortable and complicating. But, from
the nettle Danger, *alone*, we pluck the flower Safety. And he who
loves Truth first—Advantage second—will certainly find Truth at
length, and care little at what loss of Advantage. So, let every
man be fully persuaded in his own mind—with which safe and
salutary text we may take leave of matters theological, and resume
our story.

The political events which occurred during Horace Greeley's
residence in Westhaven were numerous and exciting; some of
them were of a character to attract the attention of a far less forward and thoughtful boy than he. Doubtless he read the message
of President Monroe in 1821, in which the policy of Protection

to American Industry was recommended strongly, and advocated by arguments so simple that a child could understand them; so cogent that no man could refute them—arguments, in fact, precisely similar to those which the Tribune has since made familiar to the country. In the message of 1822, the president repeated his recommendation, and again in that of 1824. Those were the years of the recognition of the South American Republics, of the Greek enthusiasm, of Lafayette's triumphal progress through the Union; of the occupation of Oregon, of the suppression of Piracy in the Gulf of Mexico; of the Clay, Adams and Jackson controversy. It was during the period we are now considering, that Henry Clay made his most brilliant efforts in debate, and secured a place in the affections of Horace Greeley, which he retained to his dying day. It was then, too, that the boy learned to distrust the party who claimed to be pre-eminently and exclusively Democratic.

How attentively he watched the course of political events, how intelligently he judged them, at the age of thirteen, may be inferred from a passage in an article which he wrote twenty years after, the facts of which he stated from his early recollection of them:

"The first political contest," he wrote in the TRIBUNE for August 29th, 1846, "in which we ever took a distinct interest will serve to illustrate this distinction [between real and sham democracy]. It was the Presidential Election of 1824. Five candidates for President were offered, but one of them was withdrawn, leaving four, all of them members in regular standing of the so-called Republican or Democratic party. But a caucus of *one-fourth* of the members of Congress had selected one of the four (William H. Crawford) as *the* Republican candidate, and it was attempted to make the support of this one a test of party orthodoxy and fealty. This was resisted, we think most justly and democratically, by three-fourths of the people, including a large majority of those of this State. But among the prime movers of the caucus wires was *Martin Van Buren* of this State, and here it was gravely proclaimed and insisted that Democracy required a blind support of Crawford in preference to Adams, Jackson, or Clay, all of the Democratic party, who were competitors for the station. A Legislature was chosen as 'Republican' before the people generally had begun to think of the Presidency, and, this Legislature, it was undoubtingly expected, would choose Crawford Electors of President. But the friends of the rival candidates at length began to bestir themselves and demand that the New York Electors should be chosen by a direct vote of the people, and not by a forestalled Legislature This demand was vehemently resisted by Martin Van Buren and those who followed his lead, including the leading 'Democratic' politicians and editors of the State, the 'Albany Argus,' 'Noah's Enquirer, or National Advocate,' &c. &c. The feeling in favor of an Election by the people became so strong and general that Gov. Yates, though himself a Crawford man, was impelled to call a special session of the Legislature for this express purpose. The Assembly passed a bill giving the choice to the people by an overwhelming majority, in defiance of the exertions of Van Buren, A. C. Flagg, &c. The bill went to the Senate, to which body *Silas Wright* had recently been elected from the Northern District, and elected by Clintonian votes on an explicit understanding that he would vote for giving the choice of the Electors to the people. He accordingly voted, on one or two abstract propositions, that the choice *ought to be* given to the people. But when it came to a direct vote, this same Silas Wright, now Governor, voted to *deprive* the people of that privilege, by postponing the whole subject to the next regular session of the Legislature, when it would be *too late* for the people to choose Electors for that time. A bare majority (17) of the Senators thus withheld from the people the right they demanded. The cabal failed in their great object, after all, for several members of the Legislature, elected as Democrats, took ground for Mr. Clay, and by uniting with the friends of Mr. Adams defeated most of the Crawford Electors, and Crawford lost the Presidency. We were but thirteen when this took place, but we looked on very earnestly, without prejudice, and tried to look beyond the mere names by which the contending parties were called. Could we doubt that Democracy was on one side and the Democratic party on the other? Will ' Democrat' attempt to gainsay it now ?

" Mr. Adams was chosen President—as thorough a Democrat, in the true sense of the word, as ever lived—a plain, unassuming, upright, and most capable statesman. He managed the public affairs so well that nobody could really give a reason for opposing him, and hardly any two gave the same reason. There was no party conflict during his time respecting the Bank, Tariff, Internal Improvements, nor anything else of a substantial character. He kept the expenses of the government very moderate. He never turned a man out of office because of a difference of political sentiment. Yet it was determined at the outset that he should be put down, no matter how well he might administer the government, and a combination of the old Jackson, Crawford, and Calhoun parties, with the personal adherents of De Witt Clinton, aided by a shamefully false and preposterous outcry that he had obtained the Presidency by a *bargain* with Mr. Clay, succeeded in returning an Opposition Congress in the middle of his term, and at its close to put in General Jackson over him by a large majority.

" The character of this man Jackson we had studied pretty thoroughly and without prejudice. His fatal duel with Dickinson about a horse-race; his pistoling Colonel Benton in the streets of Nashville; his forcing his way through the Indian country with his drove of negroes in defiance of the express order of the Agent Dinsmore; his imprisonment of Judge Hall at New Orleans, long after the British had left that quarter, and when martial law ought long since to have been set aside; his irruption into Florida and capture of Spanish posts and officers without a shadow of authority to do so; his threats to cut off the ears of Senators who censured this conduct in solemn debate—in short, his whole life convinced us that the man never was a Democrat, in any proper sense of the term, but a violent and lawless despot, after the pattern of Cæsar, Cromwell, and Napoleon, and unfit to be trusted with power. Of course, we went against him, but not against anything really Democratic in him or his party.

"That General Jackson in power justified all our previous expectations of him, need hardly be said. That he did more to destroy the Republican character of our government and render it a centralized despotism, than any other man could do, we certainly believe. But our correspondent and we would probably disagree with regard to the Bank and other questions which convulsed the Union during his rule, and we will only ask his attention to one of them, the earliest, and, in our view, the most significant.

"The Cherokee Indians owned, and had ever occupied, an extensive tract of country lying within the geographical limits of Georgia, Alabama, &c. It was theirs by the best possible title—theirs by our solemn and reiterated Treaty stipulations. We had repeatedly bought from them slices of their lands, solemnly guarantying to them all that we did not buy, and agreeing to defend them therein against all aggressors. We had promised to keep all intruders out of their territory. At least one of these Treaties was signed by Gen. Jackson himself; others by Washington, Jefferson, &c. All the usual pretexts for agression upon Indians failed in this case. The Cherokees had been our friends and allies for many years; they had committed no depredations; they were peaceful, industrious, in good part Christianized, had a newspaper printed in their own tongue, and were fast improving in the knowledge and application of the arts of civilized life. They compared favorably every way with their white neighbors. But the Georgians coveted their fertile lands, and determined to have them; they set them up in a lottery and gambled them off among themselves, and resolved to take possession. A fraudulent Treaty was made between a few Cherokees of no authority or consideration and sundry white agents, including one 'who stole the livery of Heaven to serve the devil in,' but everybody scoffed at this mockery, as did ninety-nine hundredths of the Cherokees.

"Now Georgia, during Mr. Adams' Administration, attempted to extend her jurisdiction over these poor people. Mr. Adams, finding remonstrance of no avail, stationed a part of the army at a proper point, prepared to drive all intruders out of the Cherokee country, as we had by treaty solemnly engaged to do. This answered the purpose. Georgia blustered, but dared not go further. She went *en masse* for Jackson, of course. When he came in, she proceeded at once to extend her jurisdiction over the Cherokees in very deed. They remonstrated—pointed to their broken treaties, and urged the President to perform his sworn duty, and protect them, but in vain. Georgia seized a Cherokee accused of killing another Cherokee in their own country, tried him for and convicted him of murder. He sued out a writ of error, carried the case up to the U. S. Supreme Court, and there obtained a decision in his favor, establishing the utter illegality as well as injustice of the acts of Georgia in the premises. The validity of our treaties with the Cherokees, and the consequent duty of the President to see them enforced, any thing in any State-law or edict to the contrary notwithstanding, was explicitly affirmed. But President Jackson decided that Georgia was right and the Supreme Court wrong, and refused to enforce the decision of the latter. So the Court was defied, the Cherokee hung, the Cherokee country given up to the cupidity of the Georgians, and its rightful owners driven across the Mississippi, virtually at the point of the bayonet. That case changed the nature of our Government, making the President Supreme Judge of the Law as well as its Chief Minister—in other words, Dictator. "Amen! Hurrah for Jackson!" said the Pharisaic Democracy of Party and Spoils. We could not say it after them. We considered our nation perjured in the trampling down and exile of these Cherokees; perjury would have lain heavy on our soul had we approved and promoted the deed."

On another occasion, when Silas Wright was nominated for Governor of the State of New York, the Tribune broke forth: "The 'notorious Seventeen'—what New-Yorker has not heard of them? —yet how small a proportion of our present voting population retain a vivid and distinct recollection of the outrage on Republicanism and Popular Rights which made the 'Seventeen' so unenviably notorious! The Editor of the Tribune is of that proportion, be it small or large. Though a boy in 1824, and living a mile across the Vermont line of the State, he can never forget the indignation awakened by that outrage, which made him for ever an adversary of the Albany Regency and the demagogues who here and elsewhere made use of the terms 'Democracy,' 'Democrats,' 'Democratic party,' to hoodwink and cajole the credulous and unthinking —to divert their attention from things to names—to divest them of independent and manly thought, and lead them blindfold wherever the intriguers' interests shall dictate—to establish a real Aristocracy under the abused name of Democracy. It was 1824 which taught many beside us the nature of this swindle, and fired them with unconquerable zeal and resolution to defeat the fraud by exposing it to the apprehension of a duped and betrayed people."

These extracts will assist the reader to recall the political excitements of the time.   And he may well esteem it extraordinary for a boy of thirteen—an age when a boy is, generally, most a boy—to understand them so well, and to be interested in them so deeply. It should be remembered, however, that in remote country places, where the topics of conversation are few, *all* the people take a degree of interest in politics, and talk about political questions with a frequency and pertinacity of which the busy inhabitants of cities can form little idea.

Horace's last year in Westhaven (1825) wore slowly away.   He had exhausted the schools; he was impatient to be at the types, and he wearied his father with importunities to get him a place in a printing-office.   But his father was loth to let him go, for two reasons : the boy was useful at home, and the cautious father feared he would not do well away from home ; he was so gentle, so absent, so awkward, so little calculated to make his way with stran gers.   One day, the boy saw in the " Northern Spectator," a weekly paper, published at East Poultney, eleven miles distant, an advertisement for an apprentice in the office of the "Spectator" itself. He showed it to his father, and wrung from him a reluctant consent to his applying for the place.   "I have n't got time to go and see about it, Horace; but if you have a mind to walk over to Poultney and see what you can do, why you may."

Horace *had* a mind to.

4*

CHAPTER VI.

APPRENTICESHIP.

EAST POULTNEY is not, decidedly not, a place which a traveler—if, by any extraordinary chance, a traveler should ever visit it—would naturally suspect of a newspaper. But, in one of the most densely-populated parts of the city of New York, there is a *field!* —a veritable, indubitable field, with a cow in it, a rough wooden fence around it, and a small, low, wooden house in the middle of it, where an old gentleman lives, who lived there when all was rural around him, and who means to live there all his days, pasturing his cow and raising his potatoes on ground which he could sell—but won't—at a considerable number of dollars per foot. The field in the metropolis we can account for. But that a newspaper should ever have been published at East Poultney, Rutland county, Vermont, seems, at the first view of it, inexplicable.

Vermont, however, is a land of villages; and the business which is elsewhere done only in large towns is, in that State, divided among the villages in the country. Thus, the stranger is astonished at seeing among the few signboards of mere hamlets, one or two containing most unexpected and metropolitan announcements, such as, "SILVERSMITH," "ORGAN FACTORY," "PIANO FORTES," "PRINTING OFFICE," or "PATENT MELODEONS." East Poultney, for example, is little more than a hamlet, yet it once had a newspaper, and boasts a small factory of melodeons at this moment. A foreigner would as soon expect to see there an Italian opera house or a French café.

The Poultney river is a small stream that flows through a valley, which widens and narrows, narrows and widens, all along its course; here, a rocky gorge; a grassy plain, beyond. At one of its narrow places, where the two ranges of hills approach and nod to one another, and where the river pours through a rocky channel—a torrent on a very small scale—the little village nestles, a cluster of houses at the base of an enormous hill. It is built round a small triangular green, in the middle of which is a church, with a handsome clock in its steeple, all complete except the works, and bearing on its ample face the date, 1805. No village, however minute, can get on without three churches, representing the Conservative, the Enthusiastic, and Eccentric tendencies of human nature; and, of course, East Poultney has three. It has likewise the most remarkably shabby and dilapidated school-house in all the country round. There is a store or two; but business is not brisk, and when a customer arrives in town, perhaps, his first difficulty will be to *find* the storekeeper, who has locked up his store and gone to hoe in his garden or talk to the blacksmith. A tavern, a furnace, a saw-mill, and forty dwelling houses, nearly complete the inventory of the village. The place has a neglected and 'seedy' aspect which is rare in New England. In that remote and sequestered spot, it seems to have been forgotten, and left behind in the march of progress; and the people, giving up the hope and the endeavor to catch up, have settled down to the tranquil enjoyment of Things as they Are. The village cemetery, near by,—more populous far than the village, for the village is an old one—is upon the side of a steep ascent, and whole ranks of gravestones bow, submissive to the law of gravitation, and no man sets them upright. A quiet, slow little place is East Poultney. Thirty years ago, the people were a little more wide awake, and there were a few more of them.

It was a fine spring morning in the year 1826, about ten o'clock, when Mr. Amos Bliss, the manager, and one of the proprietors, of the Northern Spectator, 'might have been seen' in the garden behind his house planting potatoes. He heard the gate open behind him, and, without turning or looking round, became dimly conscious of the presence of a boy. But the boys of country villages go into whosesoever garden their wandering fancy impels them, and supposing this boy to be one of his own neighbors, Mr. Bliss continued his work and quickly forgot that he was not alone. In a few minutes, he heard a voice close behind him, a strange voice, high-pitched and whining.

It said, "Are you the man that carries on the printing office?"

Mr. Bliss then turned, and resting upon his hoe, surveyed the person who had thus addressed him. He saw standing before him a boy apparently about fifteen years of age, of a light, tall, and slender form, dressed in the plain, farmer's cloth of the time, his garments cut with an utter disregard of elegance and fit. His trowsers were exceedingly short and voluminous; he wore no stockings; his shoes were of the kind denominated 'high-lows,' and much worn down; his hat was of felt, 'one of the old stamp, with so small a brim, that it looked more like a two-quart measure inverted than anything else;' and it was worn far back on his head; his hair was white, with a tinge of orange at its extremities, and it lay thinly upon a broad forehead and over a head 'rocking on shoulders which seemed too slender to support the weight of a member so disproportioned to the general outline.' The general effect of the figure and its costume was so *outré*, they presented such a combination of the rustic and ludicrous, and the apparition had come upon him so suddenly, that the amiable gardener could scarcely keep from laughing.

He restrained himself, however, and replied, "Yes, I'm the man."

Whereupon the stranger asked, "Don't you want a boy to learn the trade?"

"Well," said Mr. Bliss, "we have been thinking of it. Do *you* want to learn to print?"

"I've had some notion of it," said the boy in true Yankee fashion, as though he had not been dreaming about it, and longing for it for years.

Mr. Bliss was both astonished and puzzled—astonished that such a fellow as the boy *looked* to be, should have ever thought of learning to print, and puzzled how to convey to him an idea of the absurdity of the notion. So, with an expresssion in his countenance, such as that of a tender-hearted dry-goods merchant might be supposed to assume if a hod-carrier should apply for a place in the lace department, he said, " Well, my boy—but, you know, it takes considerable learning to be a printer. Have you been to school much ?"

" No," said the boy, " I have 'nt had much chance at school. I 've read some."

" What have you read ?" asked Mr. Bliss.

" Well, I 've read some history, and some travels, and a little of most everything."

" Where do you live ?"

" At Westhaven."

" How did you come over ?"

" I came on foot."

" What's your name ?"

" Horace Greeley."

Now it happened that Mr. Amos Bliss had been for the last three years an Inspector of Common Schools, and in fulfilling the duties of his office—examining and licensing teachers—he had acquired an uncommon facility in asking questions, and a fondness for that exercise which men generally entertain for any employment in which they suppose themselves to excel. The youth before him was—in the language of medical students—a 'fresh subject,' and the Inspector proceeded to try all his skill upon him, advancing from easy questions to hard ones, up to those knotty problems with which he had been wont to ' stump' candidates for the office of teacher. The boy was a match for him. He answered every question promptly, clearly and modestly. He could not be ' stumped' in the ordinary school studies, and of the books he had read he could give a correct and complete analysis. In Mr. Bliss's own account of the interview, he says, " On entering into conversation, and a partial examination of the qualifications of my new applicant, it required but little time to discover that he possessed a mind of no common order, and an acquired intelligence far beyond his years. He had had but little opportunity at the common school, but he said ' he had read some,' and what he had read he well understood and remembered. In addition to the ripe intelligence manifested in one so young, and whose instruction had been so limited, there was a single-mindedness, a truthfulness and common sense in what he said, that at once commanded my regard."

After half an hour's conversation with the boy, Mr. Bliss intimated that he thought he would do, and told him to go into the printing-office and talk to the foreman. Horace went to the printing-office, and there his appearance produced an effect on the tender minds of the three apprentices who were at work therein, which can be much better imagined than described, and which is most vividly remembered by the two who survive. To the foreman Horace addressed himself, regardless certainly, oblivious probably, of the stare and the remarks of the boys. The foreman, at first, was inclined to wonder that Mr. Bliss should, for one moment, think it possible that a boy got up in that style could perform the most ordinary duties of a printer's apprentice. Ten minutes' talk with him, however, effected a partial revolution in his mind in the boy's favor, and as he was greatly in want of another apprentice, he was not inclined to be over particular. He tore off a slip of proof-paper, wrote a few words upon it hastily with a pencil, and told the boy to take it to Mr. Bliss. That piece of paper was his fate. The words were: ' *Guess we 'd better try him.*' Away went Horace to the garden, and presented his paper. Mr. Bliss, whose curiosity had been excited to a high pitch by the extraordinary contrast between the appearance of the boy and his real quality, now entered into a long conversation with him, questioned him respecting his history, his past employments, his parents, their circumstances, his own intentions and wishes; and the longer he talked, the more his admiration grew. The result was, that he agreed to accept Horace as an apprentice, provided his father would agree to the usual terms; and then, with eager steps, and a light heart, the happy boy took the dusty road that led to his home in Westhaven.

"You 're not going to hire that tow-head, Mr. Bliss, are you?" asked one of the apprentices at the close of the day. "I am," was the reply, "and if you boys are expecting to get any fun out of him, you 'd better get it quick, or you 'll be too late. There 's something *in* that tow-head, as you 'll find out before you 're a week older."

A day or two after, Horace packed up his wardrobe in a small cotton handkerchief. Small as it was, it would have held more; for its proprietor never had more than two shirts, and one change of outer-clothing, at the same time, till he was of age. Father and son walked, side by side, to Poultney, the boy carrying his possessions upon a stick over his shoulder.

At Poultney, an unexpected difficulty arose, which for a time made Horace tremble in his high-low shoes. The terms proposed by Mr. Bliss were, that the boy should be bound for five years, and receive his board and twenty dollars a year. Now, Mr. Greeley had ideas of his own on the subject of apprenticeship, and he objected to this proposal, and to every particular of it. In the first place, he had determined that no child of his should ever be bound at all. In the second place, he thought five years an unreasonable time; thirdly, he considered that twenty dollars a year and board was a compensation ridiculously disproportionate to the services which Horace would be required to render; and finally, on each and all of these points, he clung to his opinion with the tenacity of a Greeley. Mr. Bliss appealed to the established custom of the country; five years was the usual period; the compensation offered was the regular thing; the binding was a point essential to the employer's interest. And at every pause in the conversation, the appealing voice of Horace was heard: "Father, I *guess* you 'd better make a bargain with Mr. Bliss;" or, "Father, I guess it won 't make much difference;" or, "Don't you think you 'd better do it, father?" At one moment the boy was reduced to despair. Mr. Bliss had given it as his *ultimatum* that the proposed binding was absolutely indispensable; he "could do business in no other way." "Well, then, Horace," said the father, "let us go home." The father turned to go; but Horace lingered; he could not give it up; and so the father turned again; the negotiation was re-opened, and after a prolonged discussion, a compromise was effected. What the terms were, that were finally agreed to, I cannot positively state, for the three memories which I have consulted upon the subject give three different replies. Probably, however, they were—no binding, and no money for six months; then the boy could, if he chose, bind himself for the remainder of the five years, at forty dollars a year, the apprentice to be boarded from the beginning. And so the father went home, and the son went straight to the printing office and took his first lesson in the art of setting type.

A few months after, it may be as well to mention here, Mr.

Greeley removed to Erie county, Pennsylvania, and bought some wild land there, from which he gradually created a farm, leaving Horace alone in Vermont. Grass now grows where the little house stood in Westhaven, in which the family lived longest, and the barn in which they stored their hay and kept their cattle, leans forward like a kneeling elephant, and lets in the daylight through ten thousand apertures. But the neighbors point out the tree that stood before their front door, and the tree that shaded the kitchen window, and the tree that stood behind the house, and the tree whose apples Horace liked, and the bed of mint with which he regaled his nose. And both the people of Westhaven and those of Amherst assert that whenever the Editor of the Tribune revisits the scenes of his early life, at the season when apples are ripe, one of the things that he is surest to do, is to visit the apple trees that produce the fruit which he liked best when he was a boy, and which he still prefers before all the apples of the world.

The new apprentice took his place at the font, and received from the foreman his 'copy,' composing stick, and a few words of instruction, and then he addressed himself to his task. He needed no further assistance. The mysteries of the craft he seemed to comprehend intuitively. He had thought of his chosen vocation for many years; he had formed a notion how the types *must* be arranged in order to produce the desired impression, and, therefore, all he had to acquire was manual dexterity. In perfect silence, without looking to the right hand or to the left, heedless of the sayings and doings of the other apprentices, though they were bent on mischief, and tried to attract and distract his attention, Horace worked on, hour after hour, all that day; and when he left the office at night could set type better and faster than many an apprentice who had had a month's practice. The next day, he worked with the same silence and intensity. The boys were puzzled. They thought it absolutely incumbent on them to perform an initiating rite of some kind; but the new boy gave them no handle, no excuse, no opening. He committed no greenness, he spoke to no one, looked at no one, seemed utterly oblivious of every thing save only his copy and his type. They threw type at him, but he never looked around. They talked saucily *at* him, but he threw back no retort. This would never do. Towards the close of the third day, the oldest apprentices took one of the large black balls with which printers used to *dab* the ink upon the type, and remarking that in his opinion Horace's hair was of too light a hue for so black an art as that which he had undertaken to learn, applied the ball, well inked, to Horace's head, making four distinct dabs. The boys, the journeyman, the pressman and the editor, all paused in their work to observe the result of this experiment. Horace neither spoke nor moved. He went on with his work as though nothing had happened, and soon after went to the tavern where he boarded, and spent an hour in purifying his dishonored locks. And that was all the 'fun' the boys 'got out' of their new companion on *that* occasion. They were conquered. In a few days the victor and the vanquished were excellent friends.

Horace was now fortunately situated. Ampler means of acquiring knowledge were within his reach than he had ever before enjoyed; nor were there wanting opportunities for the display of his acquisitions and the exercise of his powers.

"About this time," writes Mr. Bliss, "a sound, well-read theologian and a practical printer was employed to edit and conduct the paper. This opened a desirable school for intellectual culture to our young *debutant*. Debates ensued; historical, political, and religious questions were discussed; and often while all hands were engaged at the font of types; and here the purpose for which our young aspirant 'had read some' was made manifest. Such was the correctness of his memory in what he had read, in both biblical and profane history, that the reverend gentleman was often put at fault by his corrections. He always quoted chapter and verse to prove the point in dispute. On one occasion the editor said that money was the root of all evil, when he was corrected by the 'devil,' who said he believed it read in the Bible that the love of money was the root of all evil.

"A small town library gave him access to books, by which, together with the reading of the exchange papers of the office, he improved all his leisure hours. He became a frequent talker in our village lyceum, and often wrote dissertations.

"In the first organization of our village temperance society, the question arose as to the age when the young might become members. Fearing lest his own age might bar him, he moved that they be received when they were old enough to drink—which was adopted *nem. con.*

"Though modest and retiring, he was often led into political discussions with our ablest politicians, and few would leave the field without feeling instructed by the soundness of his views and the unerring correctness of his statements of political events.

"Having a thirst for knowledge, he bent his mind and all his energies to its acquisition, with unceasing application and untiring devotion; and I doubt if, in the whole term of his apprenticeship, he ever spent an hour in the common recreations of young men. He used to pass my door as he went to his daily meals, and though I often sat near, or stood in the way, so much absorbed did he appear in his own thoughts—his head bent forward and his eyes fixed upon the ground, that I have the charity to believe the reason why he never turned his head or gave me a look, was because he had no idea I was there!"

On one point the reminiscences of Mr. Bliss require correction. He thinks that his apprentice never spent an hour in the common recreations of young men during his residence in Poultney. Mr. Bliss, however, was his senior and his employer; and therefore observed him at a distance and from above. But I, who have conversed with those who were the friends and acquaintances of the youth, can tell a better story. He had a remarkable fondness for games of mingled skill and chance, such as whist, draughts, chess, and others; and the office was never without its dingy pack of cards, carefully concealed from the reverend editor and the serious customers, but brought out from its hiding-place whenever the coast was clear and the boys had a leisure hour. Horace never gambled, nor would he touch the cards on Sunday; but the delight of playing a game occasionally was heightened, perhaps, by the fact that in East Poultney a pack of cards was regarded as a thing accursed, not fit for saintly hands to touch. Bee-hunting, too, continued to be a favorite amusement with Horace. "He was always ready for a bee-hunt," says one who knew him well in Poultney, and bee-hunted with him often in the woods above the village. To finish with this matter of amusement, I may mention that a dancing-school was held occasionally at the village-tavern, and Horace was earnestly (ironically, perhaps) urged to join it; but he refused. Not that he disapproved of the dance—that best of all home recreations—but he fancied he was not exactly the figure for a quadrille. He occasionally looked in at the door of the dancing-room, but never could be prevailed upon to enter it.

Until he came to live at Poultney, Horace had never tried his hand at original composition. The injurious practice of writing 'compositions' was not among the exercises of any of the schools which he had attended. At Poultney, very early in his apprenticeship, he began, not indeed to write, but to compose paragraphs for the paper as he stood at the desk, and to set them in type as he composed them. They were generally items of news condensed from large articles in the exchange papers; but occasionally he composed an original paragraph of some length; and he continued to render editorial assistance of this kind all the while he remained in the office. The 'Northern Spectator' was an 'Adams paper,' and Horace was an Adams man.

The Debating Society, to which Mr. Bliss alludes, was an important feature in the life of East Poultney. There happened to be among the residents of the place, during the apprenticeship of Horace Greeley, a considerable number of intelligent men, men of some knowledge and talent—the editor of the paper, the village doctor, a county judge, a clergyman or two, two or three persons of some political eminence, a few well-informed mechanics, farmers, and others. These gentlemen had formed themselves into a 'Lyceum,' before the arrival of Horace, and the Lyceum had become so famous in the neighborhood, that people frequently came a distance of ten miles to attend its meetings. It assembled weekly, in the winter, at the little brick school-house. An original essay was read by the member whose 'turn' it was to do so, and then the question of the evening was debated; first, by four members who had been designated at the previous meeting, and after they had each spoken once, the question was open to the whole society. The questions were mostly of a very innocent and rudimental character, as, 'Is novel-reading injurious to society?' 'Has a person a right to take life in self-defense?' 'Is marriage conducive to happiness?' 'Do we, as a nation, exert a good moral influence in the world?' 'Do either of the great parties of the day carry out the principles of the Declaration of Independence?' 'Is the Union likely to be perpetuated?' 'Was Napoleon Bonaparte a great man?' 'Is it a person's duty to take the temperance pledge?' et cetera.

Horace joined the society, the first winter of his residence in Poultney, and, young as he was, soon became one of its leading members. "He was a real giant at the Debating Society," says

one of his early admirers. "Whenever he was appointed to speak
or to read an essay, he never wanted to be excused; he was always
ready. He was exceedingly *interested* in the questions which he
discussed, and stuck to his opinion against all opposition—not dis-
courteously, but still *he stuck to it*, replying with the most perfect
assurance to men of high station and of low. He had one advantage over all his fellow members; it was his memory. He had read
everything, and remembered the minutest details of important
events ; dates, names, places, figures, statistics—nothing had escaped
him. He was never treated as a *boy* in the society, but as a man
and an equal; and his opinions were considered with as much deference as those of the judge or the sheriff—more, I think. To the
graces of oratory he made no pretense, but he was a fluent and
interesting speaker, and had a way of giving an unexpected turn to
the debate by reminding members of a fact, well known but overlooked; or by correcting a misquotation, or by appealing to what
are called first principles. He was an opponent to be afraid of;
yet his sincerity and his earnestness were so evident, that those
whom he most signally floored liked him none the less for it. He
never lost his temper. In short, he spoke in his sixteenth year just
as he speaks now; and when he came a year ago to lecture in a
neighboring village, I saw before me the Horace Greeley of the
old Poultney 'Forum,' as we called it, and no other."

It is hardly necessary to record, that Horace never made the
slightest preparation for the meetings of the Debating Society in
the way of *dress*—except so far as to put on his jacket. In the
summer, he was accustomed to wear, while at work, two garments,
a shirt and trowsers; and when the reader considers that his trowsers were very short, his sleeves tucked up above his elbows, his
shirt open in front, he will have before his mind's eye the picture
of a youth attired with extreme simplicity. In his walks about the
village, he added to his dress a straw hat, valued originally at one
shilling. In the winter, his clothing was really insufficient. So, at
least, thought a kind-hearted lady who used to see him pass her
window on his way to dinner. "He never," she says, "had an
overcoat while he lived here; and I used to pity him *so* much in
cold weather. I remember him as a slender, pale little fellow,
younger looking than he really was, in a brown jacket much too

short for him. I used to think the winds would blow him away sometimes, as he crept along the fence lost in thought, with his head down, and his hands in his pockets. He was often laughed at for his homely dress, by the boys. Once, when a very interesting question was to be debated at the school-house, a young man who was noted among us for the elegance of his dress and the length of his account at the store, advised Horace to get a new ' rig out ' for the occasion, particularly as he was to lead one of the sides, and an unusually large audience was expected to be present. ' No,' said Horace, ' I guess I 'd better wear my old clothes than run in debt for new ones.' "

. Now, forty dollars a year is sufficient to provide a boy in the country with good and substantial clothing ; half the sum will keep him warm and decent. The reader, therefore, may be inclined to censure the young debater for his apparent parsimony ; or worse, for an insolent disregard of the feelings of others ; or, *worst*, for a pride that aped humility. The reader, if that be the present inclination of his mind, will perhaps experience a revulsion of feeling when he is informed—as I now do inform him, and on the best authority— that every dollar of the apprentice's little stipend which he could save by the most rigid economy, was piously sent to his father, who was struggling in the wilderness on the other side of the Alleghanies, with the difficulties of a new farm, and an insufficient capital. And this was the practice of Horace Greeley during all the years of his apprenticeship, and for years afterwards ; as long, in fact, as his father's land was unpaid for and inadequately provided with implements, buildings, and stock. At a time when filial piety may be reckoned among the extinct virtues, it is a pleasure to record a fact like this.

Twice, during his residence at Poultney, Horace visited his parents in Pennsylvania, six hundred miles distant, walking a great part of the way, and accomplishing the rest on a slow canal boat. On one of these tedious journeys he first saw Saratoga, a circumstance to which he alluded seven years after, in a fanciful epistle, written from that famous watering-place, and published in the " New Yorker " :

" Saratoga ! bright city of the present ! thou ever-during one-and-twenty of existence! a wanderer by thy stately palaces and gushing fountains salutes thee! Years, yet not many, have elapsed since, a weary roamer from a distant land, he first sought thy health-giving waters. November's sky was over earth and him, and more than all, over thee; and its chilling blasts made mournful melody amid the waving branches of thy ever-verdant pines. Then, as now, thou wert a City of Tombs, deserted by the gay throng whose light laughter re-echoes so joyously through thy summer-robed arbors. But to him, thou wert ever a fairy land, and he wished to quaff of thy Hygeian treasures as of the nectar of the poet's fables. One long and earnest draught, ere its sickening disrelish came over him, and he flung down the cup in the bitterness of disappointment and disgust, and sadly addressed him again to his pedestrian journey. Is it ever thus with thy castles, Imagination? thy pictures, Fancy? thy dreams, O Hope? Perish the unbidden thought! A health, in sparkling Congress, to the rainbow of life! even though its promise prove as shadowy as the baseless fabric of a vision. Better even the dear delusion of Hope—if delusion it must be—than the rugged reality of listless despair. (I think I could do this better in rhyme, if I had not trespassed in that line already. However, the cabin-conversation of a canal-packet is not remarkably favorable to poetry.) In plain prose, there is a great deal of mismanagement about this same village of Saratoga. The season gives up the ghost too easily," &c., &c.

During the four years that Horace lived at East Poultney, he boarded for some time at the tavern, which still affords entertainment for man and beast—*i. e.* peddler and horse—in that village. It was kept by an estimable couple, who became exceedingly attached to their singular guest, and he to them. Their recollections of him are to the following effect:—Horace at that time ate and drank whatever was placed before him; he was rather fond of good living, ate furiously, and fast, and much. He was very fond of coffee, but cared little for tea. Every one drank in those days, and there was a great deal of drinking at the tavern, but Horace never could be tempted to taste a drop of anything intoxicating. "I always," said the kind landlady, "took a great interest in young people, and when I saw they were going wrong, it used to distress me, no matter whom they belonged to; but I never feared for Horace. Whatever might be going on about the village or in the bar-room, I always knew *he* would do right." He stood on no ceremony at the table; he *fell to* without waiting to be asked or helped, devoured everything right and left, stopped as suddenly as he had begun, and vanished instantly. One day, as Horace was stretching his long arm over to the other side of the table in quest of a distant dish, the servant, wishing to hint to him in a jocular manner, that that was not exactly the most proper way of proceeding, said, "Don't trouble yourself, Horace, *I* want to help you to that dish, for, you know, I have a *particular* regard for you." He blushed, as only a boy with a very white face can blush, and, thenceforth, was less adventurous in exploring the remoter portions of the table-cloth. When any topic of interest was started at the table, he joined in it with the utmost confidence, and maintained his opinion against anybody, talking with great vivacity, and never angrily. He came, at length, to be regarded as a sort of Town Encyclopedia, and if any one wanted to know anything, he went, as a matter of course, to Horace Greeley; and, if a dispute arose between two individuals, respecting a point of history, or politics, or science, they referred it to Horace Greeley, and whomsoever *he* declared to be right, was confessed to be the victor in the controversy. Horace never went to a tea-drinking or a party of any kind, never went on an excursion, never slept away from home or was absent from one meal during the period of his residence at the tavern, except when he went to visit his parents. He seldom went to church, but spent the Sunday, usually, in reading. He was a stanch Universalist, a stanch whig, and a pre-eminently stanch anti-Mason. Thus, the landlord and landlady.

Much of this is curiously confirmed by a story often told in convivial moments by a distinguished physician of New York, who on one occasion chanced to witness at the Poultney tavern the exploits, gastronomic and encyclopedic, to which allusion has just been made. "Did I ever tell you," he is wont to begin, "how and where I first saw my friend Horace Greeley? Well, thus it happened. It was one of the proudest and happiest days of my life. I was a country boy then, a farmer's son, and we lived a few miles from East Poultney. On the day in question I was sent by my father to sell a load of potatoes at the store in East Poultney, and bring back various commodities in exchange. Now this was the first time, you must know, that I had ever been entrusted with so important an errand. I had been to the village with my father often enough, but now I was to go alone, and I felt as proud and independent as a midshipman the first time he goes ashore in command of a boat. Big with the fate of twenty bushels of potatoes, off I drove—reached the village—sold out my load—drove round to the tavern—put up my horses, and went in to dinner. This going to the tavern on my own account, all by myself, and paying my own bill, was, I thought, the crowning glory of the whole adventure. There were a good many people at dinner, the sheriff of the county and an ex-member of Congress among them, and I felt considerably abashed at first; but I had scarcely begun to eat, when my eyes fell upon an object so singular that I could do little else than stare at it all the while it remained in the room. It was a tall, pale, white-haired, *gawky* boy, seated at the further end of the table. He was in his shirt-sleeves, and he was eating with a rapidity and awkwardness that I never saw equaled before nor since. It seemed as if he was eating for a wager, and had gone in to win. He neither looked up nor round, nor appeared to pay the least attention to the conversation. My first thought was, 'This is a pretty sort of a tavern to let such a fellow as that sit at the same table with all these gentlemen; he ought to come in with the hostler.' I thought it strange, too, that no one seemed to notice him, and I supposed he owed his continuance at the table to that circumstance alone. And so I sat, eating little myself, and occupied in watching the wonderful performance of this wonderful youth. At length the conversation at the table became quite animated, turning upon some measure of an early Congress; and a question arose how certain members had voted on its final passage. There was a difference of opinion; and the sheriff, a very finely-dressed personage, I thought, to my boundless astonishment, referred the matter to the unaccountable Boy, saying, 'Aint that right, Greeley?' 'No,' said the Unaccountable, without looking up, 'you 're wrong.' 'There,' said the ex-member, 'I told you so.' 'And you 're wrong, too,' said the still-devouring Mystery. Then he laid down his knife and fork, and gave the history of the measure, explained the state of parties at the time, stated the vote in dispute, named the leading advocates and opponents of the bill, and, in short, gave a complete exposition of the whole matter. I listened and wondered; but what surprised me most was, that the company received his statement as pure gospel, and as settling the question beyond dispute—as a dictionary settles a dispute respecting the spelling of a word.   A minute after, the boy left the dining-room, and I never saw him again, till I met him, years after, in the streets of New York, when I claimed acquaintance with him as a brother Vermonter, and told him this story, to his great amusement."

One of his fellow-apprentices favors me with some interesting reminiscences.   He says, "I was a fellow-apprentice with Horace Greeley at Poultney for nearly two years.   We boarded together during that period at four different places, and we were constantly together."   The following passage from a letter from this early friend of our hero will be welcome to the reader, notwithstanding its repetitions of a few facts already known to him:—

Little did the inhabitants of East Poultney, where *Horace Greeley* went to reside in April, 1826, as an apprentice to the printing business, dream of the potent influence he was a few years later destined to exert, not only upon the politics of a neighboring State, but upon the noblest and grandest philanthropic enterprises of the age.   He was then a remarkably plain-looking unsophisticated lad of fifteen, with a slouching, careless gait, leaning away forward as he walked, as if both his head and his heels were too heavy for his body.   He wore a wool hat of the old stamp, with so small a brim, that it looked more like a two-quart measure inverted than a hat; and he had a singular, whining voice that provoked the merriment of the older apprentices, who had hardly themselves outgrown, in their brief village residence, similar peculiarities of country breeding.   But the rogues could not help pluming themselves upon their superior manners and position; and it must be confessed that the young 'stranger' was mercilessly 'taken in' by his elders in the office, whenever an opportunity for a practical joke presented itself.

But these things soon passed away, and as Horace was seen to be an unusually intelligent and honest lad, he came to be better appreciated.   The office in which he was employed was that of the   *Northern Spectator,*   a weekly paper then published by Messrs. Bliss & Dewey, and edited by E. G. Stone, brother to the late Col. Stone of the N. Y. Commercial Advertiser.   The new comer boarded in Mr. Stone's family, by whom he was well esteemed for his boyish integrity; and Mr. S. on examination found him better skilled in English grammar, even at that early age, than were the majority of school teachers in those times.   His superior intelligence also strongly commended him to the notice of Amos Bliss, Esq., one of the firm already mentioned, then and now a highly-respectable merchant of East Poultney, who has marked with pride and pleasure every successive step of the 'Westhaven boy,' from that day to this.

5

In consequence of the change of proprietors, editors and other things pertaining to the management of the Spectator office, Horace had, during the term of his apprenticeship, about as many opportunities of 'boarding round,' as ordinarily fall to the lot of a country schoolmaster. In 1827, he boarded at the 'Eagle tavern,' which was then kept by Mr. Harlow Hosford, and was the head-quarters of social and fashionable life in that pleasant old village. There the balls and village parties were had, there the oysters suppers came off, and there the lawyers, politicians and village oracles nightly congregated. Horace was no hand for ordinary boyish sports; the rough and tumble games of wrestling, running, etc., he had no relish for; but he was a diligent student in his leisure hours, and eagerly read everything in the way of books and papers that he could lay his hands on.   And it was curious to see what a power of mental application he had—a power which enabled him, seated in the bar-room, (where, perhaps, a dozen people were in earnest conversation,) to pursue undisturbed the reading of his favorite book, whatever it might be, with evidently as close attention and as much satisfaction as if he had been seated alone in his chamber.

If there ever was a self-made man, this same Horace Greeley is one, for he had neither wealthy or influential friends, collegiate or academic education, nor anything to start him in the world, save his own native good sense, an unconquerable love of study, and a determination to win his way by his own efforts. He had, however, a natural aptitude for arithmetical calculations, and could easily surpass, in his boyhood, most persons of his age in the facility and accuracy of his demonstrations; and his knowledge of grammar has been already noted.   He early learned to observe and remember political statistics, and the leading men and measures of the political parties, the various and multitudinous candidates for governor and Congress, not only in a single State, but in many, and finally in all the States, together with the location and vote of this, that, and the other congressional districts, (whig, democratic and what not,) at all manner of elections. These things he rapidly and easily mastered, and treasured in his capacious memory, till we venture to say he has few if any equals at this time, in this particular department, in this or any other country. I never knew but one man who approached him in this particular, and that was Edwin Williams, compiler of the N. Y. State Register.

Another letter from the same friend contains information still more valuable. "Judging," he writes, "from what I do certainly know of him, I can say that few young men of my acquaintance grew up with so much freedom from everything of a vicious and corrupting nature—so strong a resolution to study everything in the way of useful knowledge—and such a quick and clear percep

tion of the queer and humorous, whether in print or in actual life.
His love of the poets—Byron, Shakspeare, etc., discovered itself in
boyhood—and often have Greeley and I strolled off into the woods,
of a warm day, with a volume of Byron or Campbell in our pockets,
and reclining in some shady place, read it off to each other by the
hour. In this way, I got such a hold of 'Childe Harold,' the 'Pleasures of Hope,' and other favorite poems, that considerable portions
have remained ever since in my memory. Byron's apostrophe to
the Ocean, and some things in the [4th] canto relative to the men
and monuments of ancient Italy, were, if I mistake not, his special
favorites—also the famous description of the great conflict at
Waterloo. 'Mazeppa' was also a marked favorite. And for many
of Mrs. Hemans' poems he had a deep admiration."

The letter concludes with an honest burst of indignation;
"Knowing Horace Greeley as I do and have done for thirty years,
knowing his integrity, purity, and generosity, I can tell you one
thing, and that is, that the contempt with which I regard the slanders of certain papers with respect to his conduct, and character, is
quite *inexpressible*. There is doubtless a proper excuse for the conduct of lunatics, mad dogs, and rattlesnakes; but I know of no decent,
just, or reasonable apology for such meanness (it is a hard word, but
a very expressive one) as the presses alluded to have exhibited."

Horace came to Poultney, an ardent politician; and the events
which occurred during his apprenticeship were not calculated to
moderate his zeal, or weaken his attachment to the party he had
chosen. John Quincy Adams was president, Calhoun was vice-
president, Henry Clay was secretary of State. It was one of the
best and ablest administrations that had ever ruled in Washington;
and the most unpopular one. It is among the inconveniences of
universal suffrage, that the party which comes before the country
with the most taking popular Cry is the party which is likeliest to
win. During the existence of this administration, the Opposition
had a variety of popular Cries which were easy to vociferate, and
well adapted to impose on the unthinking, *i. e.* the majority.
'Adams had not been elected by the people.' 'Adams had gained
the presidency by a corrupt bargain with Henry Clay.' 'Adams
was lavish of the public money.' But of all the Cries of the time,
'Hurrah for Jackson' was the most effective. Jackson was a man

of the people. Jackson was the hero of New Orleans and the conqueror of Florida. Jackson was pledged to retrenchment and reform. Against vociferation of this kind, what availed the *fact*, evident, incontrovertible, that the affairs of the government were conducted with dignity, judgment and moderation?—that the country enjoyed prosperity at home, and the respect of the world?—that the claims of American citizens against foreign governments were prosecuted with diligence and success?—that treaties highly advantageous to American interests were negotiated with leading nations in Europe and South America?—that the public revenue was greater than it had ever been before?—that the resources of the country were made accessible by a liberal system of internal improvement?—that, nevertheless, there were surplus millions in the treasury?—that the administration nobly disdained to employ the executive patronage as a means of securing its continuance in power?—All this availed nothing. ' Hurrah for Jackson ' carried the day. The Last of the Gentlemen of the Revolutionary school retired. The era of wire-pulling began. That deadly element was introduced into our political system which rendered it so exquisitely vicious, that thenceforth it worked to corruption by an irresistible necessity! It is called Rotation in Office. It is embodied in the maxim, ' To the victors belong the spoils.' It has made the word *office-holder* synonymous with the word *sneak*. It has thronged the capital with greedy sycophants. It has made politics a game of cunning, with enough of chance in it to render it interesting to the low crew that play. It has made the president a pawn with which to make the first move—a puppet to keep the people amused while their pockets are picked. It has excluded from the service of the State nearly every man of ability and worth, and enabled bloated and beastly demagogues, without a ray of talent, without a sentiment of magnanimity, illiterate, vulgar, insensible to shame, to exert a *power* in this republic, which its greatest statesmen in their greatest days never wielded.

In the loud contentions of the period, the reader can easily believe that our argumentative apprentice took an intense interest. The village of East Poultney cast little more—if any more—than half a dozen votes for Jackson, but how much this result was owing to the efforts of Horace Greeley cannot now be ascertained. All agree that he contributed his full share to the general babble which the election of a President provokes. During the whole administration of Adams, the revision of the tariff with a view to the better protection of American manufactures was among the most prominent topics of public and private discussion.

It was about the year 1827 that the Masonic excitement arose Military men tell us that the bravest regiments are subject to *panic*. Regiments that bear upon their banners the most honorable distinctions, whose colors are tattered with the bullets of a hundred fights, will on a sudden falter in the charge, and fly, like a pack of cowards, from a danger which a pack of cowards might face without ceasing to be thought cowards. Similar to these causeless and irresistible panics of war are those frenzies of fear and fury mingled which sometimes come over the mind of a nation, and make it for a time incapable of reason and regardless of justice. Such seems to have been the nature of the anti-Masonic mania which raged in the Northern States from the year 1827.

A man named Morgan, a printer, had published, for gain, a book in which the harmless secrets of the Order of Free Masons, of which he was a member, were divulged. Public curiosity caused the book to have an immense sale. Soon after its publication, Morgan announced another volume which was to reveal unimagined horrors ; but, before the book appeared, Morgan disappeared, and neither ever came to light. Now arose the question, *What became of Morgan?* and it rent the nation, for a time, into two imbittered and angry factions. " Morgan !" said the Free Masons, " that perjured traitor, died and was buried in the natural and ordinary fashion." " Morgan !" said the anti-Masons, " that martyred patriot, was dragged from his home by Masonic ruffians, taken in the dead of night to the shores of the Niagara river, murdered, and thrown into the rapids." It is impossible for any one to conceive the utter delirium into which the people in some parts of the country were thrown by the agitation of this subject. Books were written. Papers were established. Exhibitions were got up, in which the Masonic ceremonies were caricatured or imitated. Families were divided. Fathers disinherited their sons, and sons forsook their fathers. Elections were influenced, not town and county elections merely, but State and national elections. There were Masonic candidates and anti-Masonic candidates in every election in the Northern States for at least two years after Morgan vanished. Hundreds of Lodges bowed to the storm, sent in their charters to the central authority, and voluntarily ceased to exist. There are families now, about the country, in which Masonry is a forbidden topic, because its introduction would revive the old quarrel, and turn the peaceful tea-table into a scene of hot and interminable contention. There are still old ladies, male and female, about the country, who will tell you with grim gravity that, if you trace up Masonry, through all its Orders, till you come to the grand, tip-top, Head Mason of the world, you will discover that that dread individual and the Chief of the Society of Jesuits are one and the same Person!

I have been tempted to use the word *ridiculous* in connection with this affair; and looking back upon it, at the distance of a quarter of a century, ridiculous seems a proper word to apply to it. But it did not seem ridiculous then. It had, at least, a serious side. It was believed among the anti-Masons that the Masons were bound to protect one another in doing injustice; even the commission of treason and murder did not, it was said, exclude a man from the shelter of his Lodge. It was alleged that a Masonic jury dared not, or would not, condemn a prisoner who, after the fullest proof of his guilt had been obtained, made the Masonic sign of distress. It was asserted that a judge regarded the oath which made him a Free Mason as more sacred and more binding than that which admitted him to the bench. It is in vain, said the anti-Masons, for one of *us* to seek justice against a Mason, for a jury cannot be obtained without its share of Masonic members, and a court cannot be found without its Masonic judge.

Our apprentice embraced the anti-Masonic side of this controversy, and embraced it warmly. It was natural that he should. It was inevitable that he should. And for the next two or three years he expended more breath in denouncing the Order of the Free-Masons, than upon any other subject—perhaps than all other subjects put together. To this day secret societies are his special aversion.

But we must hasten on. Horace had soon learned his trade. He became the best hand in the office, and rendered important assistance in editing the paper. Some numbers were almost entirely his work. But there was ill-luck about the little establishment. Several times, as we have seen, it changed proprietors, but none of them could make it prosper ; and, at length, in the month of June, 1830, the second month of the apprentice's fifth year, the Northern Spectator was discontinued ; the printing-office was broken up, and the apprentice, released from his engagement, became his own master, free to wander whithersoever he could pay his passage, and to work for whomsoever would employ him.

His possessions at this crisis were—a knowledge of the art of printing, an extensive and very miscellaneous library in his memory, a wardrobe that could be stuffed into a pocket, twenty dollars in cash, and—a sore leg. The article last named played too serious a part in the history of its proprietor, not to be mentioned in the inventory of his property. He had injured his leg a year before in stepping from a box, and it troubled him, more or less, for three years, swelling occasionally to four times its natural size, and obliging him to stand at his work, with the leg propped up in a most horizontal and uncomfortable position. It was a tantalizing feature of the case that he could walk without much difficulty, but standing was torture. As a printer, he had no particular occasion to walk ; and by standing he was to gain his subsistence.

Horace Greeley was no longer a Boy. His figure and the expression of his countenance were still singularly youthful ; but he was at the beginning of his twentieth year, and he was henceforth to confront the world as a man. So far, his life had been, upon the whole, peaceful, happy and fortunate, and he had advanced towards his object without interruption, and with sufficient rapidity. His constitution, originally weak, Labor and Temperance had rendered capable of great endurance. His mind, originally apt and active, incessant reading had stored with much that is most valuable among the discoveries, the thoughts, and the fancies of past generations. In the conflicts of the Debating Society, the printing-office, and the tavern, he had exercised his powers, and tried the correctness of his opinions. If his knowledge was incomplete, if there were wide domains of knowledge, of which he had little more than heard, yet what he did know he knew well ; he had learned it, not as a task, but because he *wanted to know it ;* it partook of the vitality of his own mind ; it was his own, and he could use it.

If there had been a PEOPLE'S COLLEGE, to which the new emancipated apprentice could have gone, and where, earning his subsistence by the exercise of his trade, he could have spent half of each day for the next two years of his life in the systematic study of Language, History and Science, under the guidance of men able to guide him aright, under the influence of women capable of attracting his regard, and worthy of it—it had been well. But there was not then, and there is not now, an institution that meets the want and the need of such as he.

At any moment there are ten thousand young men and women in this country, strong, intelligent, and poor, who are about to go forth into the world ignorant, who would gladly go forth instructed, if they could get knowledge, and earn it *as* they get it, by the labor of their hands. They are the sons and daughters of our farmers and mechanics. They are the very *elite* among the young people of the nation. There is talent, of all kinds and all degrees, among them—talent, that is the nation's richest possession—talent, that could bless and glorify the nation. Should there not be—*can* there not be, somewhere in this broad land, a UNIVERSITY-TOWN— where all trades could be carried on, all arts practiced, all knowledge accessible, to which those who have a desire to become excellent in their calling, and those who have an aptitude for art, and those who have fallen in love with knowledge, could accomplish the wish of their hearts without losing their independence, without becoming paupers, or prisoners, or debtors? Surely such a University for the People is not an impossibility. To found such an institution, or assemblage of institutions—to find out the conditions upon which it could exist and prosper—were not an easy task. A Committee could not do it, nor a 'Board,' nor a Legislature. It is an enterprise for ONE MAN—a man of boundless disinterestedness, of immense administrative and constructive talent, fertile in expedients, courageous, persevering, physically strong, and morally great—a man born for his work, and devoted to it 'with a quiet, deep enthusiasm'. Give such a man the indispensable land, and twenty-five years, and the People's College would be a dream no more, but a triumphant and *imitable* reality; and the founder thereof would have done a deed compared with which, either for its difficulty or for its results, such triumphs as those of Trafalgar and Waterloo would not be worthy of mention.

There have been self-sustaining monasteries! Will there never be self-sustaining colleges? Is there anything like an inherent *impossibility* in a thousand men and women, in the fresh strength of youth, capable of a just subordination, working together, each for all and all for each, with the assistance of steam, machinery, and a thousand fertile acres—earning a subsistence by a few hours' labor per day, and securing, at least, half their time for the acquisition of the art, or the language, or the science which they prefer? I think not. We are at present a nation of ignoramuses, our ignorance rendered only the more conspicuous and misleading, by the faint intimations of knowledge which we acquire at our schools. Are we to remain such for ever?

But if Horace Greeley derived no help from schools and teachers, he received no harm from them. He finished his apprenticeship, an uncontaminated young man, with the means of independence at his finger-ends, ashamed of no honest employment, of no decent habitation, of no cleanly garb. "There are unhappy times," says Mr. Carlyle, "in the world's history, when he that is least educated will chiefly have to say that he is least *perverted;* and, with the multitude of false eye-glasses, convex, concave, green, or even yellow, *has not lost the natural use of his eyes.*" "How were it," he asks, "if we surmised, that for a man gifted with natural vigor, with a man's character to be developed in him, more especially if in the way of literature, as thinker and writer, it is actually, in these strange days, no special misfortune to be trained up among the uneducated classes, and not among the educated; but rather, of the two misfortunes, the smaller?" And again, he observes, "The grand result of schooling is a mind with just vision to discern, with free force to do; the grand schoolmaster is PRACTICE."

5*

CHAPTER VII.

HE WANDERS.

"Well, Horace, and where are you going now?" asked the kind landlady of the tavern, as Horace, a few days after the closing of the printing-office, appeared on the piazza, equipped for the road—i. e., with his jacket on, and with his bundle and his stick in his hand.

"I am going," was the prompt and sprightly answer, "to Pennsylvania, to see my father, and there I shall stay till my leg gets well."

With these words, Horace laid down the bundle and the stick, and took a seat for the last time on that piazza, the scene of many a peaceful triumph, where, as Political Gazetteer, he had often given the information that he alone, of all the town, could give; where, as political partisan, he had often brought an antagonist to extremities; where, as oddity, he had often fixed the gaze and twisted the neck of the passing peddler.

And was there no demonstration of feeling at the departure of so distinguished a personage? There was. But it did not take the form of a silver dinner-service, nor of a gold tea ditto, nor of a piece of plate, nor even of a gold pen, nor yet of a series of resolutions. While Horace sat on the piazza, talking with his old friends, who gathered around him, a meeting of two individuals was held in the corner of the bar-room. They were the landlord and one of his boarders; and the subject of their deliberations were, an old brown overcoat belonging to the latter. The landlord had the floor, and his speech was to the following purport:—

"He felt like doing something for Horace before he went. Horace was an entirely unspeakable person. He had lived a long time in the house; he had never given any trouble, and we feel for him as for our own son. Now, there is that brown over-coat of yours. It's cold on the canal, all the summer, in the mornings and evenings. Horace is poor and his father is poor. You are owing me a little, as much as the old coat is worth, and what I say is, let us give the poor fellow the overcoat, and call our account squared." This feeling oration was received with every demonstration of approval, and the proposition was carried into effect forthwith. The landlady gave him a pocket Bible. In a few minutes more, Horace rose, put his stick through his little red bundle, and both over his shoulder, took the overcoat upon his other arm, said 'Good-by,' to his friends, promised to write as soon as he was settled again, and set off upon his long journey. His good friends of the tavern followed him with their eyes, until a turn of the road hid the bent and shambling figure from their sight, and then they turned away to praise him and to wish him well. Twenty-five years have passed; and, to this hour, they do not tell the tale of his departure without a certain swelling of the heart, without a certain glistening of the softer pair of eyes.

It was a fine, cool, breezy morning in the month of June, 1830. Nature had assumed those robes of brilliant green which she wears only in June, and welcomed the wanderer forth with that heavenly smile which plays upon her changeful countenance only when she is attired in her best. Deceptive smile! The forests upon those hills of hilly Rutland, brimming with foliage, *concealed* their granite ribs, their chasms, their steeps, their precipices, their morasses, and the reptiles that lay coiled among them; but they were *there*. So did the alluring aspect of the world hide from the wayfarer the struggle, the toil, the danger that await the man who goes out from his seclusion to confront the world ALONE—the world of which he knows nothing except by hearsay, that cares nothing for him, and takes no note of his arrival. The present wayfarer was destined to be quite alone in his conflict with the world, and he was destined to wrestle with it for many years before it yielded him anything more than a show of submission. How prodigal of help is the Devil to his scheming and guileful servants! But the Powers Celestial—

they love their chosen too wisely and too well to diminish by one
care the burthen that makes them strong, to lessen by one pang the
agony that makes them good, to prevent one mistake of the folly
that makes them wise.

Light of heart and step, the traveler walked on. In the afternoon he reached Comstock's Fording, fourteen miles from Poultney;
thence, partly on canal-boat and partly on foot, he went to Schenectady, and there took a 'line-boat' on the Erie Canal. A week of
tedium in the slow line-boat—a walk of a hundred miles through the
woods, and he had reached his father's log-house. He arrived late in
the evening. The last ten miles of the journey he performed after
dark, guided, when he could catch a glimpse of it through the
dense foliage, by a star. The journey required at that time about
twelve days : it is now done in eighteen hours. It cost Horace
Greeley about seven dollars; the present cost by railroad is eleven
dollars; distance, six hundred miles.

He found his father and brother transformed into backwoodsmen.
Their little log-cabin stood in the midst of a narrow clearing, which
was covered with blackened stumps, and smoked with burning tim·
ber. Forests, dense and almost unbroken, heavily timbered, abound-
ing in wolves and every other description of 'varmint,' extended a
day's journey in every direction, and in some directions many days'
journey. The country was then so wild and 'new,' that a hunter would
sell a man a deer before it was shot; and appointing the hour when,
and the spot where, the buyer was to call for his game, would have
it ready for him as punctually as though he had ordered it at Fulton
market. The wolves were so bold, that their howlings could be
heard at the house as they roamed about in packs in search of the
sheep; and the solitary camper-out could hear them *breathe* and see
their eye-balls glare, as they prowled about his smoldering fire.
Mr. Greeley, who had brought from Vermont a fondness for rearing
sheep, tried to continue that branch of rural occupation in the wilderness; but after the wolves, in spite of his utmost care and pre-
caution, had killed a hundred sheep for him, he gave up the attempt. But it was a level and a very fertile region—' varmint' always select a good 'location'—and it has since been subdued into a
beautiful land of grass and woods.

Horace staid at home for several weeks, assisting his father, fishing occasionally, and otherwise amusing himself : while his good mother assiduously nursed the sore leg. It healed too slowly for its impatient proprietor, who had learned 'to labor,' *not* 'to wait;' and so, one morning, he walked over to Jamestown, a town twenty miles distant, where a newspaper was struggling to get published, and applied for work. Work he obtained. It was very freely given ; but at the end of the week the workman received a promise to pay, but no payment. He waited and worked four days longer, and discovering by that time that there was really no money to be had or hoped for in Jamestown, he walked home again, as poor as before.

And now the damaged leg began to swell again prodigiously ; at one time it was as large below the knee as a demijohn. Cut off from other employment, Horace devoted all his attention to the unfortunate member, but without result. He heard about this time of a famous doctor who lived in that town of Pennsylvania which exults in the singular name of ' North-East,' distant twenty-five miles from his father's clearing. To him, as a last resort, though the family could ill afford the trifling expense, Horace went, and staid with him a month. "You don't drink liquor," were the doctor's first words as he examined the sore, "if you did, you'd have a bad leg of it." The patient thought he *had* a bad leg of it, without drinking liquor. The doctor's treatment was skillful, and finally successful. Among other remedies, he subjected the limb to the action of electricity, and from that day the cure began. The patient left North-East greatly relieved, and though the leg was weak and troublesome for many more months, yet it gradually recovered, the wound subsiding at length into a long red scar.

He wandered, next, in an easterly direction, in search of employment, and found it in the village of Lodi, fifty miles off, in Cataraugus county, New York. At Lodi, he seems to have cherished a hope of being able to remain awhile and earn a little money. He wrote to his friends in Poultney describing the paper on which he worked, "as a Jackson paper, a forlorn affair, else I would have sent you a few numbers." One of his letters written from Lodi to a friend in Vermont, contains a passage which may serve to show what was going on in the mind of the printer as he stood at the case setting up Jacksonian paragraphs. "You are aware that an important election is close at hand in this State, and of course, a great deal of interest is felt in the result. The regular Jacksonians imagine that they will be able to elect Throop by 20,000 majority; but after having obtained all the information I can, I give it as my decided opinion, that if none of the candidates decline, we shall elect Francis Granger, governor. This county will give him 1000 majority, and I estimate his vote in the State at 125,000. I need not inform you that such a result will be highly satisfactory to your humble servant, H. Greeley." It was a result, however, which he had not the satisfaction of contemplating. The confident and yet cautious manner of the passage quoted is amusing in a politician but twenty years of age.

At Lodi, as at Jamestown, our roving journeyman found work much more abundant than money. Moreover, he was in the camp of the enemy; and so at the end of his sixth week, he again took bundle and stick and marched homeward, with very little more money in his pocket than if he had spent his time in idleness. On his way home he fell in with an old Poultney friend who had recently settled in the wilderness, and Horace arrived in time to assist at the ' warming' of the new cabin, a duty which he performed in a way that covered him with glory.

In the course of the evening, a draught-board was introduced, and the stranger beat in swift succession half a dozen of the best players in the neighborhood. It happened that the place was rather noted for its skillful draught-players, and the game was played incessantly at private houses and at public. To be beaten in so scandalous a manner by a passing stranger, and he by no means an ornamental addition to an evening party, and young enough to be the son of some of the vanquished, nettled them not a little. They challenged the victor to another encounter at the tavern on the next evening. The challenge was accepted. The evening arrived, and there was a considerable gathering to witness and take part in the struggle—among the rest, a certain Joe Wilson who had been specially sent for, and whom no one had *ever* beaten, since he came into the settlement. The great Joe was held in reserve. The party of the previous evening, Horace took in turn, and beat with ease. Other players tried to foil his ' Yankee tricks,' but were themselves foiled. The reserve was brought up. Joe Wilson took his seat at the table. He played his deadliest, pausing long before he hazarded a move; the company hanging over the board, hushed and anxious. They were not kept many minutes in suspense; Joe was overthrown; the unornamental stranger was the conqueror. Another game—the same result. Another and another and another; but Joe lost every game. Joseph, however, was too good a player not to respect so potent an antagonist, and he and all the party behaved well under their discomfiture. The board was laid aside, and a lively conversation ensued, which was continued 'with unabated spirit to a late hour.' The next morning, the traveler went on his way, leaving behind him a most distinguished reputation as a draught-player and a politician.

He remained at home a few days, and then set out again on his travels in search of some one who could pay him wages for his work. He took a 'bee line' through the woods for the town of Erie, thirty miles off, on the shores of the great lake. He had exhausted the smaller towns; Erie was the last possible move in *that* corner of the board; and upon Erie he fixed his hopes. There were two printing offices, at that time, in the place. It was a town of five thousand inhabitants, and of extensive lake and inland trade.

The gentleman still lives who saw the weary pedestrian enter Erie, attired in the homespun, abbreviated and stockingless style with which the reader is already acquainted. His old black felt hat slouched down over his shoulders in the old fashion. The red cotton handkerchief still contained his wardrobe, and it was carried on the same old stick. The country frequenters of Erie were then, and are still, particularly rustic in appearance; but our hero seemed the very embodiment and incarnation of the rustic Principle; and among the crowd of Pennsylvania farmers that thronged the streets, he swung along, pre-eminent and peculiar, a marked person, the observed of all observers. He, as was his wont, observed nobody, but went at once to the office of the Erie Gazette, a weekly paper, published then and still by Joseph M. Sterrett.

"I was not," Judge Sterrett is accustomed to relate, "I was not in the printing office when he arrived. I came in, soon after, and saw him sitting at the table reading the newspapers, and so absorbed in them that he paid no attention to my entrance. My first feeling was one of astonishment, that a fellow so singularly 'green' in his

appearance should be *reading*, and above all, reading so intently
I looked at him for a few moments, and then, finding that he made
no movement towards acquainting me with his business, I took up
my composing stick and went to work. He continued to read for
twenty minutes, or more; when he got up, and coming close to my
case, asked, in his peculiar, whining voice,

"Do you want any help in the printing business?"

"Why," said I, running my eye involuntarily up and down the
extraordinary figure, "did *you* ever work at the trade?"

"Yes," was the reply; "I worked *some* at it in an office in Vermont, and I should be willing to work under instruction, if you
could give me a job."

Now Mr. Sterrett did want help in the printing business, and
could have given him a job; but, unluckily, he misinterpreted this
modest reply. He at once concluded that the timid applicant was
a runaway apprentice; and runaway apprentices are a class of their
fellow-creatures to whom employers cherish a common and decided
aversion. Without communicating his suspicions, he merely said
that he had no occasion for further assistance, and Horace, without
a word, left the apartment.

A similar reception and the same result awaited him at the other
office; and so the poor wanderer trudged home again, not in the
best spirits.

"Two or three weeks after this interview," continues Judge
Sterrett—he *is* a judge, I saw him on the bench—"an acquaintance of mine, a farmer, called at the office, and inquired if I wanted a journeyman. I did. He said a neighbor of his had a son
who learned the printing business somewhere Down East, and
wanted a place. 'What sort of a looking fellow is he?' said I.
He described him, and I knew at once that he was my supposed
runaway apprentice. My friend, the farmer, gave him a high character, however; so I said, 'Send him along,' and a day or two
after along he came."

The terms on which Horace Greeley entered the office of the
Erie Gazette were of his own naming, and therefore peculiar. He
would do the best he could, he said, and Mr. Sterrett might pay
him what he (Mr. Sterrett) thought he had earned. He had only
one request to make, and that was, that he should not be required

tc work at the press, unless the office was so much hurried that his services in that department could not be dispensed with. He had had a little difficulty with his leg, and press work rather hurt him than otherwise. The bargain included the condition that he was to board at Mr. Sterrett's house ; and when he went to dinner on the day of his arrival, a lady of the family expressed her opinion of him in the following terms :—" So, Mr. Sterrett, you 've hired that fellow to work for you, have you ? Well, you won't keep him three days." In three days she had changed her opinion ; and to this hour the good lady cannot bring herself to speak otherwise than kindly of him, though she is a stanch daughter of turbulent Erie, and ' *must* say, that certain articles which appeared in the Tribune during the WAR, did really seem *too* bad from one who had been himself an Eriean.' But then, ' he gave no more trouble in the house than if he had n't been in it.'

Erie, famous in the Last War but one, as the port whence Commodore Perry sailed out to victory—Erie, famous in the last war of all, as the place where the men, except a traitorous thirteen, and the women, except *their* faithful wives, all rose as ONE MAN against the Railway Trains, saying, in the tone which is generally described as ' not to be misunderstood ': " Thus far shalt thou go without stopping for refreshment, and no farther," and achieved as Break of Gauge men, the distinction accorded in another land to the Break o' Day boys—Erie, which boasts of nine thousand inhabitants, and aspires to become the Buffalo of Pennsylvania—Erie, which already has business enough to sustain many stores wherein not every article known to traffic is sold, and where a man cannot consequently buy coat, hat, boots, physic, plough, crackers, grindstone and penknife, over the same counter—Erie, which has a Mayor and Aldermen, a dog-law, and an ordinance against shooting off guns in the street under a penalty of five dollars for each and every offense—Erie, for the truth cannot be longer dashed from utterance, is the shabbiest and most broken-down looking large town, *I*, the present writer, an individual not wholly untraveled, ever saw, in a free State of this Confederacy.

The shores of the lake there are ' bluffy,' sixty feet or more above the water, and the land for many miles back is nearly a dead level, exceedingly fertile, and quite uninteresting. No, not quite   For much of the primeval forest remains, and the gigantic trees that were saplings when Columbus played in the streets of Genoa, tower aloft, a hundred feet without a branch, with that exquisite daintiness of taper of which the eye never tires, which architecture has never equaled, which only Grecian architecture approached, and was beautiful because it approached it. The City of Erie is merely a square mile of this level land, close to the edge of the bluff, with a thousand houses built upon it, which are arranged on the plan of a corn-field—only, not more than a third of the houses have 'come up.' The town, however, condenses to a focus around a piece of ground called 'The Park,' four acres in extent, surrounded with a low, broken board fence, that was white-washed a long time ago, and therefore now looks very forlorn and pig-pen-ny. The side-walks around 'The Park' present an animated scene. The huge hotel of the place is there—a cross between the Astor House and a country tavern, having the magnitude of the former, the quality of the latter. There, too, is the old Court-House,—its uneven brick floor covered with the chips of a mortising machine, —its galleries up near the high ceiling, kept there by slender poles,—its vast cracked, rusty stove, sprawling all askew, and putting forth a system of stovepipes that wander long through space before they find the chimney. Justice is administered in that Court-house in a truly free and easy style; and to hear the drowsy clerk, with his heels in the air, administer, 'twixt sleep and awake, the tremendous oath of Pennsylvania, to a brown, abashed farmer, with his right hand raised in a manner to set off his awkwardness to the best advantage, is worth a journey to Erie. Two sides of 'The Park' are occupied by the principal stores, before which the country wagons stand, presenting a continuous range of muddy wheels. The marble structure around the corner is not a Greek temple, though built in the style of one, and quite deserted enough to be a ruin—it is the Erie Custom House, a fine example of governmental management, as it is as much too large for the business done in it as the Custom House of New York is too small.

The Erie of the present year is, of course, not the Erie of 1831, when Horace Greeley walked its streets, with his eyes on the pavement and a bundle of exchanges in his pocket, ruminating on the prospects of the next election, or thinking out a copy of verses to send to his mother. It was a smaller place, then, with fewer brick blocks, *more* pigs in the street, and no custom-house in the Greek style. But it had one feature which has not changed. The LAKE was there!

An island, seven miles long, but not two miles wide, once a part of the main land, lies opposite the town, at an apparent distance of half a mile, though in reality two miles and a half from the shore. This island, which approaches the main land at either extremity, forms the harbor of Erie, and gives to that part of the lake the effect of a river. Beyond, the Great Lake stretches away further than the eye can reach.

A great lake in fine weather is like the ocean only in one particular—you cannot see across it. The ocean asserts itself; it is demonstrative. It heaves, it flashes, it sparkles, it foams, it roars. On the stillest day, it does not quite go to sleep; the tide steals up the white beach, and glides back again over the shells and pebbles musically, or it murmurs along the sides of black rocks, with a subdued though always audible voice. The ocean is a living and life-giving thing, 'fair, and fresh, and ever free.' The lake, on a fine day, lies dead. No tide breaks upon its earthy shore. It is as blue as a blue ribbon, as blue as the sky; and vessels come sailing out of heaven, and go sailing into heaven, and no eye can discern where the lake ends and heaven begins. It is as smooth as a mirror's face, and as dull as a mirror's back. Often a light mist gathers over it, and then the lake is *gone* from the prospect; but for an occasional sail dimly descried, or a streak of black smoke left by a passing steamer, it would give absolutely *no* sign of its presence, though the spectator is standing a quarter of a mile from the shore. Oftener the mist gathers thickly along the horizon, and then, so perfect is the illusion, the stranger will swear he sees the opposite shore, not fifteen miles off. There is no excitement in looking upon a lake, and it has no effect upon the appetite or the complexion. Yet there is a quiet, languid beauty hovering over it, a beauty all its own, a charm that grows upon the mind the longer you linger upon the shore. The Castle of Indolence should have been placed upon the bank of Lake Erie, where its inmates could have lain on the grass and gazed down, through all the slow hours of the long summer day, upon the lazy, hazy, blue expanse.

When the wind blows, the lake wakes up; and still it is not the ocean. The waves are discolored by the earthy bank upon which they break with un-oceanlike monotony. They neither advance, nor recede, nor roar, nor *swell*. A great lake, with all its charms, and they are many and great, is only an infinite pond.

The people of Erie care as much for the lake as the people of Niagara care for the cataract, as much as people generally care for anything wonderful or anything beautiful which they can see by turning their heads. In other words, they care for it as the means by which lime, coal, and lumber may be transported to another and a better market. Not one house is built along the shore, though the shore is high and level. Not a path has been worn by human feet above or below the bluff. Pigs, sheep, cows, and sweet-brier bushes occupy the unenclosed ground, which seems so *made* to be built upon that it is surprising the handsome houses of the town should have been built anywhere else. One could almost say, in a weak moment, Give me a cottage on the bluff, and I will *live* at Erie!

It was at Erie, probably, that Horace Greeley first saw the uniform of the American navy. The United States and Great Britain are each permitted by treaty to keep one vessel of war in commission on the Great Lakes. The American vessel usually lies in the harbor of Erie, and a few officers may be seen about the town. What the busy journeyman printer thought of those idle gentlemen, apparently the only quite useless, and certainly the best dressed, persons in the place, may be guessed. Perhaps, however, he passed them by, in his absent way, and saw them not.

In a few days, the new comer was in high favor at the office of the Erie Gazette. He is remembered there as a remarkably correct and reliable compositor, though not a rapid one, and his steady devotion to his work enabled him to accomplish more than faster workmen. He was soon placed by his employer on the footing of a regular journeyman, at the usual wages, twelve dollars a month and board. All the intervals of labor he spent in reading. As soon as the hour of cessation arrived, he would hurry off his apron, wash his hands, and lose himself in his book or his newspapers, often forgetting his dinner, and often forgetting whether he had had his dinner or not. More and more, he became absorbed in politics. It is said, by one who worked beside him at Erie, that he could tell the name, post-office address, and something of the history and political leanings, of every member of Congress; and that he could give the particulars of every important election that had occurred within his recollection, even, in some instances, to the county majorities.

And thus, in earnest work and earnest reading, seven profitable and not unhappy months passed swiftly away. He never lost one day's work. On Sundays, he read, or walked along the shores of the lake, or sailed over to the Island. His better fortune made no change either in his habits or his appearance; and his employer was surprised, that month after month passed, and yet his strange journeyman drew no money. Once, Mr. Sterrett ventured to rally him a little upon his persistence in wearing the hereditary .homespun, saying, "Now, Horace, you have a good deal of money coming to you; don't go about the town any longer in that outlandish rig. Let me give you an order on the store. Dress up a little, Horace." To which Horace replied, looking down at the 'outlandish rig,' as though he had never seen it before, "You see, Mr. Sterrett, my father is on a new place, and I want to help him all I can." However, a short time after, Horace *did* make a faint effort to dress up a little; but the few articles which he bought were so extremely coarse and common, that it was a question in the office whether his appearance was improved by the change, or the contrary.

At the end of the seventh month, the man whose sickness had made a temporary vacancy in the office of the Gazette, returned to his place, and there was, in consequence, no more work for Horace Greeley. Upon the settlement of his account, it appeared that he had drawn for his personal expenses during his residence at Erie, the sum of *six dollars!* Of the remainder of his wages, he took about fifteen dollars in money, and the rest in the form of a note; and with all this wealth in his pocket, he walked once more to his father's house. This note the generous fellow gave to his father, reserving the money to carry on his own personal warfare with the world.

And now, Horace was tired of dallying with fortune in country printing offices. He said, he thought it was time to *do* something, and he formed the bold resolution of going straight to New York and seeking his fortune in the metropolis. After a few days of recreation at home, he tied up his bundle once more, put his money in his pocket, and plunged into the woods in the direction of the Erie Canal.

CHAPTER VIII.

ARRIVAL IN NEW YORK.

The journey—a night on the tow-path—He reaches the city—Inventory of his property—Looks for a boarding-house—Finds one—Expends half his capital upon clothes—Searches for employment—Berated by David Hale as a runaway apprentice—Continues the search—Goes to church—Hears of a vacancy—Obtains work—The boss takes him for a '——— fool,' but changes his opinion—Nicknamed 'the Ghost'—Practical jokes—Horace metamorphosed—Dispute about commas—The shoemaker's boarding-house—Grand banquet on Sundays.

HE took the canal-boat at Buffalo and came as far as Lockport, whence he walked a few miles to Gaines, and staid a day at the house of a friend whom he had known in Vermont. Next morning he walked back, accompanied by his friend, to the canal, and both of them waited many hours for an eastward-bound boat to pass. Night came, but no boat, and the adventurer persuaded his friend to go home, and set out himself to walk on the tow-path towards Albion. It was a very dark night. He walked slowly on, hour after hour, looking anxiously behind him for the expected boat, looking more anxiously before him to discern the two fiery eyes of the boats bound to the west, in time to avoid being swept into the canal by the tow-line. Towards morning, a boat of the slower sort, a scow probably, overtook him; he went on board, and tired with his long walk, lay down in the cabin to rest. Sleep was tardy in alighting upon his eye-lids, and he had the pleasure of hearing his merits and his costume fully and freely discussed by his fellow passengers. It was Monday morning. One passenger explained the coming on board of the stranger at so unusual an hour, by suggesting that he had been *courting* all night. (Sunday evening in country places is sacred to love.) His appearance was so exceedingly unlike that of a lover, that this sally created much amusement, in which the wakeful traveler shared. At Rochester he took a faster boat. Wednesday night he reached Schenectady, where he left the canal and walked to Albany, as the canal between those two towns is much obstructed by locks. He reached Albany on Thursday morning, just in time to see the seven o'clock steamboat move out into the stream. He, therefore, took passage in a tow-boat which started at ten o'clock on the same morning. At sunrise on Friday, the eighteenth of August, 1831, Horace Greeley landed at Whitehall, close to the Battery, in the city of New York.

New York was, and is, a city of adventurers. Few of our eminent citizens were born here. It is a common boast among New Yorkers, that this great merchant and that great millionaire came to the city a ragged boy, with only three and sixpence in his pocket; and *now* look at him ! In a list of the one hundred men who are esteemed to be the most 'successful' among the citizens of New York, it is probable that seventy-five of the names would be those of men who began their career here in circumstances that gave no promise of future eminence. But among them all, it is questionable whether there was one who on his arrival had so little to help, so much to hinder him, as Horace Greeley.

Of solid cash, his stock was ten dollars. His other property consisted of the clothes he wore, the clothes he carried in his small bundle, and the stick with which he carried it. The clothes he wore need not be described ; they were those which had already astonished the people of Erie. The clothes he carried were very few, and precisely similar in cut and quality to the garments which he exhibited to the public. On the violent supposition that his wardrobe could in any case have become a salable commodity, we may compute that he was worth, on this Friday morning at sunrise, ten dollars and seventy-five cents. He had no friend, no acquaintance here. There was not a human being upon whom he had any claim for help or advice. His appearance was all against him. He looked in his round jacket like an overgrown boy. No one was likely to observe the engaging beauty of his face, or the noble round of his brow under that overhanging hat, over that

long and stooping body.   He was somewhat timorous in his intercourse with strangers.   He would not intrude upon their attention ;
he had not the faculty of pushing his way, and proclaiming his merits and his desires.   To the arts by which men are conciliated, by
which unwilling ears are forced to attend to an unwelcome tale, he
was utterly a stranger.   Moreover, he had neglected to bring with
him any letters of recommendation, or any certificate of his skill
as a printer.   It had not occurred to him that anything of the kind
was necessary, so unacquainted was he with the life of cities.

His first employment was to find a boarding-house where he
could live a long time on a small sum.   Leaving the green Battery
on his left hand, he strolled off into Broad-street, and at the corner
of that street and Wall discovered a house that in his eyes had the
aspect of a cheap tavern.   He entered the bar-room, and asked the
price of board.

"I guess we 're too high for you," said the bar-keeper, after
bestowing one glance upon the inquirer.

"Well, how much a week do you charge ?"

"Six dollars."

"Yes, that 's more than I can afford," said Horace with a laugh
at the enormous mistake he had made in inquiring at a house of
such pretensions.

He turned up Wall-street, and sauntered into Broadway.   Seeing
no house of entertainment that seemed at all suited to his circumstances, he sought the water once more, and wandered along the
wharves of the North River as far as Washington-market.   Board-
ing-houses of the cheapest kind, and drinking-houses of the lowest
grade, the former frequented chiefly by emigrants, the latter by
sailors, were numerous enough in that neighborhood.   A house,
which combined the low groggery and the cheap boarding-house
in one small establishment, kept by an Irishman named M'Gorlick,
chanced to be the one that first attracted the rover's attention.   It
looked so mean and squalid, that he was tempted to enter, and
again inquire for what sum a man could buy a week's shelter and
sustenance.

"Twenty shillings," was the landlord's reply.

"Ah," said Horace, "that sounds more like it."

He engaged to board with Mr. M'Gorlick on the instant, and

proceeded soon to test the quality of his fare by taking breakfast in the bosom of his family. The cheapness of the entertainment was its best recommendation.

After breakfast Horace performed an act which I believe he had never spontaneously performed before. He bought some clothes, with a view to render himself more presentable. They were of the commonest kind, and the garments were few, but the purchase absorbed nearly half his capital. Satisfied with his appearance, he now began the round of the printing-offices, going into every one he could find, and asking for employment—merely asking, and going away, without a word, as soon as he was refused. In the course of the morning, he found himself in the office of the Journal of Commerce, and he chanced to direct his inquiry, 'if they wanted a hand,' to the late David Hale, one of the proprietors of the paper. Mr. Hale took a survey of the person who had presumed to address him, and replied in substance as follows:—

"My opinion is, young man, that you're a runaway apprentice, and you'd better go home to your master."

Horace endeavored to explain his position and circumstances, but the impetuous Hale could be brought to no more gracious response than, "Be off about your business, and don't bother us."

Horace, more amused than indignant, retired, and pursued his way to the next office. All that day he walked the streets, climbed into upper stories, came down again, ascended other heights, descended, dived into basements, traversed passages, groped through labyrinths, ever asking the same question, 'Do you want a hand?' and ever receiving the same reply, in various degrees of civility, 'No.' He walked ten times as many miles as he needed, for he was not aware that nearly all the printing-offices in New York are in the same square mile. He went the entire length of many streets which any body could have told him did not contain one.

He went home on Friday evening very tired and a little discouraged.

Early on Saturday morning he resumed the search, and continued it with energy till the evening. But no one wanted a hand. Business seemed to be at a stand-still, or every office had its full complement of men. On Saturday evening he was still more fatigued. He resolved to remain in the city a day or two longer, and then, if

still unsuccessful, to turn his face homeward, and inquire for work
at the towns through which he passed. Though discouraged, he
was not disheartened, and still less alarmed.

The youthful reader should observe here what a sense of independence and what fearlessness dwell in the spirit of a man who has
learned the art of living on the mere necessaries of life. If Horace
Greeley had, after another day or two of trial, chosen to leave the
city, he would have carried with him about four dollars; and with
that sum he could have walked leisurely and with an unanxious
heart all the way back to his father's house, six hundred miles,
inquiring for work at every town, and feeling himself to be a free
and independent American citizen, traveling on his own honestly-
earned means, undegraded by an obligation, the equal in social rank
of the best man in the best house he passed. Blessed is the young
man who can walk thirty miles a day, and dine contentedly on half
a pound of crackers! Give him four dollars and summer weather,
and he can travel and rovel like a prince incog. for forty days.

On Sunday morning, our hero arose, refreshed and cheerful. He
went to church twice, and spent a happy day. In the morning he
induced a man who lived in the house to accompany him to a small
Universalist church in Pitt street, near the Dry Dock, not less than
three miles distant from M'Gorlick's boarding-house. In the evening
he found his way to a Unitarian church. Except on one occasion,
he had never before this Sunday heard a sermon which accorded
with his own religious opinions; and the pleasure with which he
heard the benignity of the Deity asserted and proved by able men,
was one of the highest he had enjoyed.

In the afternoon, as if in reward of the pious way in which he
spent the Sunday, he heard news which gave him a faint hope of
being able to remain in the city. An Irishman, a friend of the
landlord, came in the course of the afternoon to pay his usual Sunday visit, and became acquainted with Horace and his fruitless
search for work. He was a shoemaker, I believe, but he lived in a
house which was much frequented by journeymen printers. From
them he had heard that hands were wanted at West's, No. 85 Chatham street, and he recommended his new acquaintance to make
immediate application at that office.

Accustomed to country hours, and eager to seize the chance,

Horace was in Chatham street and on the steps of the designated house by half-past five on Monday morning. West's printing office was in the second story, the ground floor being occupied by Mc-Elrath and Bangs as a bookstore. They were publishers, and West was their printer. Neither store nor office was yet opened, and Horace sat down on the steps to wait.

Had Thomas McElrath, Esquire, happened to pass on an early walk to the Battery that morning, and seen our hero sitting on those steps, with his red bundle on his knees, his pale face supported on his hands, his attitude expressive of dejection and anxiety, his attire extremely unornamental, it would not have occurred to Thomas Mc-Elrath, Esquire, as a *probable* event, that one day he would be the PARTNER of that sorry figure, and proud of the connection! Nor did Miss Reed, of Philadelphia, when she saw Benjamin Franklin pass her father's house, eating a large roll and carrying two others under his arms, see in that poor wanderer any likeness to her future husband, the husband that made her a proud and an immortal wife. The princes of the mind always remain incog. till they come to the throne, and, doubtless, the Coming Man, when he *comes*, will appear in a strange disguise, and no man will know him.

It seemed very long before any one came to work that morning at No. 85. The steps on which our friend was seated were in the narrow part of Chatham-street, the gorge through which at morning and evening the swarthy tide of mechanics pours. By six o'clock the stream has set strongly down-town-ward, and it gradually swells to a torrent, bright with tin kettles. Thousands passed by, but no one stopped till nearly seven o'clock, when one of Mr. West's journeymen arrived, and finding the door still locked, he sat down on the steps by the side of Horace Greeley. They fell into conversation, and Horace stated his circumstances, something of his history, and his need of employment. Luckily this journeyman was a Vermonter, and a kind-hearted, intelligent man. He looked upon Horace as a countryman, and was struck with the singular candor and artlessness with which he told his tale. "I saw," says he, "that he was an honest, good young man, and being a Vermonter myself, I determined to help him if I could."

He did help him. The doors were opened, the men began to arrive; Horace and his newly-found friend ascended to the office.

and soon after seven the work of the day began.   It is hardly necessary to say that the appearance of Horace, as he sat in the office
waiting for the coming of the foreman, excited unbounded astonishment, and brought upon his friend a variety of satirical observations.
Nothing daunted, however, on the arrival of the foreman he stated
the case, and endeavored to interest him enough in Horace to give
him a trial.   It happened that the work for which a man was wanted
in the office was the composition of a Polyglot Testament; a kind
of work which is extremely difficult and tedious.   Several men had
tried their hand at it, and, in a few days or a few hours, given it up.
The foreman looked at Horace, and Horace looked at the foreman.
Horace saw a handsome man (now known to the sporting public as
Colonel Porter, editor of the Spirit of the Times.)   The foreman
beheld a youth who could have gone on the stage, that minute, as
Ezekiel Homespun without the alteration of a thread or a hair, and
brought down the house by his 'getting up' alone.   He no more
believed that Ezekiel could set up a page of a Polyglot Testament
than that he could construct a chronometer.   However, partly to
oblige Horace's friend, partly because he was unwilling to wound
the feelings of the applicant by sending him abruptly away, he consented to let him try.   "Fix up a case for him," said he, "and we'll
see if he *can* do anything."   In a few minutes Horace was at
work.

The gentleman to whose intercession Horace Greeley owed his
first employment in New-York is now known to all the dentists in
the Union as the leading member of a firm which manufactures
annually twelve hundred thousand artificial teeth.   He has made
a fortune, the reader will be glad to learn, and lives in a mansion up
town.

After Horace had been at work an hour or two, Mr. West, the
'boss,' came into the office.   What his feelings were when he saw
his new man, may be inferred from a little conversation upon the
subject which took place between him and the foreman.

"Did you hire that —— fool?" asked West with no small irritation.

"Yes; we must have hands, and he's the best I could get," said
the foreman, justifying his conduct, though he was really ashamed
of it.

"Well," said the master, "for God's sake pay him off to-night, and let him go about his business."

Horace worked through the day with his usual intensity, and in perfect silence. At night he presented to the foreman, as the cus tom then was, the 'proof' of his day's work What astonishment was depicted in the good-looking countenance of that gentleman when he discovered that the proof before him was greater in quantity, and more correct than that of any other day's work which had yet been done on the Polyglot ! There was no thought of sending the new journeyman about his business now. He was an established man at once. Thenceforward, for several months, Horace worked regularly and hard on the Testament, earning about six dollars a week.

He had got into good company. There were about twenty men and boys in the office, altogether, of whom two have since been members of Congress, three influential editors, and several others have attained distinguished success in more private vocations. Most of them are still alive; they remember vividly the coming among them of Horace Greeley, and are fond of describing his ways and works. The following paragraph the reader is requested to regard as the condensed statement of their several recollections.

Horace worked with most remarkable devotion and intensity. His task was difficult, and he was paid by the 'piece.' In order, therefore, to earn tolerable wages, it was necessary for him to work harder and longer than any of his companions, and he did so. Often he was at his case before six in the morning; often he had not left it at nine in the evening ; always, he was the first to begin and the last to leave. In the summer, no man beside himself worked before breakfast, or after tea. While the young men and older apprentices were roaming the streets, seeking their pleasure, he, by the light of a candle stuck in a bottle, was eking out a slender day's wages by setting up an extra column of the Polyglot Testament.

For a day or two, the men of the office eyed him askance, and winked at one another severely. The boys were more demonstrative, and one of the most mischievous among them named him THE GHOST, in allusion to his long white hair, and the singular fairness of his complexion. Soon, however, the men who worked near him began to suspect that his mind was better furnished than his person. Horace always had a way of talking profusely while at work, and that, too, without working with less assiduity. Conversations soon arose about masonry, temperance, politics, religion; and the new journeyman rapidly argued his way to respectful consideration. His talk was ardent, animated, and *positive*. He was perfectly confident of his opinions, and maintained them with an assurance that in a youth of less understanding and less geniality would have been thought arrogance. His enthusiasm at this time, was Henry Clay; his great subject, masonry. In a short time, to quote the language of one his fellow-workmen, 'he was the lion of the shop.' Yet for all that, the men who admired him most would have their joke, and during all the time that Horace remained in the office, it was the standing amusement to make nonsensical remarks in order to draw from him one of his shrewd, half-comic, Scotch-Irish retorts. "And we always *got* it," says one.

The boys of the office were overcome by a process similar to that which frustrated the youth of Poultney. Four or five of them, who knew Horace's practice of returning to the office in the evening and working alone by candle-light, concluded that that would be an excellent time to play a few printing-office tricks upon him. They accordingly lay in ambush one evening, in the dark recesses of the shop, and awaited the appearance of the Ghost. He had no sooner lighted his candle and got at work, than a ball, made of 'old roller,' whizzed past his ear and knocked over his candle. He set it straight again and went on with his work. Another ball, and another, and another, and finally a volley. One hit his 'stick,' one scattered his type, another broke his bottle, and several struck his head. He bore it till the balls came so fast, that it was impossible for him to work, as all his time was wasted in repairing damages. At length, he turned round and said, without the slightest ill-humor, and in a supplicating tone, "Now, boys, don't. I want to work. Please, now, let me alone." The boys came out of their places of concealment into the light of the candle, and troubled him no more.

Thus, it appears, that every man can best defend himself with the weapon that nature has provided him—whether it be fists or forgiveness. Little Jane Eyre was of opinion, that when anybody has struck another, he should himself be struck; " ...y hard," says Jane, "so hard, that he will be afraid ever to stri.. anybody again." On the contrary, thought Horace Greeley, whe... any one has wantonly or unjustly struck another, he should be ..o severely forgiven, and made so thoroughly ashamed of himself, ..hat he will ever after shrink from striking a wanton or an unjust blow. Sound maxims, *both ;* the first, for Jane, the second, for Horace.

His good humor was, in truth, naturally imperturbable. He was soon the recognized OBLIGING MAN of the office; the person relied upon always when help was needed—a most inconvenient kind of reputation. Among mechanics, money is generally abundant enough on Sundays and Mondays ; and they spend it freely on those days. Tuesday and Wednesday, they are only in moderate circumstances. The last days of the week are days of pressure and borrowing, when men are in a better condition to be treated than to treat. Horace Greeley was the man who had money always ; he was as rich apparently on Saturday afternoon as on Sunday morning, and as willing to lend. In an old memorandum-book belonging to one of his companions in those days, still may be deciphered such entries as these: 'Borrowed of Horace Greeley, 2s.' 'Owe Horace Greeley, 9s. 6d.' 'Owe Horace Greeley, 2s. 6d, for a breastpin.' He never refused to lend his money. To himself, he allowed scarcely anything in the way of luxury or amusement; unless, indeed, an occasional purchase of a small share in a lottery-ticket may be styled a luxury.

Lotteries were lawful in those days, and Chatham-street was where lottery-offices most abounded. It was regarded as a perfectly respectable and legitimate business to keep a lottery-office, and a perfectly proper and moral action to buy a lottery-ticket. The business was conducted openly and fairly, and under official supervision ; not as it now is, by secret and irresponsible agents in all parts of the city and country. Whether less money, or more, is lost by lotteries now than formerly, is a question which, it is surprising, no journalist has determined. Whether they cause less or greater demoralization is a question which it were well for moralists to consider.

Of the few incidents which occurred to relieve the monotony of

the printing-office in Chatham-street, the one which is most glee-
fully remembered is the following :—

Horace was, of course, subjected to a constant fire of jocular
observations upon his dress, and frequently to practical jokes suggested by its deficiencies and redundancies. Men stared at him in
the streets, and boys called after him. Still, however, he clung to
his linen roundabout, his short trowsers, his cotton shirt, and his
dilapidated hat. Still he wore no stockings, and made his wrist-
bands meet with twine. For all jokes upon the subject he had deaf
ears; and if any one seriously remonstrated, he would not defend
himself by explaining, that all the money he could spare was needed in the wilderness, six hundred miles away, whither he punctually
sent it. September passed and October. It began to be cold, but
our hero had been toughened by the winters of Vermont, and still
he walked about in linen. One evening in November, when business was urgent, and all the men worked till late in the evening,
Horace, instead of returning immediately after tea, as his custom
was, was absent from the office for two hours. Between eight and
nine, when by chance all the men were gathered about the 'composing stone,' upon which a strong light was thrown, a strange
figure entered the office, a tall gentleman, dressed in a complete suit
of faded broadcloth, and a shabby, over-brushed beaver hat, from
beneath which depended long and snowy locks. The garments
were fashionably cut; the coat was in the style of a swallow's
tail; the figure was precisely that of an old gentleman who had
seen better days. It advanced from the darker parts of the office,
and emerged slowly into the glare around the composing stone.
The men looked inquiringly. The figure spread out its hands,
looked down at its habiliments with an air of infinite complacency,
and said,—

"Well, boys, and how do you like me now?"

"Why, it's Greeley," screamed one of the men.

It *was* Greeley, metamorphosed into a decayed gentleman by a
second-hand suit of black, bought of a Chatham-street Jew for five
dollars.

A shout arose, such as had never before been heard at staid and
regular 85 Chatham-street. Cheer upon cheer was given, and men

laughed till the tears came, the venerable gentleman being as happy as the happiest.

"Greeley, you must treat upon *that* suit, and no mistake," said one.

"Oh, of course," said everybody else.

"Come along, boys; I'll treat," was Horace's ready response.

All the company repaired to the old grocery on the corner of Duane-street, and there each individual partook of the beverage that pleased him, the treater indulging in a glass of spruce beer. Posterity may as well know, and take warning from the fact, that this five-dollar suit was a failure. It had been worn thin, and had been washed in blackened water and ironed smooth. A week's wear brought out all its pristine shabbiness, and developed new.

Our hero was not, perhaps, quite so indifferent to his personal appearance as he seemed. One day, when Colonel Porter happened to remark that his hair had once been as white as Horace Greeley's, Horace said with great earnestness, "Was it?"—as though he drew from that fact a hope that his own hair might darken as he grew older. And on another occasion, when he had just returned from a visit to New-Hampshire, he said, "Well, I have been up in the country among my cousins; *they* are all good-looking young men enough; I do n't see why *I* should be such a curious-looking fellow."

One or two other incidents which occurred at West's are perhaps worth telling; for one well-authenticated fact, though apparently of trifling importance, throws more light upon character than pages of general reminiscence.

It was against the rules of the office for a compositor to enter the press-room, which adjoined the composing-room. Our hero, however, went on one occasion to the forbidden apartment to speak to a friend who worked there upon a hand-press that was exceedingly hard to pull.

"Greeley," said one of the men, "you're a pretty stout fellow, but you can 't pull back that lever."

"Can 't I?" said Horace; "I can."

"Try it, then," said the mischief-maker.

The press was arranged in such a manner that the lever offered no resistance whatever, and, consequently, when Horace seized it, and collected all his strength for a tremendous effort, he fell backwards on the floor with great violence, and brought away a large part of the press with him. There was a thundering noise, and all the house came running to see what was the matter. Horace got up, pale and trembling from the concussion.

"Now, that was too bad," said he.

He stood his ground, however, while the man who had played the trick gave the 'boss' a fictitious explanation of the mishap, without mentioning the name of the apparent offender. When all was quiet again, Horace went privately to the pressman and offered to *pay* his share of the damage done to the press!

With Mr. West, Horace had little intercourse, and yet they did on several occasions come into collision. Mr. West, like all other bosses and men, had a weakness; it was commas. He loved commas, he was a stickler for commas, he was irritable on the subject of commas, he thought more of commas than any other point of prosody, and above all, he was of opinion that he knew more about commas than Horace Greeley. Horace had, on his part, no objection to commas, but he loved them in moderation, and was determined to keep them in their place. Debates ensued. The journeyman expounded the subject, and at length, after much argument, convinced his employer that a redundancy of commas was possible, and, in short, that he, the journeyman, knew how to preserve the balance of power between the various points, without the assistance or advice of any boss or man in Chatham, or any other street. There was, likewise, a certain professor whose book was printed in the office, and who often came to read the proofs. It chanced that Horace set up a few pages of this book, and took the liberty of altering a few phrases that seemed to him inelegant or incorrect. The professor was indignant, and though he was not so ignorant as not to perceive that his language had been altered for the better, he thought it due to his dignity to apply opprobrious epithets to the impertinent compositor. The compositor argued the matter, but did not appease the great man.

Soon after obtaining work, our friend found a better boarding-house, at least a more convenient one. On the corner of Duane-street and Chatham there was, at that time, a large building, occupied below as a grocery and bar-room, the upper stories as a · `echanics' boarding-house. It accommodated about fifty boarders, most of whom were shoe-makers, who worked in their own rooms, or in shops at the top of the house, and paid, for room and board, two dollars and a half per week. This was the house to which Horace Greeley removed, a few days after his arrival in the city, and there he lived for more than two years. The reader of the Tribune may, perhaps, remember, that its editor has frequently displayed a particular acquaintance with the business of shoe-making, and drawn many illustrations of the desirableness and feasibility of association from the excessive labor and low wages of shoe-makers. It was at this house that he learned the mysteries of the craft. He was accustomed to go up into the shops, and sit among the men while waiting for dinner. It was here, too, that he obtained that general acquaintance with the life and habits of city mechanics, which has enabled him since to address them so wisely and so convincingly. He is remembered by those who lived with him there, only as a very quiet, thoughtful, studious young man, one who gave no trouble, never went out 'to spend the evening,' and read nearly every minute when he was not working or eating. The late Mr. Wilson, of the Brother Jonathan, who was his roommate for some months, used to say, that often he went to bed leaving his companion absorbed in a book, and when he awoke in the morning, saw him exactly in the same position and attitude, as though he had not moved all night. He had not read all night, however, but had risen to his book with the dawn. Soon after sunrise, he went over the way to his work.

Another of Mr. Wilson's reminiscences is interesting. The reader is aware, perhaps, from experience, that people who pay only two dollars and a half per week for board and lodging are not provided with all the luxuries of the season; and that, not unfrequently, a desire for something delicious steals over the souls of boarders, particularly on Sundays, between 12, M. and 1, P.M. The eating-house revolution had then just begun, and the institution of Dining Down Town was set up; in fact, a bold man established a Sixpenny Dining Saloon in Beekman-street, which was the talk of the shops in the winter of 1831. On Sundays Horace and his friends, after their return from Mr. Sawyer's (Universalist) church in Orchard-street, were accustomed to repair to this establishment, and indulge in a splendid repast at a cost of, at least, one shilling each, rising on some occasions to eighteen pence. Their talk at dinner was of the soul-banquet, the sermon, of which they had partaken in the morning, and it was a custom among them to ascertain who could repeat the substance of it most correctly. Horace attended that church regularly, in those days, and listened to the sermon with his head bent forward, his eyes upon the floor, his arms folded, and one leg swinging, quite in his old class attitude at the Westhaven school.

This, then, is the substance of what his companions remember of Horace Greeley's first few months in the metropolis. In a way so homely and so humble, New York's most distinguished citizen, the Country's most influential man, began his career.

In his subsequent writings there are not many allusions of an autobiographical nature to this period. The following is, indeed, the only paragraph of the kind that seems worth quoting. It is valuable as throwing light upon the *habit of his mind* at this time :—

"Fourteen years ago, when the editor of the TRIBUNE came to this city, there was published here a small daily paper entitled the 'Sentinel,' devoted to the cause of what was called by its own supporters 'the Working Men's Party,' and by its opponents 'the *Fanny Wright* Working Men.' Of that party we have little personal knowledge, but at the head of the paper, among several good and many objectionable avowals of principle, was borne the following :

"'*Single Districts for the choice of each Senator and Member of Assembly.*'

"We gave this proposition some attention at the time, and came to the conclusion that it was alike sound and important. It mattered little to us that it was accompanied and surrounded by others that we could not assent to, and was propounded by a party with which we had no acquaintance and little sympathy. We are accustomed to welcome truth, from whatever quarter it may approach us, and on whatever flag it may be inscribed. Subsequent experience has fully confirmed our original impression, and now we have little doubt that this principle, which was utterly slighted when presented under unpopular auspices, will be engrafted on our reformed Constitution without serious opposition."—*Tribune, Dec.,* 1845.

CHAPTER IX.

FROM OFFICE TO OFFICE.

HORACE GREELEY was a journeyman printer in this city for fourteen months. Those months need not detain us long from the more eventful periods of his life.

He worked for Mr. West in Chatham street till about the first of November (1831). Then the business of that office fell off, and he was again a seeker for employment. He obtained a place in the office of the 'Evening Post,' whence, it is *said*, he was soon dismissed by the late Mr. Leggett, on the ground of his sorry appearance. The story current among printers is this: Mr. Leggett came into the printing-office for the purpose of speaking to the man whose place Horace Greeley had taken.

" Where 's Jones ?" asked Mr. Leggett.

" He 's gone away," replied one of the men.

" Who has taken his place, then ?" said the irritable editor.

" There 's the man," said some one, pointing to Horace, who was ' bobbing' at the case in his peculiar way.

Mr. Leggett looked at ' the man,' and said to the foreman, " For God's sake discharge him, and let 's have decent-*looking* men in the office, at least."

Horace was accordingly—so goes the story—discharged at the end of the week.

He worked, also, for a few days upon the ' Commercial Advertiser,' as a ' sub,' probably. Then, for two weeks and a half, upon a little paper called ' The Amulet,' a weekly journal of literature and art. The ' Amulet' was discontinued, and our hero had to wait ten years for his wages.

His next step can be given in his own words. The following is the beginning of a paragraph in the New Yorker of March 2d, 1839:

"Seven years ago, on the first of January last—that being a holiday, and the writer being then a stranger with few social greetings to exchange in New York—he inquired his way into the ill-furnished, chilly, forlorn-looking attic printing-office in which William T. Porter, in company with another very young man, who soon after abandoned the enterprise, had just issued the 'Spirit of the Times,' the first weekly journal devoted entirely to sporting intelligence ever attempted in this country. It was a moderate-sized sheet of indifferent paper, with an atrocious wood-cut for the head—about as uncomely a specimen of the 'fine arts' as our 'native talent' has produced. The paper was about in proportion; for neither of its conductors had fairly attained his majority, and each was destitute of the experience so necessary in such an enterprise, and of the funds and extensive acquaintance which were still more necessary to its success. But one of them possessed a persevering spirit and an ardent enthusiasm for the pursuit to which he had devoted himself."

And, consequently, the 'Spirit of the Times' still exists and flourishes, under the proprietorship of its originator and founder, Colonel Porter. For this paper, our hero, during his short stay in the office, composed a multitude of articles and paragraphs, most of them short and unimportant. As a specimen of his style at this period, I copy from the 'Spirit' of May 5th, 1832, the following epistle, which was considered extremely funny in those innocent days:

"MESSRS. EDITORS:—Hear me you shall, pity me you must, while I proceed to give a short account of the dread calamities which this vile habit of turning the whole city upside down, 'tother side out, and wrong side before, on the First of May, has brought down on my devoted head.

"You must know, that having resided but a few months in your city, I was totally ignorant of the existence of said custom. So, on the morning of the eventful, and to me disastrous day, I rose, according to immemorial usage, at the dying away of the last echo of the breakfast bell, and soon found myself seated over my coffee, and my good landlady exercising her powers of volubility (no weak ones) apparently in my behalf; but so deep was the reverie in which my half-awakened brain was then engaged, that I did not catch a single idea from the whole of her discourse. I smiled and said, "Yes, ma'am," "certainly ma'am," at each pause; and having speedily dispatched my breakfast, sallied immediately out, and proceeded to attend to the business which engrossed my mind. Dinner-time came, but no time for dinner; and it was late before I was at liberty to wend my way, over wheel-barrows, barrels, and all manner of obstructions, towards my boarding-house. All here was still ; but by the help of my night-keys, I soon introduced myself to my chamber, dreaming of nothing but sweet repose ; when, horrible to relate ! my ears were instantaneously saluted by a most piercing female shriek, proceeding exactly from my own bed, or at least from the place where it should have been ; and scarcely had sufficient time elapsed for my hair to bristle on my head, before the shriek was answered by the loud vociferations of a ferocious mastiff in the kitchen beneath, and re-echoed by the outcries of half a dozen inmates of the house, and these again succeeded by the rattle of the watchman ; and the next moment, there was a round dozen of them (besides the dog) at my throat, and commanding me to tell them instantly what the devil all this meant.

"You do well to ask that," said I, as soon as I could speak, "after falling upon me in this fashion in my own chamber."

"O take him off," said the one who assumed to be the master of the house ; "perhaps he 's not a thief after all ; but, being too tipsy for starlight, he has made a mistake in trying to find his lodgings,"—and in spite of all my remonstrances, I was forthwith marched off to the watch-house, to pass the remainder of the night. In the morning, I narrowly escaped commitment on the charge of 'burglary with intent to steal (I verily believe it would have gone hard with me if the witnesses could have been got there at that unseasonable hour), and I was finally discharged with a solemn admonition to guard *for the future* against intoxication (think of that, sir, for a member of the Cold Water Society !)

"I spent the next day in unraveling the mystery ; and found that my landlord had removed his goods and chattels to another part of the city, on the established day, supposing me to be previously acquainted and satisfied with his intention of so doing ; and another family had immediately taken his place ; of which changes, my absence of mind and absence from dinner had kept me ignorant ; and thus had I been led blindfold into a 'Comedy' (or rather tragedy) of Errors. Your unfortunate,

"TIMOTHY WIGGINS."

His connection with the office of a sporting paper procured him occasionally an order for admission to a theater, which he used. He appeared to have had a natural liking for the drama ; all intelligent persons have when they are young ; and one of his companions of that day remembers well the *intense* interest with which he once witnessed the performance of Richard III., at the old Chatham theater. At the close of the play, he said there was another of Shakespeare's tragedies which he had long wished to see, and that was Hamlet.

Soon after writing his letter, the luckless Wiggins, tempted by the prospect of better wages, left the Spirit of the Times, and went back to West's, and worked for some weeks on Prof. Bush's Notes on Genesis, 'the worst manuscript ever seen in a printing-office.' That finished, he returned to the Spirit of the Times, and remained till October, when he went to visit his relatives in New Hampshire. He reached his uncle's farm in Londonderry in the apple-gathering season, and going at once to the orchard found his cousins engaged in that pleasing exercise. Horace jumped over the fence, saluted them in the hearty and unornamental Scotch-Irish style, sprang into a tree, and assisted them till their task for the day was done, and then all the party went frolicking into the woods on a grape-hunt. Horace was a welcome guest. He was full of fun in those days, and kept the boys roaring with his stories, or agape with descriptions of city scenes.

Back to the city again early in November, in time and on purpose to vote at the fall elections.

He went to work, soon after, for Mr. J. S. Redfield, now an eminent publisher of this city, then a stereotyper. Mr. Redfield favors me with the following note of his connection with Horace Greeley: —" My recollections of Mr. Greeley extend from about the time he first came to the city to work as a compositor. I was carrying on the stereotyping business in William street, and having occasion one day for more compositors, one of the hands brought in Greeley, remarking 'sotto voce' as he introduced him, that he was a " boyish and rather odd looking genius," (to which remark I had no difficulty in assenting,) 'but he had understood that he was a good workman.' Being much in want of help at the time, Greeley was set to work, and I was not a little surprised to find on Saturday night, that his bills were much larger than those of any other compositor in the office, and oftentimes nearly double those at work by the side of him on the same work. He would accomplish this, too, *and talk all the time!* The same untiring industry, and the same fearlessness and independence, which have characterized his course as Editor of the New York Tribune, were the distinguishing features of his character as a journeyman."

He remained in the office of Mr. Redfield till late in December, when the circumstance occurred which gave him his FIRST LIFT in the world. There is a tide, it is said, in the affairs of every man, *once* in his life, which taken at the flood leads on to fortune:

Horace Greeley's First Lift happened to take place in connection with an event of great, world-wide and lasting consequence; yet one which has never been narrated to the public. It shall, therefore, have in this work a short chapter to itself.

CHAPTER X.

THE FIRST PENNY PAPER—AND WHO THOUGHT OF IT.

Importance of the cheap daily press—The originator of the idea—History of the idea —Dr. Sheppard's Chatham-street cogitations—The idea is conceived—It is born— Interview with Horace Greeley—The Doctor thinks he is 'no common boy'—The schemer baffled—Daily papers twenty-five years ago—Dr. Sheppard comes to a resolution—The firm of Greeley and Story—The Morning Post appears—And fails —The sphere of the cheap press—Fanny Fern and the pea-nut merchant.

WHEN the Historian of the United States shall have completed the work that has occupied so many busy and anxious years, and, in the tranquil solitude of his study, he reviews the long series of events which he has narrated, the question may arise in his mind,—Which of the events that occurred during the first seventy years of the Republic is likely to exert the greatest and most lasting influence upon its future history? Surely, he will not pause long for a reply. For, there is one event, which stands out so prominently beyond and above all others, the consequences of which, to this country and all other countries, must be so immense, and, finally, so beneficial, that no other can be seriously placed in com petition with it. It was the establishment of the first penny daily paper in the city of New York in the year 1838. Its results, in this country, have already been wonderful indeed, and it is destined to play a great part in the history of every civilized nation, and in that of every nation yet to be civilized.

Not that Editors are, in all cases, or in most, the wisest of men ; not that editorial writing has a greater value than hasty composition in general.   Editors are a useful, a laborious, a generous, an honorable class of men and women, and their writings have their due effect.   But, that part of the newspaper which interests, awakens, moves, warns, inspires, instructs and educates all classes and conditions of people, the wise and the unwise, the illiterate and the learned, is the NEWS !   And the News, the same news, at nearly the same instant of time, is communicated to all the people of this fair and vast domain which we inherit, by the instrumentality of the Cheap Press, aided by its allies the Rail and the Wire.

A catastrophe happens to-day in New York.   New Orleans shudders to-morrow at the recital ; and the Nation shudders before the week ends.   A 'Great Word,' uttered on any stump in the land, soon illuminates a million minds.   A bad deed is perpetrated, and the shock of disgust flies with electric rapidity from city to city, from State to State—from the heart that records it to every heart that beats.   A gallant deed or a generous one is done, or a fruitful idea is suggested, and it falls, like good seed which the wind scatters, over all the land at once.   Leave the city on a day when some stirring news is rife, travel as far and as fast as you may, rest not by day nor night ; you cannot easily get where that News is not, where it is not the theme of general thought and talk, where it is not doing its part in informing, or, at least, exciting the public mind.   Abandon the great lines of travel, go rocking in a stage over corduroy roads, through the wilderness, to the newest of new villages, a cluster of log-houses, in a field of blackened stumps, and even there you must be prompt with your news, or it will have flown out from a bundle of newspapers under the driver's seat, and fallen in flakes all over the settlement.

The Cheap Press—its importance cannot be estimated !   It puts every mind in direct communication with the greatest minds, which all, in one way or another, speak through its columns.   It brings the *Course of Events* to bear on the progress of every individual.   It is the great leveler, elevator and democraticizer.   It makes this huge Commonwealth, else so heterogeneous and disunited, think with one mind, feel with one heart, and talk with one tongue. Dissolve the Union into a hundred petty States, and the Press will still keep us. in heart and soul and habit, One People.

Pardon this slight digression, dear reader. Pardon it, because the beginnings of the greatest things are, in appearance, so insig nificant, that unless we look at them in the light of their conse quences, it is impossible to take an interest in them.

There are not, I presume, twenty-five persons alive, who know in whose head it was, that the idea of a cheap daily paper origin ated. Nor has the proprietor of that head ever derived from his idea, which has enriched so many others, the smallest pecuniary advantage. He walks these streets, this day, an unknown man, and poor. His name—the reader may forget it, History will not—is HORATIO DAVIS SHEPPARD. The story of his idea, amply confirmed in every particular by living and unimpeachable witnesses, is the following :

About the year 1880, Mr. Sheppard, recently come of age and into the possession of fifteen hundred dollars, moved from his native New Jersey to New York, and entered the Eldridge Street Medical School as a student of medicine. He was ambitious and full of ideas. Of course, therefore, his fifteen hundred dollars *burned* in his vest pocket—(where he actually used to carry it, until a fellow stu dent almost compelled him to deposit it in a place of safety). He took to dabbling in newspapers and periodicals, a method of getting rid of superfluous cash, which is as expeditious as it is fascinating. He soon had an interest in a medical magazine, and soon after, a share in a weekly paper. By the time he had completed his medi cal studies, he had gained some insight into the nature of the news paper business, and lost the greater part of his money.

People who live in Eldridge street, when they have occasion to go 'down town,' must necessarily pass through Chatham street, a thoroughfare which is noted, among many other things, for the ex traordinary number of articles which are sold in it for a 'penny a piece.' Apple-stalls, peanut-stalls, stalls for the sale of oranges, melons, pine-apples, cocoanuts, chestnuts, candy, shoe-laces, cakes, pocket-combs, ice-cream, suspenders, lemonade, and oysters, line the sidewalk. In Chatham street, those small trades are carried on, on a scale of magnitude, with a loudness of vociferation, and a

flare of lamp-light, unknown to any other part of the town. Along
Chatham street, our medical student ofttimes took his way, musing
on the instability of fifteen hundred dollars, and observing, possibly
envying, the noisy merchants of the stalls. He was struck with
the rapidity with which they sold their penny ware. A small boy
would sell half a dozen penny cakes in the course of a minute.
The difference between a cent, and no money, did not seem to be
appreciated by the people. If a person saw something, wanted it,
knew the price to be only a cent, he was almost as certain to buy
it as though it were offered him for nothing. Now, thought he, to
make a fortune, one has nothing more to do than to produce a
tempting article which can be sold profitably for a cent, place it
where everybody can see it, and buy it, without stopping—and lo !
the thing is done ! If it were only *possible* to produce a small, spicy
daily paper for a cent, and get boys to sell it about the streets, *how*
it would sell ! How many pennies that now go for cakes and pea-
nuts would be spent for news and paragraphs !

The idea was born—the twin ideas of the penny paper and the
newsboy. But, like the young of the kangaroo, they crawled into
the mental pouch of the teeming originator, and nestled there for
months, before they were fully formed and strong enough to confront the world.

Perhaps it *is* possible, continued the musing man of medicine, on
a subsequent walk in Chatham street. He went to a paper ware-
house, and made inquiries touching the price of the cheaper kinds
of printing paper. He figured up the cost of composition. He
computed office expenses and editorial salaries. He estimated the
probable circulation of a penny paper, and the probable income to
be derived from advertising. Surely, he could sell four or five
thousand a day ! *There*, for instance, is a group of people ; suppose
a boy were at this moment to go up to *them* with an armful of papers, 'only one cent,' I am positive, thought the sanguine projector,
that six of the nine would buy a copy ! His conclusion was, that
he could produce a newspaper about twice the size of an average
sheet of letter-paper, half paragraphs and half advertisements, and
sell it at a cent per copy, with an ample profit to himself. He was
sure of it ! He had tried all his arithmetic upon the project, and
the figures gave the same result always. The twins leaped from

the pouch, and taking their progenitor by the throat, led him a fine dance before he could shake them off. For the present, they possessed him wholly.

As most of his little inheritance had vanished, it was necessary for him to interest some one in the scheme who had either capital or a printing office. The Spirit of the Times was then in its infancy. To the office of that paper, where Horace Greeley was then a journeyman, Mr. Sheppard first directed his steps, and there he first unfolded his plans and exhibited his calculations. Mr. Greeley was not present on his first entrance. He came in soon after, and began telling in high glee a story he had picked up of old Isaac Hill, who used to read his speeches in the House, and one day brought the wrong speech, and got upon his legs, and half way into a swelling exordium before he discovered his mistake. The narrator told his story extremely well, taking off the embarrassment of the old gentleman as he gradually came to the knowledge of his misfortune, to the life. The company were highly amused, and Mr. Sheppard said to himself, "That's no common *boy*." Perhaps it was an unfortunate mo‧ment to introduce a bold and novel idea; but it is certain that every individual present, from the editor to the devil, regarded the notion of a penny paper as one of extreme absurdity,—foolish, ridiculous, frivolous! They took it as a joke, and the schemer took his leave.

Nor is it at all surprising that they should have regarded it in that light. A daily newspaper in those days was a solemn thing. People in moderate circumstances seldom saw, never bought one. The price was ten dollars a year. Cut the present Journal of Commerce in halves, fold it, fancy on its second page half a column of serious editorial, a column of news, half a column of business and shipping intelligence, and the rest of the ample sheet covered with advertisements, and you have before your mind's eye the New York daily paper of twenty-five years ago. It was not a thing for the people; it appertained to the counting-house; it was taken by the wholesale dealer; it was cumbrous, heavy, solemn. The idea of making it an article to be cried about the streets, to be sold for a cent, to be bought by workingmen and boys, to come into competition with cakes and apples, must have seemed to the respectable New Yorkers of 1831, unspeakably absurd. When the respectable

New Yorker first saw a penny paper, he gazed at it (I saw him) with a feeling similar to that with which an ill-natured man may be supposed to regard General Tom Thumb, a feeling of mingled curiosity and contempt; he put the ridiculous little thing into his waistcoat pocket to carry home for the amusement of his family; and he wondered what nonsense would be perpetrated *next.*

Dr. Sheppard—he had now taken his degree—was not disheartened by the merry reception of his idea at the office of the Spirit of the Times. He went to other offices—to nearly *every* other office ! For eighteen months it was his custom, whenever opportunity offered, to expound his project to printers and editors, and, in fact, to any one who would listen to him long enough. *He could not convince one man of the feasibility of his scheme,—not one!* A few people thought it a good idea for the instruction of the million, and recommended him to get some society to take hold of it. But not a human being could be brought to believe that it would *pay* as a business, and only a few of the more polite and complaisant printers could be induced to consider the subject in a serious light at all.

Reader, possessed with an Idea, reader, 'in a minority of one,' take courage from the fact.

Despairing of getting the assistance he required, Dr. Sheppard resolved, at length, to make a desperate effort to start the paper himself. His means were fifty dollars in cash and a promise of credit for two hundred dollars' worth of paper. Among his printer friends was Mr. Francis Story, the foreman of the Spirit of the Times office, who, about that time, was watching for an opportunity to get into business on his own account. To him Dr. Sheppard announced his intention, and proposed that he should establish an office and print the forthcoming paper, offering to pay the bill for composition every Saturday. Mr. Story hesitated; but, on obtaining from Mr. Sylvester a promise of the printing of his *Bank Note Reporter*, he embraced Dr. Sheppard's proposal, and offered Horace Greeley, for whom he had long entertained a warm friendship and a great admiration, an equal share in the enterprise. Horace was not favorably impressed with Dr. Sheppard's scheme. In the first place, he had no great faith in the practical ability of that gentleman; and, secondly, he was of opinion that the smallest price for which a daily paper could be profitably sold was two cents.

His arguments on the latter point did not convince the ardent doctor; but, with the hope of overcoming his scruples and enlisting his co-operation, he consented to give up his darling idea, and fix the price of his paper at two cents. Horace Greeley agreed, at length, to try his fortune as a master printer, and in December, the firm of Greeley and Story was formed.

Now, experience has since proved that two cents is the best price for a cheap paper. But the point, the charm, the *impudence* of Dr. Sheppard's project all lay in those magical words, 'PRICE ONE CENT,' which his paper was to have borne on its heading—but did not. And the capital to be invested in the enterprise was so ludicrously inadequate, that it was necessary for the paper to pay at once, or cease to appear. Horace Greeley's advice, therefore, though good as a general principle, was not applicable to the case in hand. Not that the proposed paper would, or could, have succeeded upon any terms. Its failure was inevitable. Dr. Sheppard is one of those projectors who have the faculty of suggesting the most valuable and fruitful ideas, without possessing, in any degree, the qualities needful for their realization.

The united capital of the two printers was about one hundred and fifty dollars. They were both, however, highly respected in the printing world, and both had friends among those whose operations keep that world in motion. They hired part of a small office at No. 54 Liberty street. Horace Greeley's candid story prevailed with Mr. George Bruce, the great type founder, so far, that he gave the new firm credit for a small quantity of type—an act of trust and kindness which secured him one of the best customers he has ever had. (To this day the type of the Tribune is supplied by Mr. Bruce.) Before the new year dawned, Greeley and Story were ready to execute every job of printing which was not too extensive or intricate, on favorable terms, and with the utmost punctuality and dispatch.

On the morning of January 1st, 1833, the MORNING POST, and a snow-storm of almost unexampled fury, came upon the town together. The snow was a wet blanket upon the hopes of newsboys and carriers, and quite deadened the noise of the new paper, filling up areas, and burying the tiny sheet at the doors of its few subscribers. For several days the streets were obstructed with snow. It was very cold. There were few people in the streets, and those few were not easily tempted to stop and fumble in their pockets for two cents. The newsboys were soon discouraged, and were fain to run shivering home. Dr. Sheppard was wholly unacquainted with the details of editorship, and most of the labor of getting up the numbers fell upon Mr. Greeley, and they were produced under every conceivable disadvantage. Yet, with all these misfortunes and drawbacks, several hundred copies were daily sold, and Dr. Sheppard was able to pay all the expenses of the first week. On the second Saturday, however, he paid his printers half in money and half in promises. On the third day of the third week, the faith and the patience of Messrs. Greeley and Story gave out, and the 'Morning Post' ceased to exist.

The last two days of its short life it was sold for a cent, and the readiness with which it was purchased convinced Dr. Sheppard, but him alone, that if it had been started at that price, it would not have been a failure. His money and his credit were both gone, and the error could not be retrieved. He could not even pay his printers the residue of their account, and he had, in consequence, to endure some emphatic observations from Mr. Story on the madness and presumption of his scheme. "Did n't I tell you so?" said the other printers. "Everybody," says Dr. Sheppard, "abused me, except Horace Greeley. He spoke very kindly, and told me not to mind what Story said." The doctor, thenceforth, washed his hands of printers' ink, and entered upon the practice of his profession.

Nine months after, the SUN appeared, a penny paper, a dingy sheet a little larger than a sheet of letter paper. Its success demonstrated the correctness of Dr. Sheppard's calculations, and justified the enthusiasm with which he had pursued his Idea. The office from which the Sun was issued was one of the last which Dr. Sheppard had visited for the purpose of enlisting co-operation. Neither of the proprietors was present, but the ardent schemer expounded his plans to a journeyman, and thus planted the seed which, in September, produced fruit in the form of the Sun, which 'shines for all.'

This morning, the cheap daily press of this city has issued a hundred and fifty thousand sheets, the best of which contain a history of the world for one day, so completely given, so intelligently com mented upon, as to place the New York Press at the head of the journalism of the world. The Cheap Press, be it observed, had, first of all, to create *itself*, and, secondly, to create its *Public.* The papers of the old school have gone on their way prospering. They are read by the class that read them formerly. But—mark that long line of hackmen, each seated on his box waiting for a customer, and *each reading his morning paper !* Observe the paper that is thrust into the pocket of the omnibus driver. Look into shops and factories at the dinner hour, and note how many of the men are reading their newspaper as they eat their dinner. All *this* is new. All this has resulted from the Chatham-street cogitations of Horatio Davis Sheppard.

A distinguished authoress of this city relates the following circumstance, which occurred last summer :

THE MAN WHO DOES TAKE THE PAPER.

To the Editor of The N. Y. Tribune.

Sir :—Not long since I read in your paper an article headed "the man who never took a newspaper." In contrast to this I would relate to you a little incident which came under my own observation :

Having been disappointed the other morning in receiving that part of my breakfast contained in The N. Y. Daily Tribune, I dispatched a messenger to see what could be done in the way of satisfaction. After half an hour's diligent search he returned, much to my chagrin, empty-handed. Recollecting an old copy set me at school after this wise : "If you want a thing done do it yourself," I seized my bonnet and sallied forth. Not far from my domicil appears each morning, with the rising sun, an old huckster-man, whose stock in trade consists of two empty barrels, across which is thrown a *pro tem* counter in the shape of a plank, a pint of pea-nuts, six sticks of peppermint candy, half a dozen choleric looking pears and apples, copies of the daily papers, and an old stubby broom, with which the owner carefully brushes up the nut-shells dropped by graceless urchins to the endangerment of his sidewalk lease.

"Have you this morning's Tribune?" said I, looking as amiable as I knew how.

"No *Ma'am*," was the decided reply.

"Why—yes, you have," said I, laying my hand on the desired number.

"Well, you *can't* have *that*, Ma'am," said the disconcerted peanut merchant, "for I have n't read it myself!"

"I'll give you *three* cents for it," said I.

7

(A shake of the head.)

"Four cents ?"

(Another shake.)

"Sixpence ?" (I was getting excited.)

"It 's no use, Ma'am," said the persistent old fellow. "It 's the only number I could get, and I tell you that nobody shall have *that* TRIBUNE till I have read it myself !"

You should have seen, Mr. Editor, the shapeless hat, the mosaic coat, the tattered vest, and the *extraordinary* pair of trousers that were educated up to that TRIBUNE—it was a picture ! FANNY FERN.

CHAPTER XI.

THE FIRM CONTINUES

Lottery printing — The Constitutionalist—Dudley S. Gregory—The lottery suicide— The firm prospers—Sudden death of Mr. Story—A new partner—Mr. Greeley as a master—A dinner story—Sylvester Graham—Horace Greeley at the Graham House—The New Yorker projected—James Gordon Bennett.

THE firm of Greeley and Story was not seriously injured by the failure of the Morning Post. They stopped printing it in time, and their loss was not more than fifty or sixty dollars. Meanwhile, their main stay was Sylvester's Bank Note Reporter, which yielded about fifteen dollars' worth of composition a week, payment for which was sure and regular. In a few weeks Mr. Story was fortunate enough to procure a considerable quantity of lottery printing. This was profitable work, and the firm, thenceforth, paid particular attention to that branch of business, and our hero acquired great dexterity in setting up and arranging the list of prizes and drawings.

Among other things, they had, for some time, the printing of a small tri-weekly paper called the *Constitutionalist*, which was the organ of the great lottery dealers, and the vehicle of lottery news, a small, dingy quarto of four pages, of which one page only was devoted to reading matter, the rest being occupied by lottery tables and advertisements. The heading of this interesting peri odical was as follows: "THE CONSTITUTIONALIST, Wilmington, Delaware. Devoted to the Interests of Literature, Internal Improvement, Common Schools, &c., &c." The last half square of the last column of the Constitutionalist's last page contained a standing advertisement, which read thus:—

"Greeley and Story, No. 54 Liberty-street, New York, respectfully solicit the patronage of the public to their business of Letter-Press Printing, particularly Lottery Printing, such as schemes, periodicals, &c., which will be executed on favorable terms."

Horace Greeley, who had by this time become an inveterate paragraphist, and was scribbler-general to the circle in which he moved, did not disdain to contribute to the first page of the Constitutionalist. The only set of the paper which has been preserved I have examined; and though many short articles are pointed out by its proprietor, as written by Mr. Greeley, I find none of the slightest present interest, and none which throw any light upon his feelings, thoughts or habits, at the time when they were written. He wrote well enough, however, to impress his friends with a high idea of his talent; and his prompt fidelity in all his transactions, at this period, secured him one friend, who, in addition to a host of other good qualities, chanced to be the possessor, or wielder, of extensive means. This friend, at various subsequent crises of our hero's life, proved to be a friend indeed, because a friend in need. They sat together, long after, the printer and the patron, in the representative's hall at Washington, as members of the thirtieth Congress. Why shall I not adorn this page by writing on it the name of the kindly, the munificent Dudley S. Gregory, to whose wise generosity, Jersey City, and Jersey citizens, owe so much; in whose hands large possessions are far more a public than a private good?

Mr. Gregory was, in 1833, the agent or manager of a great lottery association, and he had much to do with arranging the tables and schemes published in the Constitutionalist. This brought him in contact with the senior member of the firm of Greeley and Story, to whose talents his attention was soon called by a particular circumstance. A young man, who had lost all his property by the lottery, in a moment of desperation committed suicide. A great hue and cry arose all over the country against lotteries; and many

newspapers clamored for their suppression by law. The lottery
dealers were alarmed. In the midst of this excitement, Horace
Greeley, while standing at the case, composed an article on the
subject, the purport of which is said to have been, that the argument for and against lotteries was not affected by the suicide of that
young man; but it simply proved, that he, the suicide, was a person of weak character, and had nothing to do with the question
whether the State ought, or ought not, to license lotteries. This
article was inserted in one of the lottery papers, attracted considera-
able attention, and made Mr. Gregory aware that his printer was
not an ordinary man. Soon after, Mr. Greeley changed his opi-
ion on the subject of lotteries, and advocated their suppression
by law.

Greeley and Story were now prosperous printers. Their business
steadily increased, and they began to accumulate capital. The term
of their copartnership, however, was short. The great dissolver of
partnerships, King Death himself, dissolved theirs in the seventh
month of its existence. On the 9th of July, Francis Story went
down the bay on an excursion, and never returned alive. He was
drowned by the upsetting of a boat, and his body was brought back
to the city the same evening. There had existed between these
young partners a warm friendship. Mr. Story's admiration of the
character and talents of our hero amounted to enthusiasm; and
he, on his part, could not but love the man who so loved him. When
he went up to the coffin to look for the last time on the marble
features that had never turned to his with an unkind expression, he
said, "Poor Story! shall I ever meet with any one who will bear
with me as he did?" To the bereaved family Horace Greeley behaved with the most scrupulous justice, sending Mr. Story's mother
half of all the little outstanding accounts as soon as they were paid,
and receiving into the vacant place a brother-in-law of his deceased
partner, Mr. Jonas Winchester, a gentleman now well known to the
press and the people of this country.

A short time before, he had witnessed the marriage of Mr. Winchester by the Episcopal form. He was deeply impressed with the
ceremony, listening to it in an attitude expressive of the profoundest
interest; and when it was over, he exclaimed aloud, "That's the

most beautiful service I ever saw. If ever I am married it shall be by that form."

The business of "Greeley and Co." went on prospering through the year; but increase of means made not the slightest difference in our hero's habits or appearance. His indifference to dress was a chronic complaint, and the ladies of his partner's family tried in vain to coax and laugh him into a conformity with the usages of society. They hardly succeeded in inducing him to keep his shirt buttoned over his white bosom. "He was always a clean man, you know," says one of them. There was not even the show or pretence of discipline in the office. One of the journeymen made an outrageous caricature of his employer, and showed it to him one day as he came from dinner. "Who's that?" asked the man. "That's me," said the master, with a smile, and passed in to his work. The men made a point of appearing to differ in opinion from him on every subject, because they liked to hear him talk; and, one day, after a long debate, he exclaimed, "Why, men, if I were to say that that black man there was black, you'd all swear he was white." He worked with all his former intensity and absorption. Often, such conversations as these took place in the office about the middle of the day:

(H. G., looking up from his work)—Jonas, have I been to dinner?

(Mr. Winchester)—You ought to know best. I don't know

(H. G.)—John, have I been to dinner?

(John)—I believe not. Has he, Tom?

To which Tom would reply 'no,' or 'yes,' according to his own recollection or John's wink; and if the office generally concurred in Tom's decision, Horace would either go to dinner or resume his work, in unsuspecting accordance therewith.

It was about this time that he embraced the first of his two "isms" (he has never had but two). Graham arose and lectured, and made a noise in the world, and obtained followers. The substance of his message was that We, the people of the United States, are in the habit of taking our food in too concentrated a form. Bulk is necessary as well as nutriment; brown bread *is* better than white; and meat should be eaten only once a day, or never, said the Rev. Dr. Graham. Stimulants, he added, were pernicious, and their apparent necessity arises solely from too concentrated, and therefore indigestible food.   A simple message, and one most obviously true.   The wonder is, not that he should have obtained followers, but that there should have been found one human being so besottedly ignorant and so incapable of being instructed as to deny the truth of his leading principles.   Graham was a remarkable man. He was one of those whom nature has gifted with the power of taking an interest in human welfare.   He was a *discoverer* of the facts, that most of us are sick, and that none of us need be; that disease is impious and *disgraceful*, the result, in almost every instance, of folly or crime.   He exonerated God from the aspersions cast upon His wisdom and goodness by those who attribute disease to *His* "mysterious dispensations," and laid all the blame and shame of the ills that *flesh* endures at the door of those who endure them. Graham was one of the two or three men to whom this nation might, with some propriety, erect a monument.   Some day, perhaps, a man will take the trouble to read Graham's two tough and wordy volumes, and present the substance of them to the public in a form which will not repel, but win the reader to perusal and conviction.

Horace Greeley, like every other thinking person that heard Dr. Graham lecture, was convinced that upon the whole he was right. He abandoned the use of stimulants, and took care in selecting his food, to see that there was the proper proportion between its bulk and its nutriment; *i. e.* he ate Graham bread, little meat, and plenty of rice, Indian meal, vegetables and fruit.   He went, after a time, to board at the Graham house, a hotel conducted, as its name imported, on Graham principles, the rules and regulations having been written by Dr. Graham himself.   The first time our friend appeared at the table of the Graham House, a silly woman who lived there tried her small wit upon him.

"It's lucky," said she to the landlady, "that you've no cat in the house."

"Why?" asked the landlady.

"Because," was the killing reply, "if you had, the cat would certainly take that man with the white head for a gosling, and fly at him."

Gentlemen who boarded with him at the Graham House, remember him as a Portentious Anomaly, one who, on ordinary occasions, said nothing, but was occasionally roused to most vehement argument; a man much given to reading and cold-water baths.

In the beginning of the year 1834, the dream of editorship revived in the soul of Horace Greeley. A project for starting a weekly paper began to be agitated in the office. The firm, which then consisted of three members, H. Greeley, Jonas Winchester, and E. Sibbett, considered itself worth three thousand dollars, and was further of opinion, that it contained within itself an amount of editorial talent sufficient to originate and conduct a family paper superior to any then existing. The firm was correct in both opinions, and the result was—the New Yorker.

An incident connected with the job office of Greeley & Co. is, perhaps, worth mentioning here. One James Gordon Bennett, a person then well known as a smart writer for the press, came to Horace Greeley, and exhibiting a fifty-dollar bill and some other notes of smaller denomination as his cash capital, invited him to join in setting up a new daily paper, the New York Herald. Our hero declined the offer, but recommended James Gordon to apply to another printer, naming one, who he thought would like to share in such an enterprise. To him the editor of the Herald did apply, and with success. The Herald appeared soon after, under the joint proprietorship of Bennett and the printer alluded to. Upon the subsequent burning of the Herald office, the partners separated, and the Herald was thenceforth conducted by Bennett alone.

CHAPTER XII.

EDITOR OF THE NEW YORKER.

Character of the Paper—Its Early Fortunes—Happiness of the Editor—Scene in the Office—Specimens of Horace Greeley's Poetry—Subjects of his Essays—His Opinions then—His Marriage—The Silk-stocking Story—A day in Washington—His Impressions of the Senate—Pecuniary difficulties—Causes of the New-Yorker's ill-success as a Business—The missing letters—The Editor gets a nickname—The Agonies of a Debtor—Park Benjamin—Henry J. Raymond.

LUCKILY for the purposes of the present writer, Mr. Greeley is the most autobiographical of editors. He takes his readers into his

confidence, his sanctum, and his iron safe.   He has not the least objection to tell the public the number of his subscribers, the amount
of his receipts, the excess of his receipts over his expenditures, or
the excess of his expenditures over his receipts.   Accordingly, the
whole history of the New Yorker, and the story of its editor's joys
and sorrows, his trials and his triumphs, lie plainly and fully written in the New Yorker itself.

The New Yorker was, incomparably, the best newspaper of its
kind that had ever been published in this country.   It was printed,
at first, upon a large folio sheet; afterwards, in two forms, folio and
quarto, the former at two dollars a year, the latter at three.   Its
contents were of four kinds; literary matter, selected from home
and foreign periodicals, and well selected; editorial articles by the
editor, vigorously and courteously expressed; news, chiefly political, compiled with an accuracy new to American journalism; city,
literary, and miscellaneous paragraphs.   The paper took no side in
politics, though the ardent convictions of the editor were occasionally manifest, in spite of himself.   The heat and fury of some of
his later writings never characterize the essays of the New Yorker.
He was always gentle, however strong and decided; and there was
a modesty and candor in his manner of writing that made the subscriber a friend.   For example, in the very first number, announcing the publication of certain mathematical books, he says, " As we
are not ourselves conversant with the higher branches of mathemat-
ics, we cannot pretend to speak authoritatively upon the merits of
these publications"—a kind of avowal which omniscient editors are
not prone to make.

A paper, that lived long, never stole into existence more quietly
than the New Yorker.   Fifteen of the personal friends of the editors had promised to become subscribers; and when, on the 22d of
March, 1834, the first number appeared, it sold to the extent of one
hundred copies.   No wonder.   Neither of the proprietors had any
reputation with the public; all of them were very young, and the
editor evidently supposed that it was only necessary to make a good
paper in order to sell a great many copies.   The 'Publishers' Ad
dress,' indeed, expressly said :—

" There is one disadvantage attending our *debut* which is seldom encoun

tered in the outset of periodicals aspiring to general popularity and patronage. Ours is not blazoned through the land as, 'The Cheapest Periodical in
the World,' 'The Largest Paper ever Published,' or any of the captivating
clap-traps wherewith enterprising gentlemen, possessed of a convenient stock
of assurance, are wont to usher in their successive experiments on the gulli-
bility of the Public. No likenesses of eminent and favorite authors will em-
bellish our title, while they disdain to write for our columns. No 'distinguished literary and fashionable characters' have been dragged in to bolster
up a rigmarole of preposterous and charlatan pretensions. And indeed so
serious is this deficiency, that the first (we may say the only) objection which
has been started by our most judicious friends in the discussion of our plans
and prospects, has invariably been this:—'You do not indulge sufficiently in
high-sounding pretensions. You cannot succeed without *humbug*.' Our answer has constantly been:—'*We shall try*,' and in the spirit of this determination, we respectfully solicit of our fellow-citizens the extension of that
share of patronage which they shall deem warranted by our performances
rather than our promises."

The public took the New Yorker at its word. The second number had a sale of nearly two hundred copies, and for three months,
the increase averaged a hundred copies a week. In September, the
circulation was 2,500; and the second volume began with 4,500.
During the first year, three hundred papers gave the New Yorker
a eulogistic notice. The editor became, at once, a person known
and valued throughout the Union. He enjoyed his position thoroughly, and he labored not more truly with all his might, than with
all his heart.

The spirit in which he performed his duties, and the glee with
which he entered into the comicalities of editorial life, cannot be
more agreeably shown than by transcribing his own account of a
Scene which was enacted in the office of the New Yorker, soon
after its establishment. The article was entitled 'Editorial Luxuries.'

We love not the ways of that numerous class of malcontents who are perpetually finding fault with their vocation, and endeavoring to prove themselves the most miserable dogs in existence. If they really think so, why
under the sun do they not abandon their present evil ways and endeavor to
hit upon something more endurable? Nor do we not deem these grumblers
more plentiful among the brethren of the quill than in other professions, sim
ply because the groanings uttered through the press are more widely circu

lated than when merely breathed to the night-air of some unsympathising friend who forgets all about them the next minute; but we do think the whole business is in most ridiculously bad taste. An Apostle teaches us of "groanings which cannot be uttered"—it would be a great relief to readers, if editorial groanings were of this sort. Now, *we* pride ourselves rather on the delights of our profession; and we rejoice to say, that we find them neither few nor inconsiderable. There is one which even now flitted across our path, which, to tell the truth, was rather above the average—in fact, so good, that we can not afford to monopolize it, even though we shall be constrained to allow our reader a peep behind the curtain. So, here it is:

[SCENE. Editorial Sanctum—Editor *solus—i. e.* immersed in thought and newspapers, with a journal in one hand and busily spoiling white paper with the other—only two particular friends talking to him at each elbow. Devil calls for 'copy' at momentary intervals. Enter a butternut-colored gentleman, who bows most emphatically.]

Gent. Are you the editor of the New Yorker, sir?

Editor. The same, sir, at your service.

Gent. Did you write this, sir?

Editor. Takes his scissored extract and reads—'So, when we hear the brazen vender of quack remedies boldly trumpeting his miraculous cures, or the announcement of the equally impudent experimenter on public credulity (*Goward*) who announces, that he 'teaches music in six lessons, and half a dozen distinct branches of science in as many weeks,' we may be grieved, and even indignant, that such palpable deceptions of the simple and unwary should not be discountenanced and exposed.'

That reads like me, sir. I do not remember the passage; but if you found it in the editorial columns of the New Yorker, I certainly *did* write it.

Gent. It was in No. 15. "The March of Humbug."

Editor. Ah! *now* I recollect it—there is no mistake in my writing that article.

Gent. Did you allude to *me*, sir, in those remarks?

Editor. You will perceive that the name '*Goward*' has been introduced by yourself—there is nothing of the kind in my paper.

Gent. Yes, sir; but I wish to know whether you intended those remarks to apply to me.

Editor. Well, sir, without pretending to recollect exactly what I may have been thinking of while writing an article three months ago, I will frankly say, that I think I must have had you in my eye while penning that paragraph.

Gent. Well, sir, do you know that such remarks are grossly unjust and impertinent to me?

Editor. I know nothing of you, sir, but from the testimony of friends and your own advertisements in the papers—and these combine to assure me that you are a quack.

Gent. That is what my enemies say, sir; but if you examine my certificates, sir, you will know the contrary.

Editor. I am open to conviction, sir.

Gent. Well, sir, I have been advertising in the Traveler for some time, and have paid them a great deal of money, and here they come out this week and abuse me—so, I have done with them; and, now, if you will say you will not attack me in this fashion, I will patronize you (holding out some tempting advertisements).

Editor. Well, sir, I shall be very happy to advertise for you; but I can give no pledge as to the course I shall feel bound to pursue.

Gent. Then, I suppose you will continue to call me a quack.

Editor. I do not know that I am accustomed to attack my friends and patrons; but if I have occasion to speak of you at all, it shall be in such terms as my best judgment shall dictate.

Gent. Then, I am to understand you as my enemy.

Editor. Understand me as you please, sir; I shall endeavor to treat you and all men with fairness.

Gent. But do you suppose I am going to pay money to those who ridicule me and hold me up as a quack?

Editor. You will pay it where you please, sir—I must enjoy my opinions.

Gent. Well, but is a man to be judged by what his enemies say of him? Every man has his enemies.

Editor. I hope not, sir; I trust I have not an enemy in the world.

Gent. Yes, you have—*I'm your enemy!*—and the enemy of every one who misrepresents me. I can get no justice from the press, except among the penny dailies. I'll start a paper myself before a year. I'll show that some folks can edit newspapers as well as others.

Editor. The field is open, sir,—go ahead.

[Exit in a rage, *Rev.* J. R. Goward, A. M., Teacher (in six lessons) of everything.]

Another proof of the happiness of the early days of our hero's editorial career might be found in the habit he then had of writing verses. It will, perhaps, surprise some of his present readers, who know him only as one of the most practical of writers, one given to politics, sub-soil plows, and other subjects supposed to be unpoetical, to learn that he was in early life a very frequent, and by no means altogether unsuccessful poetizer. Many of the early numbers of the New-Yorker contain a poem by "H. G." He has published, in all, about thirty-five poems, of which the New-Yorker contains twenty; the rest may be found in the Southern Literary Messenger, and various other magazines, annuals, and occasional volumes. I have seen no poem of his which does not contain the *material* of poetry—thought, feeling, fancy; but in few of them was the poet enabled to give his thought, feeling and fancy complete expression. A specimen or two of his poetry it would be an unpardonable omission not to give, in a volume like this, particularly as his poetic period is past.

The following is a tribute to the memory of one who was the ideal hero of his youthful politics. It was published in the first number of the New-Yorker:

ON THE DEATH OF WILLIAM WIRT.

Rouse not the muffled drum,
Wake not the martial trumpet's mournful sound
  For him whose mighty voice in death is dumb;
Who, in the zenith of his high renown,
  To the grave went down.

Invoke no cannon's breath
To swell the requiem o'er his ashes poured—
  Silently bear him to the house of death:—
The aching hearts by whom he was adored,
  He won not with the sword.

No! let affection's tear
Be the sole tribute to his memory paid;
  Earth has no monument so justly dear
To souls like his in purity arrayed—
  Never to fade.

I loved thee, patriot Chief!
I battled proudly 'neath thy banner pure;
  Mine is the breast of woe—the heart of grief,
Which suffer on unmindful of a cure—
  Proud to endure.

But vain the voice of wail
For thee, from this dim vale of sorrow fled—

Earth has no spell whose magic shall not fail
To light the gloom that shrouds thy narrow bed,
  Or woo thee from the dead.

  Then take thy long repose
Beneath the shelter of the deep green sod:
  Death but a brighter halo o'er thee throws—
Thy fame, thy soul alike have spurned the clod—
  Rest thee in God.

A series of poems, entitled "Historic Pencilings," appear in the first volume of the New Yorker, over the initials "H. G." These were the poetized reminiscences of his boyish historical reading. Of these poems the following is, perhaps, the most pleasing and characteristic:

NERO'S TOMB.

"When Nero perished by the justest doom,
*   *   *   *   *
Some hand unseen strewed flowers upon his grave.

BYRON.

The tyrant slept in death;
His long career of blood had ceased forever,
  And but an empire's execrating breath
Remained to tell of crimes exampled never.
  Alone remained? Ah! no;
Rome's scathed and blackened walls retold the story
  Of conflagrations broad and baleful glow.
Such was the halo of the despot's glory!

  And round his gilded tomb
Came crowds of sufferers—but not to weep—
  Not theirs the wish to light the house of gloom
With sympathy. No! Curses wild and deep
  His only requiem made.
But soft! see, strewed around his dreamless bed
  The trophies bright of many a verdant glade,
The living's tribute to the honored dead.

What mean those gentle flowers ?
So sweetly smiling in the face of wrath—
  Children of genial suns and fostering showers.
Now crushed and trampled in the million's path—
  What do they, withering here ?
Ah ! spurn them not ? they tell of sorrow's flow—
  There has been *one* to shed affection's tear,
And 'mid a nation's joy, to feel a pang of woe !

No ! scorn them not, those flowers,
They speak too deeply to each feeling heart—
  They tell that Guilt hath still its holier hours—
That none may e 'er from earth unmourned depart ;
  That none hath *all* effaced
The spell of Eden o 'er his spirit cast,
  The heavenly image in his features traced—
Or quenched the love unchanging to the last !

Another of the 'Historic Pencilings,' was on the 'Death of Pericles.' This was its last stanza :—

No ! let the brutal conqueror
  Still glut his soul with war,
And let the ignoble million
  With shouts surround his car ;
But dearer far the lasting fame
  Which twines its wreaths with peace—
Give *me* the tearless memory
  Of the mighty one of Greece.

Only one of his poems seems to have been inspired by the tender passion. It is dated May 31st, 1834. Who this bright Vision was to whom the poem was addressed, or whether it was ever visible to any but the poet's eye, has not transpired.

FANTASIES.

They deem me cold, the thoughtless and light-hearted,
  In that I worship not at beauty's shrine ;

They deem me cold, that through the years departed,
 I ne'er have bowed me to some form divine.
They deem me proud, that, where the world hath flattered,
 I ne'er have knelt to languish or adore ;
They think not that the homage idly scattered
 Leaves the heart bankrupt, ere its spring is o'er.

No ! in my soul there glows but one bright vision,
 And o'er my heart there rules but one fond spell,
Bright'ning my hours of sleep with dreams Elysian
 Of one unseen, yet loved, aye cherished well ;
Unseen ? Ah ! no ; her presence round me lingers,
 Chasing each wayward thought that tempts to rove ;
Weaving Affection's web with fairy fingers,
 And waking thoughts of purity and love.

Star of my heaven ! thy beams shall guide me ever,
 Though clouds obscure, and thorns bestrew my path ;
As sweeps my bark adown life's arrowy river
 Thy angel smile shall soothe misfortune's wrath ;
And ah ! should Fate ere speed her deadliest arrow,
 Should vice allure to plunge in her dark sea,
Be this the only shield my soul shall borrow—
 One glance to Heaven—one burning thought of thee !

1 ne'er on earth may gaze on those bright features,
 Nor drink the light of that soul-beaming eye ;
But wander on 'mid earth's unthinking creatures,
 Unloved in life, and unlamented die ;
But ne'er shall fade the spell thou weavest o'er me,
 Nor fail the star that lights my lonely way ;
Still shall the night's fond dreams that light restore me,
 Though Fate forbid its gentler beams by day.

I have not dreamed that gold or gems adorn thee—
 That Flatt'ry's voice may vaunt thy matchless form ;
I little reck that worldlings all may scorn thee,
 Be but thy soul still pure, thy feelings warm ;

Be thine bright Intellect's unfading treasures,
   And Poesy's more deeply-hallowed spell,
And Faith the zest which heightens all thy pleasures,
   With trusting love—Maid of my soul! farewell!

One more poem claims place here, if from its autobiographical character alone. Those who believe there *is* such a thing as regeneration, who know that a man *can* act and live in a disinterested spirit, will not read this poem with entire incredulity. It appeared in the Southern Literary Messenger for August, 1840.

THE FADED STARS.

I mind the time when Heaven's high dome
   Woke in my soul a wondrous thrill—
When every leaf in Nature's tome
   Bespoke creation's marvels still;
When mountain cliff and sweeping glade,
   As morn unclosed her rosy bars,
Woke joys intense—but naught e'er bade
   My heart leap up, like you, bright stars!

Calm ministrants to God's high glory!
   Pure gems around His burning throne!
Mute watchers o'er man's strange, sad story
   Of Crime and Woe through ages gone!
'Twas yours the mild and hallowing spell
   That lured me from ignoble gleams—
Taught me where sweeter fountains swell
   Than ever bless the worldling's dreams.

How changed was life! a waste no more,
   Beset by Want, and Pain, and Wrong;
Earth seemed a glad and fairy shore,
   Vocal with Hope's inspiring song.
But ye, bright sentinels of Heaven!
   Far glories of Night's radiant sky!
Who, as ye gemmed the brow of Even,
   Has ever deemed Man born to die?

   *   *   *   *

'Tis faded now, that wondrous grace
 That once on Heaven's forehead shone;
I read no more in Nature's face
 A soul responsive to my own.
A dimness on my eye and spirit,
 Stern time has cast in hurrying by;
Few joys my hardier years inherit,
 And leaden dullness rules the sky.

Yet mourn not I—a stern, high duty
 Now nerves my arm and fires my brain;
Perish the dream of shapes of beauty,
 So that *this* strife be not in vain;
To war on Fraud entrenched with Power—
 On smooth Pretense and specious Wrong—
This task be mine, though Fortune lower;
 For this be banished sky and song.

The subjects upon which the editor of the New Yorker used to descant, as editor, contrast curiously with those upon which, as poet, he aspired to sing. Turning over the well-printed pages of that journal, we find calm and rather elaborate essays upon 'The Interests of Labor,' 'Our Relations with France,' 'Speculation,' 'The Science of Agriculture,' 'Usury Laws,' 'The Currency,' 'Overtrading,' 'Divorce of Bank and State,' 'National Conventions,' 'International Copyright,' 'Relief of the Poor,' 'The Public Lands,' 'Capital Punishment,' 'The Slavery Question,' and scores of others equally unromantic. There are, also, election returns given with great minuteness, and numberless paragraphs recording nominations. The New Yorker gradually became *the* authority in the department of political statistics. There were many people who did not consider an election 'safe,' or 'lost,' until they saw the figures in the New Yorker. And the New Yorker deserved this distinction; for there never lived an editor more scrupulous upon the point of literal and absolute correctness than Horace Greeley. To quote the language of a proof-reader—"If there *is* a thing that will make Horace furious, it is to have a name spelt wrong, or a mistake in election returns." In fact, he was morbid on the subject, till time toughened him; time, and proof-readers.

The opinions which he expressed in the columns of the New Yorker are, in general, those to which he still adheres, though on a few subjects he used *language* which he would not now use. His opinions on those subjects have rather advanced than changed. For example : he is now opposed to the punishment of death in all cases, except when, owing to peculiar circumstances, the immediate safety of the community demands it. In June, 1836, he wrote :—
" And now, having fully expressed our conviction that the punishment of death is one which should sometimes be inflicted, we may add, that we would have it resorted to as unfrequently as possible. Nothing, in our view, but cold-blooded, premeditated, unpalliated murder, can fully justify it. Let this continue to be visited with the sternest penalty."

Another example. The following is part of an article on the Slavery Question, which appeared in July, 1834. It differs from his present writings on the same subject, not at all in doctrine, though very much in tone. Then, he thought the North the aggressor. Since then, we have had Mexican Wars, Nebraska bills, etc., and he now writes as one assailed.

"To a philosophical observer, the existence of domestic servitude in one portion of the Union while it is forbidden and condemned in another, would indeed seem to afford no plausible pretext for variance or alienation. The Union was formed with a perfect knowledge, on the one hand, that slavery existed at the south, and, on the other, that it was utterly disapproved and discountenanced at the north. But the framers of the constitution saw no reason for distrust and dissension in this circumstance. Wisely avoiding all discussion of a subject so delicate and exciting, they proceeded to the formation of 'a more perfect union,' which, leaving each section in the possession of its undoubted right of regulating its own internal government and enjoying its own speculative opinions, provided only for the common benefit and mutual well-being of the whole. And why should not this arrangement be satisfactory and perfect? Why should not even the existing evils of one section be left to the correction of its own wisdom and virtue, when pointed out by the unerring finger of experience?

    *   *   *   *   *   *   *   *   *

We entertain no doubt that the system of slavery is at the bottom of most of the evils which afflict the communities of the south—that it has occasioned the decline of Virginia, of Maryland, of Carolina. We see it even retarding the growth of the new State of Missouri, and causing her to fall far behind her sister Indiana in improvement and population. And we venture to assert, that if the objections to slavery, drawn from a correct and enlightened political economy, were once fairly placed before the southern public, they would need no other inducements to impel them to enter upon an immediate and effective course of legislation, with a view to the ultimate extinction of the evil. But, right or wrong, no people have a greater disinclination to the lectures or even the advice of their neighbors; and we venture to predict, that whoever shall bring about a change of opinion in that quarter, must, in this case, reverse the proverb which declares, that 'a prophet hath honor except in his own country.' "

* * * * * * *

After extolling the Colonization Society, and condemning the formation of anti-slavery societies at the North, as irritating and useless, the editor proceeds:—"We hazard the assertion, that there never existed two distinct races—so diverse as to be incapable of amalgamation—inhabiting the same district of country, and in open and friendly contact with each other, that maintained a perfect equality of political and social condition. * * * It remains to be proved, that the history of the nineteenth century will afford a direct contradiction to all former experience. * *. * We cannot close without reiterating the expression of our firm conviction, that if the African race are ever to be raised to a degree of comparative happiness, intelligence, and freedom, it must be in some other region than that which has been the theater of their servitude and degradation. They must 'come up *out* of the land of Egypt and out of the house of bondage;' even though they should be forced to cross the sea in their pilgrimage and wander forty years in the wilderness."

Again. In 1835, he had not arrived at the Maine Law, but was feeling his way towards it. He wrote thus:

" Were we called upon to indicate simply the course which *should* be pursued for the eradication of this crying evil, our compliance would be a far easier matter. We should say, unhesitatingly, that the vending of alcohol, or of liquors of which alcohol forms a leading component, should be regulated by the laws which govern the sale of other insidious, yet deadly, poisons. It should be kept for sale only by druggists, and dealt out in small portions, and with like regard to the character and ostensible purpose of the applicant as in the case of its counterpart. * * * * But we must not forget, that we are to determine simply what *may* be done by the friends of temperance for the advancement of the noble cause in which they are engaged, rather than what the more ardent of them (with whom we are proud to rank ourselves) would desire to see accomplished. We are to look at things as they *are;* and, in that view, all attempts to interdict the sale of intoxicating liquors in our hotels, our country stores, and our steam-boats, in the present state of public opinion, must be hopelessly, ridiculously futile. * * * * The only available provision bearing on this branch of the traffic, which could be urged with the least prospect of success, is the imposition of a *real* license-tax—say from $100 to $1000 per annum—which would have the effect of diminishing the evil by rendering less frequent and less universal the temptations which lead to it. But even that, we apprehend, would meet with strenuous opposition from so large and influential a portion of the community, as to render its adoption and efficiency extremely doubtful."

The most bold and stirring of his articles in the New Yorker, was one on the "Tyranny of Opinion," which was suggested by the extraordinary enthusiasm with which the Fourth of July was celebrated in 1837. A part of this article is the only specimen of the young editor's performance, which, as a specimen, can find place in this chapter. The sentiments which it avows, the country has not yet caught up with; nor will it, for many a year after the hand that wrote them is dust. After an allusion to the celebration, the article proceeds:

"The great pervading evil of our social condition is the worship and the bigotry of Opinion. While the theory of our political institutions asserts or implies the absolute freedom of the human mind—the right not only of free thought and discussion, but of the most unrestrained action thereon within the wide boundaries prescribed by the laws of the land, yet the *practical commentary* upon this noble text is as discordant as imagination can conceive. Beneath the thin veil of a democracy more free than that of Athens in her glory, we cloak a despotism more pernicious and revolting than that of Turkey or China. It is the despotism of Opinion. Whoever ventures to propound opinions strikingly at variance with those of the majority, must be content to brave obloquy, contempt and persecution. If political, they exclude him from public employment and trust; if religious, from social intercourse and general regard, if not from absolute rights. However moderately heretical in his political views, he cannot be a justice of the peace, an officer of the customs, or a lamp-lighter; while, if he be positively and frankly skeptical in his theology, grave judges pronounce him incompetent to give testimony in courts of justice, though his character for veracity be indubitable. That is but a narrow view of the subject which ascribes all this injustice to the errors of parties or individuals; it flows naturally from the vice of the age and country—the tyranny of Opinion. It can never be wholly rectified until the whole community shall be brought to feel and acknowledge, that the only security for public liberty is to be found in the absolute and unqualified freedom of thought and expression, confining penal consequences to *acts* only which are detrimental to the welfare of society.

"The philosophical observer from abroad may well be astounded by the gross inconsistencies which are presented by the professions and the conduct of our people. Thousands will flock together to drink in the musical periods of some popular disclaimer on the inalienable rights of man, the inviolability of the immunities granted us by the Constitution and Laws, and the invariable reverence of freemen for the majesty of law. They go away delighted with our institutions, the orator and themselves. The next day they may be engaged in 'lynching' some unlucky individual who has fallen under their sovereign displeasure, breaking up a public meeting of an obnoxious cast, or tarring and feathering some unfortunate lecturer or propagandist, whose views do not square with their own, but who has precisely the same right to enjoy and propagate his opinions, however erroneous, as though he inculcated nothing but what every one knows and acknowledges already. The shamelessness of this incongruity is sickening; but it is not confined to this glaring exhibition. The sheriff, town-clerk, or constable, who finds the political majority in his district changed, either by immigration or the course of events, must be content to change too, or be hurled from his station. Yet what necessary connection is there between his politics and his office? Why might it not as properly be insisted that a town-officer should be six feet high, or have red hair, if the majority were so distinguished, as that he should think with them respecting the men in high places and the measures projected or opposed by them? And how does the proscription of a man in any way for obnoxious opinions differ from the most glaring tyranny?"

In the New Yorker of July 16th, 1836, may be seen, at the head of a long list of recent marriages, the following interesting announcement:

"In Immanuel church, Warrenton, North Carolina, on Tuesday morning, 5th inst., by Rev. William Norwood, Mr. Horace Greeley, editor of the New Yorker, to Miss Mary Y. Cheney, of Warrenton, formerly of this city."

The lady was by profession a teacher, and to use the emphatic language of one of her friends, 'crazy for knowledge.' The acquaintance had been formed at the Graham House, and was continued by correspondence after Miss Cheney, in the pursuit of her vocation, had removed to North Carolina. Thither the lover hied; the two became one, and returned together to New York. They were married, as he said he would be, by the Episcopal form. Sumptuous was the attire of the bridegroom; a suit of fine black broadcloth, and "on this occasion only," a pair of silk stockings! It appears that silk stockings and matrimony were, in his mind, associated ideas, as rings and matrimony, orange blossoms and matrimony, are in the minds of people in general. Accordingly, he bought a pair of silk stockings; but trying on his wedding suit previous to his departure for the south, he found, to his dismay, that the stockings were completely hidden by the affluent terminations of another garment. The question now at once occurred to his logical mind, 'What is the use of *having* silk stockings, if nobody can *see* that you have them?' He laid the case, it is said, before his tailor, who, knowing his customer, immediately removed the difficulty by cutting away a crescent of cloth from the front of the aforesaid terminations, which rendered the silk stockings obvious to the most casual observer. Such is the *story*. And I regret that other stories, and true ones, highly honorable to his head and heart, delicacy forbids the telling of in this place.

The editor, of course, turned his wedding tour to account in the way of his profession. On his journey southward, Horace Greeley first saw Washington, and was impressed favorably by the houses of Congress, then in session. He wrote admiringly of the Senate:—"That the Senate of the United States is unsurpassed in intellectual greatness by any body of fifty men ever convened, is a trite observation. A phrenologist would fancy a strong confirmation of his doctrines in the very appearance of the Senate; a physiognomist would find it. The most striking person on the floor is Mr. Clay, who is incessantly in motion, and whose spare, erect form betrays an easy dignity approaching to majesty, and a perfect gracefulness, such as I have never seen equaled. His countenance is intelligent and indicative of character; but a glance at his figure while his face was completely averted, would give assurance that he was no common man. Mr. Calhoun is one of the plainest men and certainly the dryest, hardest speaker I ever listened to. The flow of his ideas reminded me of a barrel filled

with pebbles, each of which must find great difficulty in escaping
from the very solidity and number of those pressing upon it and
impeding its natural motion. Mr. Calhoun, though far from being
a handsome, is still a very remarkable personage; but Mr. Benton
has the least intellectual countenance I ever saw on a senator. Mr.
Webster was not in his place." * * * * "The best
speech was that of Mr. Crittenden, of Kentucky. That man is not
appreciated so highly as he should and must be. He has a
rough readiness, a sterling good sense, a republican manner and
feeling, and a vein of biting, though homely satire, which will
yet raise him to distinction in the National Councils."

Were Greeley and Co.' making their fortune meanwhile? Far
from it. To edit a paper well is one thing; to make it pay as a
business is another. The New Yorker had soon become a famous,
an admired, and an influential paper. Subscriptions poured in; the
establishment looked prosperous; but it was not. The sorry tale
of its career as a business is very fully and forcibly told in the various addresses to, and chats with, Our Patrons, which appear in the
volumes of 1837, that 'year of ruin,' and of the years of slow recovery from ruin which followed. In October, 1837, the editor
thus stated his melancholy case:

" Ours is a plain story; and it shall be plainly told. The New Yorker was
established with very moderate expectations of pecuniary advantage, but
with strong hopes that its location at the head-quarters of intelligence for the
continent, and its cheapness, would insure it, if well conducted, such a patronage as would be ultimately adequate, at least, to the bare expenses of its publication. Starting with scarce a shadow of patronage, it had four thousand
five hundred subscribers at the close of the first year, obtained at an outlay of
three thousand dollars beyond the income in that period. This did not materially disappoint the publishers' expectations. Another year passed, and their
subscription increased to seven thousand, with a further outlay, beyond all receipts, of two thousand dollars. A third year was commenced with two editions—folio and quarto—of our journal; and at its close, their conjoint subscriptions amounted to near nine thousand five hundred; yet our receipts had
again fallen two thousand dollars behind our absolutely necessary expenditures. Such was our situation at the commencement of this year of ruin;
and we found ourselves wholly unable to continue our former reliance on the
honor and ultimate good faith of our backward subscribers. Two thousand five
hundred of them were stricken from our list, and every possible retrenchment of

our expenditures effected.   With the exercise of the most parsimonious frugal
ity, and aided by the extreme kindness and generous confidence of our friends,
we have barely and with great difficulty kept our bark afloat.   For the future, we
have no resource but in the justice and generosity of our patrons.   Our humble
portion of this world's goods has long since been swallowed up in the all-devour-
ing vortex; both of the Editor's original associates in the undertaking have
abandoned it with loss, and those who now fill their places have invested to the
full amount of their ability.   Not a farthing has been drawn from the concern
by any one save for services rendered; and the allowance to the proprietors
having charge respectively of the editorial and publishing departments has
been far less than their services would have commanded elsewhere.   The last six
months have been more disastrous than any which preceded them, as we have
continued to fall behind our expenses without a corresponding increase of patronage.   A large amount is indeed due us; but we find its collection almost
impossible, except in inconsiderable portions and at a ruinous expense.   All
appeals to the honesty and good faith of the delinquents seem utterly fruitless.   As a last resource, therefore, and one beside which we have no alterna-
tive, we hereby announce, that from and after this date, the price of the New
Yorker will be three dollars per annum for the folio, and four dollars for the
quarto edition.

"Friends of the New Yorker! Patrons! we appeal to you, not for charity,
but for justice.   Whoever among you is in our debt, no matter how small the
sum, is guilty of a moral wrong in withholding the payment.   We bitterly
need it—we have a right to expect it.   Six years of happiness could not atone
for the horrors which blighted hopes, agonizing embarrassments, and gloomy
apprehensions—all arising in great measure from your neglect—have con-
spired to heap upon us during the last six months.   We have borne all in silence: we now tell you we *must* have our pay.   Our obligations for the next
two months are alarmingly heavy, and they must be satisfied, at whatever sacrifice.   We shall cheerfully give up whatever may remain to us of property,
and mortgage years of future exertion, sooner than incur a shadow of dishonor,
by subjecting those who have credited us to loss or inconvenience.   We must
pay; and for the means of doing it we appeal most earnestly to you.   It is
possible that we might still further abuse the kind solicitude of our friends;
but the thought is agony.   We should be driven to what is but a more delicate
mode of beggary, when justice from those who withhold the hard earnings of
our unceasing toil would place us above the revolting necessity!   At any rate,
we will not submit to the humiliation without an effort.

"We have struggled until we can no longer doubt that, with the present
currency—and there seems little hope of an immediate improvement—we cannot live at our former prices.   The suppression of small notes was a blow to
cheap city papers, from which there is no hope of recovery.   With a currency
including notes of two and three dollars, one half our receipts would come to

us directly from the subscribers; without such notes, we must submit to an agent's charge on nearly every collection. Besides, the notes from the South Western States are now at from twenty to thirty per cent. discount; and have been more: those from the West range from six to twenty. All notes beyond the Delaware River range from twice to ten times the discount charged upon them when we started the New Yorker. We cannot afford to depend exclusively upon the patronage to be obtained in our immediate neighborhood; we cannot retain distant patronage without receiving the money in which alone our subscribers can pay. But one course, then, is left us—to tax our valuable patronage with the delinquencies of the worse than worthless—the paying for the non-paying, and those who send us par-money, with the evils of our present depraved and depreciated currency."

Two years after, there appeared another chapter of pecuniary history, written in a more hopeful strain. A short extract will complete the reader's knowledge of the subject:

"Since the close of the year of ruin (1837), we have pursued the even tenor of our way with such fortune as was vouchsafed us; and, if never elated with any signal evidence of popular favor, we have not since been doomed to gaze fixedly for months into the yawning abyss of Ruin, and feel a moral certainty that, however averted for a time, that must be our goal at last. On the contrary, our affairs have slowly but steadily improved for some time past, and we now hope that a few months more will place us beyond the reach of pecuniary embarrassments, and enable us to add new attractions to our journal.

"And this word 'attraction' brings us to the confession that the success of our enterprise, if success there has been, has not been at all of a pecuniary cast thus far. Probably we lack the essential elements of that very desirable kind of success. There have been errors, mismanagement and losses in the conduct of our business. We mean that we lack, or do not take kindly to, the arts which contribute to a newspaper sensation. When our journal first appeared, a hundred copies marked the extent to which the public curiosity claimed its perusal. Others establish new papers, (the New World and Brother Jonathan Mr. Greeley might have instanced,) even without literary reputation, as we were, and five or ten thousand copies are taken at once—just to see what the new thing is. And thence they career onward on the crest of a towering wave.

"Since the New Yorker was first issued, seven copartners in its publication have successively withdrawn from the concern, generally, we regret to say, without having improved their fortunes by the connection, and most of them with the conviction that the work, however valuable, was not calculated to prove lucrative to its proprietors. 'You don't humbug enough,' has been the complaint of more than one of our retiring associates: 'you ought to make more noise, and vaunt your own merits. The world will never believe you print a good paper unless you tell them so.' Our course has not been changed by these representations. We have endeavored in all things to maintain our self-respect and deserve the good opinion of others ; if we have not succeeded in the latter particular, the failure is much to be regretted, but hardly to be amended by pursuing the vaporous course indicated. If our journal be a good one, those who read it will be very apt to discover the fact ; if it be not, our assertion of its excellence, however positive and frequent, would scarcely outweigh the weekly evidence still more abundantly and convincingly furnished. We are aware that this view of the case is controverted by practical results in some cases ; but we are content with the old course, and have never envied the success which Merit or Pretense may attain by acting as its own trumpeter."

The New Yorker never, during the seven years of its existence, became profitable ; and its editor, during the greater part of the time, derived even his means of subsistence either from the business of job printing or from other sources, which will be alluded to in a moment. The causes of the New Yorker's signal failure as a business seem to have been these :

1. It was a very *good* paper, suited only to the more intelligent class of the community, which, in all times and countries, is a small class. "We have a pride," said the editor once, and truly, "in believing that we might, at any time, render our journal more attractive to the million by rendering it less deserving ; and that by merely considering what would be sought after and read with avidity, without regard to its moral or its merit, we might easily become popular at the mere expense of our own self-approval."

2. It seldom praised, never puffed, itself. The editor, however, seems to have thought, that he might have done both with propriety. Or was he speaking in pure irony, when he gave the Mirror this 'first-rate notice.' "There is one excellent quality," said he, "which has always been a characteristic of the *Mirror*—the virtue of self-appreciation. We call it a virtue, and it is not merely one in itself, but the parent of many others. As regards our vocation, it is alike necessary and just. The world should be made to understand, that the aggregate of talent, acquirement, tact, industry, and general intelligence which is required to sustain creditably the character of a public journal, might, if judiciously parceled out, form the stamina of, at least, one professor of languages, two brazen lec-

turers on science, ethics, or phrenology, and three average congress
ional or other demagogues.   Why, then, should starvation wave
his skeleton scepter *in terrorem* over such a congregation of available excellences?"

3. The leading spirit of the New Yorker had a singular, a constitutional, an incurable inability to conduct business.   His character
is the exact opposite of that 'hard man' in the gospel, who reaped
where he had not sown.   He was too amiable, too confiding, too
absent, and too 'easy,' for a business man.   If a boy stole his letters from the post-office, he would admonish him, and either let him
go or try him again.   If a writer in extremity offered to do certain
paragraphs for three dollars a week, he would say, "No, that's too
little; I'll give you five, till you can get something better."   On
one occasion, he went to the post-office himself, and receiving a
large number of letters, put them, it is said, into the pockets of
his overcoat.   On reaching the office, he hung the overcoat on its
accustomed peg, and was soon lost in the composition of an article.
It was the last of the chilly days of spring, and he thought no more
either of his overcoat or its pockets, till the autumn.   Letters kept
coming in complaining of the non-receipt of papers which had been
ordered and paid for; and the office was sorely perplexed.   On the
first cool day in October, when the editor was shaking a summer's
dirt from his overcoat, the missing letters were found, and the mystery was explained.   Another story gives us a peep into the office
of the New Yorker.   A gentleman called, one day, and asked to
see the editor.   "I am the editor," said a little coxcomb who was
temporarily in charge of the paper.   "You are not the person I
want to see," said the gentleman.   "Oh!" said the puppy, "you
wish to see the *Printer*.   He's not in town."   The men in the composing-room chanced to overhear this colloquy, and thereafter, our
hero was called by the nickname of 'The Printer,' and by that
alone, whether he was present or absent.   It was "Printer, how
will you have this set?" or "Printer, we're waiting for copy."   All
this was very pleasant and amiable; but, businesses which *pay* are
never carried on in that style.   It is a pity, but a fact, that businesses which pay, are generally conducted in a manner which is
exceedingly disagreeable to those who assist in them.

4. The Year of Ruin.

5. The 'cash principle,' the only safe one, had not been yet applied to the newspaper business. The New Yorker lost, on an average, 1,200 dollars a year by the removal of subscribers to parts unknown, who left without paying for their paper, or notifying the office of their departure.

Of the unnumbered pangs that mortals know, pecuniary anxiety is to a sensitive and honest *young* heart the bitterest. To live upon the edge of a gulf that yawns hideously and always at our feet, to feel the ground giving way under the house that holds our happiness, to walk in the pathway of avalanches, to dwell under a volcano rumbling prophetically of a coming eruption, is not pleasant. But welcome yawning abyss, welcome earthquake, avalanche, volcano! They can crush, and burn, and swallow a man, but not degrade him. The terrors they inspire are not to be compared with the deadly and withering FEAR that crouches sullenly in the soul of that honest man who owes much money to many people, and cannot think how or when he can pay it. That alone has power to take from life *all* its charm, and from duty all its interest. For other sorrows there is a balm. *That* is an evil unmingled, while it lasts; and the light which it throws upon the history of mankind and the secret of man's struggle with fate, is purchased at a price fully commensurate with the value of that light.

The editor of the New Yorker suffered all that a man could suffer from this dread cause. In private letters he alludes, but only alludes, to his anguish at this period. "Through most of the time," he wrote years afterward, "I was very poor, and for four years really bankrupt; though always paying my notes and keeping my word, but living as poorly as possible." And again: "My embarrassments were sometimes dreadful; not that I feared destitution, but the fear of involving my friends in my misfortunes was very bitter." He came one afternoon into the house of a friend, and handing her a copy of his paper, said: "There, Mrs. S., that is the last number of the New Yorker you will ever see. I can secure my friends against loss if I stop now, and I'll not risk their money by holding on any longer." He went over that evening to Mr. Gregory, to make known to him his determination; but that constant and invincible friend would not listen to it. He insisted on his continuing the struggle, and offered his assistance with such frank and earnest cordiality, that our hero's scruples were at length removed, and he came home elate, and resolved to battle another year with delinquent subscribers and a depreciated currency.

During the early years of the New Yorker, Mr. Greeley had little regular assistance in editing the paper. In 1839, Mr. Park Benjamin contributed much to the interest of its columns by his lively and humorous critiques; but his connection with the paper was not of long duration. It was long enough, however, to make him acquainted with the character of his associate. On retiring, in October, 1839, he wrote: " Grateful to my feelings has been my intercourse with the readers of the New Yorker and with its principal editor and proprietor. By the former I hope my humble efforts will not be unremembered; by the latter I am happy to believe that the sincere friendship which I entertain for him is reciprocated. I still insist upon my editorial right so far as to say in opposition to any veto which my coadjutor may interpose, that I cannot leave the association which has been so agreeable to me without paying to sterling worth, unbending integrity, high moral principle and ready kindness, their just due. These qualities exist in the character of the man with whom now I part; and by all, to whom such qualities appear admirable, must such a character be esteemed. His talents, his industry, require no commendation from me; the readers of this journal know them too well; the public is sufficiently aware of the manner in which they have been exerted. What I have said has flowed from my heart, tributary rather to its own emotions than to the subject which has called them forth; his plain good name is his best eulogy."

A few months later, Mr. Henry J. Raymond, a recent graduate of Burlington College, Vermont, came to the city to seek his fortune. He had written some creditable sketches for the New Yorker, over the signature of "Fantome," and on reaching the city called upon Horace Greeley. The result was that he entered the office as an assistant editor "till he could get something better," and it may encourage some young, hard-working, unrecognized, ill-paid journalist, to know that the editor of the New York Daily Times began his editorial career upon a salary of eight dollars a week. The said unrecognized, however, should further be informed, that Mr. Raymond is the hardest and swiftest worker connected with the New York Press.

CHAPTER XIII.

THE JEFFERSONIAN.

Objects of the Jeffersonian—Its character—A novel Glorious-Victory paragraph—The
Graves and Cilley duel—The Editor overworked.

THE slender income derived from the New Yorker obliged its
editor to engage in other labors. He wrote, as occasion offered, for
various periodicals. The Daily Whig he supplied with its leading
article for several months, and in 1838 undertook the entire editorial charge of the Jeffersonian, a weekly paper of the 'campaign'
description, started at Albany on the third of March, and continuing in existence for one year.

With the conception and the establishment of the Jeffersonian,
Horace Greeley had nothing to do. It was published under the
auspices and by the direction of the Whig Central Committee of
the State of New York, and the fund for its establishment was contributed by the leading politicians of the State in sums of ten dollars. "I never sought the post of its editor," wrote Mr. Greeley in
1848, "but was sought for it by leading whigs whom I had never
before personally known." It was afforded at fifty cents a year,
attained rapidly a circulation of fifteen thousand; the editor, who
spent three days of each week in Albany, receiving for his year's
services a thousand dollars. The ostensible object of the paper was
—to quote the language of its projectors—"to furnish to every
person within the State of New York a complete summary of political intelligence, at a rate which shall place it absolutely within the
reach of every man who will read it." But, according to the subsequent explanation of the Tribune, "it was established on the impulse of the whig tornado of 1837, to secure a like result in 1838,
so as to give the Whig party a Governor, Lieutenant Governor,
Senate, Assembly, U. S. Senator, Congressmen, and all the vast executive patronage of the State, then amounting to millions of dollars a year."

The Jeffersonian was a good paper. It was published in a neat . to form of eight pages. Its editorials, generally few and brief, were written to convince, not to inflame, to enlighten, not to blind. It published a great many of the best speeches of the day, some for, some against, its own principles. Each number contained a full and well-compiled digest of political intelligence, and one page, or more, of general intelligence. It was not, in the slightest degree, like what is generally understood by a 'campaign paper.' Capital letters and po'nts of admiration were as little used as in the sedate and courteous columns of the New Yorker; and there is scarcely anything to be found of the 'Glorious-Victory' sort except this:

"Glorious Victory! 'We have met the enemy, and they are ours!' Our whole ticket, with the exception of town clerk, one constable, three fence-viewers, a pound-master and two hog-reeves elected! There never was such a ·iumph!"

Stop, my friend. Have you elected the best men to the several offices to be filled? Have you chosen men who have hitherto evinced not only capacity but integrity?—men whom you would trust implicity in every relation and business of life? Above all, have you selected the very best person in the township for the important office of Justice of the Peace? If yea, we rejoice with you. If the men whose election will best subserve the cause of virtue and public order have been chosen, even your opponents will have little reason for regret. If it be otherwise, *you* have achieved but an empty and dubious triumph.

It would be gratifying to know what the Whig Central Committee thought of such unexampled 'campaign' language. In a word, the Jeffersonian was a better fifty cents' worth of thought and fact than had previously, or has since, been afforded, in the form of a weekly paper.

The columns of the Jeffersonian afford little material for the purposes of this volume. There are scarcely any of those characteristic touches, those autobiographical allusions, that contribute so much to the interest of other papers with which our hero has been connected. This is one, however:

(Whosoever may have picked up the wallet of the editor of this paper—lost somewhere near State street, about the 20th ult., shall receive half the contents, all round, by returning the balance to this office.)

I will indulge the reader with one article entire from the Jeffersonian ; 1, because it is interesting ; 2, because it will serve to show the spirit and the manner of the editor in recording and commenting upon the topics of the day. He has since written more emphatic, but not more effective articles, on similar subjects :

THE TRAGEDY AT WASHINGTON.

THE whole country is shocked, and its moral sensibilities outraged, by the horrible tragedy lately perpetrated at Washington, of which a member of Congress was the victim. It was, indeed, an awful, yet we will hope not a profitless catastrophe ; and we blush for human nature when we observe the most systematic efforts used to pervert to purposes of party advantage and personal malignity, a result which should be sacred to the interests of humanity and morality—to the stern inculcation and enforcement of a reverence for the laws of the land and the mandates of God.

Nearly a month since, a charge of corruption, or an offer to sell official influence and exertion for a pecuniary consideration, against some unnamed member of Congress, was transmitted to the New York Courier and Enquirer by its correspondent, ‘ the Spy in Washington.’ Its appearance in that journal called forth a resolution from Mr. Wise, that the charge be investigated by the House. On this an irregular and excited debate arose, which consumed a day or two, and which was signalized by severe attacks on the Public Press of this country, and on the letter-writers from Washington. In particular, the Courier and Enquirer, in which this charge appeared, its chief Editor, and its correspondent the Spy, were stigmatized ; and Mr. Cilley, a member from Maine, was among those who gave currency to the charges. Col. Webb, the Editor, on the appearance of these charges, instantly proceeded to Washington, and there addressed a note to Mr. Cilley on the subject. That note, it appears, was courteous and dignified in its language, merely inquiring of Mr. C. if his remarks, published in the Globe, were intended to convey any personal disrespect to the writer, and containing no menace of any kind. It was handed to Mr. Cilley by Mr. Graves, a member from Kentucky, but declined by Mr. C., on the ground, as was understood, that he did not choose to be drawn into controversy with Editors of public journals in regard to his remarks in the House. This was correct and honorable ground. The Constitution expressly provides that members of Congress shall not be responsible elsewhere for words spoken in debate, and the provision is a most noble and necessary one.

But Mr. Graves considered the reply as placing him in an equivocal position. If a note transmitted through his hands had been declined, as was liable to be understood, because the writer was not worthy the treatment of a gentleman, the dishonor was reflected on himself as the bearer of a disgraceful message. Mr. Graves, therefore, wrote a note to Mr. C., asking him if he were correct in his understanding that the letter in question was declined because Mr. C. could not consent to hold himself accountable to public journalists for words spoken in debate, and not on grounds of personal objection to Col. Webb as a gentleman. To this note Mr. Cilley replied, on the advisement of his friends, that he declined the note of Col. Webb, because he "chose to be drawn into no controversy with *him*," and added that he "neither affirmed nor denied anything in regard to his character." This was considered by Mr. Graves as involving him fully in the dilemma which he was seeking to avoid, and amounting to an impeachment of his veracity, and he now addressed another note to inquire, "*whether you declined to receive his* (Col. Webb's) *communication on the ground of any personal objection to him as a gentleman of honor?*" To this query Mr. Cilley declined to give an answer, denying the right of Mr. G. to propose it. The next letter in course was a challenge from Mr. Graves by the hand of Mr. Wise, promptly responded to by Mr. Cilley through Gen. Jones of Wisconsin.

The weapons selected by Mr. Cilley were rifles; the distance eighty yards. (It was said that Mr. Cilley was practicing with the selected weapon the morning of accepting the challenge, and that he lodged eleven balls in succession in a space of four inches square.) Mr. Graves experienced some difficulty in procuring a rifle, and asked time, which was granted; and Gen. Jones, Mr. Cilley's second, tendered him the use of his own rifle; but, meantime, Mr. Graves had procured one.

The challenge was delivered at 12 o'clock on Friday; the hour selected by Mr. Cilley was 12 of the following day. His unexpected choice of rifles, however, and Mr. Graves' inability to procure one, delayed the meeting till 2 o'clock.

The first fire was ineffectual. Mr. Wise, as second of the challenging party, now called all parties together, to effect a reconciliation. Mr. C. declining to negotiate while under challenge, it was suspended to give room for explanation. Mr. Wise remarked—"Mr. Jones, these gentlemen have come here without animosity towards each other; they are fighting merely upon a point of honor; cannot Mr. Cilley assign some reason for not receiving at Mr. Graves' hands Colonel Webb's communication, or make some disclaimer which will relieve Mr. Graves from his position?" The reply was—"I am authorized by my friend, Mr. Cilley, to say that in declining to receive the note from Mr. Graves, purporting to be from Colonel Webb, he meant no disrespect to Mr. Graves, because he entertained for him then, as he now does, the highest respect and the most kind feelings; but that he declined to receive the note because he chose not to be drawn into any controversy with Colonel Webb.' This is Mr. Jones' version; Mr. Wise thinks he said, "My friend refuses to disclaim disrespect to Colonel Webb, because he does not choose to be drawn into an expression of opinion as to him." After consultation, Mr Wise re-

turned to Mr. Jones and said, " Mr. Jones, this answer leaves Mr. Graves pre
cisely in the position in which he stood when the challenge was sent."

Another exchange of shots was now had to no purpose, and another attempt
at reconciliation was likewise unsuccessful. The seconds appear to have been
mutually and anxiously desirous that the affair should here terminate, but no
arrangement could be effected. Mr. Graves insisted that his antagonist should
place his refusal to receive the message of which he was the bearer on some
grounds which did not imply such an opinion of the writer as must reflect disgrace on the bearer. He endeavored to have the refusal placed on the ground
that Mr. C. "did not hold himself accountable to Colonel Webb for words
spoken in debate." This was declined by Mr. Cilley, and the duel proceeded.

The official statement, drawn up by the two seconds, would seem to import
that but three shots were exchanged; but other accounts state positively that
Mr. Cilley fell at the fourth fire. He was shot through the body, and died in
two minutes. On seeing that he had fallen, badly wounded, Mr. Graves expressed a wish to see him, and was answered by Mr. Jones—" My friend is
dead, sir !"

Colonel Webb first heard of the difficulty which had arisen on Friday evening, but was given to understand that the meeting would not take place for
several days. On the following morning, however, he had reason to suspect
the truth. He immediately armed himself, and with two friends proceeded to
Mr. Cilley's lodgings, intending to force the latter to meet him before he did
Mr. Graves. He did not find him, however, and immediately proceeded to the
old dueling ground at Bladensburgh, and thence to several other places, to
interpose himself as the rightful antagonist of Mr. Cilley. Had he found the
parties, a more dreadful tragedy still would doubtless have ensued. But the
place of meeting had been changed, and the arrangements so secretly made,
that though Mr. Clay and many others were on the alert to prevent it, the
duel was not interrupted.

"We believe we have here stated every material fact in relation to this
melancholy business. It is suggested, however, that Mr. Cilley was less disposed to concede anything from the first in consideration of his own course
when a difficulty recently arose between two of his colleagues, Messrs. Jarvis
and Smith, which elicited a challenge from the former, promptly and nobly
declined by the latter. This refusal, it is said, was loudly and vehemently
stigmatized as cowardly by Mr. Cilley. This circumstance does not come to
us well authenticated, but it is spoken of as notorious at Washington.

"But enough of detail and circumstance. The reader who has not seen the
official statement will find its substance in the foregoing. He can lay the
blame where he chooses. We blame only the accursed spirit of False Honor
which required this bloody sacrifice—the horrid custom of Dueling which ex-
acts and palliates this atrocity. It appears evident that Mr. Cilley's course
must have been based on the determination that Col. Webb was not entitled

to be regarded as a gentleman; and if so, there was hardly an escape from a bloody conclusion after Mr. Graves had once consented, however unconsciously, to bear the note of Col. Webb. Each of the parties, doubtless, acted as he considered due to his own character; each was right in the view of the duelist's code of honor, but fearfully wrong in the eye of reason, of morality, of humanity, and the imperative laws of man and of God. Of the principals, one sleeps cold and stiff beneath the icy pall of winter and the clods of the valley; the other—far more to be pitied—lives to execrate through years of anguish and remorse the hour when he was impelled to imbrue his hands in the blood of a fellow-being.

Mr. Graves we know personally, and a milder and more amiable gentleman is rarely to be met with. He has for the last two years been a Representative from the Louisville District, Kentucky, and is universally esteemed and beloved. Mr. Cilley was a young man of one of the best families in New Hampshire; his grandfather was a Colonel and afterwards a General of the Revolution. His brother was a Captain in the last War with Great Britain, and leader of the desperate bayonet charge at Bridgewater. Mr. Cilley himself, though quite a young man, has been for two years Speaker of the House of Representatives of Maine, and was last year elected to Congress from the Lincoln District, which is decidedly opposed to him in politics, and which recently gave 1,200 majority for the other side. Young as he was, he had acquired a wide popularity and influence in his own State, and was laying the foundations of a brilliant career in the National Councils. And this man, with so many ties to bind him to life, with the sky of his future bright with hope, without an enemy on earth, and with a wife and three children of tender age whom his death must drive to the verge of madness—has perished miserably in a combat forbidden by God, growing out of a difference so pitiful in itself, so direful in its consequences.

Could we add anything to render the moral more terribly impressive?

The year of the Jeffersonian was a most laborious and harassing one. No one but a Greeley would or could have endured such continuous and distracting toils. He had two papers to provide for; papers diverse in character, papers published a hundred and fifty miles apart, papers to which expectant thousands looked for their weekly supply of mental pabulum. As soon as the agony of getting the New Yorker to press was over, and copy for the outside of the next number given out, away rushed the editor to the Albany boat; and after a night of battle with the bed-bugs of the cabin, or the politicians of the hurricane-deck, he hurried off to new duties at the office of the Jeffersonian. The Albany boat of 1838 was a very different style of conveyance from the Albany boat of the present year of our Lord.　It was, in fact, not much more than six times as elegant and comfortable as the steamers that, at this hour, ply in the seas and channels of Europe.　The sufferings of our hero may be imagined.

But, not his labors.　*They* can be understood only by those who know, by blessed experience, what it *is* to get up, or try to get up, a good, correct, timely, and entertaining weekly paper.　The subject of editorial labor, however, must be reserved for a future page.

CHAPTER XIV.

THE LOG-CABIN.

"TIPPECANOE AND TYLER TOO."

Wire-pulling—The delirium of 1840—The Log-Cabin—Unprecedented hit—A glance at its pages—Log-Cabin jokes—Log-Cabin songs—Horace Greeley and the cake-basket—Pecuniary difficulties continue—The Tribune announced.

WIRE-PULLING is a sneaking, bad, demoralizing business, and the people hate it.　The campaign of 1840, which resulted in the election of General Harrison to the presidency, was, at bottom, the revolt of the people of the United States against the wire-pulling principle, supposed to be incarnate in the person of Martin Van Buren.　Other elements entered into the delirium of those mad months.　The country was only recovering, and that slowly, from the disasters of 1836 and 1837, and the times were still 'hard.' But the fire and fury of the struggle arose from the fact, that General Harrison, a man who had done something, was pitted against Martin Van Buren, a man who had pulled wires.　The hero of Tippecanoe and the farmer of North Bend, against the wily diplomatist who partook of sustenance by the aid of gold spoons.　The Log-Cabin against the White House.

Great have been the triumphs of wire-pulling in this and other countries; and yet it is an unsafe thing to engage in.　As bluff King Hal melted away, with one fiery glance, all the greatness of

Wolsey; as the elephant, with a tap of his trunk, knocks the breath out of the little tyrant whom he had been long accustomed implicitly to obey,—so do the People, in some quite unexpected moment, blow away, with one breath, the elaborate and deep-laid schemes of the republican wire-puller; and *him!* They have done it, O wire-puller! and will do it again.

Who can have forgotten that campaign of 1840? The 'mass meetings,' the log-cabin raisings, the 'hard cider' drinking, the song singing, the Tippecanoe clubs, the caricatures, the epigrams, the jokes, the universal excitement! General Harrison was *sung* into the presidential chair. Van Buren was laughed out of it. Every town had its log-cabin, its club, and its chorus. Tippecanoe song-books were sold by the hundred thousand. There were Tippecanoe medals, Tippecanoe badges, Tippecanoe flags, Tippecanoe handkerchiefs, Tippecanoe almanacs, and Tippecanoe shaving-soap. All other interests were swallowed up in the one interest of the election. All noises were drowned in the cry of Tippecanoe and Tyler too.

The man who contributed most to keep alive and increase the popular enthusiasm, the man who did most to feed that enthusiasm with the substantial fuel of fact and argument, was, beyond all question, Horace Greeley.

On the second of May, the first number of the Log-Cabin appeared, by 'H. Greeley & Co.,' a weekly paper, to be published simultaneously at New York and Albany, at fifty cents for the campaign of six months. It was a small paper, about half the size of the present Tribune; but it was conducted with wonderful spirit, and made an unprecedented hit. Of the first number, an edition of twenty thousand was printed, which Mr. Greeley's friends thought a far greater number than would be sold; but the edition vanished from the counter in a day. Eight thousand more were struck off; they were sold in a morning. Four thousand more were printed, and still the demand seemed unabated. A further supply of six thousand was printed, and the types were then distributed. In a few days, however, the demand became so urgent, that the number was re-set, and an edition of ten thousand struck off. Altogether, forty-eight thousand of the first number were sold. Subscribers came pouring in at the rate of seven hundred a day. The list lengthened in a few weeks to sixty thousand names, and kept increasing till the weekly issue was between eighty and ninety thousand. ' H. Greeley and Co.' were really overwhelmed with their success. They had made no preparations for such an enormous increase of business, and they were troubled to hire clerks and folders fast enough to get their stupendous edition into the mails.

The Log Cabin is not dull reading, even now, after the lapse of fifteen years ; and though the men and the questions of that day are, most of them, dead. But *then*, it was devoured with an eagerness, which even those who remember it can hardly realize. Let us glance hastily over its pages.

The editor explained the ' objects and scope' of the little paper, thus :—

" The Log Cabin will be a zealous and unwavering advocate of the rights, interests and prosperity of our whole country, but especially those of the hardy subduers and cultivators of her soil. It will be the advocate of the cause of the Log Cabin against that of the Custom House and Presidential Palace. It will be an advocate of the interests of unassuming industry against the schemes and devices of functionaries ' drest in a little brief authority,' whose salaries are trebled in value whenever Labor is forced to beg for employment at three or four shillings a day. It will be the advocate of a sound, uniform, *adequate* Currency for our whole country, against the visionary projects and ruinous experiments of the official Dousterswivels of the day, who commenced by promising Prosperity, Abundance, and Plenty of Gold as the sure result of their policy; and lo! we have its issues in disorganization, bankruptcy, low wages and treasury rags. In fine, it will be the advocate of Freedom, Improvement, and of National Reform, by the election of Harrison and Tyler, the restoration of purity to the government, of efficiency to the public will, and of Better Times to the People. Such are the objects and scope of the Log Cabin."

The contents of the Log Cabin were of various kinds. The first page was devoted to Literature of an exclusively Tippecanoe character, such as " Sketch of Gen. Harrison," " Anecdote of Gen. Harrison," " General Harrison's Creed," " Slanders on Gen. Harrison refuted," " Meeting of the Old Soldiers," &c. The first number had *twenty-eight* articles and paragraphs of this description. The second page contained editorials and correspondence. The third was where the "Splendid Victories," and "Unprecedented Triumphs," were recorded. The fourth page contained a Tippecanoe song with music, and a few articles of a miscellaneous character. Dr. Channing's lecture upon the Elevation of the Laboring Classes ran through several of the early numbers. Most of the numbers contain an engraving or two, plans of General Harrison's battles, portraits of the candidates, or a caricature. One of the caricatures represented Van Buren caught in a trap, and over the picture was the following explanation:—"The New Era has prepared and pictured a Log Cabin Trap, representing a Log Cabin—set as a figure-4-trap, and baited with a barrel of hard cider. By the following it will be seen that the trap has been SPRUNG, and a sly nibbler from Kinderhook is looking out through the gratings. Old Hickory is intent on prying him out; but it is manifestly no go." The editorials of the Log Cabin were mostly of a serious and argumentative cast, upon the Tariff, the Currency, and the Hard Times. They were able and timely. The *spirit* of the campaign, however, is contained in the other departments of the paper, from which a few brief extracts may amuse the reader for a moment, as well as illustrate the feeling of the time.

The Log Cabins that were built all over the country, were 'raised' and inaugurated with a great show of rejoicing. In one number of the paper, there are accounts of as many as six of these hilarious ceremonials, with their speechifyings and hard-cider drinkings. The humorous paragraph annexed appears in an early number, under the title of "Thrilling Log Cabin Incident :"—

"The whigs of Erie, Pa., raised a Log Cabin last week from which the banner of Harrison and Reform was displayed. While engaged in the dedication of their Cabin, the whigs received information which led them to apprehend a hostile demonstration from Harbor Creek, a portion of the borough whose citizens had ever been strong Jackson and Van Buren men. Soon afterwards a party of horsemen, about forty in number, dressed in Indian costume, armed with tomahawks and scalping knives, approached the Cabin! The whigs made prompt preparations to defend their banner. The scene became intensely exciting. The assailants rode up to the Cabin, dismounted, and surrendered themselves up as voluntary prisoners of war. On inquiry, they proved to be stanch Jackson men from Harbor Creek, who had taken that mode of arraying themselves under the HARRISON BANNER! The tomahawk was then buried ; after which *the string of the latch was pushed out*, and the Harbor-Creek ers were ushered into the Cabin, where they pledged their support to Harrison in a bumper of good old hard cider."

The great joker of that election, as of every other since, was Mr. Prentice, of the Louisville Journal, the wittiest of editors, living or dead. Many of his good things appear in the Log Cabin, but most of them allude to men and events that have been forgotten, and the point of the joke is lost. The following are three of the Log Cabin jokes ; they sparkled in 1840, flat as they may seem now :—

" The Globe says that ' there are but two parties in the country, the poor man's party and the rich man's party,' and that ' Mr. Van Buren is the friend of the former.' The President is certainly in favor of strengthening the poor man's party, *numerically!* He goes for impoverishing the whole country— except the office-holders."

" What do the locofocos expect by vilifying the Log Cabin ? Do they not know that a Log Cabin is all the better for being daubed with mud ?"

" A whig passing through the streets of Boston a few mornings ago, espied a custom-house officer gazing ruefully at a bulletin displaying the latest news of the Maine election. ' Ah! Mr. ———, taking your *bitters* this morning, I see.' The way the loco scratched gravel was a pattern for sub-treasurers."

One specimen paragraph from the department of political news will suffice to show the *frenzy* of those who wrote for it. A letter-writer at Utica, describing a ' mass meeting ' in that city, bursts upon his readers in this style:

" This has been the proudest, brightest day of my life ! Never—no, never, have I before seen the people in their majesty ! Never were the foundations of popular sentiment so broken up ! The scene from early dawn to sunset, has been one of continued, increasing, bewildering enthusiasm. The hearts of TWENTY-FIVE THOUSAND FREEMEN have been overflowing with gratitude, and gladness, and joy. It has been a day of jubilee—an ERA OF DELIVERANCE FOR CENTRAL NEW YORK ! The people in waves have poured in from the valleys and rushed down from the mountains. The city has been vocal with eloquence, with music, and with acclamations. Demonstrations of strength, and emblems of victory, and harbingers of prosperity are all around us, cheering and animating, and assuring a people who are finally and effectually aroused. I will not now *attempt* to describe the procession of the people. Suffice it to say that

thore was an ocean of them! The procession was over FIVE MILES LONG. *
* * Governor Seward and Lieut. Gov. Bradish were unanimously nominated by resolution for re-election. The result was communicated to the people
assembled in Mass in Chancery Square, whose response to the nomination was
spontaneous, loud, deep and resounding."

The profusion of the presidential mansion was one of the standing topics of those who wished to eject its occupant. In one number of the Log-Cabin is a speech, delivered in the House of Representatives by a member of the opposition, in which the bills of the
persons who supplied the White House are given at length. Take
these specimens :

34 table knives ground, ...	$1,37½
2 new knife blades, ...	75
2 cook's knife blades, ...	2,50
	4,62½
2 dozen brooms, ...	$3,75
1-2 do. hard scrubs, ...	2,37
1-2 do. brooms, ...	1,38
	6,50
2 tin buckets, ...	$2,00
Milk strainer and skimmer, ...	92½
Chamber bucket, ...	2,00
2 dozen tart pans, ...	2,50
	7,12½

This seems like putting an extremely fine point upon a political ar
gument. What the orator wished to show, however, was, that such
articles as the above ought to be paid for out of the presidential
salary, not the public treasury. The speech exhibited some columns
of these 'house-bills.' It made a great sensation, and was enough
to cure any decent man of a desire to become a servant of the
people.

But, as I have observed, Gen. Harrison was *sung* into the presidential chair. The Log Cabin preserves a large number of the political ditties of the time; the editor himself contributing two. A very
few stanzas will suffice to show the quality of the Tippecanoe poetry
The following is one from the 'Wolverine's Song' ·

We know that Van Buren can ride in his coach,
With servants, forbidding the Vulgar's approach—
We know that his fortune such things will allow,
And we know that our candidate follows the plough ;
But what if he does ?   Who was bolder to fight
In his country's defense on that perilous night,
When naught save his valor sufficed to subdue
Our foes at the battle of Tippecanoe ?
                    Hurrah for Tippecanoe !
He dropped the red Locos at Tippecanoe !

From the song of the 'Buckeye Cabin,' these are two stanzas :

Oh ! where, tell me where, was your Buckeye Cabin made ?
Oh ! where, tell me where, was your Buckeye Cabin made ?
'Twas made among the merry boys that wield the plough and spade
Where the Log Cabins stand in the bonnie Buckeye shade.

Oh ! what, tell me what, is to be your Cabin's fate ?
Oh ! what, tell me what, is to be your Cabin's fate ?
We 'll wheel it to the Capitol and place it there elate,
For a token and a sign of the bonnie Buckeye State.

The 'Turn Out Song' was very popular, and easy to sing :

From the White House, now Matty, turn out, turn out,
From the White House, now Matty, turn out !
        Since there you have been
        No peace we have seen,
So Matty, now please to turn out, turn out,
So Matty, now please to turn out !
*   *   *   *   *   *   *
    Make way for old Tip ! turn out, turn out !
    Make way for old Tip, turn out !
        'Tis the people's decree,
        Their choice he shall be,
So, Martin Van Buren, turn out, turn out,
So, Martin Van Buren, turn out !

But of all the songs ever sung, the most absurd and the most tell
ing, was that which began thus :

> What has caused this great commotion-motion-motion
> Our country through?
> It is the ball a-rolling on
> For Tippecanoe and Tyler too,
> For Tippecanoe and Tyler too;
> And with them we'll beat little Van;
> Van, Van, Van is a used-up man,
> And with them we'll beat little Van.

This song had two advantages. The tune—half chant, half jig—was adapted to bring out all the absurdities of the words, and, in particular, those of the last two lines. The second advantage was, that stanzas could be multiplied to any extent, on the spot, to suit the exigences of any occasion. For example:

> "The beautiful girls, God bless their souls, souls, souls,
> The country through,
> Will all, to a man, do all they can
> For Tippecanoe and Tyler too;
> And with them," etc., etc.

During that summer, ladies attended the mass meetings in thousands, and in their honor the lines just quoted were frequently sung.

These few extracts from the Log Cabin show the nature of the element in which our editor was called upon to work in the hot months of 1840. His own interest in the questions at issue was intense, and his labors were incessant and most arduous. He wrote articles, he made speeches, he sat on committees, he traveled, he gave advice, he suggested plans; while he had two newspapers on his hands, and a load of debt upon his shoulders. His was a willing servitude. From the days of his apprenticeship he had observed the course of 'Democratic' administrations with disgust and utter disapproval, and he had borne his full share of the consequences of their bad measures. His whole soul was in this contest. He fought fairly too. His answer to a correspondent, that 'articles assailing the personal character of Mr. Van Buren or any of his supporters cannot be published in the Cabin,' was in advance of the politics of 1840.

One scene, if it could be portrayed on the printed page as visibly as it exists in the memories of those who witnessed it, would show better than declaratory words, how *absorbed* Mr. Greeley was in politics during this famous 'campaign.' It is a funny story, and literally true.

Time,—Sunday evening. Scene,—the parlor of a friend's house. Company,—numerous and political, except the ladies, who are gracious and hospitable. Mr. Greeley is expected to tea, but does not come, and the meal is transacted without him. Tea over, he arrives, and plunges headlong into a conversation on the currency. The lady of the house thinks he 'had better take some tea,' but cannot get a hearing on the subject; is distressed, puts the question at length, and has her invitation hurriedly declined; brushed aside, in fact, with a wave of the hand.

"Take a cruller, any way," said she, handing him a cake-basket containing a dozen or so of those unspeakable, Dutch indigestibles.

The expounder of the currency, dimly conscious that a large object was approaching him, puts forth his hands, still vehemently talking, and takes, not a cruller, but the cake-basket, and deposits it in his lap. The company are inwardly convulsed, and some of the weaker members retire to the adjoining apartment, the expounder continuing his harangue, unconscious of their emotions or its cause. Minutes elapse. His hands, in their wandering through the air, come in contact with the topmost cake, which they take and break. He begins to eat; and eats and talks, talks and eats, till he has finished a cruller. Then he feels for another, and eats that, and goes on, slowly consuming the contents of the basket, till the last crum is gone. The company look on amazed, and the kind lady of the house fears for the consequences. She had heard that cheese is an antidote to indigestion. Taking the empty cake-basket from his lap, she silently puts a plate of cheese in its place, hoping that instinct will guide his hand aright. The experiment succeeds. Gradually, the blocks of white new cheese disappear. She removes the plate. No ill consequences follow. Those who saw this sight are fixed in the belief, that Mr. Greeley was not then, nor has since become, aware, that on that evening he partook of sustenance.

The reader, perhaps, has concluded that the prodigious sale of the Log Cabin did something to relieve our hero from his pecuniary embarrassments. Such was not the fact. He paid some debts, but he incurred others, and was not, for any week, free from anxiety. The price of the paper was low, and its unlooked-for sale involved the proprietors in expenses which might have been avoided, or much lessened, if they had been prepared for it. The mailing of single numbers cost a hundred dollars. The last number of the campaign series, the great "O K" number, the number that was all staring with majorities, and capital letters, and points of admiration, the number that announced the certain triumph of the Whigs, and carried joy into a thousand Log Cabins, contained a most moving "Appeal" to the "Friends who owe us." It was in small type, and in a corner remote from the victorious columns. It ran thus:—" We were induced in a few instances to depart from our general rule, and forward the first series of the Log Cabin on credit—having in almost every instance a promise, that the money should be sent us before the first of November. That time has passed, and we regret to say, that many of those promises have not been fulfilled. To those who owe us, therefore, we are compelled to say, Friends! *we need our money*—our paper-maker needs it! and has a right to ask us for it. The low price at which we have published it, forbids the idea of gain from this paper: we only ask the means of paying what we owe. Once for all, we *implore* you to do us justice, and enable us to do the same." This tells the whole story. Not a word need be added.

The Log Cabin was designed only for the campaign, and it was expected to expire with the twenty-seventh number. The zealous editor, however, desirous of presenting the complete returns of the victory, issued an extra number, and sent it gratuitously to all his subscribers. This number announced, also, that the Log Cabin would be resumed in a few weeks. On the fifth of December the new series began, as a family political paper, and continued, with moderate success, till both it and the New Yorker were merged in the Tribune.

For his services in the campaign—and no man contributed *as much* to its success as he—Horace Greeley accepted no office; nor did he even witness the inauguration. This is not strange. But it *is* somewhat surprising that the incoming administration had not the decency to *offer* him something. Mr. Fry (W. H.) made a speech one evening at a political meeting in Philadelphia. The next morning, a committee waited upon him to k now for what office he intended to become an applicant. " Office ?" said the astonished composer—" No office." " Why, then," said the committee, "*what the h—ll did you speak last night for ?*" Mr. Greeley had not even the honor of a visit from a committee of this kind.

The Log Cabin, however, gave him an immense reputation in all parts of the country, as an able writer and a zealous politician—a reputation which soon became more valuable to him than pecuniary capital. The Log Cabin of April 8d contained the intelligence of General Harrison's death ; and, among a few others, the following advertisement :

" NEW YORK TRIBUNE.

" On Saturday, the tenth day of April instant, the Subscriber will publish the first number of a New Morning Journal of Politics, Literature, and General Intelligence.

" The TRIBUNE, as its name imports, will labor to advance the interests of the People, and to promote their Moral, Social, and Political well-being. The immoral and degrading Police Reports, Advertisements and other matter which have been allowed to disgrace the columns of our leading Penny Papers, will be carefully excluded from this, and no exertion spared to render it worthy of the hearty approval of the virtuous and refined, and a welcome visitant at the family fireside.

" Earnestly believing that the political revolution which has called William Henry Harrison to the Chief Magistracy of the Nation was a triumph of Right Reason and Public Good over Error and Sinister Ambition, the Tribune will give to the New Administration a frank and cordial, but manly and inde pendent support, judging it always by its acts, and commending those only so far as they shall seem calculated to subserve the great end of all govern ment—the welfare of the People.

" The Tribune will be published every morning on a fair royal sheet—(size of the Log-Cabin and Evening Signal)—and transmitted to its city subscribers at the low price of *one cent* per copy. Mail subscribers, $4 per annum. It will contain the news by the morning's Southern Mail, which is contained in no other Penny Paper. Subscriptions are respectfully solicited by

HORACE GREELEY, 30 ANN ST.

CHAPTER XV.

STARTS THE TRIBUNE.

The Capital—The Daily Press of New York in 1841—The Tribune appears—The Omens unpropitious—The first week—Conspiracy to put down the Tribune—The Tribune triumphs—Thomas McElrath—The Tribune alive—Industry of the Editors—Their independence—Horace Greeley and John Tyler—The Tribune a Fixed Fact.

Who furnished the capital? Horace Greeley. But he was scarcely solvent on the day of the Tribune's appearance. True; and yet it is no less the fact that nearly all the large capital required for the enterprise was supplied by him.

A large capital is indispensable for the establishment of a good daily paper; but it need not be a capital of money. It may be a capital of reputation, credit, experience, talent, opportunity. Horace Greeley was trusted and admired by his party, and by many of the party to which he was opposed. In his own circle, he was known to be a man of incorruptible integrity—one who *would* pay his debts at any and at every sacrifice—one who was quite incapable of contracting an obligation which he was not *confident* of being able to discharge. In other words, his credit was good. He had talent and experience. Add to these a thousand dollars lent him by a friend, (James Coggeshall,) and the evident need there was of just such a paper as the Tribune proved to be, and we have the capital upon which the Tribune started. All told, it was equivalent to a round fifty thousand dollars.

In the present year, 1855, there are two hundred and three periodicals published in the city of New York, of which twelve are daily papers. In the year 1841, the number of periodicals was one hundred, and the number of daily papers twelve. The Courier and Enquirer, New York American, Express, and Commercial Advertiser were Whig papers, at ten dollars a year. The Evening Post and Journal of Commerce, at the same price, leaned to the 'Democratic' side of politics, the former avowedly, the latter not. The

Signal, Tatler, and Star were cheap papers, the first two neutral, the latter dubious. The Herald, at two cents, was—the Herald! The Sun, a penny paper of immense circulation, was affectedly neutral, really 'Democratic,' and very objectionable for the gross character of many of its advertisements. A cheap paper, of the Whig school of politics, did not exist. On the 10th of April, 1841, the Tribune appeared—a paper one-third the size of the present Tribune, price one cent; office No. 30 Ann-street; Horace Greeley, editor and proprietor, assisted in the department of literary criticism, the fine arts, and general intelligence, by H. J. Raymond. Under its heading, the new paper bore, as a motto, the dying words of Harrison: "I DESIRE YOU TO UNDERSTAND THE TRUE PRINCIPLES OF THE GOVERNMENT. I WISH THEM CARRIED OUT. I ASK NOTHING MORE."

The omens were not propitious. The appallingly sudden death of General Harrison, the President of so many hopes, the first of the Presidents who had died in office, had cast a gloom over the whole country, and a prophetic doubt over the prospects of the Whig party.

The editor watched the preparation of his first number all night, nervous and anxious, withdrawing this article and altering that, and never leaving the form till he saw it, complete and safe, upon the press. The morning dawned sullenly upon the town. "The sleety atmosphere," wrote Mr. Greeley, long after, "the leaden sky, the unseasonable wintriness, the general gloom of that stormy day, which witnessed the grand though mournful pageant whereby our city commemorated the blighting of a nation's hopes in the most untimely death of President Harrison, were not inaptly miniatured in his own prospects and fortunes. Having devoted the seven preceding years almost wholly to the establishment of a weekly compend of literature and intelligence, (The New Yorker,) wherefrom, though widely circulated and warmly praised, he had received no other return than the experience and wider acquaintance thence accruing, he entered upon his novel and most precarious enterprise, most slenderly provided with the external means of commanding subsistence and success in its prosecution. With no partner or business associate, with inconsiderable pecuniary resources, and only a promise from political friends of aid to the extent of two thousand dollars, of which but one half was ever realized, (and that long since repaid, but the sense of obligation to the far from wealthy friend who made the loan is none the less fresh and ardent,) he undertook the enterprise—at all times and under any circumstances hazardous—of adding one more to the already amply extensive list of daily newspapers issued in this emporium, where the current expenses of such papers, already appalling, were soon to be doubled by rivalry, by stimulated competition, by the progress of business, the complication of interests, and especially by the general diffusion of the electric telegraph, and where at least nineteen out of every twenty attempts to establish a new daily have proved disastrous failures. Manifestly, the prospects of success in this case were far from flattering."

The Tribune began with about six hundred subscribers, procured by the exertions of a few of the editor's personal and political friends. Five thousand copies of the first number were printed, and "we found some difficulty in giving them away," says Mr. Greeley in the article just quoted. The expenses of the first week were five hundred and twenty-five dollars; the receipts, ninety-two dollars. A sorry prospect for an editor whose whole cash capital was a thousand dollars, and that borrowed.

But the Tribune was a live paper. FIGHT was the word with it from the start; FIGHT has been the word ever since; FIGHT is the word this day! If it had been let alone, it would not have died; its superiority both in quantity and the quality of its matter to any other of the cheap papers would have prevented that catastrophe; but its progress was amazingly accelerated in the first days of its existence by the efforts of an enemy to put it down. That enemy was the Sun.

"The publisher of the Sun," wrote Park Benjamin in the Evening Signal, "has, during the last few days, got up a conspiracy to crush the New York Tribune. The Tribune was, from its inception, very successful, and, in many instances, persons in the habit of taking the Sun, stopped that paper—wisely preferring a sheet which gives twice the amount of reading matter, and always contains the latest intelligence. This fact afforded sufficient evidence to Beach, as it did to all others who were cognizant of the circumstances, that the Tribune would, before the lapse of many weeks, supplant the Sun. To prevent this, and, if possible, to destroy the

9

circulation of the Tribune altogether, an attempt was made to bribe
the carriers to give up their routes ; fortunately this succeeded only
in the cases of two men who were likewise carriers of the Sun
In the next place, all the newsmen were threatened with being de
prived of the Sun, if, in any instance, they were found selling the
Tribune.   But these efforts were not enough to gratify Beach.   He
instigated boys in his office, or others, to whip the boys engaged
in selling the Tribune.   No sooner was this fact ascertained at the
office of the Tribune, than young men were sent to defend the
sale of that paper.   They had not been on their station long, before a boy from the Sun office approached and began to flog the
lad with the Tribune ; retributory measures were instantly resorted
to ; but, before a just chastisement was inflicted, Beach himself,
and a man in his employ, came out to sustain their youthful emis-
sary.   The whole matter will, we understand, be submitted to the
proper magistrates."

The public took up the quarrel with great spirit, and this was *one*
reason of the Tribune's speedy and striking success.   For three
weeks subscribers poured in at the rate of three hundred a day !
It began its fourth week with an edition of six thousand ; its seventh week, with eleven thousand, which was the utmost that could
be printed with its first press.   The advertisements increased in
proportion.   The first number contained four columns ; the twelfth,
nine columns ; the hundredth, thirteen columns.   Triumph ! triumph ! nothing but triumph !   New presses capable of printing
the astounding number of thirty-five hundred copies an hour are
duly announced.   The indulgence of advertisers is besought 'for
this day only ;' 'to-morrow, their favors *shall* appear.'   The price
of advertising was raised from four to six cents a line.   Letters of
approval came by every mail.   "We have a number of requests,"
said the Editor in an early paragraph, "to blow up all sorts of
abuses, which shall be attended to as fast as possible."   In another,
he returns his thanks "to the friends of this paper and the principles it upholds, for the addition of over a thousand substantial
names to its subscription list last week."   Again : "The Sun is rush-
ing rapidly to destruction.   It has lost even the groveling sagacity,
the vulgar sordid instinct with which avarice once gifted it."
Again : "Everything appears to work well with us.   True, we

have not heard (except through the veracious Sun) from any gentlemen proposing to give us a $2,500 press ; but if any gentlemen *have* such an intention, and proceed to put it in practice, the public may rest assured that they will not be ashamed of the act, while we shall be most eager to proclaim it and acknowledge the kindness. But even though we wait for such a token of good-will and sympathy until the Sun shall cease to be the slimy and venomous instrument of loco-focoism it is, jesuitical and deadly in politics and groveling in morals—we shall be abundantly sustained and cheered by the support we are regularly receiving." Editors wrote in the English language in those days. Again : "The Sun of yesterday gravely informed its readers that '*It is doubtful whether the Land Bill can pass the House.*' The Tribune of the same date contained the news of the *passage* of that very bill!" Triumph! saucy triumph! nothing but triumph!

One thing only was wanting to *secure* the Tribune's brilliant success ; and that was an efficient business partner. Just in the nick of time, the needed and predestined man appeared, the man of all others for the duty required. On Saturday morning, July 31st, the following notices appeared under the editorial head on the second page :

The undersigned has great pleasure in announcing to his friends and the public that he has formed a copartnership with THOMAS McELRATH, and that THE TRIBUNE will hereafter be published by himself and Mr. M. under the firm of GREELEY & McELRATH. The principal Editorial charge of the paper will still rest with the subscriber ; while the entire business management of the concern henceforth devolves upon his partner. This arrangement, while it relieves the undersigned from a large portion of the labors and cares which have pressed heavily upon him for the last four months, assures to the paper efficiency and strength in a department where they have hitherto been needed ; and I cannot be mistaken in the trust that the accession to its conduct of a gentleman who has twice been honored with their suffrages for an important station, will strengthen THE TRIBUNE in the confidence and affections of the Whigs of New York. Respectfully,

July 31st. HORACE GREELEY.

The undersigned, in connecting himself with the conduct of a public journal, invokes a continuance of that courtesy and good feeling which has been extended to him by his fellow-citizens. Having heretofore received evidence of kindness and regard from the conductors of the Whig press of this city and rejoicing in the friendship of most of them, it will be his aim in his new vocation to justify that kindness and strengthen and increase those friendships. His hearty concurrence in the principles, Political and Moral, on which THE TRIBUNE has thus far been conducted, has been a principal incitement to the connection here announced; and the statement of this fact will preclude the necessity of any special declaration of opinions. With gratitude for past favors, and an anxious desire to merit a continuance of regard, he remains,

The Public's humble servant,   THOMAS McELRATH.

A strict disciplinarian, a close calculator, a man of method and order, experienced in business, Mr. McElrath possessed in an eminent degree the very qualities in which the editor of the Tribune was most deficient. Roll Horace Greeley and Thomas McElrath into one, and the result would be, a very respectable approximation to a Perfect Man. The two, united in partnership, have been able to produce a very respectable approximation to a perfect newspaper. As Damon and Pythias are the types of perfect friendship, so may Greeley and McElrath be of a perfect partnership; and one may say, with a sigh at the many discordant unions the world presents, Oh! that every Greeley could find his McElrath! and blessed is the McElrath that finds his Greeley!

Under Mr. McElrath's direction, order and efficiency were soon introduced into the business departments of the Tribune office. It became, and has ever since been, one of the best-conducted newspaper establishments in the world. Early in the fall, the New Yorker and Log Cabin were merged into the Weekly Tribune, the first number of which appeared on the 20th of September. The concern, thus consolidated, knew, thenceforth, nothing but prosperity. The New Yorker had existed seven years and a half; the Log Cabin, eighteen months.

The Tribune, I repeat, was a live paper. It was, also, a variously interesting one. Its selections, which in the early volumes occupied several columns daily, were of high character. It gave the philosophers of the Dial an ample hearing, and many an appreciating notice. It made liberal extracts from Carlyle, Cousin, and others, whose works contained the spirit of the New Time. The eighth number gave fifteen songs from a new volume of Thomas Moore. Barnaby Rudge was published entire in the first volume. Mr. Raymond's notices of new books were a conspicuous and interesting fea-tare. Still more so, were his clear and able sketches and reports of public lectures. In November, the Tribune gave a fair and courteous report of the Millerite Convention. About the same time, Mr. Greeley himself reported the celebrated McLeod trial at Utica, sending on from four to nine columns a day.

Amazing was the industry of the editors. Single numbers of the Tribune contained eighty editorial paragraphs. Mr. Greeley's average day's work was three columns, equal to fifteen pages of foolscap; and the mere writing which an editor does, is *not* half his daily labor. In May, appeared a series of articles on Retrenchment and Reform in the City Government, a subject upon which the Tribune has since shed a considerable number of barrels of ink. In the same month, it disturbed a hornet's nest by saying, that " the whole moral atmosphere of the Theater, as it actually exists among us, is in our judgment unwholesome, and therefore, while we do not propose to war upon it, we seek no alliance with it, and cannot conscientiously urge our readers to visit it, as would be expected if we were to solicit and profit by its advertising patronage."

Down came all the hornets of the press. The Sun had the effrontery to assert, in reply, that " most of the illegitimate births in New York owe their origin to acquaintances formed at 'Evening Churches,' and that 'Class-meetings' have done more to *people* the House of Refuge than twenty times the number of theaters." This discussion might have been turned to great advantage by the Tribune, if it had not, with obstinate honesty, given the religious world a rebuff by asserting its right to advertise heretical books.

"As to our friend," said the Tribune, "who complains of the advertising of certain Theological works which do not square with his opinions, we must tell him plainly that he is unreasonable. No other paper that we ever heard of establishes any test of the Orthodoxy of works advertised in its columns; even the Commercial Advertiser and Journal of Commerce advertise for the very sect proscribed by him. If one were to attempt a discrimination, where would he end ? One man considers Universalism immoral; but another is equally positive that Arminianism is so; while a third holds the same bad opinion of Calvinism. Who shall decide between them ? Certainly not the Editor of a daily newspaper, un less he prints it avowedly under the patronage of a particular sect. Our friend inquires whether we should advertise infidel books also. We answer, that if any one should offer an advertisement of lewd, ribald, indecent, blasphemous or law-prohibited books, we should claim the right to reject it. But a work no otherwise objectionable than as controverting the Christian record and doctrine, would not be objected to by us. True Christianity neither fears refutation nor dreads discussion—or, as JEFFERSON has forcibly said, ‘Error of opinion may be tolerated where Reason is left free to combat it.’ ”

In politics, the Tribune was strongly, yet not blindly whig. It appealed, in its first number, to the whig party for support. The same number expressed the decided opinion, that Mr. Tyler would prove to be, as president, all that the whigs desired, and that opinion the Tribune was one of the last to yield. In September it justified Daniel Webster in retaining office, after the ‘treachery’ of Tyler was manifest, and when all his colleagues had resigned in disgust. It justified him on the ground that he could best bring to a conclusion the Ashburton negotiations. This defense of Webster was deeply offensive to the more violent whigs, and it remained a pretext of attack on the Tribune for several years. With regard to his course in the Tyler controversy, Mr. Greeley wrote in 1845 a long explanation, of which the material passage was as follows:—“In December, 1841, I visited Washington upon assurances that John Tyler and his advisers were disposed to return to the Whig party, and that I could be of service in bringing about a complete reconciliation between the Administration and the Whigs in Congress and in the country. I never proposed to ‘connect myself with the cause of the Administration,’ but upon the understanding that it should be heartily and faithfully a WHIG Administration. * * Finally, I declined utterly and absolutely, to ‘connect myself with the cause of the Administration’ the moment I became satisfied, as I did during that visit, that the *Chief* of the Government did not desire a reconciliation, upon the basis of sustaining Whig principles and Whig measures, with the party he had so deeply wronged, but was treacherously coqueting with Loco-Focoism, and fooled with the idea of a re-election.”

Against Repudiation, then an exciting topic, the Tribune went dead in many a telling article. In behalf of Protection to American Industry, the editor wrote columns upon columns.

In a word, the Tribune was equal to its opportunity; it lived up to its privileges. In every department it steadily and strikingly improved throughout the year. It began its second year with twelve thousand subscribers, and a daily average of thirteen columns of advertisements. The Tribune was a Fixed Fact.

The history of a daily paper is the history of the world. It is obviously impossible in the compass of a work like this to give anything like a complete history of the Tribune. For that purpose ten octavo volumes would be required, and most interesting volumes they would be. All that I can do is to select the leading events of its history which were most intimately connected with the history of its editor, and dwell with some minuteness upon them, connecting them together only by a slender thread of narrative, and omitting even to mention many things of real interest. It will be convenient, too, to group together in separate chapters events similar in their nature, but far removed from one another in the time of their occurrence. Indeed, I am overwhelmed with the mass of materials, and must struggle out as best I can.

A great book is a great evil, says the Greek Reader. This book was fore-ordained to be a small one.

CHAPTER XVI.

THE TRIBUNE AND FOURIERISM.

What made Horace Greeley a Socialist—The hard winter of 1838—Albert Brisbane-The subject broached—Series of articles by Mr. Brisbane begun—Their effect—Cry of Mad Dog—Discussion between Horace Greeley and Henry J. Raymond—How it arose—Abstract of it in a conversational form.

THE editor of the Tribune was a Socialist years before the Tribune came into existence.

The winter of 1838 was unusually severe. The times were hard, fuel and food were dear, many thousands of men and women **were** out of employment, and there was general distress. As the cold months wore slowly on, the sufferings of the poor became so aggravated, and the number of the unemployed increased to such a degree, that the ordinary means were inadequate to relieve even those who were destitute of every one of the necessaries of life. Some died of starvation. Some were frozen to death. Many, through exposure and privation, contracted fatal diseases. A large number, who had never before known want, were reduced to beg. Respectable mechanics were known to offer their services as waiters in eating-houses for their food only. There never had been such a time of suffering in New York before, and there has not been since. Extraordinary measures were taken by the comfortable classes to alleviate the sufferings of their unfortunate fellow-citizens. Meetings were held, subscriptions were made, committees were appointed; and upon one of the committees Horace Greeley was named to serve, and did serve, faithfully and laboriously, for many weeks. The district which his committee had in charge was the Sixth Ward, the 'bloody' Sixth, the squalid, poverty-stricken Sixth, the pool into which all that is worst in this metropolis has a tendency to reel and slide. It was his task, and that of his colleagues, to see that no one froze or starved in that forlorn and polluted region. More than this they could not do, for the subscriptions, liberal as they were, were not more than sufficient to relieve actual and pressing distress. In the better parts of the Sixth Ward a large number of mechanics lived, whose cry was, not for the bread and the fuel of charity, but for Work! Charity their honest souls disdained. Its food choked them, its fire chilled them. Work, give us work! was their eager, passionate demand.

All this Horace Greeley heard and saw. He was a young man—not quite twenty-six—compassionate to weakness, generous to a fault. He had known what it was to beg for work, from shop to shop, from town to town; and, that very winter, he was struggling with debt, at no safe distance from bankruptcy. *Why* must these things be? *Are* they inevitable? Will they *always* be inevitable? Is it in human wisdom to devise a remedy? in human virtue to apply it? *Can* the beneficent God have designed this, who, with such wonderful profusion, has provided for the wants, tastes, and luxuries of all his creatures, and for a hundred times as many creatures as yet have lived at the same time? Such questions Horace Greeley pondered, in silence, in the depths of his heart, during that winter of misery.

From Paris came soon the calm, emphatic answer, These things need NOT be! They are due alone to the short-sightedness and injustice of man! Albert Brisbane brought the message. Horace Greeley heard and believed it. He took it to his heart. It became a part of him.

Albert Brisbane was a young gentleman of liberal education, the son of wealthy parents. His European tour included, of course, a residence at Paris, where the fascinating dreams of Fourier were the subject of conversation. He procured the works of that amiable and noble-minded man, read them with eager interest, and became completely convinced that his captivating theories were capable of speedy realization—not, perhaps, in slow and conservative Europe, but in progressive and unshackled America. He returned home a Fourierite, and devoted himself with a zeal and disinterestedness that are rare in the class to which he belonged, and that in any class cannot be too highly praised, to the dissemination of the doctrines in which he believed. He wrote essays and pamphlets. He expounded Fourierism in conversation. He started a magazine called the Future, devoted to the explanation of Fourier's plans, published by Greeley & Co. He delivered lectures. In short, he did all that a man could do to make known to his fellow men what he believed it became them to know. He made a few converts, but only a few, till the starting of the Tribune gave him access to the public ear.

Horace Greeley made no secret of his conversion to Fourierism. On the contrary, he avowed it constantly in private, and occasionally in public print, though never in his own paper till towards the end of the Tribune's first year. His native sagacity taught him that before Fourierism could be realized, a complete revolution in public sentiment must be effected, a revolution which would require many years of patient effort on the part of its advocates.

The first mention of Mr. Brisbane and Fourierism in the Tribune, appeared October 21st, 1841. It was merely a notice of one of Mr. Brisbane's lectures:

" Mr. A. Brisbane delivered a lecture at the Stuyvesant Institute last evening upon the Genius of Christianity considered in its bearing on the Social Insti- tutions and Terrestrial Destiny of the Human Race. He contended that the mission of Christianity upon earth has hitherto been imperfectly understood, and that the doctrines of Christ, carried into practical effect, would free the world of Want, Misery, Temptation and Crime. This, Mr. B. believes, will be effected by a system of Association, or the binding up of individual and fam- ily interests in Social and Industrial Communities, wherein all faculties may be developed, all energies usefully employed, all legitimate desires satisfied, and idleness, want, temptation and crime be annihilated. In such Associa- tions, individual property will be maintained, the family be held sacred, and every inducement held out to a proper ambition. Mr. B. will lecture hereafter on the practical details of the system of *Fourier*, of whom he is a zealous dis- ciple, and we shall then endeavor to give a more clear and full account of his doctrines."

A month later, the Tribune copied a flippant and sneering arti- cle from the London Times, on the subject of Fourierism in France. In his introductory remarks the editor said:

" We have written something, and shall yet write much more, in illustra- tion and advocacy of the great Social revolution which our age is destined to commence, in rendering all useful Labor at once attractive and honorable, and banishing Want and all consequent degradation from the globe. The germ of this revolution is developed in the writings of Charles Fourier, a phil- anthropic and observing Frenchman, who died in 1837, after devoting thirty years of a studious and unobtrusive life to inquiries, at once patient and pro- found, into the causes of the great mass of Social evils which overwhelm Hu- manity, and the true means of removing them. These means he proves to be a system of Industrial and Household Association, on the principle of Joint Stock Investment, whereby Labor will be ennobled and rendered attractive and universal, Capital be offered a secure and lucrative investment, and Tal- ent and Industry find appropriate, constant employment, and adequate re- ward, while Plenty, Comfort, and the best means of Intellectual and Moral Improvement is guaranteed to all, regardless of former acquirements or con- dition. This grand, benignant plan is fully developed in the various works of M. Fourier, which are abridged in the single volume on ' The Social Des- tiny of Man,' by Mr. A. Brisbane, of this State. Some fifteen or sixteen other works in illustration and defense of the system have been given to the world, by Considerant, Chevalier, Paget, and other French writers, and by Hugh Do- herty, Dr. H. McCormack. and others in English. A tri-weekly journal (' *La Phalange*') devoted to the system, is published by M. Victor Considerant in

Paris, and another (the 'London Phalanx') by Hugh Doherty, in London,
each ably edited."

Early in 1842, a number of gentlemen associated themselves together for the purpose of bringing the schemes of Fourier fully and
prominently before the public; and to this end, they purchased the
right to occupy one column daily on the first page of the Tribune
with an article, or articles, on the subject, from the pen of Mr.
Brisbane. The first of these articles appeared on the first of March,
1842, and continued, with some interruptions, at first daily, afterwards three times a week, till about the middle of 1844, when Mr.
Brisbane went again to Europe. The articles were signed with the
letter B, and were known to be communicated. They were calm
in tone, clear in exposition. At first, they seem to have attracted
little attention, and less opposition. They were regarded (as far as
my youthful recollection serves) in the light of articles to be skipped, and by most of the city readers of the Tribune, I presume,
they were skipped with the utmost regularity, and quite as a matter
of course. Occasionally, however, the subject was alluded to editorially, and every such allusion was of a nature to be read. Gradually, Fourierism became one of the topics of the time. Gradually
certain editors discovered that Fourierism was unchristian. Gradually, the cry of Mad Dog arose. Meanwhile, the articles of Mr.
Brisbane were having their effect upon the People.

In May, 1843, Mr. Greeley wrote, and with perfect truth:

"The Doctrine of Association is spreading throughout the country with a
rapidity which we did not anticipate, and of which we had but little hope.
We receive papers from nearly all parts of the Northern and Western States,
and some from the South, containing articles upon Association, in which general views and outlines of the System are given. They speak of the subject
as one 'which is calling public attention,' or, 'about which so much is now
said,' or, 'which is a good deal spoken of in this part of the country,' &c.,
showing that our Principles are becoming a topic of public discussion. From
the rapid progress of our Doctrines during the past year, we look forward
with hope to their rapid continued dissemination. We feel perfectly confident
that never, in the history of the world, has a philosophical doctrine, or the plan
of a great reform, spread with the rapidity which the Doctrine of Association
has spread in the United States for the last year or two. There are now a
large number of papers, and quite a number of lecturers in various parts of

the country, who are lending their efforts to the cause, so that the onward movement must be greatly accelerated.

"Small Associations are springing up rapidly in various parts of the country. The Sylvania Association in Pike country, Pa., is now in operation; about seventy persons are on the domain, erecting buildings, &c., and preparing for the reception of other members.

"An Association has been organized in Jefferson county. Our friend, A. M. Watson, is at the head of it; he has been engaged for the last three years in spreading the principles in that part of the State, and the result is the formation of an Association. Several farmers have put in their farms and taken stock; by this means the Domain has been obtained. About three hundred persons, we are informed, are on the lands. They have a very fine quarry on their Domain, and they intend, among the branches of Industry which they will pursue, to take contracts for erecting buildings out of the Association. They are now erecting a banking-house in Watertown, near which the Association is located.

"Efforts are making in various parts of this State, in Vermont, in Pennsylvania, Indiana, and Illinois, to establish Associations, which will probably be successful in the course of the present year. We have heard of these movements; there may be others of which we are not informed."

About the same time, he gave a box on the ear to the editors who wrote of Fourierism in a hostile spirit:—"The kindness of our friends of the New York Express, Rochester Evening Post, and sundry other Journals which appear inclined to wage a personal controversy with us respecting Fourierism, (the Express without knowing how to spell the word,) is duly appreciated. Had we time and room for disputation on that subject, we would prefer opponents who would not be compelled to confess frankly or betray clearly their utter ignorance of the matter, whatever might be their manifestations of personal pique or malevolence in unfair representations of the little they *do* understand. We counsel our too belligerent friends to possess their souls in patience, and not be too eager to rival the fortune of him whose essay proving that steamships could *not* cross the Atlantic happened to reach us in the first steamship that *did* cross it. 'The proof of the pudding' is not found in wrangling about it."

We also find, occasionally, a paragraph in the Tribune like this: "T. W. Whitley and H. Greeley will address such citizens of Newark as choose to hear them on the subject of 'Association' at 7½ o'clock this evening at the Relief Hall, rear of J. M. Quimby's Repository."

Too fast. Too fast. I need not detail the progress of Fourierism—the many attempts made to establish Associations—the failure of all of them but one, which still exists—the ruin that ensued to many worthy men—the ridicule with which the Associationists were assailed—the odium excited in many minds against the Tribune—the final relinquishment of the subject. All this is perfectly well known to the people of this country.

Let us come, at once, to the grand climax of the Tribune's Fourierism, the famous discussion of the subject between Horace Greeley and H. J. Raymond, of the Courier and Enquirer, in the year 1846. That discussion *finished* Fourierism in the United States.

Mr. Raymond had left the Tribune, and joined the Courier and Enquirer, at the solicitation of Col. Webb, the editor of the latter. It was a pity the Tribune *let* him go, for he is a born journalist, and could have helped the Tribune to attain the position of the great, only, undisputed Metropolitan Journal, many years sooner than it will. Horace Greeley is not a born journalist. He is too much in earnest to be a perfect editor. He has too many opinions and preferences. He is a BORN LEGISLATOR, a Deviser of Remedies, a Suggester of Expedients, a Framer of Measures. The most successful editor is he whose great endeavor it is to tell the public *all it wants to know*, and whose comments on passing events best express the *feeling of the country* with regard to them. Mr. Raymond is not a man of first-rate talent—great talent would be in his way—he is most interesting when he attacks; and of the varieties of composition, polished vituperation is not the most difficult. But he has the right *notion* of editing a daily paper, and when the Tribune lost him, it lost more than it had the slightest idea of—as events have since shown.

However, Horace Greeley and Henry J. Raymond, the one naturally liberal, the other naturally conservative—the one a Universalist, the other a Presbyterian—the one regarding the world as a place to be made better by living in it, the other regarding it as an oyster to be opened, and bent on opening it—would have found it hard to work together on equal terms. They separated amicably, and each went his way. The discussion of Fourierism arose thus :

Mr. Brisbane, on his return from Europe, renewed the agitation of his subject. The Tribune of August 19th, 1846, contained a letter by him, addressed to the editors of the Courier and Enquirer, proposing several questions, to which answers were requested, respecting Social Reform. The Courier replied. The Tribune rejoined editorially, and was answered in turn by the Courier. Mr. Brisbane addressed a second letter to the Courier, and sent it direct to the editor of that paper in manuscript. The Courier agreed to publish it, if the Tribune would give place to its reply. The Tribune declined doing so, but challenged the editor of the Courier to a public discussion of the whole subject.

"Though we cannot now," wrote Mr. Greeley, "open our columns to a set discussion by others of social questions (which may or may not refer mainly to points deemed relevant by us), we readily close with the *spirit* of the Courier's proposition. * * As soon as the State election is fairly over—say Nov. 10th—we will publish an entire article, filling a column of the Tribune, very nearly, in favor of Association as we understand it ; and, upon the Courier copying this and replying, we will give place to its reply, and respond ; and so on, till each party shall have published twelve articles on its own side, and twelve on the other, which shall fulfill the terms of this agreement. All the twelve articles of each party shall be published without abridgment or variation in the Daily, Weekly, and Semi-weekly editions of both papers. Afterward each party will, of course, be at liberty to comment at pleasure in his own columns. In order that neither paper shall be crowded with this discussion, one article per week, only, on either side, shall be published, unless the Courier shall prefer greater dispatch. Is not this a fair proposition ? What says the Courier ? It has, of course, the advantage of the defensive position and of the last word."

The Courier said, after much toying and dallying, and a preliminary skirmish of paragraphs, COME ON! and, on the 20th of November, the Tribune came on. The debate lasted six months. It was conducted on both sides with spirit and ability, and it attracted much attention. The twenty-four articles, of which it consisted, were afterwards published by the Harpers in a pamphlet of eighty-three closely-printed, double-columned pages, which had a considerable sale, and has long been out of print. On one side we see earnestness and sincerity; on the other tact and skill. One strove to convince, the other to triumph. The thread of argument is often lost in a maze of irrelevancy. The subject, indeed, was peculiarly ill calculated for a public discussion. When men converse on a scheme which has for its object the good of mankind, let them confer in awful whispers—apart, like conspirators; not distract themselves in dispute in the hearing of a nation; for they who would benefit mankind must do it either by stealth or by violence.

I have tried to condense this tremendous pamphlet into the form and brevity of a conversation, with the following result. Neither of the speakers, however, are to be held responsible for the language employed.

Horace Greeley. Nov. 20th. The earth, the air, the waters, the sunshine, with their natural products, were divinely intended and appointed for the sustenance and enjoyment of the whole human family. But the present *fact* is, that a very large majority of mankind are landless; and, by law, the landless have no inherent right to stand on a single square foot of their native State, except in the highways. Perishing with cold, they have no legal right to a stick of decaying fuel in the most unfrequented morass. Famishing, they have no legal right to pluck and eat the bitterest acorn in the depths of the remotest forest. But the Past cannot be recalled. What has been done, has been done. The legal rights of individuals must be held sacred. But those whom society has divested of their natural right to a share in the soil, are entitled to *Compensation,* i. e. to continuous opportunity to earn a subsistence by Labor. To own land is to possess this opportunity. The majority own no land. Therefore the minority, who own *legally* all the land, which *naturally* belongs to all men alike, are bound to secure to the landless majority a compensating security of remunerating Labor. But, as society is now organized, this is not, and cannot be, done. "Work, work! give us something to do! anything that will secure us honest bread," is at this moment the prayer of not less than thirty thousand human beings within the sound of the City-Hall bell. Here is an enormous waste and loss. We must devise a remedy and that remedy, I propose to show, is found in Association.

H. J. Raymond. Nov. 23*d.* Heavens ! Here we have one of the leading Whig presses of New York advocating the doctrine that *no man can rightfully own land !* Fanny Wright was of that opinion. The doctrine is erroneous and *dangerous.* If a man cannot rightfully own land, he cannot rightfully own anything which the land produces; that is, he cannot rightfully own anything at all. The blessed institution of property, the basis of the social fabric, from which arts, agriculture, commerce, civilization spring, and without which they could not exist, is threatened with destruction, and by a leading Whig paper too. Conservative Powers, preserve us !

Horace Greeley. Nov. 26*th.* Fudge ! What I said was this : Society, having divested the majority of any right to the soil, is bound to compensate them by guaranteeing to each an opportunity of earning a subsistence by Labor. Your vulgar, clap-trap allusion to Fanny Wright does not surprise me. I shall neither desert nor deny a truth because she, or any one else, has proclaimed it. But to proceed. By association I mean a Social Order, which shall take the place of the present Township, to be composed of some hundreds or some thousands of persons, who shall be united together in interest and industry for the purpose of securing to each individual the following things : 1, an elegant and commodious house ; 2, an education, complete and thorough ; 3, a secure subsistence ; 4, opportunity to labor ; 5, fair wages ; 6, agreeable social relations ; 7, progress in knowledge and skill. As society is at present organized, these are the portion of a very small minority. But by association of capital and industry, they might become the lot of all ; inasmuch as association tends to *Economy* in all departments, economy in lands, fences, fuel, household labor, tools, education, medicine, legal advice, and commercial exchanges. My opponent will please observe that his article is three times as long as mine, and devoted in good part to telling the public that the Tribune is an exceedingly mischievous paper ; which is an imposition.

H. J. Raymond. Nov. 30*th.* A home, fair wages, education, etc., are very desirable, we admit ; and it is the unceasing aim of all good men in society, as it now exists, to place those blessings within the reach of all. The Tribune's claim that it can be accomplished only by association is only a claim. Substantiate it. Give us proof of its effi.acy. Tell us in whom the property is to be vested, how labor is to be remunerated, what share capital is to have in the concern, by what device men are to be induced to labor, how moral offenses are to be excluded or punished. Then we may be able to discuss the subject. Nothing was stipulated about the length of the articles; and we *do* think the Tribune a mischievous paper.

Horace Greeley. Dec. 1st. The property of an association will be vested in those who contributed the capital to establish it, represented by shares of stock, just as the property of a bank, factory, or railroad now is. Labor, skill and talent, will be remunerated by a fixed proportion of their products, or of its proceeds, if sold. Men will be induced to labor by a knowledge that its rewards will be a certain and major proportion of the product, which of course will be less or more according to the skill and industry of each individual. The slave has no motive to diligence except fear; the hireling is tempted to eye-service; the solitary worker for himself is apt to become disheartened; but men working for themselves, in groups, will find labor not less attractive than profitable. Moral offenses will be punished by legal enactment, and they will be rendered unfrequent by plenty and education.

H. J. Raymond. Dec. 8th. Oh—then the men of capital are to own the land, are they? Let us see. A man with money enough may buy an entire domain of five thousand acres; men without money will cultivate it on condition of receiving a fixed proportion of its products; the major part, says the Tribune; suppose we say *three-fourths.* Then the contract is simply this:—*One rich man (or company) owns five thousand acres of land, which he leases forever to two thousand poor men at the yearly rent of one-fourth of its products.* It is an affair of landlord and tenant—the lease perpetual, payment in kind; and the landlord to own the cattle, tools, and furniture of the tenant, as well as the land. Association, then, is merely a plan for extending the relation of landlord and tenant over the whole arable surface of the earth.

Horace Greeley. Dec. 10th. By no means. The capital of a mature association would be, perhaps, half a million of dollars; it an infant association, fifty thousand dollars; and this increase of value would be both created and *owned* by Labor. In an ordinary township, however, the increase, though all created by Labor, is chiefly owned by Capital. The majority of the inhabitants remain poor; while a few—merchants, land-owners, mill-owners, and manufacturers—are enriched. That this is the fact in recently-settled townships, is undeniable. That it would not be the fact in a township settled and cultivated on the principle of association, seems to me equally so.

H. J. Raymond. Dec 14th. But not to me. Suppose fifty men furnish fifty thousand dollars for an association upon which a hundred and fifty others are to labor and to live. With that sum they buy the land, build the houses, and procure everything needful for the start. The capitalists, bear in mind, are the absolute owners of the entire property of the association. In twenty years, that property may be worth half a million, and it still remains the property of the capitalists, the laborers having annually drawn their share of the products. They may have saved a portion of their annual share, and thus have accumulated property; but they have no more title to the *domain* than they had at first. If the concern should not prosper, the laborers could not buy shares; if it should, the capitalists would not sell except at their increased value. What advantage, then, does association offer for the poor man's acquiring property superior to that afforded by the present state of things? None, that we can see. On the contrary, the more rapidly the domain of an association should increase in value, the more difficult it would be for the laboring man to rise to the class of proprietors; and this would simply be an *aggravation* of the worst features of the social system. And how you associationists *would* quarrel! The skillful would be ever grumbling at the awkward, and the lazy would shirk their share of the work, but clamor for their share of the product. There would be ten occasions for bickerings where now there is one. The fancies of the associationist, in fact, are as baseless, though not as beautiful, as More's Utopia, or the Happy Valley of Rasselas.

Horace Greeley Dec. 16th. No, *Sir!* In association, those who furnish the original capital are the owners merely of *so much stock* in the concern—not of all the land and other property, as you represent. Suppose that capital to be fifty thousand dollars. At the end of the first year it is found that twenty-five thousand dollars have been added to the value of the property by Labor. For this amount *new stock* is issued, which is apportioned to Capital, Labor and Skill as impartial justice shall dictate—to the non-resident capitalist a certain proportion; to the working capitalist the same proportion, plus the excess of his earnings over his expenses; to the laborer that excess only. The apportionment is repeated every year; and the proportion of the new stock assigned to Capital is such that when the property of the association is worth half a million, Capital will own about one-fifth of it. With regard to the practical working of association, I point you to the fact that association and civilization are one. They advance and recede together. In this age we have large steamboats, monster hotels, insurance, partnerships, joint stock companies, public schools, libraries, police, Odd Fellowship—all of which are exemplifications of the *idea* upon which association is based; all of which work well as institutions, and are productive of incalculable benefits to mankind.

H. J. Raymond. Dec. 24th. Of course;—but association assumes to shape and govern the details of *social life*, which is a very different affair. One '*group*,' it appears, is to do all the cooking, another the gardening, another the ploughing. But suppose that some who want to be cooks are enrolled in the gardening group. They will naturally sneer at the dishes cooked by their rivals, perhaps form a party for the expulsion of the cooks, and so bring about a kitchen war. Then, who will consent to be a member of the boot-blacking, ditch-digging and sink-cleaning groups? Such labors must be done, and groups must be detailed to do them. Then, who is to settle the wages question? Who is to determine upon the *comparative* efficiency of each laborer, and settle the comparative value of his work? There is the religious difficulty too, and the educational difficulty, the medical difficulty, and numberless other difficulties, arising from differences of opinion, so radical and so earnestly entertained as to preclude the *possibility* of a large number of persons living together in the intimate relation contemplated by association.

Horace Greeley. Dec. 28th. Not so fast. After the first steamship had crossed the Atlantic all the demonstrations of the impossibility of that fact fell to the ground. Now, with regard to associations, *the first steamship has crossed!* The communities of Zoar and Rapp have existed from twenty to forty years, and several associations of the kind advocated by me have survived from two to five years, not only without being broken up by the difficulties alluded to, but without their presenting themselves in the light of *difficulties* at all. No inter-kitchen war has disturbed their peace, no religious differences have marred their harmony, and men have been found willing to perform ungrateful offices, required by the general good. Passing over your objections, therefore, I beg you to consider the enormous difficulties, the wrongs, the waste, the misery, occasioned by and inseparable from society as it is now organized. For example, the coming on of winter contracts business and throws thousands out of employment. They and their families suffer, the dealers who supply them are losers in custom, the almshouse is crowded, private charity is taxed to the extreme, many die of diseases induced by destitution, some are driven by despair to intoxication; and all this, while every ox and horse is well fed and cared for, while there is inaccessible plenty all around, while capital is luxuriating on the products of the very labor which is now palsied and suffering. Under the present system, capital is everything, man nothing, except as a means of accumulating capital. Capital founds a factory, and for the *single* purpose of increasing capital, taking no thought of the human beings by whom it is increased. The fundamental ideas of association, on the other hand, is to effect a just *distribution* of products among capital, talent and labor.

H. J. Raymond. Jan. 6th. The *idea* may be good enough; but the means are impracticable; the details are absurd, if not inhumane and impious. The Tribune's admission, that an association of indolent or covetous persons could not endure *without a moral transformation of its members,* seems to us fatal to the whole theory of association. It implies that *individual* reform must precede *so cial* reform, which is precisely our position. But how *s* individual reform to be effected? *By association*, says the Tribune. That is, the motion of the water-wheel is to *produce* the water by which alone it can be *set* in motion—the action of the watch is to produce the main-spring without which it cannot move. Absurd.

Horace Greeley. Jan. 18*th*. Incorrigible mis-stater of my positions! I am as well aware as you are that the mass of the ignorant and destitute are, at present, incapable of so much as understanding the social order I propose, much less of becoming efficient members of an association. What I say is, let those who *are* capable of understanding and promoting it, *begin* the work, found associations, and *show* the rest of mankind how to live and thrive in harmonious industry. You tell me that the sole efficient agency of Social Reform is Christianity. I answer that association *is* Christianity; and the dislocation *now* existing between capital and labor, between the capitalist and the laborer, is as atheistic as it is inhuman.

H. J. Raymond. Jan. 20*th*. Stop a moment. The test of true benevolence is practice, not preaching; and we have no hesitation in saying that the members of any one of our city churches do more every year for the practical relief of poverty and suffering than any phalanx that ever existed. There are in our midst hundreds of female sewing societies, each of which clothes more nakedness and feeds more hunger, than any 'association' that ever was formed. There is a single individual in this city whom the Tribune has vilified as a selfish, grasping despiser of the poor, who has expended more money in providing the poor with food, clothing, education, sound instruction in morals and religion, than all the advocates of association in half a century. While association has been *theorizing* about starvation, Christianity has been *preventing* it. Associationists tell us, that giving to the poor deepens the evil which it aims to relieve, and that the bounty of the benevolent, as society is now organized, is very often abused. We assure them, it is not the social system which abuses the bounty of the benevolent; it is simply the dishonesty and indolence of individuals, and they would do the same under any system, and especially in association.

Horace Greeley. Jan. 29th. Private benevolence is good and necessary ; the Tribune has ever been its cordial and earnest advocate. But benevolence relieves only the *effects* of poverty, while Association proposes to reach and finally eradicate its *causes.* The charitable are doing nobly this winter for the re'ief of the destitute ; but will there be in this city *next* winter fewer objects of charity than there are now ? And let me tell you, sir, if you do not know it already, that the advocates of association, in proportion to their number, and their means, are, at least, *as* active and *as* ready in feeding the hungry and clothing the naked, as any class in the community. Make the examinations as close as you please, bring it as near home as you like, and you will find the fact to be as I have asserted.

H. J. Raymond. Feb. 10th. You overlook one main objection. Association aims, not merely to re-organize Labor, but to revolutionize Society, to change radically Laws, Government, Manners and Religion. It pretends to be a new Social Science, *discovered* by Fourier. In our next article we shall show what its principles are, and point out their inevitable tendency.

Horace Greeley. Feb. 17th. Do so. Meanwhile let me remind you, that there is *need* of a new Social System, when the old one works so villanously and wastefully. There is Ireland, with three hundred thousand able-bodied men, willing to work, yet unemployed. Their labor is worth forty-five millions of dollars a year, which they need, and Ireland needs, but which the present Social System dooms to waste. There is work enough in Ireland to do, and men enough willing to do it ; but the spell of a vicious Social System broods over the island, and keeps the workmen and the work apart. Four centuries ago, the English laborer could earn by his labor a good and sufficient subsistence for his family. Since that time Labor and Talent have made England rich 'beyond the dreams of avarice ;' and, at this day, the Laborer, as a rule, cannot, by unremitting toil, fully supply the necessities of his family. His bread is coarse, his clothing scanty, his home a hovel, his children uninstructed, his life cheerless. He lives from hand to mouth in abject terror of the poor-house, where, he shudders to think, he must end his days. Precisely the same causes are in operation here, and, in due time, will produce precisely the same effects. There is NEED of a Social Re-formation !

H. J. Raymond. March 3d. You are mistaken. The statement that the laborers of the present day are worse off than those of former ages, has been exploded. They are *not*. On the contrary, their condition is *better* in every respect. Evils under the present Social System exist, great evils—evils, for the removal of which the most constant and zealous efforts ought to be made ; yet they are very far from being *as* great or as *general* as the Associationists assert. The fact is indisputable, that, as a rule throughout the country, no honest man, able and willing to work, need stand idle from lack of opportunity. The exceptions to this rule are comparatively few, and arise from temporary and local causes. But we proceed to examine the fundamental principle of the Social System proposed to be substituted for that now established. In one word, that principle is *Self-Indulgence !* "Reason and Passion," writes Parke Godwin, the author of one of the clearest expositions of Socialism yet published, " will be in perfect accord : duty and pleasure will have the same meaning ; without inconvenience or calculation, *man will follow his bent :* hearing only of Attraction, he will never act from necessity, and *never curb himself by restraints.*" What becomes of the *self-denial* so expressly, so frequently, so emphatically enjoined by the New Testament ? Fourierism and Christianity, Fourierism and Morality, Fourierism and Conjugal Constancy are in palpable hostility ! We are told, that if a man has a passion for a dozen kinds of work, he joins a dozen *groups ;* if for a dozen kinds of study, he joins a dozen *groups ;* and, if for a dozen women, the System requires that there must be a dozen different *groups* for his full gratification ! For man will follow his *bent,* and never curb himself by *restraints !*

Horace Greeley. March 12th. Not so. I re-assert what I before proved, that the English laborers of to-day are worse off than those of former centuries ; and I deny with disgust and indignation that there is in Socialism, as American Socialists understand and teach it, any provision or license for the gratification of criminal passions or

unlawful desires.   Why not quote Mr. Godwin fully and fairly?
Why suppress his remark, that, "So long as the Passions may
bring forth Disorder—*so long as Inclination may be in opposition
to Duty*—we reprobate as strongly as any class of men all indulgence of the inclinations and feelings; and where Reason is unable
to guide them, have no objection to other means"?   Socialists know
nothing of Groups, organized, or to be organized, for the perpetra-
tion of crimes, or the practice of vices.

H. J. Raymond.   March 19*th.*   Perhaps not.   But *I* know, from
the writings of leading Socialists, that the law of Passional Attraction, *i. e.* Self-Indulgence, is the essential and fundamental principle
of Association; and that, while Christianity pronounces the free
and full gratification of the passions a *crime*, Socialism extols it as
a *virtue.*

Horace Greeley.   March 26*th.*   Impertinent.   Your articles are all
entitled "The Socialism of the *Tribune* examined"; and the Tribune has never contained a line to justify your unfair inferences
from garbled quotations from the writings of Godwin and Fourier.
What the Tribune advocates is, simply and solely, such an organization of Society as will secure to every man the opportunity of uninterrupted and profitable labor, and to every child nourishment and
culture.   These things, it is undeniable, the present Social System
does not secure; and hence the necessity of a new and better organization.   So no more of your ' Passional Attraction.'

H. J. Raymond.   April 16*th.*   I tell you the scheme of Fourier is
essentially and fundamentally *irreligious !* by which I mean that it
does not follow my Catechism, and apparently ignores the Thirty-
Nine Articles.   Shocking.

Horace Greeley,   April 28*th.*   Humph !

H. J. Raymond.   May 20*th.*   The Tribune is doing a great deal of
harm.   The editor does not know it—but it *is.*

Thus ended Fourierism.   Thenceforth, the Tribune alluded to the subject occasionally, but only in reply to those who sought to make political or personal capital by reviving it. By its discussion of the subject it rendered a great service to the country : first, by affording one more proof that, for the ills that flesh is heir to, there is, there can be, no panacea ; secondly, by exhibiting the economy of association, and familiarizing the public mind with the idea of association—an idea susceptible of a thousand applications, and capable, in a thousand ways, of alleviating and preventing human woes. We see its perfect triumph in Insurance, whereby a loss which would crush an individual falls upon the whole company of insurers, lightly and unperceived. Future ages will witness its successful application to most of the affairs of life.

CHAPTER XVII.

THE TRIBUNE'S SECOND YEAR.

Increase of price—The Tribune offends the Sixth Ward fighting-men—The office threatened—Novel preparations for defense—Charles Dickens defended — The Editor travels—Visits Washington, and sketches the Senators—At Mount Vernon—At Niagara—A hard hit at Major Noah.

THE Tribune, as we have seen, was started as a penny paper. It began its second volume, on the eleventh of April, 1842, at the increased price of nine cents a week, or two cents for a single number, and effected this serious advance without losing two hundred of its twelve thousand subscribers. At the same time, Messrs. Greeley and McElrath started the ʻAmerican Laborer,ʼ a monthly magazine, devoted chiefly to the advocacy of Protection. It was published at seventy-five cents for the twelve numbers which the prospectus announced.

When it was remarked, a few pages back, that the word with the Tribune was FIGHT, no allusion was intended to the use of carnal weapons. " The pen is mightier than the sword," claptraps Bulwer in one of his plays ; and the Pen was the only fighting implement referred to. It came to pass, however, in the first month of the Tribune's second year, that the pointed nib of the warlike journal gave deadly umbrage to certain fighting men of the Sixth Ward, by exposing their riotous conduct on the day of the Spring elections. The office was, in consequence, threatened by the offended parties with a nocturnal visit, and the office, alive to the duty of hospitality, prepared to give the expected guests a suitable reception by arming itself to the chimneys.

This (I believe) was one of the paragraphs deemed most offensive :

"It appears that some of the 'Spartan Band,' headed by Michael Walsh, after a fight in the 4th District of the Sixth Ward, paraded up Centre street, opposite the Halls of Justice, to the neighborhood of the poll of the 3d District, where, after marching and counter-marching, the leader Walsh re-commenced the work of violence by knocking down an unoffending individual, who was following near him. This was the signal for a general attack of this band upon the Irish population, who were knocked down in every direction, until the street was literally strewed with their prostrate bodies. After this demonstration of 'Spartan valor,' the Irish fled, and the band moved on to another poll to re-enact their deeds of violence. In the interim the Irish proceeded to rally their forces, and, armed with sticks of cord-wood and clubs, paraded through Centre street, about 300 strong, attacking indiscriminately and knocking down nearly all who came in their way—some of their victims, bruised and bloody, having to be carried into the Police Office and the prison, to protect them from being murdered. A portion of the Irish then dispersed, while another portion proceeded to a house in Orange street, which they attacked and riddled from top to bottom. Re-uniting their scattered forces, the Irish bands again, with increased numbers, marched up Centre street, driving all before them, and when near the Halls of Justice, the cry was raised, 'Americans, stand firm!' when a body of nearly a thousand voters surrounded the Irish bands, knocked them down, and beat them without mercy—while some of the fallen Irishmen were with difficulty rescued from the violence that would have destroyed them, had they not been hurried into the Police Office and prison as a place of refuge. In this encounter, or the one that preceded it, a man named Ford, and said to be one of the 'Spartans,' was carried into the Police Office beaten almost to death, and was subsequently transferred to the Hospital."

On the morning of the day on which this appeared, two gentlemen, more muscular than civil, called at the office to say, that the Tribune's account of the riot was incorrect, and did injustice to

Individuals, who expected to see a retraction on the following day. No retraction appeared on the following day, but, on the contrary, a fuller and more emphatic repetition of the charge. The next morning, the office was favored by a second visit from the muscular gentlemen. One of them seized a clerk by the shoulder, and requested to be informed whether *he* was the offspring of a female dog who had put *that* into the paper, pointing to the offensive article. The clerk protested his innocence; and the men of muscle swore, that, *whoever* put it in, if the next paper did not do them justice, the Bloody Sixth would come down and 'smash the office.' The Tribune of the next day contained a complete history of the riot, and denounced its promoters with more vehemence than on the days preceding. The Bloody Sixth was ascertained to be in a ferment, and the office prepared itself for defense.

One of the compositors was a member of the City Guard, and through his interest, the muskets of that admired company of citizen-soldiers were procured; as soon as the evening shades prevailed, they were conveyed to the office, and distributed among the men. One of the muskets was placed near the desk of the Editor, who looked up from his writing and said, he 'guessed they 'wouldn't come down,' and resumed his work. The foreman of the press-room in the basement caused a pipe to be conveyed from the safety valve of the boiler to the steps that led up to the sidewalk. The men in the Herald office, near by, made common cause, for this occasion only, with their foemen of the Tribune, and agreed, on the first alarm, to rush through the sky-light to the flat roof, and rain down on the heads of the Bloody Sixth a shower of brick-bats to be procured from the surrounding chimneys. It was thought, that what with volleys of musketry from the upper windows, a storm of bricks from the roof, and a blast of hot steam from the cellar, the Bloody Sixth would soon have enough of smashing the Tribune office. The men of the allied offices waited for the expected assault with the most eager desire. At twelve o'clock, the partners made a tour of inspection, and expressed their perfect satisfaction with all the arrangements. But, unfortunately for the story, the night wore away, the paper went to press, morning dawned, and yet the Bloody Sixth had not appeared! Either the Bloody Sixth had thought better of it, or the men of muscle had had no right to speak in its awful name. From whatever cause—these masterly preparations were made in vain; and the Tribune went on its belligerent way, unsmashed. For some weeks, 'it kept at' the election frauds, and made a complete exposure of the guilty persons

Let us glance hastily over the rest of the volume.

It was the year of Charles Dickens' visit to the United States. The Tribune ridiculed the extravagant and unsuitable honors paid to the amiable novelist, but spoke strongly in favor of international copyright, which Mr. Dickens made it his 'mission' to advocate. When the 'American Notes for General Circulation' appeared, the Tribune was one of the few papers that gave it a 'favorable notice.' "We have read the book," said the Tribune, "very carefully, and we are forced to say, in the face of all this stormy denunciation, that, so far as its tone toward this country is concerned, it *is one of the very best works of its class we have ever seen.* There is not a sentence it which seems to have sprung from ill-nature or contempt; not a word of censure is uttered for its own sake or in a fault-finding spirit; the whole is a calm, judicious, gentlemanly, unexceptionable record of what the writer saw—and a candid and *correct* judgment of its worth and its defects. How a writer could look upon the broadly-blazoned and applauded slanders of his own land which abound in this—how he could run through the pages of LESTER's book—filled to the margin with the grossest, most unfounded and illiberal assaults upon all the institutions and the social phases of Great Britain—and then write so calmly of this country, with so manifest a freedom from passion and prejudice, as DICKENS has done, is to us no slight marvel. That he has done it is infinitely to his credit, and confirms us in the opinion we had long since formed of the soundness of his head and the goodness of his heart."

In the summer of 1842, Mr. Greeley made an extensive tour, visiting Washington, Mount Vernon, Poultney, Westhaven, Londonderry, Niagara, and the home of his parents in Pennsylvania, from all of which he wrote letters to the Tribune. His letters from Washington, entitled 'Glances at the Senate,' gave agreeable sketches of Calhoun, Preston, Benton, Evans, Crittenden, Wright. and others. Silas Wright he thought the 'keenest logician in the Senate,' the 'Ajax of plausibility,' the 'Talleyrand of the forum.'

Calhoun he described as the 'compactest speaker' in the Senate; Preston, as the 'most forcible declaimer;' Evans, as the 'most dexterous and diligent legislator;' Benton, as an individual, "gross and burly in person, of countenance most unintellectual, in manner pompous and inflated, in matter empty, in conceit a giant, in influence a cipher!"

From Mount Vernon, Mr. Greeley wrote an interesting letter, chiefly descriptive. It concluded thus:—"Slowly, pensively, we turned our faces from the rest of the mighty dead to the turmoil of the restless living—from the solemn, sublime repose of Mount Vernon to the ceaseless intrigues, the petty strifes, the ant-hill bustle of the Federal City. Each has its own atmosphere; London and Mecca are not so unlike as they. The silent, enshrouding woods, the gleaming, majestic river, the bright, benignant sky—it is fitly here, amid the scenes he loved and hallowed, that the man whose life and character have redeemed Patriotism and Liberty from the reproach which centuries of designing knavery and hollow profession had cast upon them, now calmly awaits the trump of the archangel. Who does not rejoice that the original design of removing his ashes to the city has never been consummated—that they lie where the pilgrim may reverently approach them, unvexed by the light laugh of the time-killing worldling, unannoyed by the vain or vile scribblings of the thoughtless or the base? Thus may they repose forever! that the heart of the patriot may be invigorated, the hopes of the philanthropist strengthened and his aims exalted, the pulse of the American quickened and his aspirations purified by a visit to Mount Vernon!"

From Niagara, the traveller wrote a letter to Graham's Magazine:

"Years," said he, ' though not many, have weighed upon me since first, in boyhood, I gazed from the deck of a canal-boat upon the distant cloud of white vapor which marked the position of the world's great cataract, and listened to catch the rumbling of its deep thunders. Circumstances did not then permit me to gratify my strong desire of visiting it; and now, when I am tempted to wonder at the stolidity of those who live within a day's journey, yet live on through half a century without one glance at the mighty torrent, I am checked by the reflection that I myself passed within a dozen miles of it no less than five times before I was able to enjoy its magnificence. The propitious hour came at last, however; and, after a disappointed gaze from the upper terrace on the British side, (in which I half feared that the sheet of broken and boiling water above was all the cataract that existed,) and rapid tortuous descent by the woody declivity, I stood at length on Table Rock, and the whole immensity of the tremendous avalanche of waters burst at once on my arrested vision, while awe struggled with amazement for the mastery of my soul.

"This was late in October; I have twice visited the scene amid the freshness and beauty of June; but I think the late Autumn is by far the better season. There is then a sternness in the sky, a plaintive melancholy in the sighing of the wind through the mottled forest foliage, which harmonizes better with the spirit of the scene; for the Genius of Niagara, O friend! is never a laughter-loving spirit. For the gaudy vanities, the petty pomps, the light follies of the hour, he has small sympathy. Let not the giddy heir bring here his ingots, the selfish aspirant his ambition, the libertine his victim, and hope to find enjoyment and gaiety in the presence. Let none come here to nurse his pride, or avarice, or any other low desire. God and His handiwork here stand forth in lone sublimity; and all the petty doings and darings of the ants at the base of the pyramid appear in their proper insignificance. Few can have visited Niagara and left it no humbler, no graver than they came."

On his return to the city, Horace Greeley subsided, with curious abruptness, into the editor of the Tribune. This note appears on the morning after his arrival:

"The senior editor of this paper has returned to his post, after an absence of four weeks, during which he has visited nearly one half of the counties of this State, and passed through portions of Pennsylvania, Vermont, Massachusetts, etc. During this time he has written little for the Tribune save the casual and hasty letters to which his initials were subscribed; but it need hardly be said that the general course and conduct of the paper have been the same as if he had been at his post.

"Two deductions only from the observations he has made and the information he has gathered during his tour, will here be given. They are these:

"1. The cause of Protection to Home Industry is much stronger throughout this and the adjoining States than even the great party which mainly upholds it; and nothing will so much tend to *ensure* the election of Henry Clay next President as the veto of an efficient Tariff bill by John Tyler.

"2. The strength of the Whig party is unbroken by recent disasters and treachery, and only needs the proper opportunity to manifest itself in all the energy and power of 1840. If a distinct and unequivocal issue can be made upon the great leading questions at issue between the rival parties—on Protection to Home Industry and Internal Improvement—the Whig ascendency will be triumphantly vindicated in the coming election."

I need not dwell on the politics of that year. For Protection—for Clay—against Tyler—against his vetoes—for a law to punish se duction—against capital punishment—imagine countless columns.

In October, died Dr. Channing. "Deeply," wrote Mr. Greeley, "do we deplore his loss, most untimely, to the faithless eye of man does it seem—to the cause of truth, of order and of right, and still more deeply do we lament that he has left behind him, in the same department of exertion, so few, in proportion to the number needed, to supply the loss occasioned by his death." Soon after, the Tribune gave Theodore Parker a hearing by publishing sketches of his lectures.

An affair of a personal nature made considerable noise about this time, which is worth alluding to, for several reasons. Major Noah, then the editor of the 'Union,' a Tylerite paper of small circulation and irritable temper, was much addicted to attacks on the Tribune. On this occasion, he was unlucky enough to publish a ridiculous story, to the effect that Horace Greeley had taken his breakfast in company with two colored men at a boarding-house in Barclay street. The story was eagerly copied by the enemies of the Tribune, and at length Horace Greeley condescended to notice it. The point of his most happy and annihilating reply is contained in these, its closing sentences: "We have never associated with blacks; never eaten with them; and yet it is quite probable that if we *had* seen two cleanly, decent colored persons sitting down at a second table in another room just as we were finishing our breakfast, we might have gone away without thinking or caring about the matter. We choose our own company in all things, and that of our own race, but cherish little of that spirit which for eighteen centuries has held the kindred of M. M. Noah accursed of God and man, outlawed and outcast, and unfit to be the associates of Christians, Mussulmen, or even self-respecting Pagans. Where there are thousands who would not eat with a negro, there are (or lately were) tens of thousands who would not eat with a Jew. We leave to such renegades as the Judge of Israel the stirring up of prejudices and the prating of 'usages of society,' which over half the world make him an abhorrence, as they not long since would have done here; we treat all men according to what they are and not whence they spring. That he is a knave, we think much to his discredit; that he is a Jew nothing, however unfortunate it may be for that luckless people." This was a hit not more hard than fair. The 'Judge of Israel,' it is said, felt it acutely.

The Tribune continued to prosper. It ended the second volume with a circulation of twenty thousand, and an advertising patronage so extensive as to compel the issue of frequent supplements. The position of its chief editor grew in importance. His advice and co-operation were sought by so many persons and for so many objects, that he was obliged to keep a notice standing, which requested "all who would see him personally in his office, to call between the hours of 8 and 9 A. M., and 5 and 6 P. M., unless the most imperative necessity dictate a different hour. If this notice be disregarded, he will be compelled to abandon his office and seek elsewhere a chance for an hour's uninterrupted devotion to his daily duties."

His first set lecture in New York is thus announced, January 3d, 1843: "Horace Greeley will lecture before the New York Lyceum at the Tabernacle, this evening. Subject, 'Human Life.' The lecture will commence at half past 7, precisely. If those who care to hear it will sit near the desk, they will favor the lecturer's weak and husky voice."

CHAPTER XVIII.

THE TRIBUNE AND J. FENIMORE COOPER.

The libel—Horace Greeley's narrative of the trial—He reviews the opening speech of Mr. Cooper's counsel—A striking illustration—He addresses the jury—Mr. Cooper sums up—Horace Greeley comments on the speech of the novelist—In doing so he perpetrates new libels—The verdict—Mr. Greeley's remarks on the same—Strikes a bee-line for New York—A new suit—An imaginary case.

A MAN is never so characteristic as when he sports. There was something in the warfare waged by the author of the Leatherstocking against the press, and particularly in his suit of the Tribune for libel, that appealed so strongly to Horace Greeley's sense of the comic, that he seldom alluded to it without, apparently, falling into a paroxysm of mirth. Some of his most humorous passages were written in connection with what he called ' the Cooperage of the Tribune.' To that affair, therefore, it is proper that a short chapter should be devoted, before pursuing further the History of the Tribune.

The matter alleged to be libelous appeared in the Tribune, Nov. 17th, 1841. The trial took place at Saratoga, Dec. 9th, 1842. Mr. Greeley defended the suit in person, and, on returning to New York, wrote a long and ludicrous account of the trial, which occupied eleven columns and a quarter in the Tribune of Dec. 12th. For that number of the paper there was such a demand, that the account of the trial was, soon after, re-published in a pamphlet, of which this chapter will be little more than a condensation.

The libel—such as it was—the reader may find lurking in the following epistle :

" MR. FENIMORE COOPER AND HIS LIBELS.

" FONDA, Nov. 17, 1841.

" TO THE EDITOR OF THE TRIBUNE :—

" The Circuit Court now sitting here is to be occupied chiefly with the legal griefs of Mr. Fenimore Cooper, who has determined to avenge himself upon the Press for having contributed by its criticisms to his waning popularity as a novelist.

" The 'handsome Mr. Effingham' has three cases of issue here, two of which are against Col. Webb, Editor of the Courier and Enquirer, and one against Mr. Weed, Editor of the Albany Evening Journal.

" Mr. Weed not appearing on Monday, (the first day of court,) Cooper moved for judgment by default, as Mr. Weed's counsel had not arrived. Col. Webb, who on passing through Albany, called at Mr. Weed's house, and learned that his wife was seriously and his daughter dangerously ill, requested Mr. Sacia to state the facts to the Court, and ask a day's delay. Mr. Sacia made, at the same time, an appeal to Mr. Cooper's humanity. But that appeal, of course, was an unavailing one. The novelist pushed his advantage. The Court, however, ordered the cause to go over till the next day, with the understanding that the default should be entered then if Mr. Weed did not appear. Col. Webb then despatched a messenger to Mr. Weed with this information. The messenger returned with a letter from Mr. Weed, stating that his daughter lay very ill, and that he would not leave her while she was suffering or in danger Mr. Cooper, therefore, immediately moved for his default. Mr. Sacia interposed again for time, but it was denied. A jury was empan-

10*

eled to assess Mr. Effingham's damages. · The trial, of course, was ex-parte, Mr. Weed being absent and defenceless.   Cooper's lawyer made a wordy, windy, abusive appeal for exemplary damages.   The jury retired, under a strong charge against Mr. Weed from Judge Willard, and after remaining in their room till twelve o'clock at night, sealed a verdict for $400 for Mr. Effing-ham, which was delivered to the Court this morning.

"This meager verdict, under the circumstances, is a severe and mortifying rebuke to Cooper, who had everything his own way.

"The value of Mr. Cooper's character, therefore, has been judicially ascer-tained.

"It is worth exactly four hundred dollars.

"Col. Webb's trial comes on this afternoon ; his counsel, A. L. Jordan, Esq., having just arrived in the up train.   Cooper will be blown sky high.   This experiment upon the Editor of the Courier and Enquirer, I predict, will cure the ' handsome Mr. Effingham' of his monomania for libels."

The rest of the story shall be given here in Mr. Greeley's own words.   He begins the narrative thus :—

"The responsible Editor of the Tribune returned yesterday morning from a week's journey to and sojourn in the County of Saratoga, having been thereto urgently persuaded by a Supreme Court writ, requiring him to answer to the declaration of Mr. J. Fenimore Cooper in an action for Libel.

"This suit was originally to have been tried at the May Circuit at Ballston ; but neither Fenimore (who was then engaged in the Coopering of Col. Stone of the Commercial) nor we had time to attend to it—so it went over to this term, which opened at Ballston Spa on Monday, Dec. 5th.   We arrived on the ground at eleven o'clock of that day, and found the plaintiff and his lawyers ready for us, our case No. 10 on the calendar, and of course a good prospect of an early trial ; but an important case involving Water-rights came in ahead of us (No. 8) taking two days, and it was half-past 10, A.M., of Friday, before ours was reached—very fortunately for us, as we had no lawyer, had never talked over the case with one, or made any preparation whatever, save in thought, and had not even found time to read the papers pertaining to it till we arrived at Ballston.

"The delay in reaching the case gave us time for all ; and that we did not employ lawyers to aid in our conduct or defense proceeded from no want of confidence in or deference to the many eminent members of the Bar there in attendance, beside Mr. Cooper's three able counsel, but simply from the fact that we wished to present to the Court some considerations which we thought had been overlooked or overborne in the recent Trials of the Press for Libel before our Supreme and Circuit Courts, and which, since they appealed more directly and forcibly to the experience of Editors than of Lawyers, we presumed an ordinary editor might present as plainly and fully as an able lawyer. We wished to place before the Court and the country those views which we understand the Press to maintain with us of its own position, duties, responsibilities, and rights, as affected by the practical construction given of late years in this State to the Law of Libel, and its application to editors and journals. Understanding that we could not appear both in person and by counsel, we chose the former; though on trial we found our opponent was permitted to do what we supposed we could not. So much by way of explanation to the many able and worthy lawyers in attendance on the Circuit, from whom we received every kindness, who would doubtless have aided us most cheerfully if we had required it, and would have conducted our case far more skillfully than we either expected or cared to do. We had not appeared there to be saved from a verdict by any nice technicality or legal subtlety.

"The case was opened to the Court and Jury by Richard Cooper, nephew and attorney of the plaintiff, in a speech of decided pertinence and force. * * * Mr. R. Cooper has had much experience in this class of cases, and is a young man of considerable talent. His manner is the only fault about him, being too elaborate and pompous, and his diction too bombastic to produce the best effect on an unsophisticated auditory. If he will only contrive to correct this, he will yet make a figure at the Bar—or rather, he will make less figure and do more execution. The force of his speech was marred by Fenimore's continually interrupting to dictate and suggest to him ideas when he would have done much better if left alone. For instance: Fenimore instructed him to say, that our letter from Fonda above recited purported to be from the 'correspondent of the Tribune,' and thence to draw and press on the Jury the inference that the letter was written by some of our own *corps*, whom we had sent to Fonda to report these trials. This inference we were obliged to repel in our reply, by showing that the article plainly read 'correspondence of the Tribune,' just as when a fire, a storm, or some other notable event occurs in any part of the country or world, and a friend who happens to be there, sits down and dispatches us a letter by the first mail to give us early advices, though he has no connection with us but by subscription and good will, and perhaps never wrote a line to us in his life till now.

* * * * * * * * *

"The next step in Mr. R. Cooper's opening: We had, to the Declaration against us, pleaded the General Issue—that is Not Guilty of libeling Mr. Cooper, at the same time fully admitting that we had published all that he *called* our libels on him, and desiring to put in issue only the fact of their being or not being libels, and have the verdict turn on that issue. But Mr. Cooper told the Jury (and we found, to our cost, that this was New York Supreme and Circuit Court law) that *by pleading Not Guilty we had legally admitted ourselves to be Guilty*—that all that was necessary for the plaintiff under that plea was to put in our admission of publication, and then the Jury had nothing to do but to assess the plaintiff's damages under the direction of the Court. In short, we were made to understand that there was no way under Heaven—we beg pardon; under New York Supreme Court Law—in which the editor of a newspaper could plead to an action for libel that the matter charged upon him as libelous was not in its nature or intent a libel, but simply a statement, according to the best of his knowledge and belief, of some notorious and every way public transaction, or his own honest comments thereon; and ask the Jury to decide whether the plaintiff's averment or his answers thereto be the truth! To illustrate the beauties of 'the perfection of human reason'—always intending New York Circuit and Supreme Court reason—on this subject, and to show the perfect soundness and pertinence of Mr. Cooper's logic according to the decisions of these Courts, we will give an example.

"Our police reporter, say this evening, shall bring in on his chronicle of daily occurrences the following:

" 'A hatchet-faced chap, with mouse-colored whiskers, who gave the name of John Smith, was brought in by a watchman who found him lying drunk in the gutter. After a suitable admonition from the Justice, and on payment of the usual fine, he was discharged.'

"Now, our reporter, who, no more than we, ever before heard of *this* John Smith, is only ambitious to do his duty correctly and thoroughly, to make his description accurate and graphic, and perhaps to protect better men who rejoice in the cognomen of John Smith, from being confounded with this one in the popular rumor of his misadventure. If the paragraph should come under our notice, we should probably strike it out altogether, as relating to a subject of no public moment, and likely to crowd out better matter. But we do not see it, and in it goes: Well: John Smith, who ' acknowledges the corn ' as to being accidentally drunk and getting into the watch-house, is not willing to rest under the imputation of being hatched-faced and having mouse-colored whiskers, retains Mr. Richard Cooper—for he could not do better—and commences an action for libel against us. We take the best legal advice, and are told that we must *demur* to the Declaration—that is, go before a court without jury, where no facts can be shown, and maintain that the matter charged as uttered by us is not libelous. But Mr. R. Cooper meets us there and says justly : ' How is the court to decide without evidence that this matter is not libelous ? If it was written and inserted for the express purpose of ridiculing and bringing into contempt my client, it clearly *is* libelous. And then as to damages : My client is neither rich nor a great man, but his character, in his own circle, is both dear and valuable to him. We shall be able to show on trial that he was on the point of contracting marriage with the daughter of the keeper of the most fashionable and lucrative oyster-cellar in Orange street, whose nerves were so shocked at the idea of her intended having a ' hatchet face and mouse-colored whiskers,' that she fainted outright on reading the paragraph (copied from your paper into the next day's 'Sun'), and was not brought to until a whole bucket of oysters which she had just opened had been poured over her in a hurried mistake for water. Since then, she has frequent relapses and shuddering, especially when my client's name is mentioned, and utterly refuses to see or speak of him. The match is dead broke, and my client loses thereby a capital home, where victuals are more plentiful and the supply more steady than it has been his fortune to find them for the last year or two. He loses, with all this, a prospective interest in the concern, and is left utterly without business or means of support except this suit. Besides, how can you tell, in the absence of all testimony, that the editor was not paid to insert this villanous description of my client, by some envious rival for the affections of the oyster-maid, who calculates both to gratify his spite and advance his lately hopeless wooing? In that case, it certainly is a libel. We affirm this to be the case, and you are bound to presume that it is. The demurrer must be overruled.' And so it must be. No judge could decide otherwise.

"Now we are thrown back upon a dilemma : Either we must plead *Justification*, in which case *we admit that our publication was on its face a libel;* and now, woe to us if we cannot prove Mr. Cooper's client's face as sharp, and his whiskers of the precise color as stated. A shade more or less ruins us. For, be it known, by attempting a Justification we have not merely admitted our offense to be a libel, but *our plea is an aggravation of the libel*, and entitles the plaintiff to recover higher and more exemplary damages. But we have just one chance more : to plead the *general issue*—to wit, that we *did not* libel the said John Smith, and go into court prepared to show that we had no malice toward or intent to injure Mr. Smith, never heard of him before, and have done all we knew how to make him reparation—in short, that we have done and intended nothing which brings us fairly within the iron grasp of the law of libel. But here again, while trying our best to get in somehow a plea of Not Guilty, we have actually pleaded Guilty!—so says the Supreme Court law of New York—our admitted publication (no matter of what) concerning John Smith proves irresistibly that we *have* libeled him—we are not entitled in any way whatever to go to the Jury with evidence tending to show that our publication is *not* a libel—or, in overthrow of the legal *presumption* of malice, to show that there actually *was* none. All that we possibly can offer must be taken into account merely in mitigation of damages. *Our* hide is on the fence, you see, any how.

"But to return to Richard's argument at Ballston. He put very strongly against us the fact that our Fonda correspondent (see Declaration above) considered Fenimore's verdict there a meager one. 'Gentlemen of the jury,' said he, 'see how these editors rejoice and exult when they get off with so light a verdict as $400 ! They consider it a triumph over the law and the defendant They don't consider that amount anything. If you mean to vindicate the law and the character of my client, you see you must give much more than this.'

This was a good point, but not quite fair. The exultation over the ' meager verdizt' was expressly in view of the fact, that the cause was *undefended*—that Fenimore and his counsel had it all their own way, evidence, argument, charge, and all. Still, Richard had a good chance here to appeal for a large verdict, and he did it well.

" On one other point Richard talked more like a cheap lawyer and less like a—like what we had expected of him—than through the general course of his argument. In his pleadings, he had set forth Horace Greeley and Thomas Mc-Elrath as *Editors* and Proprietors of the Tribune, and we readily enough admitted whatever he chose to assert about us except the essential thing in dis pute between us. Well, on the strength of this he puts it to the Court and Jury, that Thomas McElrath is one of the Editors of the Tribune, and that he, being (having been) a lawyer, would have been in Court to defend this suit, if there was any valid defense to be made. This, of course, went very hard against us ; and it was to no purpose that we informed him that Thomas McElrath, though legally implicated in it, had nothing to do practically with this matter—(all which he knew very well long before)—and that the other defendant is the man who does whatever libeling is done in the Tribune, and holds himself everywhere responsible for it. We presume there is not much doubt even so far off as Cooperstown as to who edits the Tribune, and who wrote the editorial about the Fonda business. (In point of fact, the real and palpable defendant in this suit never even conversed with his partner a quar-ter of an hour altogether about this subject, considering it entirely his own job ; and the plaintiff himself, in conversation with Mr. McElrath, in the pres-ence of *his attorney*, had fully exonerated Mr. M. from anything more than legal liability.) But Richard was on his legs as a lawyer—he pointed to the seal on his bond—and therefore insisted that Thomas McElrath was art and part in the alleged libel, not only legally, but actually, and would have been present to respond to it if he had deemed it susceptible of defense ! As a lawyer, we suppose this was right ; but, as an Editor and a man, we could not have done it."

' Richard' gave way, and ' Horace' addressed the jury in a speech of fifty minutes, which need not be inserted here, because all its leading ideas are contained in the narrative. It was a convincing argument, so far as the reason and justice of the case were concern-ed ; and, in any court where reason and justice bore sway, would have gained the case. " Should you find, gentleman," concluded Mr. Greeley, " that I had no right to express an opinion as to the honor and magnanimity of Mr. Cooper, in pushing his case to a trial as related, you will of course compel me to pay whatever damage has been done to his character by such expression, followed and accompanied by his own statement of the whole matter. I will not predict your estimate, gentlemen, but I may express my profound conviction that no opinion which Mr. Cooper might choose to express of any act of my life—no construction he could put upon my conduct or motives, could possibly damage me to an extent which would entitle or incline me to ask damages at your hands.

"But, gentlemen, you are bound to consider—you cannot refuse to consider, that if you condemn me to pay any sum whatever for this expression of my opinions on his conduct, you thereby seal your own lips, with those of your neighbors and countrymen, against any such expression in this or any other case ; you will no longer have a right to censure the rich man who harasses his poor neighbor with vexatious lawsuits merely to oppress and ruin him, but will be liable by your own verdict to prosecution and damages whenever you shall feel constrained to condemn what appears to you injustice, oppression, or littleness, no matter how flagrant the case may be.

"Gentlemen of the Jury, my character, my reputation are in your hands. I think I may say that I commit them to your keeping untarnished ; I will not doubt that you will return them to me unsullied. I ask of you no mercy, but justice. I have not sought this issue ; but neither have I feared nor shunned it. Should you render the verdict against me, I shall deplore far more than any pecuniary consequence the stigma of libeler which your verdict would tend to cast upon me—an imputation which I was never, till now, called to repel before a jury of my countrymen. But, gentlemen, feeling no consciousness of *deserving* such a stigma—feeling, at this moment, as ever, a profound conviction that I *do not* deserve it, I shall yet be consoled by the reflection that many nobler and worthier than I have suffered far more than any judgment here could inflict on me for the Rights of Free Speech and Opinion—the right of rebuking oppression and meanness in the language of manly sincerity and honest feeling. By their example, may I still be upheld and strengthened. Gentlemen, I fearlessly await your decision !"

Mr. Greeley resumes his narrative :

"Mr. J. Fenimore Cooper summed up in person the cause for the prosecution. He commenced by giving at length the reasons which had induced him to bring this suit in Saratoga. The last and only one that made any impression

on our mind was this, that he had heard a great deal of good of the people of
Saratoga, and wished to form a better acquaintance with them. (Of course
this desire was very flattering; but we hope the Saratogans won't feel too
proud to speak to common folks hereafter, for we want liberty to go there again
next summer.)

" Mr. Cooper now walked into the Public Press and its alleged abuses, arro-
gant pretensions, its interference in this case, probable motives, etc., but the
public are already aware of his sentiments respecting the Press, and would
not thank us to recapitulate them. His stories of editors publishing truth and
falsehood with equal relish may have foundation in individual cases, but certainly none in general practice. No class of men spend a tenth part so much
time or money in endeavoring to procure the earliest and best information
from all quarters, as it is their duty to do. Occasionally an erroneous or utterly false statement gets into print and is copied—for editors cannot intuitively separate all truth from falsehood—but the evil arises mainly from the circumstance that others than editors are often the spectators of events demand-
ing publicity; since we cannot tell where the next man is to be killed, or the
next storm rage, or the next important cause to be tried: if we had the
power of prophecy, it would then be time to invent some steam-lightning
balloon, and have a reporter ready on the spot the moment before any notable
event should occur. This would do it; but now we luckless editors must too
often depend on the observation and reports of those who are less observant,
less careful, possibly in some cases less sagacious, than those of our own tribe.
Our limitations are not unlike those of Mr. Weller, Junior, as stated while
under cross-examination in the case of Bardell vs. Pickwick :

" ' Yes, I have eyes,' replied Sam, ' and that's just it. If they was a pair
of patent double million magnifyin' gas microscopes of hextra power, p'raps
I might be able to see through a flight of stairs and a deal door, but bein'
only eyes, you see, my wision's limited.'

" Fenimore proceeded to consider our defense, which he used up in five minutes, by pronouncing it no defence at all! It had nothing to do with the matter in issue whatever, and we must be very green if we meant to be serious
in offering it. (We *were* rather green in Supreme Court libel law, that's a
fact; but we were put to school soon after, and have already run up quite a
little bill for tuition, which is one sign of progress.) His Honor the Judge
would tell the Jury that our law was no law whatever, or had nothing to do
with this case. (So he did—Cooper was right here.) In short, our speech
could not have been meant to apply to this case, but was probably the scrap-
ings of our editorial closet—mere odds and ends—what the editors call ' Balaam.' Here followed a historical digression, concerning what editors call
' Balaam,' which, as it was intended to illustrate the irrelevancy of our whole
argument, we thought very pertinent. It wound up with what was meant for
a joke about Balaam and his ass, which of course was a good thing; but its

point wholly escaped us, and we believe the auditors were equally unfortunate. However, the wag himself appreciated and enjoyed it.

"There were several other jokes (we suppose they were) uttered in the course of this lively speech, but we did n't get into their merits, (probably not being in the best humor for joking;) but one we remembered because it was really good, and came down to our comprehension. Fenimore was replying to our remarks about the 'handsome Mr. Effingham,' (see speech,) when he observed that if we *should* sue him for libel in 'pronouncing us not handsome, he should not plead the *General Issue*, but *Justify.*' That was a neat hit, and well planted. We can tell him, however, that if the Court should rule as hard against him as it does against editors when they undertake to justify, he would find it difficult to get in the testimony to establish a matter even so plain as our plainness.

"Fenimore now took up the Fonda libel suit, and fought the whole battle over again, from beginning to end. Now we had scarcely touched on this, supposing that, since we did not justify, we could only refer to the statements contained in the publications put in issue between us, and that the Judge would check us, if we went beyond these. Fenimore, however, had no trouble; said whatever he pleased—much of which would have been very pertinent if *he*, instead of we, had been on trial—showed that he did not believe anything of Mr. Weed's family being sick at the time of the Fonda Trials, why he did not, &c., &c. We thought he might have reserved all this till we got down to dinner, which everybody was now hungry for, and where it would have been more in place than addressed to the Jury.

"Knowing what we positively did and do of the severe illness of the wife of Mr. Weed, and the dangerous state of his eldest daughter at the time of the Fonda Trials in question—regarding them as we do—the jokes attempted to be cut by Fenimore over their condition—his talk of the story grewing up from one girl to the mother and three or four daughters—his fun about their probably having the Asiatic cholera among them or some other contagious disease, &c., &c., however it may have sounded to others, did seem to us rather inhu——— Hallo there! we had like to have put our foot right into it again, after all our tuition. We mean to say, considering that, just the day before, Mr. Weed had been choked by his counsel into surrendering at discretion to Fenimore, being assured (correctly) by said counsel that, as the law is now expounded and administered by the Supreme Court, he had no earthly choice but to bow his neck to the yoke, pay all that might be claimed of him and publish whatever humiliations should be required, or else prepare to be immediately ruined by the suits which Fenimore and Richard had already commenced or were getting ready for him—considering all this, and how much Mr. Weed has paid and must pay towards his subsistence—how keenly W. has had to smart for speaking his mind of him—we did not think that Fenimore's talk at this time and place of Weed's family, and of Weed himself as a man so paltry that he would pretend sickness in his family as an excuse to keep away from Court, and resort to trick after trick to put off his case for a day or two—it seemed to us, considering the present relations of the parties, most ungen—— There we go again! We mean to say that the whole of this part of Mr. Cooper's speech grated upon our feelings rather harshly. We believe *that* isn't a libel. (This talking with a gag in the mouth is rather awkward at first, but we'll get the hang of it in time. Have patience with us, Fenimore on one side and the Public on the other, till we nick it.)

*　　*　　*　　*　　*　　*　　*　　*　　*

" Personally, Fenimore treated us pretty well on this trial—let us thank him for that—and so much the more that he did it quite at the expense of his consistency and his logic. For, after stating plumply that he considered us the best of the whole Press-gang he had been fighting with, he yet went on to argue that all we had done and attempted with the intent of rendering him strict justice, had been in *aggravation* of our original trespass! Yes, there he stood, saying one moment that we were, on the whole, rather a clever fellow, and every other arguing that we had done nothing but to injure him wantonly and maliciously at first, and then all in our power to aggravate that injury! (What a set the rest of us must be!)

" And here is where he hit us hard for the first time. He had talked over an hour without gaining, as we could perceive, an inch of ground. When his compliment was put in, we supposed he was going on to say he was satisfied with our explanation of the matter and our intentions to do him justice, and would now throw up the case. But instead of this he took a sheer the other way, and came down upon us with the assertion that our publishing his statement of the Fonda business with our comments, was an aggravation of our original offense—was in effect adding insult to injury!

.　*　　*　　*　　*　　*　　*　　*

" There was a little point made by the prosecution which seemed to us *too* little. Our Fonda letter had averred that Cooper had three libel-suits coming off there at that Circuit—two against Webb, one against Weed. Richard and Fenimore argued that this was a lie—the one against Weed was all. The nicety of the distinction here taken will be appreciated when we explain that the suits against Webb were *indictments* for libels on J. Fenimore Cooper!

" We supposed that Fenimore would pile up the law against us, but were disappointed. He merely cited *the last case* decided against an Editor by the Supreme Court of this State. Of course, it was very fierce against Editors and their libels, but did not strike us as at all meeting the issue we had raised, or covering the grounds on which this case ought to have been decided.

" Fenimore closed very effectively with an appeal for his character, and a picture of the sufferings of his wife and family—his grown-up daughters often suffused in tears by these attacks on their father. Some said this was mawkish, but we consider it good, and think it told. We have a different theory as to what the girls were crying for, but we won't state it lest another dose of Supreme Court law be administered to us. ('Not any more at present, I thank ye.')

"Fenimore closed something before two o'clock, having spoken over an hour and a half. If he had not wasted so much time in promising to make but a short speech and to close directly, he could have got through considerably sooner. Then he did wrong to Richard by continually recurring to and fulsome eulogiums on the argument of 'my learned kinsman.' Richard had made a good speech and an effective one—no mistake about it—and Fenimore must mar it first by needless, provoking interruptions, and then by praises which, though deserved, were horribly out of place and out of taste. Fenimore, my friend, you and I had better abandon the Bar—we are not likely either of us to cut much of a figure there. Let us quit before we make ourselves ridiculous.

"His Honor Judge Willard occupied a brief half hour in charging the Jury. We could not decently appear occupied in taking down this Charge, and no one else did it—so we must speak of it with great circumspection. That he would go dead against us on the Law of the case we knew right well, from his decisions and charges on similar trials before. Not having his Law points before us, we shall not venture to speak of them. Suffice it to say, that they were New York Supreme and Circuit Court Law—no better and no worse than he has measured off to several editorial culprits before us. They are the settled maxims of the Supreme Court of this State in regard to the law of libel as applied to Editors and Newspapers, and we must have been a goose to expect any better than had been served out to our betters. The Judge was hardly, if at all, at liberty to know or tolerate any other.

*　　　*　　　*　　　*　　　*　　　*　　　*

"But we have filled our paper, and must close. The Judge charged very hard against us on the facts of the case, as calling for a pretty sizable verdict—our legal guilt had of course been settled long before in the Supreme Court.

"When the Charge commenced, we would not have given Fenimore the first red cent for his verdict; when it closed, we understood that we were booked to suffer some. If the Jury had returned a verdict in our favor, the Judge must have been constrained by his charge to set it aside, as contrary to law.

"The Jury retired about half-past two, and the rest of us went to dinner. The Jury were hungry too, and did not stay out long. On comparing notes, there were *seven* of them for a verdict of $100, *two* for $200, and *three* for $500. They added these sums up—total $2,600—divided by 12, and the dividend was a little over $200; so they called it $200 damages and six cents costs, which of course carries full costs against us. We went back from dinner, took the verdict in all meekness, took a sleigh, and struck a bee-line for New York."

"Thus for the Tribune the rub-a-dub is over; the adze we trust laid aside, the staves all in their places; the hoops tightly driven; and the heading not particularly out of order. Nothing remains but to pay piper, or cooper, or whatever; and that shall be promptly attended to.

"Yes, Fenimore shall have his $200. To be sure, we don't exactly see how we came to owe him that sum; but he has won it, and shall be paid. 'The court awards it, and the law doth give it.' We should like to meet him and have a social chat over the whole business, now it is over. There has been a good deal of fun in it, come to look back; and if he has as little ill-will toward us as we bear to him, there shall never be another hard thought between us. We don't blame him a bit for the whole matter; he thought we injured him, sued us, and got his pay. Since the Jury have cut down his little bill from $3,000 to $200, we won't higgle a bit about the balance, but pay it on sight. In fact, we rather like the idea of being so munificent a patron (for our means) of American Literature; and are glad to do anything for one of the most creditable (of old) of our authors, who are now generally reduced to any shift for a living by that grand National rascality and greater folly, the denial of International Copyright. ('My pensive public,' don't flatter yourself that we are to be rendered mealy-mouthed toward you by our buffeting. We shall put it to your iniquities just as straight as a loon's leg, calling a spade a spade, and not an oblong garden implement, until the judicial construction of the law of libel shall take another hitch, and its penalties be invoked to shield communities as well as individuals from censure for their transgressions. Till then, keep a bright look out!)

"And Richard, too, shall have *his* share of 'the spoils of victory.' He has earned them fairly, and, in the main, like a gentleman—making us no needless trouble, and we presume no needless expense. All was fair and above board, save some little specks in his opening of the case, which we noticed some hours ago, and have long since forgiven. For the rest, we rather like what we have seen of him; and if anybody has any law business in Otsego, or any libel suits to prosecute anywhere, we heartily recommend Richard to do the work, warranting the client to be handsomely taken in and done for throughout. (There's a puff, now, a man may be proud of. We don't give such every day out of pure kindness. It was Fenimore, we believe, that said on the trial, that our word went a great way in this country.) Can we say a good word for *you*, gallant foeman? We'll praise any thing of yours we have read except the Monikins.

"But sadder thoughts rush in on us in closing. Our case is well enough, or of no moment; but we cannot resist the conviction that by the result of these Cooper libel-suits, and by the Judicial constructions which produce that result, the Liberty of the Press—its proper influence and respectability, its power to rebuke wrong and to exert a salutary influence upon the Public Morals is fearfully impaired. We do not see how any paper can exist, and speak and act worthily and usefully in this State, without subjecting itself daily to innumerable, unjust and crushing prosecutions and indictments for libel. Even if Juries could have nerves of iron to say and do what they really think right between man and man, the costs of such prosecution would ruin any journal. But the Liberty of the Press has often been compelled to appeal from the bench to the people. It will do so now, and we will not doubt with success. Let not, then, the wrong-doer who is cunning enough to keep the blind side of the law, the swindling banker who has spirited away the means of the widow and orphan, the libertine who has dragged a fresh victim to his lair, imagine that they are permanently shielded, by this misapplication of the law of libel, from fearless exposure to public scrutiny and indignation by the eagle gaze of an unfettered Press. Clouds and darkness may for the moment rest upon it, but they cannot, in the nature of things, endure. In the very gloom of its present humiliation we read the prediction of its speedy and certain restoration to its rights and its true dignity—to a sphere not of legal sufferance merely, but of admitted usefulness and honor."

This narrative, which came within three-quarters of a column of filling the entire inside of the Tribune, and must have covered fifty pages of foolscap, was written at the rate of about a column an hour. It set the town laughing, elicited favorable notices from more than two hundred papers, and provoked the novelist to new anger, and another suit; in which the damages were laid at three thousand dollars. "We have a lively trust, however," said the offending editor, "that we shall convince the jury that we do not owe him the first red cent of it." This is one paragraph of the new complaint :

"And the said plaintiff further says and avers that the syllables inhu, followed by a dash, when they occur in the publication hereinafter set forth, as follows, to wit, inhu——, were meant and intended by the said defendants for the word inhuman, and that the said defendants, in using the aforesaid syllables, followed by a dash as aforesaid, in connection with the context, intended to convey, and did convey, the idea that the said plaintiff, on the occasion referred to in that part of said publication, had acted in an inhuman manner. And the said plaintiff also avers that the syllable ungen, followed by a dash, as follows, to wit, ungen——, when they occur in the publication hereinafter set forth, were meant and intended by the said defendants either for the word ungenerous or the word ungentlemanly, and that the said defendants, in using the syllables last aforesaid, followed by a dash as aforesaid, in connection with the context, intended to convey, and did convey, the idea that the said plaintiff, on the occasion referred to in that part of said publication, had acted either in a most ungenerous or a most ungentlemanly manner, to wit, at the place and in the county aforesaid.''

In an article commenting upon the writ, the editor, after repelling the charge, that his account of the trial was 'replete with errors of fact,' pointedly addressed his distinguished adversary thus:

"But, Fenimore, *do* hear reason a minute. This whole business is ridiculous. If you would *simply* sue those of the Press-gang who displease you, it would not be so bad; but you sue and write too, which is not the fair thing. What use in belittling the profession of Literature by appealing from its courts to those of Law? We ought to litigate *upward*, not down. Now, Fenimore, you push a very good quill of your own except when you attempt to be funny—there you break down. But in the way of cutting and slashing you are No. one, and you don't seem averse to it either. Then why not settle this difference at the point of the pen? We hereby tender you a column a day of The Tribune for ten days, promising to publish *verbatim* whatever you may write and put your name to—and to publish it in both our daily and weekly papers. You may give your view of the whole controversy between yourself and the Press, tell your story of the Ballston Trial, and cut us up to your heart's content. We will further agree not to write over two columns in reply to the whole. Now why is not this better than invoking the aid of John Doe and Richard Roe (no offense to Judge W. and your 'learned kinsman!') in the premises? Be wise, now, most chivalrous antagonist, and don't detract from the dignity of your profession!"

Mr. Cooper, we may infer, *became* wise; for the suit never came to trial; nor did he accept the Tribune's offer of a column a day for ten days. For one more editorial article on the subject room must be afforded, and with that, our chapter on the Cooperage of the Tribune may have an end.

"Our friend Fenimore Cooper, it will be remembered, chivalrously declared, in his summing up at Ballston, that if we were to sue him for a libel in asserting our personal uncomeliness, he should not plead the *General Issue*, but *Justify*. To a plain man, this would seem an easy and safe course. But let us try it: Fenimore has the audacity to say we are not handsome; we employ Richard—we presume he has no aversion to a good fee, even if made of the Editorial 'sixpences' Fenimore dilated on—and commence our action, laying the venue in St. Lawrence, Alleghany, or some other county where our personal appearance is not notorious; and, if the Judge should be a friend of ours, so much the better. Well: Fenimore boldly pleads *Justification*, thinking it as easy as not. But how is he to establish it? We of course should not be so green as to attend the Trial in person on such an issue—no man is obliged to make out his adversary's case—but would leave it all to Richard, and the help the Judge might properly give him. So the case is on, and Fenimore undertakes the Justification, which of course admits and aggravates the libel; so our side is all made out. But let us see how *he* gets along: of course, he will not think of offering witnesses to swear point-blank that we are homely—that, if he did not know it, the Judge would soon tell him would be a simple *opinion*, which would not do to go to a Jury; he must present *facts*.

"*Fenimore*.—'Well, then, your Honor, I offer to prove by this witness that the plaintiff is tow-headed, and half bald at that; he is long-legged, gaunt, and most cadaverous of visage—*ergo*, homely.'

"*Judge*.— How does that follow? Light hair and fair face bespeak a purely Saxon ancestry, and were honorable in the good old days: *I* rule that they are comely. Thin locks bring out the phrenological developments, you see, and give dignity and massiveness to the aspect; and as to slenderness, what do our dandies lace for if *that* is not graceful? *They* ought to know what is attractive, I reckon. No, sir, your proof is irrelevant, and I rule it out.'

"*Fenimore* (the sweat starting).—'Well, your Honor, I have evidence to prove the said plaintiff slouching in dress; goes bent like a hoop, and so rocking in gait that he walks down both sides of a street at once.'

"*Judge*.—'*That* to prove homeliness? I hope you don't expect a man of ideas to spend his precious time before a looking-glass? It would be robbing the public. "Bent," do you say? Isn't the curve the true line of beauty, I'd like to know? Where were you brought up? As to walking, you don't expect "a man of mark," as you called him at Ballston, to be quite as dapper and pert as a footman, whose walk is his hourly study and his nightly dream —its perfection the sum of his ambition! Great ideas of beauty *you* must have! That evidence won't answer.'

"Now, Fenimore, brother in adversity! wouldn't you begin to have a realizing sense of your awful situation? Wouldn't you begin to wish yourself somewhere else, and a great deal further, before you came into Court to justify legally an *opinion*? Wouldn't you begin to perceive that the application of the Law of Libel in its strictness to a mere expression of opinion is absurd, mistaken, and tyrannical?

"Of course, we shan't take advantage of your exposed and perilous condition, for we are meek and forgiving, with a hearty disrelish for the machinery of the law. But if we *had* a mind to take hold of you, with Richard to help us, and the Supreme Court's ruling in actions of libel at our back, *wouldn't* you catch it? We should get the whole Fund back again, and give a dinner to the numerous Editorial contributors. *That* dinner would be worth attending, Fenimore; and we'll warrant the jokes to average a good deal better than those you cracked in your speech at Ballston."

CHAPTER XIX.

THE TRIBUNE CONTINUES.

The Special Express system—Night adventures of Enoch Ward—Gig Express—Express from Halifax—Baulked by the snow-drifts—Party warfare then—Books published by Greeley and McElrath—Course of the Tribune—The Editor travels—Scenes in Washington—An incident of travel—Clay and Frelinghuysen—The exertions of Horace Greeley—Results of the defeat—The Tribune and Slavery—Burning of the Tribune Building—The Editor's reflections upon the fire.

WHAT gunpowder, improved fire-arms, and drilling have done for war, the railroad and telegraph have done for the daily press, namely, reduced success to an affair of calculation and expenditure. Twelve years ago, there was a chance for the display of individual enterprise, daring, prowess, in procuring news, and, above all, in being the *first* to announce it; which was, is, and ever will be, the point of competition with daily papers. Those were the days of the Special Expresses, which appear to have been run, regardless of expense, horseflesh, and safety, and in the running of which incredible things were achieved. Not reporters alone were then sent to remote places to report an expected speech. The reporters were accompanied, sometimes, by a rider, sometimes by a corps of printers with fonts of type, who set up the speech on the special steamboat as fast as the reporters could write it out, and had it ready for the press before the steamboat reached the city. Wonderful things were done by special express in those days; for the competition between the rival papers was intense beyond description.

Take these six paragraphs from the Tribune as the sufficient and striking record of a state of things long past away. They need no explanation or connecting remark. Perhaps they will astonish the young reader rather:

"The Governor's Message reached Wall street last evening, at nine. The contract was for three riders and ten relays of horses, and the Express was to start at 12 o'clock, M., and reach this city at 10 in the evening. It is not known here whether the arrangements at the other end of the route were strictly adhered to; but if they were, and the Express started at the hour agreed upon, it came through in nine hours, making but a fraction less than eighteen miles an hour, which seems almost incredible. It is not impossible that it started somewhat before the time agreed upon, and quite likely that extra riders and horses were employed; but be that as it may, the dispatch is almost—if not quite—unparalleled in this country."

"Our express, (Mr. Enoch Ward,) with returns of the Connecticut Election, left New Haven Monday evening, in a light sulky, at twenty-five minutes before ten o'clock, having been detained thirty-five minutes by the non-arrival of the Express locomotive from Hartford. He reached Stamford—forty miles from New Haven—in three hours. Here it commenced snowing, and the night was so exceedingly dark that he could not travel without much risk. He kept on, however, with commendable zeal, determined not to be conquered by any ordinary obstacles. Just this side of New Rochelle, and while descending a hill, he had the misfortune to run upon a horse which was apparently standing still in the road. The horse was mounted by a man who must have been asleep; otherwise he would have got out of the way. The breast of the horse came in contact with the sulky between the wheel and the shaft. The effect of the concussion was to break the wheel of the sulky by wrenching out nearly all the spokes. The night was so dark that nothing whatever could be seen, and it is not known whether the horse and the stranger received any material injury. Mr. Ward then took the harness from his horse, mounted him without a saddle, and came on to this city, a distance of seventeen miles, arriving at five o'clock on Tuesday morning."

"It will be recollected that a great ado was made upon the receipt in this city of the Acadia's news by two of our journals, inasmuch as no other paper received the advices, one of them placarding the streets with announcements that the news was received by special and exclusive express. Now, the facts are these: The Acadia arrived at Boston at half-past three o'clock, the cars leaving at four; in coming to her wharf she struck her bow against the dock and immediately reversed her wheels, put out again into the bay, and did not reach her berth until past four. But two persons, belonging to the offices of the Atlas and Times, jumped on board at the moment the ship struck the wharf, obtained their packages, and threw them into the water, whence they were taken and put into a gig and taken to the depôt. 'Thus,' said the Commercial, from which we gather the facts stated above 'the gig was the "Special Express," and its tremendous run was from Long Wharf to the depôt—about one mile!'"

"The news by the next steamer is looked for with intense interest, and in

11

order to place it before our readers at an early moment, we made arrangements some weeks since to start a horse Express from Halifax across Nova Scotia to the Bay of Fundy, there to meet a powerful steamer which will convey our Agent and Messenger to Portland. At the latter place we run a Locomotive Express to Boston, whence we express it by steam and horse-power to New York. Should no unforeseen accident occur, we will be enabled by this Express to publish the news in New York some ten, or perhaps fifteen or twenty hours before the arrival of the steamer in Boston. The extent of this enterprise may in part be judged of by the fact, that we pay no less than Eighteen Hundred Dollars for the single trip of the steamer on the Bay of Fundy! It is but fair to add that, in this Express, we were joined from the commencement by the Sun of this city, and the North American of Philadelphia; and the Journal of Commerce has also since united with us in the enterprise."

" We were beaten with the news yesterday morning, owing to circumstances which no human energy could overcome. In spite of the great snow-storm, which covered Nova Scotia with drifts several feet high, impeding and often overturning our express-sleigh—in defiance of hard ice in the Bay of Fundy and this side, often 18 inches thick, through which our steamboat had to plow her way—we brought the news through to Boston in thirty-one hours from Halifax, several hours ahead of the Cambria herself. Thence it ought to have reached this city by 6 o'clock yesterday morning, in ample season to have gone south in the regular mail train. It was delayed, however, by unforeseen and unavoidable disasters, and only reached New Haven after it should have been in this city. From New Haven it was brought hither in *four hours and a half* by our ever-trusty rider, Enoch Ward, who never lets the grass grow to the heels of *his* horses. He came in a little after 11 o'clock, but the rival express had got in over two hours earlier, having made the shortest run from Boston on record."

" The Portland Bulletin has been unintentionally led into the gross error of believing the audacious fabrication that Bennett's express came through to this city in *seven* hours and five minutes from Boston, beating ours *five* or *six* hours! That express left Boston at 11 P. M. of Wednesday, and arrived here 20 minutes past 9 on Thursday—actual time on the road, over ten hours. The Bulletin further says that our express was *sixteen* hours on the road. No such thing. We lost some fifteen minutes at the ferry on the east side of Boston. Then a very short time (instead of an hour and a half, as is reported by the express) in finding our agent in Boston; then an hour in firing up an engine and getting away from Boston, where all should have been ready for us, but was not. The locomotive was over two hours in making the run to Worcester—42 miles— though the Herald runner who came through on the arrival of the Cambria some time after, was carried over it in about half the time, with not one-fourth the delay we encountered at the depôt in Boston. (We could *guess* how all this was brought about, but it would answer no purpose now.) At Worcester, Mr. Twitchell (whom our agent on this end had only been able to find on Tuesday, having been kept two days on the route to Boston by a storm, and then finding Mr. T. absent in New Hampshire) was found in bed, but got up and put off, intending to ride but one stage. At its end, however, he found the rider he had hired sick, and had to come along himself. At one stopping-place, he found his horse amiss, and had to buy one before he could proceed. When he reached Hartford (toward morning) there was no engine fired up, no one ready, and another hour was lost *there*. At New Haven our rider was asleep, and much time was lost in finding him and getting off. Thus we lost in delays, which *we* could not foresee or prevent, over *three hours* this side of Boston ferry,—the Cambria having arrived two or three days earlier than she was expected, before our arrangements could be perfected, and on the only night of the week that the rival express could have beaten even *our* bad time, —the Long Island Railroad being obstructed with snow both before and afterward. The Herald express came in at 20 minutes past 9; our express was here at 15 minutes past 12, or *less than three* hours afterward. Such are the facts. The express for the U. S. Gazette crossed the ferry to Jersey City at 10½ instead of 11½, as we mis-stated recently."

That will do for the curiosities of the Special Express. Another feature has vanished from the press of this country, since those paragraphs were written. The leading journals are no longer *party* journals. There are no parties; and this fact has changed the look, and tone, and manner of newspapers in a remarkable degree. As a curiosity of old-fashioned party politics, and as an illustration of the element in which and with which our hero was compelled occasionally to labor, I am tempted to insert here a few paragraphs of one of his day-of-the-election articles. Think of the Tribune of *to-day*, and judge of the various progress it and the country have made, since an article like the following could have seemed at home in its columns.

THE WARDS ARE AWAKE!

" OLD FIRST! Steady and true! A split on *men* has aroused her to bring out her whole force, which will tell nobly on the Mayor. Friends! fight out your Collector, split fairly, like men, and be good friends as ever at sunset to-day; but be sure not to throw away your Assistant Alderman. We set you down 600 for Robert Smith.

"SAUCY SECOND! Never a Loco has a look here! Our friends are united, and have done their work, though making no noise about it. We count on 400 for Smith.

"GALLANT THIRD! You are wanted for the full amount! Things are altogether too sleepy here. Why won't somebody run stump, or get up a volunteer ticket? We see that the Loco-Foco Collector *has Whig ballots printed with his name on them!* This ought to arouse all the friends of the clean Whig Ticket. Come out, Whigs of the Third! and pile up 700 majority for Robert Smith! One less is unworthy of you; and you can give more if you try. But let it go at 700."

*   *   *   *   *   *   *   *   *

"BLOODY SIXTH! We won't tell all we hope from this ward, but we know Ald. CROLIUS is popular, as is OWEN W. BRENNAN, our Collector, and we feel quite sure of *their* election. We know that yesterday the Locos were afraid Shaler *would* decline, as they said his friends would vote for Crolius rather than Emmons, who is rather *too well known.* We concede 300 majority to Morris, but our friends can reduce it to 200 if they work right."

*   *   *   *   *   *   *   *   *

"EMPIRE EIGHTH! shall your faithful GEDNEY be defeated? Has he not deserved better at your hands? And SWEET, too, he was foully cheated out of his election last year by Loco-Foco fire companies brought in from the Fifteenth, and prisoners imported from Blackwell's Island. *Eighteen* of them in one house! You owe it to your candidates to elect them—you owe it still more to yourselves—and yet your Collector quarrel makes us doubt a little. Whigs of the Eighth! resolve to carry your Alderman and you WILL! Any how, Robert Smith will have a majority—we'll state it moderately at 200."

*   *   *   *   *   *   *   *   *

"BLOOMING TWELFTH! The Country Ward is steadily improving, politically as well as physically. The Whigs run their popular Alderman of last year; the Locos have made a most unpopular Ticket, which was only forced down the throats of many by virtue of the bludgeon. Heads were cracked like walnuts the night the ticket was agreed to. We say 50 for Smith, and the clean Whig ticket."

*   *   *   *   *   *   *   *   *

"Whigs of New York! THE DAY IS YOURS IF YOU WILL! But if you skulk to your chimney corners and let such a man as ROBERT SMITH be beaten by *Robert H. Morris*, you will *deserve* to be cheated, plundered and trampled on as you have been. But, No! YOU WILL NOT! On for SMITH AND VICTORY!"

We now turn over, with necessary rapidity, the pages of the third and fourth volumes of the Tribune, pausing, here and there, when something of interest respecting its editor catches our eye.

Greeley and McElrath, we observe, are engaged, somewhat extensively, in the business of publishing books. The Whig Almanac appears every year, and sells from fifteen to twenty thousand copies.
It contains statistics without end, and much literature of what may
be called the Franklin School—short, practical articles on agriculture, economy, and morals. 'Travels on the Prairies,' Ellsworth's
' Agricultural Geology,' 'Lardner's Lectures,' ' Life and Speeches of
Henry Clay,' ' Tracts on the Tariff' by Horace Greeley, ' The Farmers' Library,' are among the works published by Greeley and McElrath in the years 1843 and 1844. The business was not profitable,
I believe, and gradually the firm relinquished all their publications,
except only the Tribune and Almanac. September 1st, 1843, the
Evening Tribune began; the Semi-Weekly, May 17th, 1845.

Carlyle's Past and Present, one of the three or four Great Books
of the present generation, was published in May 1843, from a private copy, entrusted to the charge of Mr. R. W. Emerson. The
Tribune saw its merit, and gave the book a cordial welcome.
"This is a great book, a noble book," it said, in a second notice,
" and we take blame to ourself for having rashly asserted, before we
had read it thoroughly, that the author, keen-sighted at discovering
Social evils and tremendous in depicting them, was yet blind as to
their appropriate remedies. He *does* see and indicate those remedies—not entirely and in detail, but in spirit and in substance very
clearly and forcibly. There has no new work of equal practical
value with this been put forth by any writer of eminence within
the century. Although specially addressed to and treating of the
People of England, its thoughts are of immense value and general
application here, and we hope many thousand copies of the work
will instantly be put into circulation."

Later in the year the Tribune introduced to the people of the
United States, the system of Water-Cure, copying largely from European journals, and dilating in many editorial articles on the manifold and unsuspected virtues of cold water. The Erie Railroad—
that gigantic enterprise—had then and afterwards a powerful friend
and advocate in the Tribune. In behalf of the unemployed poor,
the Tribune spoke wisely, feelingly, and often. To the new Native
American Party, it gave no quarter. For Irish Repeal, it fought like
a tiger. For Protection and Clay, it could not say enough. Upon

farmers it urged the duty and policy of high farming. To the strong
unemployed young men of cities, it said repeatedly and in various
terms, 'Go forth into the Fields and Labor with your Hands.'

In the autumn, Mr. Greeley made a tour of four weeks in the Far
West, and wrote letters to the Tribune descriptive and suggestive.
In December, he spent a few days in Washington, and gave a sorry
account of the state of things in that ' magnificent mistake.'

"To a new comer," he wrote, "the Capitol wears an imposing appearance :
Nay, more. Let him view it for the first time by daylight, with the flag of
the Union floating proudly above it, (indicating that Congress is in session,)
and, if he be an American, I defy him to repress a swelling of the heart—a
glow of enthusiastic feeling. Under these free-flowing Stripes and Stars the
Representatives of the Nation are assembled in Council—under the emblem
of the National Sovereignty is in action the collective energy and embodiment
of that Sovereignty. Proud recollections of beneficent and glorious events
come thronging thickly upon him—of the Declaration of Independence, the
struggles of the Revolution, and the far more glorious peaceful advances of
the eagles of Freedom from the Alleghanies to the Falls of St. Anthony and
the banks of the Osage. An involuntary cheer rushes from his heart to his
lips, and he hastens at once to the Halls of Legislation to witness and listen
to the displays of patriotic foresight, wisdom and eloquence, there evolved.

"But here his raptures are chilled *instanter*. Entering the Capitol, he
finds its passages a series of blind, gloomy, and crooked labyrinths, through
which a stranger threads his devious way with difficulty, and not at all without inquiry and direction, to the door of the Senate or House. Here he is
met, as everywhere through the edifice, by swarms of superserviceable underlings, numerous as the frogs of Egypt, eager to manifest their official zeal
and usefulness by keeping him out or kicking him out again. He retires disgusted, and again threads the bewildering maze to the gallery, where (if of
the House) he can only look down on the noisy Bedlam in action below him—
somebody speaking and nobody listening, but a buzz of conversation, the trot-
ting of boys, the walking about of members, the writing and folding of letters, calls to order, cries of question, calls for Yeas and Nays, &c., give him
large opportunities for headache, meager ones for edification. Half an hour
will usually cure him of all passion for listening to debates in the House.
There are, of course, occasions when it is a privilege to be here, but I speak of
the general scene and impression.

" To-day, but more especially yesterday, a deplorable spectacle has been
presented here—a glaring exemplification of the terrible growth and diffusion
of office-begging. The Loco-Foco House has ordered a clean sweep of all its
underlings—door-keepers, porters, messengers, wood-carriers, &c., &c. I care

nothing for this, so far as the turned-out are concerned—let them earn a living, like other folks—but the swarms of aspirants that invaded every avenue and hall of the Capitol, making doubly hideous the dissonance of its hundred echoes, were dreadful to contemplate. Here were hundreds of young boys, from twenty down to twelve years of age, deep in the agonies of this debasing game, ear-wigging and button-holding, talking of the services of their fathers or brothers to 'the party,' and getting members to intercede for them with the appointing power. The new door-keeper was in distraction, and had to hide behind the Speaker's chair, where he could not be hunted except by proxy.

*   *   *   *   *   *   *

"The situation of the greater number of Clerks in the departments and other subordinate office-holders here is deplorable. No matter what are their respective salaries, the great mass of them are always behind-hand and getting more so. When one is dismissed from office, he has no resource, and no ability to wait for any, and considers himself, not unnaturally, a ruined man. He usually begs to be reinstated, and his wife writes or goes to the President or Secretary to cry him back into place with an 'ower-true tale' of a father without hope and children without bread; if repulsed, their prospect is dreary indeed. Where office is the sole resource, and its retention dependent on another's interest or caprice, there is no slave so pitiable as the officer.

"Of course, where every man's livelihood is dependent on a game of chance and intrigue, outright gambling is frightfully prevalent. This city is full of it in every shape, from the flaunting lottery-office on every corner to the secret card-room in every dark recess. Many who come here for office lose their last cent in these dens, and have to borrow the means of getting away. Such is Washington."

One incident of travel, and we turn to the next volume. It occurred on 'a Sound steamboat' in the year of our Lord, 1843:

"Two cleanly, well-behaved black men, who had just finished a two years' term of service to their country on a ship-of-war, were returning from Boston to their homes in this city. They presented their tickets, showing that they had paid full passage through at Boston, and requested berths. But there was no place provided for blacks on the boat; they could not be admitted to the common cabin, and the clerk informed them that they must walk the deck all night, returning them seventy-five cents of their passage-money. We saw the captain, and remonstrated on their behalf, and were convinced that the fault was not his. There was no space on the boat for a room specially for blacks (which would probably cost $20 for every $1 it yielded, as it would rarely be required, and he could not put whites into it); he had tried to make such a room, but could find no place; and he but a few days before gave

a berth in the cabin to a decent, cleanly colored man, when the other passengers appointed a committee to wait on him, and tell him that would not
answer—so he had to turn out the 'nigger' to pace the deck through the
night, count the slow hours, and reflect on the glorious privilege of living in
a land of liberty, where Slavery and tyranny are demolished, and all men are
free and equal!

"Such occurrences as this might make one ashamed of Human Nature.
We do not believe there is a steamboat in the South where a negro passing a
night upon it would not have found a place to sleep."

The year 1844 was the year of Clay and Frelinghuysen, Polk and
Dallas, the year of Nativism and the Philadelphia riots, the year
of delirious hope and deep despair, the year that finished one era of
politics and began another, the year of Margaret Fuller and the
burning of the Tribune office, the year when Horace Greeley showed his friends how hard a man can work, how little he can sleep,
and yet live. The Tribune began its fourth volume on the tenth of
April, enlarged one-third in size, with new type, and a modest flourish of trumpets. It returned thanks to the public for the liberal
support which had been extended to it from the beginning of its
career. " Our gratitude," said the editor, " is the deeper from our
knowledge that many of the views expressed through our columns
are unacceptable to a large proportion of our readers. We know
especially that our advocacy of measures intended to meliorate the
social condition of the toiling millions (not the purpose, but the
means), our ardent sympathy with the people of Ireland in their
protracted, arduous, peaceful struggle to recover some portion of
the common rights of man, and our opposition to the legal extinction of human life, are severally or collectively regarded with extreme aversion by many of our steadfast patrons, whose liberality
and confidence is gratefully appreciated." To the Whig party, of
which it was " not an organ, but an humble advocate," its " obligations were many and profound." The Tribune, in fact, had become
the leading Whig paper of the country.

Horace Greeley had long set his heart upon the election of Henry
Clay to the presidency; and for some special reasons besides the
general one of his belief that the policy identified with the name
of Henry Clay was the true policy of the government. Henry Clay
was one of the heroes of his boyhood's admiration. Yet, in 1840

believing that Clay could not be elected, he had used his influence to promote the nomination of Gen. Harrison. Then came the death of the president, the 'apostasy' of Tyler, and his pitiful attempts to secure a re-election. The annexation of Texas loomed up in the distance, and the repeal of the tariff of 1842. For these and other reasons, Horace Greeley was inflamed with a desire to behold once more the triumph of his party, and to see the long career of the eminent Kentuckian crowned with its suitable, its coveted reward. For this he labored as few men have ever labored for any but personal objects. He attended the convention at Baltimore that nominated the Whig candidates—one of the largest (and quite the most excited) political assemblages that ever were gathered in this country. During the summer, he addressed political meetings three, four, five, six times a week. He travelled far and wide, advising, speaking, and in every way urging on the cause. He wrote, on an average, *four columns a day* for the Tribune. He answered, on an average, twenty letters a day. He wrote to such an extent that his right arm broke out into biles, and, at one time, there were twenty between the wrist and the elbow. He lived, at that time, a long distance from the office, and many a hot night he protracted his labors till the last omnibus had gone, and he was obliged to trudge wearily home, after sixteen hours of incessant and intense exertion. The whigs were very confident. They were *sure* of victory. But Horace Greeley knew the country better. If every Whig had worked as he worked, how different had been the result! how different the subsequent history of the country! how different its future! We had had no annexation of Texas, no Mexican war, no tinkering of the tariff to keep the nation provincially dependent on Europe, no Fugitive Slave Law, no Pierce, no Douglas, no Nebraska!

The day before the election, the Tribune had a paragraph which shows how excited and how anxious its editor was: " Give to-morrow," he said, " *entirely* to your country. Grudge her not a moment of the daylight. Let not a store or shop be opened—nobody can want to trade or work till the contest is decided. It needs every man of us, and our utmost exertions, to save the CITY, the STATE and the UNION. A tremendous responsibility rests upon us —an electrifying victory or calamitous defeat awaits us. *Two days* only are before us. Action! Action!" On the morning of the decisive day, he said, "Don't mind the rain. It may be bad weather, but nothing to what the election of Polk would bring upon us. Let no Whig be deterred by rain from doing his whole duty! Who values his coat more than his country?"

All in vain. The returns came in slowly to what they now do. The result of a presidential election is now known in New York within a few hours of the closing of the polls. But then it was three days before the whigs certainly knew that Harry of the West had been beaten by Polk of Tennessee, before Americans knew that *their* voice in the election of president was not the controlling one.

"Each morning," said the Tribune, a few days after the result was known, "convincing proofs present themselves of the horrid effects of Loco-focoism, in the election of Mr. Polk. Yesterday it was a countermanding of orders for $8000 worth of stoves; to-day the Pittsburg Gazette says, that two Scotch gentlemen who arrived in that city last June, with a capital of £12,000, which they wished to invest in building a large factory for the manufacture of woolen fabrics, left for Scotland, when they learnt that the Anti-Tariff champion was elected. They will return to the rough hills of Scotland, build a factory, and pour their goods into this country when Polk and his break-down party shall consummate their political iniquity. These are the small first-fruits of Polk's election, the younglings of the flock,—mere hints of the confusion and difficulties which will rush down in an overwhelming flood, after the Polk machine gets well in motion."

The election of Polk and Dallas changed the tone of the Tribune on one important subject. Until the threatened annexation of Texas, which the result of this election made a certainty, the Tribune had meddled little with the question of slavery. To the *silliness* of slavery as an institution, to its infinite absurdity and impolicy, to the marvelous stupidity of the South in clinging to it with such pertinacity, Horace Greeley had always been keenly alive. But he had rather deprecated the agitation of the subject at the North, as tending to the needless irritation of the southern mind, as more likely to rivet than to unloose the shackles of the slave. It was not till slavery became aggressive, it was not till the machinery of politics was moved but with the single purpose of adding slave States to the Union, slave members to Congress, that the Tribune assumed an attitude of hostility to the South, and its pet Blunder. To a southerner who wrote about this time, inquiring what right the North had to intermeddle with slavery, the Tribune replied, that " when we find the Union on the brink of a most unjust and rapacious war, instigated wholly (as is officially proclaimed) by a determination to uphold and fortify Slavery, then we do not see how it can longer be rationally disputed that the North has much, very much, to do with Slavery. If we may be drawn in to fight for it, it would be hard indeed that we should not be allowed to talk of it." Thenceforth, the Tribune fought the aggressions of the slave power, inch by inch.

The Tribune continued on its way, triumphant in spite of the loss of the election, till the morning of Feb. 5th, 1845, when it had the common New York experience of being burnt out. It shall tell its own story of the catastrophe :

" At 4 o'clock, yesterday morning, a boy in our employment entered our publication office, as usual, and kindled a fire in the stove for the day, after which he returned to the mailing-room below, and resumed folding newspapers. Half an hour afterward a clerk, who slept on the counter of the publication office, was awoke by a sensation of heat, and found the room in flames. He escaped with a slight scorching. A hasty effort was made by two or three persons to extinguish the fire by casting water upon it, but the fierce wind then blowing rushed in as the doors were opened, and drove the flames through the building with inconceivable rapidity. Mr. Graham and our clerk, Robert M. Strebeigh, were sleeping in the second story, until awakened by the roar of the flames, their room being full of smoke and fire. The door and stairway being on fire, they escaped with only their night-clothes, by jumping from a rear window, each losing a gold watch, and Mr. Graham nearly $500 in cash, which was in his pocket-book under his pillow. Robert was somewhat cut in the face, on striking the ground, but not seriously. In our printing-office, fifth story, two compositors were at work making up the Weekly Tribune for the press, and had barely time to escape before the stairway was in flames. In the basement our pressmen were at work on the Daily Tribune of the morning, and had printed about three-fourths of the edition. The balance of course went with everything else, including a supply of paper, and the Weekly Tribune, printed on one side. A few books were hastily caught up and saved, but nothing else—not even the daily form, on which the pressmen were working So complete a destruction of a daily newspaper office was never known. From the editorial rooms, not a paper was saved; and, besides all the editor's own

manuscripts, correspondence, and collection of valuable books, some manuscripts belonging to friends, of great value to them, are gone.

" Our loss, so far as money can replace it, is about $18,000, of which $10,000
was covered by insurance. The loss of property which insurance would not
cover, we feel more keenly. If our mail-books come out whole from our Salamander safe, now buried among the burning ruins, we shall be gratefully
content.

" It is usual on such occasions to ask, ' Why were you not fully insured ?'
It was impossible, from the nature of our business, that we should be so ; and
no man could have imagined that such an establishment, in which men were
constantly at work night and day, could be wholly consumed by fire. There
has not been another night, since the building was put up, when it could have
been burned down, even if deliberately fired for that purpose. But when this
fire broke out, under a strong gale and snow-storm of twenty-four hours' continuance, which had rendered the streets impassable, it was well-nigh impossible to drag an engine at all. Some of them could not be got out of their
houses ; others were dragged a few rods and then given up of necessity ; and
those which reached the fire found the nearest hydrant frozen up, and only to
be opened with an axe. Meantime, the whole building was in a blaze."

The mail books were saved in the ' roasted Herring.' The proprietors of the morning papers, even those most inimical, editorially, to the Tribune, placed their superfluous materials at its disposal.
An office was hired temporarily. Type was borrowed and bought.
All hands worked ' with a will.' The paper appeared the next
morning at the usual hour, and the number was one of the best of
that volume. In three months, the office was rebuilt on improved
plans, and provided with every facility then known for the issue of
a daily paper. These were The Tribune's ' Reflections over the Fire,'
published a few days after its occurrence:

" We have been called, editorially, to scissor out a great many fires, both
small and great, and have done so with cool philosophy, not reflecting how
much to some one man the little paragraph would most assuredly mean. The
late complete and summary burning up of our office, licked up clean as it was
by the red flames, in a few hours, has taught us a lesson on this head. Aside
from all pecuniary loss, how great is the suffering produced by a fire ! A hundred little articles of no use to any one save the owner, things that people
would look at day after day, and see nothing in, that we ourselves have contemplated with cool indifference, now that they are irrevocably destroyed,
come up in the shape of reminiscences, and seem as if they had been worth
their weight in gold.

"We would not indulge in unnecessary sentiment, but even the old desk at which we sat, the ponderous inkstand, the familiar faces of files of Correspondence, the choice collection of pamphlets, the unfinished essay, the charts by which we steered—can they all have vanished, never more to be seen? Truly your fire makes clean work, and is, of all executive officers, super-eminent. Perhaps that last choice batch of letters may be somewhere on file; we are almost tempted to cry, 'Devil! find it up!' Poh! it is a mere cinder now; some

"'Fathoms deep my letter lies;
Of its lines is tinder made.'

"No Arabian tale can cradle a wilder fiction, or show better how altogether illusory life is. Those solid walls of brick, those five decent stories, those steep and difficult stairs, the swinging doors, the Sanctum, scene of many a deep political drama, of many a pathetic tale, utterly whiffed out, as one summarily snuffs out a spermaceti on retiring for the night. And all perfectly true.

"One always has some private satisfaction in his own particular misery. Consider what a night it was that burnt us out, that we were conquered by the elements, went up in flames heroically on the wildest, windiest, stormiest night these dozen years, not by any fault of human enterprise, but fairly conquered by stress of weather;—there was a great flourish of trumpets at all events.

"And consider, above all, that Salamander safe; how, after all, the fire, assisted by the elements, only came off second best, not being able to reduce that safe into ashes. That is the streak of sunshine through the dun wreaths of smoke, the combat of human ingenuity against the desperate encounter of the seething heat. But those boots, and Webster's Dictionary—well! we *were* handsomely whipped there, we acknowledge."

CHAPTER XX.

MARGARET FULLER.

Her writings in the Tribune—She resides with Mr. Greeley—His narrative—Dietetic Sparring—Her manner of writing—Woman's Rights—Her generosity—Her independence—Her love of children—Margaret and Pickie—Her opinion of Mr. Greeley—Death of Pickie.

MARGARET FULLER'S first article in the Tribune, a review of Emerson's Essays, appeared on the seventh of December, 1844; her

last, "Farewell to New York," was published August 1st, 1846, on
the eve of her departure for Europe. From Europe, however, she
sent many letters to the Tribune, and continued occasionally, though
at ever-increasing intervals, to correspond with the paper down
nearly to the time of her embarkation for her native land in 1850.

During the twenty months of her connection with the Tribune,
she wrote, on an average, three articles a week. Many of them
were long and elaborate, extending, in several instances, to three and
four columns ; and, as they were Essays upon authors, rather than
Reviews of Books, she indulged sparingly in extract. Among her
literary articles, we observe essays upon Milton, Shelley, Carlyle,
George Sand, the countess Hahn Hahn, Sue, Balzac, Charles Wes-
ley, Longfellow, Richter, and other magnates. She wrote, also, a
few musical and dramatic critiques. Among her general contributions, were essays upon the Rights, Wrongs, and Duties of Women,
a defense of the 'Irish Character,' articles upon 'Christmas,' 'New
Year's Day,' 'French Gayety,' 'the Poor Man,' 'the Rich Man,'
'What fits a man to be a Voter'—genial, fresh, and suggestive
essays all. Her defense of the Irish character was very touching
and just. Her essay on George Sand was discriminating and courageous. She dared to speak of her as 'one of the best exponents
of the difficulties, the errors, the weaknesses, and regenerative
powers of the present epoch.' "Let no man," continued Miss Fuller, "confound the bold unreserve of Sand with that of those who
have lost the feeling of beauty and the love of good. With a bleed-
ing heart and bewildered feet she sought the Truth, and if she lost
the way, returned as soon as convinced she had done so, but she
would never hide the fact that she had lost it. 'What God knows
I dare avow to man,' seems to be her motto. It is impossible not
to see in her, not only the distress and doubts of the intellect, but
the temptations of a sensual nature ; but we see, too, the courage of
a hero, and a deep capacity for religion. The mixed nature, too,
fits her peculiarly to speak to men so diseased as men are at present.
They feel she knows their ailment, and, if she finds a cure, it will
really be by a specific remedy."

To give George Sand her due, ten years ago, required more courage in a reviewer than it would now to withhold it.

Margaret Fuller, in the knowledge of literature, was the most

learned woman of her country, perhaps of her time. Her understanding was greater than her gift. She could appreciate, not
create. She was the noblest victim of that modern error, which
makes Education and Book-knowledge synonymous terms. Her
brain was terribly stimulated in childhood by the study of works
utterly unfit for the nourishment of a child's mind, and in after life,
it was further stimulated by the adulation of circles who place the
highest value upon Intelligence, and no value at all upon Wisdom.
It cost her the best years of her life to unlearn the errors, and to
overcome the mental habits of her earlier years. But she did it.
Her triumph was complete. She attained modesty, serenity, disinterestedness, self-control. "The spirit in which we work," says
Goëthe, "is the highest matter." What charms and blesses the
reader of Margaret Fuller's essays, is not the knowledge they
convey, nor the understanding they reveal, but the ineffably sweet,
benign, tenderly humane and serenely high *spirit* which they
breathe in every paragraph and phrase.

During a part of the time of her connection with the Tribune,
Miss Fuller resided at Mr. Greeley's house, on the banks of the East
river, opposite the lower end of Blackwell's island. "This place,"
she wrote, "is to me entirely charming; it is so completely in the
country, and all around is so bold and free. It is two miles or more
from the thickly-settled parts of New York, but omnibuses and cars
give me constant access to the city, and, while I can readily see
what and whom I will, I can command time and retirement. Stopping on the Harlem road, you enter a lane nearly a quarter of a
mile long, and going by a small brook and pond that locks in the
place, and ascending a slightly rising ground, get sight of the house,
which, old-fashioned and of mellow tint, fronts on a flower-garden
filled with shrubs, large vines, and trim box borders. On both
sides of the house are beautiful trees, standing fair, full-grown, and
clear. Passing through a wide hall, you come out upon a piazza, stretching the whole length of the house, where one can walk in
all weathers.   *   *   The beauty here, seen by moonlight, is truly
transporting. I enjoy it greatly, and the *genius loci* receives me as
to a home."

Mr. Greeley has written a singularly interesting account of the
rise and progress of his friendship with Margaret Fuller, which was

published, a few years ago, in her fascinating memoirs. A man *is*, in a degree, that which he loves to praise; and the narrative referred to, tells much of Margaret Fuller, but more of Horace Greeley. Whatever else should be omitted from this volume, that should not be; and it is, accordingly, presented here without abridgment.

"My first acquaintance with Margaret Fuller was made through the pages of *The Dial*. The lofty range and rare ability of that work, and its un-American richness of culture and ripeness of thought, naturally filled the 'fit audience, though few,' with a high estimate of those who were known as its conductors and principal writers. Yet I do not now remember that any article, which strongly impressed me, was recognized as from the pen of its female editor, prior to the appearance of 'The Great Law-suit,' afterward matured into the volume more distinctively, yet not quite accurately, entitled 'Woman in the Nineteenth Century.' I think this can hardly have failed to make a deep impression on the mind of every thoughtful reader, as the production of an original, vigorous and earnest mind. 'Summer on the Lakes,' which appeared some time after that essay, though before its expansion into a book, struck me as less ambitious in its aim, but more graceful and delicate in its execution; and as one of the clearest and most graphic delineations ever given of the Great Lakes, of the Prairies, and of the receding barbarism, and the rapidly-advancing, but rude, repulsive semi-civilization, which were contending with most unequal forces for the possession of those rich lands. I still consider 'Summer on the Lakes' unequaled, especially in its pictures of the Prairies, and of the sunnier aspects of Pioneer life.

"Yet, it was the suggestion of Mrs. Greeley—who had spent some weeks of successive seasons in or near Boston, and who had there made the personal acquaintance of Miss Fuller, and formed a very high estimate of and warm attachment for her—that induced me, in the autumn of 1844, to offer her terms, which were accepted, for her assistance in the literary department of *The Tribune*. A home in my family was included in the stipulation. I was myself barely acquainted with her when she thus came to reside with us, and I did not fully appreciate her nobler qualities for some months afterward Though we were members of the same household, we scarcely met save at breakfast; and my time and thoughts were absorbed in duties and cares, which left me little leisure or inclination for the amenities of social intercourse. Fortune seemed to delight in placing us two in relations of friendly antagonism—or rather, to develop all possible contrasts in our ideas and social habits. She was naturally inclined to luxury, and a good appearance before the world. My pride, if I had any, delighted in bare walls and rugged fare. She was addicted to strong tea and coffee, both of which I rejected and condemned, even in the most homeopathic dilutions; while, my general health being sound, and hers sadly impaired, I could not fail to find in her dietetic habits the causes of her almost habitual illness; and once, while we were still barely acquainted, when she came to the breakfast-table with a very severe headache, I was tempted to attribute it to her strong potations of the Chinese leaf the night before. She told me quite frankly that she 'declined being lectured on the food or beverage she saw fit to take,' which was but reasonable in one who had arrived at her maturity of intellect and fixedness of habits. So the subject was thenceforth tacitly avoided between us; but, though words were suppressed, looks and involuntary gestures could not so well be; and an utter divergency of views on this and kindred themes created a perceptible distance between us.

"Her earlier contributions to The Tribune were not her best, and I did not at first prize her aid so highly as I afterward learned to do. She wrote always freshly, vigorously, but not always clearly; for her full and intimate acquaintance with continental literature, especially German, seemed to have marred her felicity and readiness of expression in her mother tongue. While I never met another woman who conversed more freely or lucidly, the attempt to commit her thoughts to paper seemed to induce a singular embarrassment and hesitation. She could write only when in the vein, and this needed often to be waited for through several days, while the occasion sometimes required an immediate utterance. The new book must be reviewed before other journals had thoroughly dissected and discussed it, else the ablest critique would command no general attention, and perhaps be, by the greater number, unread. That the writer should wait the flow of inspiration, or at least the recurrence of elasticity of spirits and relative health of body, will not seem unreasonable to the general reader; but to the inveterate hack-horse of the daily press, accustomed to write at any time, on any subject, and with a rapidity limited only by the physical ability to form the requisite pen-strokes, the notion of waiting for a brighter day, or a happier frame of mind, appears fantastic and absurd. He would as soon think of waiting for a change in the moon. Hence, while I realized that her contributions evinced rare intellectual wealth and force, I did not value them as I should have done had they been written more fluently and promptly. They often seemed to make their appearance 'a day after the fair.'

"One other point of tacit antagonism between us may as well be noted. Margaret was always a most earnest, devoted champion of the Emancipation of Women from their past and present condition of inferiority, to an independence of Men. She demanded for them the fullest recognition of Social and Political Equality with the rougher sex; the freest access to all stations, professions, employments, which are open to any. To this demand I heartily acceded. It seemed to me, however, that her clear perceptions of abstract right were often overborne, in practice, by the influence of education and habit; that while she demanded absolute equality for Woman, she exacted a

deference and courtesy from men to women, *as* women, which was entirely inconsistent with that requirement. In my view, the equalizing theory can be
enforced only by ignoring the habitual discrimination of men and women, as
forming separate *classes*, and regarding all alike as simply *persons*,—as human beings. So long as a lady shall deem herself in need of some gentleman's
arm to conduct her properly out of a dining or ball-room,—so long as she
shall consider it dangerous or unbecoming to walk half a mile alone by night,
—I cannot see how the ' Woman's Rights ' theory is ever to be anything more
than a logically defensible abstraction. In this view Margaret did not at all
concur, and the diversity was the incitement to much perfectly good-natured, but
nevertheless sharpish sparring between us. Whenever she said or did anything
implying the usual demand of Woman on the courtesy and protection of Manhood, I was apt, before complying, to look her in the face and exclaim with
marked emphasis,—quoting from her ' Woman in the Nineteenth Century,'—
' LET THEM BE SEA-CAPTAINS IF THEY WILL !' Of course, this was given and
received as raillery, but it did not tend to ripen our intimacy or quicken my
esteem into admiration. Though no unkind word ever passed between us,
nor any approach to one, yet we two dwelt for months under the same roof, as
scarcely more than acquaintances, meeting once a day at a common board, and
having certain business relations with each other. Personally, I regarded her
rather as my wife's cherished friend than as my own, possessing many lofty
qualities and some prominent weaknesses, and a good deal spoiled by the unmeasured flattery of her little circle of inordinate admirers. For myself,
burning no incense on any human shrine, I half-consciously resolved to ' keep
my eye-beam clear,' and escape the fascination which she seemed to exert
over the eminent and cultivated persons, mainly women, who came to our
out-of-the-way dwelling to visit her, and who seemed generally to regard her
with a strangely Oriental adoration.

" But as time wore on, and I became inevitably better and better acquainted with her, I found myself drawn, almost irresistibly, into the general current. I found that her faults and weaknesses were all superficial and obvious
to the most casual, if undazzled, observer. They rather dwindled than expanded upon a fuller knowledge ; or rather, took on new and brighter aspects
in the light of her radiant and lofty soul. I learned to know her as a most
fearless and unselfish champion of Truth and Human Good at all hazards,
ready to be their standard-bearer through danger and obloquy, and if need be,
their martyr. I think few have more keenly appreciated the material goods
of life,—Rank, Riches, Power, Luxury, Enjoyment ; but I know none who
would have more cheerfully surrendered them all, if the well-being of our
Race could thereby have been promoted. I have never met another in
whom the inspiring hope of Immortality was so strengthened into profoundest conviction. She did not *believe* in our future and unending existence,—
she *knew* it, and lived ever in the broad glare of its morning twilight. With

a limited income and liberal wants, she was yet generous beyond the bounds of reason. Had the gold of California been all her own, she would have disbursed nine-tenths of it in eager and well-directed efforts to stay, or at least diminish, the flood of human misery. And it is but fair to state, that the liberality she evinced was fully paralleled by the liberality she experienced at the hands of others. Had she needed thousands, and made her wants known, she had friends who would have cheerfully supplied her. I think few persons, in their pecuniary dealings, have experienced and evinced more of the better qualities of human nature than Margaret Fuller. She seemed to inspire those who approached her with that generosity which was a part of her nature.

"Of her writings I do not propose to speak critically. I think most of her contributions to the Tribune, while she remained with us, were characterized by a directness, terseness, and practicality, which are wanting in some of her earlier productions. Good judges have confirmed my own opinion, that while her essays in the Dial are more elaborate and ambitious, her reviews in the Tribune are far better adapted to win the favor and sway the judgment of the great majority of readers. But, one characteristic of her writings I feel bound to commend,—their absolute truthfulness. She never asked how this would sound, nor whether that would do, nor what would be the effect of saying anything; but simply, 'Is it the truth? Is it such as the public should know?' And if her judgment answered, 'Yes,' she uttered it; no matter what turmoil it might excite, nor what odium it might draw down on her own head. Perfect conscientiousness was an unfailing characteristic of her literary efforts. Even the severest of her critiques,—that on Longfellow's Poems,— for which an impulse in personal pique has been alleged, I happen with certainty to know had no such origin. When I first handed her the book to review, she excused herself, assigning the wide divergence of her views of Poetry from those of the author and his school, as her reason. She thus induced me to attempt the task of reviewing it myself. But day after day sped by, and I could find no hour that was not absolutely required for the performance of some duty that *would not* be put off, nor turned over to another. At length I carried the book back to her in utter despair of ever finding an hour in which even to look through it; and, at my renewed and earnest request, she reluctantly undertook its discussion. The statement of these *facts* is but an act of justice to her memory.

"Profoundly religious,—though her creed was, at once, very broad and very short, with a genuine love for inferiors in social position, whom she was habitually studying, by her counsel and teachings, to elevate and improve,—she won the confidence and affection of those who attracted her, by unbounded sympathy and trust. She probably knew the cherished secrets of more hearts than any one else, because she freely imparted her own. With a full share both of intellectual and of family pride, she pre-eminently recognized and responded to the essential brotherhood of all human kind, and needed to know that a fellow-being required her counsel or assistance, to render her, not merely willing, but eager to impart it. Loving ease, luxury, and the world's good opinion, she stood ready to renounce them all, at the call of pity or of duty. I think no one, not radically averse to the whole system of domestic servitude, would have treated servants, of whatever class, with such uniform and thoughtful consideration,—a regard which wholly merged their factitious condition in their antecedent and permanent humanity. I think few servants ever lived weeks with her, who were not dignified and lastingly benefited by her influence and her counsels. They might be at first repelled, by what seemed her too stately manner and exacting disposition, but they soon learned to esteem and love her.

"I have known few women, and scarcely another maiden, who had the heart and the courage to speak with such frank compassion, in mixed circles, of the most degraded and outcast portion of the sex. The contemplation of their treatment, especially by the guilty authors of their ruin, moved her to a calm and mournful indignation, which she did not attempt to suppress nor control. Others were willing to pity and deplore; Margaret was more inclined to vindicate and to redeem. She did not hesitate to avow that on meeting some of these abused, unhappy sisters, she had been surprised to find them scarcely fallen morally below the ordinary standard of Womanhood,—realizing and loathing their debasement; anxious to escape it; and only repelled by the sad consciousness that for them sympathy and society remained only so long as they should persist in the ways of pollution. Those who have read her 'Woman,' may remember some daring comparisons therein suggested between these Pariahs of society and large classes of their respectable sisters; and that was no fitful expression,—no sudden outbreak,—but impelled by her most deliberate convictions. I think, if she had been born to large fortune, a house of refuge for all female outcasts desiring to return to the ways of Virtue, would have been one of her most cherished and first realized conceptions.

" Her love of children was one of her most prominent characteristics. The pleasure she enjoyed in their society was fully counterpoised by that she imparted. To them she was never lofty, nor reserved, nor mystical; for no one had ever a more perfect faculty for entering into their sports, their feelings, their enjoyments. She could narrate almost any story in language level to their capacities, and in a manner calculated to bring out their hearty and often boisterously-expressed delight. She possessed marvelous powers of observation and imitation or mimicry; and, had she been attracted to the stage, would have been the first actress America has produced, whether in tragedy or comedy. Her faculty of mimicking was not needed to commend her to the hearts of children, but it had its effect in increasing the fascinations of her genial nature and her heartfelt joy in their society. To amuse and instruct them was an achievement for which she would readily forego any personal object; and her intuitive perception of the toys, games, stories, rhymes, &c., best adapted to arrest and enchain their attention, was unsurpassed. Between her and my only child, then living, who was eight months old when she came to us, and something over two years when she sailed for Europe, tendrils of affection gradually intertwined themselves, which I trust Death has not severed. but rather multiplied and strengthened. She became his teacher, playmate, and monitor; and he requited her with a prodigality of love and admiration.

"I shall not soon forget their meeting in my office, after some weeks' separation, just before she left us forever. His mother had brought him in from the country, and left him asleep on my sofa, while she was absent making purchases, and he had rolled off and hurt himself in the fall, waking with the shock in a frenzy of anger, just before Margaret, hearing of his arrival, rushed into the office to find him. I was vainly attempting to soothe him as she entered; but he was running from one end to the other of the office, crying passionately, and refusing to be pacified. She hastened to him, in perfect confidence that her endearments would calm the current of his feelings,—that the sound of her well-remembered voice would banish all thought of his pain,— and that another moment would see him restored to gentleness; but, half-wakened, he did not heed her, and probably did not even realize who it was that caught him repeatedly in her arms and tenderly insisted that he should restrain himself. At last she desisted in despair; and, with the bitter tears streaming down her face, observed:—'Pickie, many friends have treated me unkindly, but no one had ever the power to cut me to the heart as you have!' Being thus let alone, he soon came to himself, and their mutual delight in the meeting was rather heightened by the momentary estrangement.

"They had one more meeting; the last on earth! 'Aunty Margaret' was to embark for Europe on a certain day, and 'Pickie' was brought into the city to bid her farewell. They met this time also at my office, and together we thence repaired to the ferry-boat, on which she was returning to her residence in Brooklyn to complete her preparations for the voyage. There they took a tender and affecting leave of each other. But soon his mother called at the office, on her way to the departing ship, and we were easily persuaded to accompany her thither, and say farewell once more, to the manifest satisfaction of both Margaret and the youngest of her devoted friends. Thus they parted, never to meet again in time. She sent him messages and presents repeatedly from Europe; and he, when somewhat older, dictated a letter in return, which was joyfully received and acknowledged. When the mother of our great-souled friend spent some days with us nearly two years afterward, 'Pickie' talked to her often and lovingly of 'Aunty Margaret,' proposing that they two should 'take a boat and go over and see her,'—for, to his infantile conception, the low coast of Long Island, visible just across the East River, was that Europe to which she had sailed, and where she was unaccountably detained so

long. Alas! a far longer and more adventurous journey was required to re-
unite those loving souls! The 12th of July, 1849, saw him stricken down
from health to death, by the relentless cholera; and my letter, announcing
that calamity, drew from her a burst of passionate sorrow, such as hardly any
bereavement but the loss of a very near relative could have impelled. Another year had just ended, when a calamity, equally sudden, bereft a wide
circle of her likewise, with her husband and infant son. Little did I fear,
when I bade her a confident Good-by, on the deck of her outward-bound ship,
that the sea would close over her earthly remains ere we should meet again;
far less that the light of my eyes and the cynosure of my hopes, who then
bade her a tenderer and sadder farewell, would precede her on the dim pathway to that 'Father's house' whence is no returning! Ah, well! God is above
all, and gracious alike in what He conceals and what He discloses;—benignant
and bounteous, as well when He reclaims as when He bestows. In a few years,
at farthest, our loved and lost ones will welcome us to their home."

Margaret Fuller, on her part, was fully sensible of the merits of
him who has so touchingly embalmed her memory. "Mr. Greeley,"
she wrote in a private letter, "is a man of genuine excellence, honorable, benevolent, and of an uncorrupted disposition. He is sagacious, and, in his way, of even great abilities. In modes of life and
manner he is a man of the people, and of the American people."
And again: "Mr. Greeley is in many ways very interesting for me
to know. He teaches me things, which my own influence on those
who have hitherto approached me, has prevented me from learning.
In our business and friendly relations, we are on terms of solid
good-will and mutual respect. With the exception of my own
mother, I think him the most disinterestedly generous person I have
ever known." And later she writes: "You have heard that the
Tribune Office was burned to the ground. For a day I thought it
must make a difference, but it has served only to increase my admiration for Mr. Greeley's smiling courage. He has really a strong
character."

In another letter, written at Rome in 1849, there is another allusion to Mr. Greeley and his darling boy. "Receiving," she said, "a
few days since, a packet of letters from America, I opened them
with more feeling of hope and good cheer, than for a long time
past. The first words that met my eye were these, in the hand of
Mr. Greeley: 'Ah, Margaret, the world grows dark with us! You
grieve, for Rome is fallen; I mourn, for Pickie is dead.'

"I have shed rivers of tears over the inexpressibly affecting letter thus begun. One would think I might have become familiar enough with images of death and destruction; yet somehow the image of Pickie's little dancing figure, lying, stiff and stark, between his parents, has made me weep more than all else. There was little hope he could do justice to himself, or lead a happy life in so perplexed a world; but never was a character of richer capacity,—never a more charming child. To me he was most dear, and would always have been so. Had he become stained with earthly faults, I could never have forgotten what he was when fresh from the soul's home, and what he was to me when my soul pined for sympathy, pure and unalloyed."

A few months after these words were written, Margaret Fuller *saw* her native shores; but she was destined never to tread them again. The vessel in which she was a passenger was wrecked on the coast of Long Island. The body of her infant son was washed on shore, but she and her husband found death, burial, requiem, all in the deep.

CHAPTER XXI.

EDITORIAL REPARTEES.

At war with all the world—The spirit of the Tribune—Retorts vituperative—The Tribune and Dr. Potts—Some prize tracts suggested—An atheist's oath—A word for domestics—Irish Democracy—The modern drama—Hit at Dr. Hawks—Dissolution of the Union—Dr. Franklin's story—A Picture for Polk—Charles Dickens and Copyright—Charge of Malignant falsehood—Preaching and Practice—Col. Webb severely hit—Hostility to the Mexican war—Violence incited—A few sparks—The course of the Tribune—Wager with the Herald.

THE years 1845, 1846, and 1847, were emphatically the fighting years of the New York Tribune. If it was not at war with all the world, all the world seemed to be at war with it, and it was kept constantly on the defensive. With the 'democratic' press, of course, it could not be at peace. The whig press of the city denounced it, really because it was immovably prosperous, ostensibly on the ground of its Fourierite and progressive tendencies. Its opposition to capital punishment, the freedom of its reviews, and the hospitality it gave to every new thought,' gave offense to the religious press. Its tremendous hostility to the Mexican war excited the animosity of all office-holders and other patriots, including the president, who made a palpable allusion to the course of the Tribune in one of his messages. There was talk even of mobbing the office, at one of the war meetings in the Park. Its zeal in behalf of Irish repeal alienated the English residents, who naturally liked the 'pluck' and independence of the Tribune. Its hostility to the slave power provoked the south, and all but destroyed its southern circulation. It offended bigots by giving Thomas Paine his due; it offended unbelievers by refusing to give him more. Its opposition to the drama, as it is, called forth many a sneer from the papers who have the honor of the drama in their special keeping. The extreme American party abhorred its enmity to Nativism. The extreme Irish party distrusted it, because in sentiment and feeling it was thoroughly Protestant. The extreme liberal party disliked its opposition to their views of marriage and divorce. In a word, if the course of the Tribune had been suggested by a desire to give the greatest offense to the greatest number, it could hardly have made more enemies than it did.

In the prospectus to the fifth volume, the editor seemed to anticipate a period of inky war.

"Our conservatism," he said, "is not of that Chinese tenacity which insists that the bad must be cherished simply because it is old. We insist only that the old must be proved bad and never condemned merely because it *is* old; and that, even if defective, it should not be overthrown till something better has been provided to replace it. The extremes of blind, stubborn resistance to change, and rash, sweeping, convulsive innovation, are naturally allies, each paving the way for the other. The supple courtier, the wholesale flatterer of the Despot, and the humble servitor and bepraiser of the dear People, are not two distinct characters, but essentially the same. Thus believing, we, while we do not regard the judgment of any *present* majority as infallible, cannot attribute infallibility to any acts or institutes of a *past* generation, but look undoubtingly for successive improvements as Knowledge, Virtue, Philanthropy, shall be more and more diffused among men.

*　　*　　*　　*　　*　　*　　*　　*　　*

"Full of error and suffering as the world yet is, we cannot afford to reject unexamined any idea which proposes to improve the Moral, Intellectual, or Social condition of mankind. Better incur the trouble of testing and exploding a thousand fallacies than by rejecting stifle a single beneficent truth. Especially on the vast theme of an improved Organization of Industry, so as to secure constant opportunity and a just recompense to every human being able and willing to labor, we are not and cannot be indifferent.

*   *   *   *   *   *   *   *   *

"No subject can be more important than this; no improvement more certain of attainment. The plans hitherto suggested may all prove abortive; the experiments hitherto set on foot may all come to nought, (as many of them doubtless will;) yet these mistakes shall serve to indicate the true means of improvement, and these experiments shall bring nearer and nearer the grand consummation which they contemplate. The securing of thorough Education, Opportunity and just Reward to all, cannot be beyond the reach of the nineteenth century. To accelerate it, the Tribune has labored and will labor resolutely and hopefully. Those whose dislike to or distrust of the investigations in this field of human effort impel them to reject our paper, have ample range for a selection of journals more acceptable."

In the spirit of these words the Tribune was conducted. And every man, in any age, who conducts his life, his newspaper, or his business in that spirit, will be misunderstood, distrusted and hated, in exact proportion to his fidelity to it. Perfect fidelity, the world will so entirely detest that it will destroy the man who attains to it. The world will not submit to be so completely put out of countenance.

My task, in this chapter, is to show how the editor of the Tribune comported himself when he occupied the position of target-general to the Press, Pulpit, and Stump of the United States. He was not in the slightest degree distressed or alarmed. On the contrary, I think he enjoyed the position; and, though he handled his enemies without gloves, and called a spade a spade, and had to dispatch a dozen foemen at once, and could not pause to select his weapons, yet I can find in those years of warfare no trace of bitterness on his part. There is no malice in his satire, no spite in his anger. He seems never so happy as when he is at bay, and is never so funny as when he is repelling a personal assault. I have before me several hundreds of his editorial hits and repartees, some serious, more comic, some refuting argument, others exposing slander, some merely vituperative, others very witty, all extremely readable,

12

though the occasions that called them forth have long passed by. My plan is to select and condense a few of each kind, presenting only the *point* of each.

Many of our editor's replies are remarkable chiefly for their 'free and easy' manner, their ignoring of 'editorial dignity.' A specimen or two:

In reply to a personal attack by Major Noah, of the Union, he begins, "We ought not to notice this old villain again." On another occasion, "What a silly old joker this last hard bargain of Tylerism is!" On another, "Major Noah! why *won't* you tell the truth once in a century, for the variety of the thing." On another, "And it is by such poor drivel as this that the superannuated renegade from all parties and all principles attempts to earn his forced contributions and 'Official' advertisements! Surely his latest purchasers must despise their worn-out tool, and most heartily repent of their hard bargain."

Such mild openings as the following are not uncommon:

"The Journal of Commerce is the most self-complacent and dogmatic of all possible newspapers."

"The villain who makes this charge against me well knows that it is the basest falsehood."

"We defy the Father of lies himself to crowd more stupendous falsehoods into a paragraph than this contains."

"Mr. Benton! each of the above observations is a deliberate falsehood, and you are an unqualified villain!"

"The Express is surely the basest and paltriest of all possible journals."

"Having been absent from the city for a few days, I perceive with a pleasurable surprise on my return that the Express has only perpetrated two new calumnies upon me of any consequence since Friday evening."

"'Ephraim,' said a grave divine, taking his text from one of the prophets, 'is a cake not turned. (Hosea, vii. 8.) Let us proceed, therefore, brethren, to turn Ephraim—first, inside out; next, back-side before; and, thirdly, 'tother end up.'

"We are under the imperative necessity of performing on Samuel of this day a searching operation like unto that of the parson on Ephraim of old."

That will suffice for the vituperative. We proceed to those of another description:

PROVOCATION.

A Sermon by Dr. Potts, denouncing the Tribune as agrarian, &c., reported in the Courier and Enquirer.

REPLY.

"It is quite probable that we have some readers among the pew-holders of a church so wealthy and fashionable as the Dr.'s, though few, we presume, among divines as well salaried as he is. We will only ask those of our patrons who may obey his command to read for their next Scripture lesson the xxvth Chapter of Leviticus, and reflect upon it for an hour or so. We are very sure they will find the exercise a profitable one, in a sense higher than they will have anticipated. Having then stopped the Tribune, they will meditate at leisure on the abhorrence and execration with which one of the Hebrew Prophets must have regarded any kind of an Agrarian or Anti-Renter; that is, one opposed to perpetuating and extending the relation of Landlord and Tenant over the whole arable surface of the earth. Perhaps the contemplation of a few more passages of Sacred Writ may not be unprofitable in a moral sense—for example:

" 'Woe unto them that join [add] house to house, that lay field to field that there be no place, that they be placed alone in the midst of the earth.' —Isaiah, v. 8.

" 'One thing thou lackest: go thy way, sell whatever thou hast, and give to the poor, and thou shalt have treasure in heaven; and come, take up the the cross, and follow me:

" 'And Jesus looked round about, and saith unto his disciples, How hardly shall they that have riches enter into the kingdom of God!'—Mark, x. 21-23.

" 'And all that believed were together, and had all things common; and sold their possessions and goods, and parted them to all, as every man had need.'—Acts, ii. 44, 45.

"We might cite columns of this sort from the Sacred Volume, showing a deplorable lack of Doctors of Divinity in ancient times, to be employed at $3,500 a year in denouncing, in sumptuous, pew-guarded edifices costing $75,000 each, all who should be guilty of 'loosening the faith of many in the *established order of things.*' Alas for their spiritual blindness! the ancient Prophets—God's Prophets—appear to have slight faith in or reverence for that 'established order' themselves! Their 'schemes' appear to have been regarded as exceedingly 'disorganizing' and hostile to 'good order' by the spiritual rulers of the people in those days.

"That Dr. Potts, pursuing (we trust) the career most congenial to his feelings, surrounded by every comfort and luxury, enjoying the best society, and enabled to support and educate his children to the hight of his desires, should be inclined to reprobate all 'nostrums' for the cure of Social evils, and sneer at 'labor-saving plans' of cooking, washing, schooling, &c., is rather deplorable than surprising. Were he some poor day-laborer, subsisting his family and paying rent on the dollar a day he could get when the weather permitted and some employer's necessity or caprice gave him a chance to earn it, we believe he would view the subject differently. As to the spirit which can denounce by wholesale all who labor in behalf of a Social Reform, in defiance of general obloquy, rooted prejudice, and necessarily serious personal sacrifices, as enemies of Christianity and Good Morals, and call upon the public to starve them into silence, does it not merit the rebuke and loathing of every generous mind? Heaven aid us to imitate, though afar off, that Divinest charity which could say for its persecutors and murderers, 'Father, forgive them, for they know not what they do!'

* * * * * * * * *

"We are profoundly conscious that the moral tone and bearing of the Press fall very far beneath their true standard, and that it too often panders to popular appetites and prejudices when it should rather withstand and labor to correct them. We, for example, remember having wasted many precious columns of this paper, whereby great good might have been done, in the publication of a controversy on the question, 'Can there be a Church without a Bishop?'—a controversy unprofitable in its subject, verbose and pointless in its logic, and disgraceful to our common Christianity in its exhibitions of uncharitable temper and gladiatorial tactics. The Rev. Dr. Potts may also remember that controversy. We ask the Pulpit to strengthen our own fallible resolution never to be tempted by any hope of pecuniary profit, (pretty sure to be delusive, as it ought,) into meddling with such another discreditable performance.

"We do not find, in the Courier's report of this sermon, any censures upon that very large and popularly respectable class of journals which regularly hire out their columns, Editorial and Advertising, for the enticement of their readers to visit groceries, theaters, horse-races, as we sometimes have thoughtlessly done, but hope never, unless through deplored inadvertence, to do again. The difficulty of entirely resisting all temptations to these lucrative vices is so great, and the temptations themselves so incessant, while the moral mischief thence accruing is so vast and palpable, that we can hardly think the Rev. Dr. slurred over the point, while we can very well imagine that his respected disciple and reporter did so. At this moment, when the great battle of Temperance against Liquid Poison and its horrible sorceries is convulsing our State, and its issue trembles in the balance, it seems truly incredible that a Doctor of Divinity, lecturing on the iniquities of the Press, can have altogether overlooked this topic. Cannot the Courier from its reporter's notes supply the omission?"

PROVOCATION.

An advertisement offering a prize of fifty dollars for the best tract on the Impropriety of Dancing by members of churches, the tract to be published by the American Tract Society.

REPLY.

" The notice copied above suggests to us some other subjects on which we think Tracts are needed—subjects which are beginning to attract the thoughts of not a few, and which are, like dancing, of practical moment. We would suggest premiums to be offered, as follows :

" $20 for the best Tract on 'The rightfulness and consistency of a Christian's spending $5,000 to $10,000 a year on the appetites and enjoyments of himself and family, when there are a thousand families within a mile of him who are compelled to live on less than $200 a year.

" $10 for the best Tract on the rightfulness and Christianity of a Christian's building a house for the exclusive residence of himself and family, at a cost of $50,000 to $100,000, within sight of a hundred families living in hovels worth less than $100.

" $5 for the best Tract on the Christianity of building Churches which cost $100,000 each, in which *poor* sinners can only worship on sufferance, and in the most out-of-the-way corners.

" We would not intimate that these topics are by any means so important as that of Dancing—far from it. The sums we suggest will shield us from that imputation. Yet we think these subjects may also be discussed with profit, and, that there may be no pecuniary hindrance, we will pay the premiums if the American Tract Society will publish the Tracts."

PROVOCATION.

An assertion in the Express, that the Tribune bestows " peculiar commendation upon that part of the new Constitution which takes away the necessity of believing in a Supreme Being, on the part of him who may be called to swear our lives or property away."

REPLY.

" ' The necessity of *believing* in a Supreme Being,' in order to be a legal witness, never existed ; but only the necessity of *professing* to believe it. Now, a thorough villain who was at the same time an Atheist would be pretty apt to keep to himself a belief, the avowal of which would subject him to legal penalties and popular obloquy, but a sincere, honest man, whose mind had become confused or clouded with regard to the evidence of a Universal Father, would be very likely to confess his lack of faith, and thereby be disabled from testifying. Such disability deranges the administration of justice and facilitates the escape of the guilty."

PROVOCATION.

An assertion that it is *false pride*, that makes domestic service so abhorrent to American girls.

REPLY.

"You, Madam, who talk so flippantly of the folly or false pride of our girls, have you ever attempted to put yourself in their place and consider the matter? Have you ever weighed in the balance a crust and a garret *at home*, with better food and lodging in the house of a stranger? Have you ever thought of the difference between doing the most arduous and repulsive work for those you love, and who love you, and doing the same in a strange place for those to whom your only bond of attachment is six dollars a month? Have you ever considered that the words of reproof and reproach, so easy to utter, are very hard to bear, especially from one whose right so to treat you is a thing of cash and of yesterday? Is the difference between freedom and service nothing to you? How many would you like to have ordering you?"

PROVOCATION.

A vain-glorious claim to pure democracy on the part of a pro-slavery Irish paper.

REPLY.

"We like Irish modesty—it is our own sort—but Irish ideas of Liberty are not always so thorough and consistent as we could wish them. To hate and resist the particular form of Oppression to which we have been exposed, by which we have suffered, is so natural and easy that we see little merit in it; to loathe and defy *all* Tyranny evermore, is what few severe sufferers by Oppression ever attain to. Ages of Slavery write their impress on the souls of the victims—we must not blame them, therefore, but cannot stifle our consciousness nor suppress our sorrow. It is sad to see how readily the great mass of our Irish-born citizens, themselves just escaped from a galling, degrading bondage, lend themselves to the iniquity of depressing and flouting the down-trodden African Race among us—it was specially sad to see them come up to the polls in squads, when our present State Constitution was adopted, and vote in solid mass against Equal Suffrage to all Citizens, shouting, 'Down with the Nagurs! Let them go back to Africa, *where they belong!*'—for such was the language of Adopted Citizens of one or two years' standing with regard to men born here, with their ancestors before them for several generations. We learn to hate Despotism and Enslavement more intensely when we are thus confronted by their ineffaceable impress on the souls of too many of their victims."

PROVOCATION.

An article in the Sunday Mercury condemning the Tribune for excluding theatrical criticism.

REPLY.

"The last time but one that we visited a theater—it was from seven to ten years ago—we were insulted by a ribald, buffoon song, in derision of total abstinence from intoxicating liquors. During the last season we understand that Mr. Brougham—whom we are specially blamed by the Mercury for not helping to a crowded benefit—has made a very nice thing of ridiculing *Socialism*. We doubt whether any great, pervading reform has been effected since there was a stage, which that stage has not ridiculed, misrepresented, and held up to popular odium. It is in its nature the creature of the mob—that is, of the least enlightened and least earnest portion of the community—and flatters the prejudices, courts the favor, and varnishes the vices of that portion. It bellows lustily for Liberty—meaning license to do as you please—but has small appetite for self-sacrifice, patient industry, and an unselfish devotion to duty. We fear that we shall not be able to like it, even with its groggeries and assignation-rooms shut up—but without this we cannot even begin."

PROVOCATION.

A sermon by Dr. Hawks denouncing Socialism in the usual style of well-fed thoughtlessness.

REPLY.

"If 'the Socialists,' as a body, were called upon to pronounce upon the propriety of taking the property of certain doctors of divinity and dividing it among the mechanics and laborers, to whom they have run recklessly and heavily in debt, we have no doubt they would vote very generally and heartily in the affirmative."

PROVOCATION.

A letter bewailing the threatened dissolution of the Union.

REPLY.

"*The dissolution of the Union would not be the dreadful affair he represents it.* It would be a very absurd act on the part of the seceding party, and would work great inconvenience and embarrassment, especially to the people of the great Mississippi Valley. In time, however, matters would accommodate themselves to the new political arrangements, and we should grow as many bushels of corn to the acre, and get as many yards of cloth from a hundred pounds of wool, as we now do. The Union is an excellent thing—quite too advantageous to be broken up in an age so utilitarian as this; but it is possible to exaggerate even *its* blessings."

PROVOCATION.

An article in a Southern paper recommending the secession of the Slave States from the Union.

REPLY.

" Dr. Franklin used to tell an anecdote illustrative of his idea of the folly of dueling, substantially thus : A man said to another in some public place, ' Sir, I wish you would move a little away from me, for a disagreeable odor proceeds from you.' 'Sir,' was the stern response, 'that is an insult, and you must fight me !' ' Certainly,' was the quiet reply, 'I will fight you if you wish it; but I don't see how that can mend the matter. If you kill me, I also shall smell badly ; and if I kill you, you will smell worse than you do now.'

" We have not yet been able to understand what our Disunionists, North or South, really expect to *gain* by dissolving the Union. * * * 'Three valuable slaves escaped,' do you say ? Will slaves be any less likely to run away when they know that, once across Mason and Dixon's line, they are safe from pursuit, and can never be reclaimed ? ' Every slaveholder is in continual ap-apprehension,' say you ? In the name of wonder, how is Disunion to soothe their nervous excitement ? They 'won't stand it,' eh ? Have they never heard of getting ' out of the frying-pan into the fire' ? Do let us hear how Slavery is to be fortified and perpetuated by Disunion !"

PROVOCATION.

The excessive *confidence* of Whigs in the election of Henry Clay.

REPLY.

" There is an old legend that once on a time all the folks in the world entered into an agreement that at a specified moment they would give one unanimous shout, just to see what a noise they *could* make, and what tremendous effects it would produce. The moment came—everybody was expecting to see trees, if not houses, thrown down by the mighty concussion ; when lo! the only sound was made by a dumb old woman, whose tongue was loosed by the excitement of the occasion. The rest had all stood with mouths and ears wide open to *hear* the great noise, and so forgot to make any !

" The moral we trust our Whig friends everywhere will take to heart."

PROVOCATION.

The passage in the President's Message which condemned those who opposed the Mexican war as *unpatriotic.*

REPLY.

Picture for the President's Bed-room.

"IS THIS WAR?"

"MONTEREY, Oct. 7, 1846.

"While I was stationed with our left wing in one of the forts, on the evening of the 21st, I saw a Mexican woman busily engaged in carrying bread and water to the wounded men of both armies. I saw this ministering angel raise the head of a wounded man, give him water and food, and then carefully bind up his wound with a handkerchief she took from her own head. After having exhausted her supplies, she went back to her own house to get more bread and water for others. As she was returning on her mission of mercy, to comfort other wounded persons, I heard the report of a gun, and saw the poor innocent creature fall dead! I think it was an accidental shot that struck her. I would not be willing to believe otherwise. It made me sick at heart, and, turning from the scene, I involuntarily raised my eyes towards heaven, and thought, great God! and *is this War?* Passing the spot next day, I saw her body still lying there with the bread by her side, and the broken gourd, with a few drops of water still in it—emblems of her errand. We buried her, and while we were digging her grave, cannon balls flew around us like hail."—*Cor. Louisville Cour.*

PROVOCATION.

Complaints of Charles Dickens' Advocacy of International Copyright at public dinners.

REPLY.

"We trust he will not be deterred from speaking the frank, round truth by any mistaken courtesy, diffidence, or misapprehension of public sentiment. He ought to speak out on this matter, for who shall protest against robbery

12*

if those who are robbed may not? Here is a man who writes for a living and writes nobly; and we of this country greedily devour his writings, are entertained and instructed by them, yet refuse so to protect his rights as an author that he can realize a single dollar from all their vast American sale and popularity. Is this right? Do we look well offering him toasts, compliments, and other syllabub, while we refuse him naked justice? while we say that every man may take from him the fruits of his labors without recompense or redress? It does very well in a dinner speech to say that fame and popularity, and all that, are more than sordid gold; but he has a wife and four children, whom his death may very possibly leave destitute, perhaps dependent for their bread, while publishers, who have grown rich on his writings, roll by in their carriages, and millions who have been instructed by them contribute not one farthing to their comfort. But suppose him rich, if you please, the justice of the case is unaltered. He is the just owner of his own productions as much as though he had made axes or horse-shoes; and the people who refuse to protect his right, ought not to insult him with the mockery of thriftless praise. Let us be just, and then generous. Good reader! if you think our guest ought to be enabled to live by and enjoy the fruits of his talents and toil, just put your names to a petition for an International Copyright Law, and then you can take his hand heartily if it comes in your way, and say, if need be, 'I have done what is in my power to protect you from robbery!' The passage of this act of long-deferred justice will be a greater tribute to his worth and achievements than acres of inflated compliments soaked in hogsheads of champagne.''

PROVOCATION.

A paragraph recommending a provision *for life* for the soldiers disabled in the Mexican war.

REPLY.

"Uncle Sam! you bedazzled old hedge-hog! don't you see 'glory' is cheap as dirt, only you never get done paying for it! Forty years hence, your boys will be still paying taxes to support the debt you are now piling up, and the cripples and other pensioners you are now manufacturing. How much more of this will satisfy you?''

PROVOCATION.

An accusation of 'malignant falsehood.'

REPLY.

"There lives not a man who knows the editor of this paper who can be made to believe that we have been guilty of 'malignant falsehood.'
    *   *   *   *   *   *   *   *

" We seek no controversy with the Sun; but, since it chooses to be personal, we defy its utmost industry and malice to point out a single act of our life inconsistent with integrity and honor. We dare it, in this respect, to do its worst!"

PROVOCATION.

This sentence in the Express: "If the editor of the Tribune believed a word of what he says, he would convert his profitable printing establishment into a Fourier common-stock concern."

REPLY.

" If our adviser will just point us to any passage, rule, maxim or precept of Fourier (of whom he appears to know so much) which prescribes a pro rata division of proceeds among all engaged in producing them, regardless of ability, efficiency, skill, experience, etc., we will assent to almost any absurdity he shall dictate.

  *   *   *   *   *   *   *   *

" As to ' carrying out his theories of Fourierism,' etc., he (the editor of the Tribune) has expended for this specific purpose some thousands of dollars, and intends to make the same disposition of more as soon as he has it to expend. Whether he ought to be guided by his own judgment or that of the Express man respecting the time and manner of thus testifying his faith, he will consider in due season. He has never had a dollar which was not the fair product of his own downright labor, and for whatever of worldly wealth may accrue to him beyond the needs of those dependent on his efforts he holds himself but the steward of a kind Providence, and bound to use it all as shall seem most conducive to the good of the Human Race. It is quite probable, however, that he will never satisfy the Express that he is either honest, sincere, or well-meaning, but that is not material. He has chosen, once for all, to answer a sort of attack which has become fashionable with a certain class of his enemies, and can hardly be driven to notice the like again."

PROVOCATION.

An allusion in the Courier and Enquirer to Mr. Greeley's diet, attire, socialism, philosophy, etc.

REPLY.

" It is true that the editor of the Tribune chooses mainly (not entirely) vegetable food ; but he never troubles his readers on the subject; it does not worry them ; why should it concern the Colonel ?   *   *   *   It is hard for *Philosophy* that so humble a man shall be made to stand as its exemplar; while *Christianity* is personified by the here of the Sunday duel with Hon. Tom. Marshall; but such luck will happen.

"As to our personal appearance, it does seem time that we should say something, to stay the flood of nonsense with which the town must by this time be nauseated. Some donkey a while ago, apparently anxious to assail or annoy the editor of this paper, and not well knowing with what, originated the story of his carelessness of personal appearances; and since then every blockhead of the same disposition and distressed by a similar lack of ideas, has repeated and exaggerated the foolery; until from its origin in the Albany Microscope it has sunk down at last to the columns of the Courier and Enquirer, growing more absurd at every landing. Yet all this time the object of this silly raillery has doubtless worn better clothes than two-thirds of those who thus assailed him—better than any of them could honestly wear, if they paid their debts otherwise than by bankruptcy; while, if they are indeed more cleanly than he, they must bathe very thoroughly not less than twice a day. The editor of the Tribune is the son of a poor and humble farmer; came to New York a minor, without a friend within 200 miles, less than ten dollars in his pocket, and precious little besides; he has never had a dollar from a relative, and has for years labored under a load of debt, (thrown on him by others' misconduct and the revulsion of 1837,) which he can now just see to the end of. Thenceforth he may be able to make a better show, if deemed essential by his friends; for himself, he has not much time or thought to bestow on the matter. That he ever *affected* eccentricity is most untrue; and certainly no costume he ever appeared in would create such a sensation in Broadway as that James Watson Webb would have worn but for the clemency of Governor Seward. Heaven grant our assailant may never hang with such weight on another Whig Executive! We drop him."

(Colonel Webb had been sentenced to two years' imprisonment for fighting a duel. Governor Seward pardoned him before he had served one day of his term.)

PROVOCATION.

A charge of 'infidelity,' in the Express.

REPLY.

"The editor of the Tribune has never been anything else than a believer in the Christian Religion, and has for many years been a member of a Christian Church. He never wrote or uttered a syllable in favor of Infidelity But truth is lost on the Express, which can never forgive us the 'Infidelity' of circulating a good many more copies, Daily and Weekly, than are taken of that paper."

PROVOCATION.

Letters complaining of the Tribune's hostility to the Mexican war

REPLY.

"Our faith is strong and clear that we serve our country best by obeying our Maker in all things, and that He requires us to bear open, unequivocal testimony against every iniquity, however specious, and to expose every lying pretense whereby men are instigated to imbrue their hands in each other's blood. We do not believe it possible that our country *can* be prospered in such a war as this. It may be victorious; it may acquire immense accessions of territory; but these victories, these acquisitions, will prove fearful calamities, by sapping the morals of our people, inflating them with pride and corrupting them with the lust of conquest and of gold, and leading them to look to the Commerce of the Indies and the Dominion of the Seas for those substantial blessings which follow only in the wake of peaceful, contented Labor. So sure as the Universe has a Ruler will every acre of territory we acquire by this war prove to our Nation a curse and the source of infinite calamities."

PROVOCATION.

An attempt on the part of Col. Webb to excite violence against the Tribune and its editor.

REPLY.

"This is no new trick on the part of the Courier. It is not the first nor the second time that it has attempted to excite a mob to violence and outrage against those whom it hates. In July, 1834, when, owing to its ferocious denunciations of the Abolitionists, a furious and law-defying mob held virtual possession of our city, assaulting dwellings, churches and persons obnoxious to its hate, and when the Mayor called out the citizens by Proclamation to assist in restoring tranquillity, the Courier (11th July) proclaimed:

"'It is time, for the reputation of the city, and perhaps for the welfare of themselves, that these Abolitionists and Amalgamationists should know the ground on which they stand. They are, we learn, always clamorous with the Police for protection, and demand it as a right inherent to their characters as American citizens. *Now we tell them* that, when they openly and publicly outrage public feeling, *they have no right to demand protection from the People they thus insult.* When they endeavor to disseminate opinions which, if generally imbibed, must infallibly destroy our National Union, and produce scenes of blood and carnage horrid to think of; when they thus preach up treason and murder, the *ægis of the Law indignantly withdraws its shelter from them.*

" ' When they vilify our religion by classing the Redeemer of the world in the lowest grade of the human species ; when they debase the noble race from which we spring—that race which called civilization into existence, and from which have proceeded all the great, the brave, and the good that have ever lived—and place it in the same scale as the most stupid, ferocious and cowardly of the divisions into which the Creator has divided mankind, then they place themselves *beyond the pale of all law*, for they violate every law, divine and human. Ought not, we ask, our City authorities to make them understand this ; to tell them that they prosecute their treasonable and beastly plans at their *own peril ?'*

" Such is the man, such the *means*, by which he seeks to bully Freemen out of the rights of Free Speech and Free Thought. There are those who cower before his threats and his ruffian appeals to mob violence—here is one who never will ! All the powers of Land-jobbing and Slave-jobbing cannot drive us one inch from the ground we have assumed of determined and open hostility to this atrocious war, its contrivers and abettors. Let those who threaten us with assassination understand, once for all, that we pity while we despise their baseness."

PROVOCATION.

The following, from the Express: " For woman we think the fittest place is home, ' sweet home '—by her own fireside and among her own children ; but the Tribune would put her in trowsers, or on stilts as a *public* woman, or tumble her pell-mell into some Fourier establishment."

REPLY.

The following, from the Express of *the same date :* " At the Park this evening the graceful Augusta, (whose benefit, last night, notwithstanding the weather, was fashionably and numerously attended,) takes her leave of us for the present. We can add nothing to what we have already said in praise of this charming artist's performances, farther than to express the hope that it may not be long ere we are again permitted to see her upon our boards. As in beauty, grace, delicacy, and refinement, she stands alone in her profession, so in private life she enjoys, and most justly, too, the highest reputation in all her relations."

PROVOCATION.

To what a low degree of debasement must the Coons have indeed fallen, when even so notorious a reprobate as Nick Biddle is disgusted with them.—*Plebeian.*

REPLY.

" All the ' notorious reprobates ' in the country were ' disgusted ' with the Whigs long ago. They have found their proper resting-place in the embraces of Loco-Focoism."

PROVOCATION.

Our whole national debt is less than sixty days' interest on that of Great Britain, yet, with all our resources the English call us bankrupt !—*Boston Post.*

REPLY.

"But England pays her interest—large as it is ; and if our States will not pay even their debts, small as they are, why should they not be called bankrupt ?"

PROVOCATION.

A charge that the Tribune sacrified the Right to the Expedient.

REPLY.

" Old stories very often have a forcible application to present times. The following anecdote we met with lately in an exchange paper :

" ' How is it, John, that you bring the wagon home in such a condition ?'

" ' I broke it driving over a stump.'

" ' Where ?'

" ' Back in the woods, half a mile or so.'

" ' But why did you run against the stump ?   Could n't you see how to drive straight ?'

" ' I *did* drive straight, sir, and that is the very reason that I drove over it The stump was directly in the middle of the road.'

" ' Why, then, did you not go round it ?'

" ' Because, sir, the stump had no right in the middle of the road, and I *had* a right in it.'

" ' True, John, the stump ought not to have been in the road, but I wonder that you were so foolish as not to consider that it *was* there, and that it was stronger than your wagon.'

" ' Why, father, do you think that I am always going to yield up my rights?   Not I.   I am determined to stick up to them, come what will.'

" ' But what is the use, John, of standing up to rights, when you only get a greater wrong by so doing ?'

" ' I shall stand up for them at all hazards.'

" ' Well, John, all I have to say is this—hereafter you must furnish your own wagon."

PROVOCATION.

The application. of the word ' Bah ' to one of the Tribune's arguments.

REPLY.

" We are quite willing that every animal should express its emotions in the language natural to it."

PROVOCATION.

Conservatism in general.

REBUKE.

"The stubborn conservative is like a horse on board a ferry-boat.   The horse may back, but the boat moves on, and the animal with it."

PROVOCATION.

A correspondent, to illustrate his position, that slave-owners have a right to move with their slaves into new territories, compared those territories to a village common, upon which every villager has an equal right to let his animals graze.

REPLY.

"No, sir.   A man may choose to pasture his *geese* upon the common, which would *spoil the pasture* for cows and horses.   The other villagers would be right in keeping out the geese, even by violence."

And thus the Tribune warred, and warring, prospered.   Repeated supplements, ever-increasing circulation, the frequent omission of advertisements, all testified that a man *may* be independent in the expression of the most unpopular opinions, and yet *not* be 'starved into silence.'

One more glance at the three volumes from which most of the above passages are taken, and we accompany our hero to new scenes.   In the Fifty-four-forty-or-Fight controversy, the Tribune of course took the side of peace and moderation.   Its obituary of General Jackson in 1845, being not *wholly* eulogistic, called forth angry comment from the democratic press.   In the same year, it gave to the advocates respectively of phonography, the phonetic system, and the magnetic telegraph, an ample hearing, and occasional encouragement.   In 1846, its Reporters were excluded from the gallery of the House of Representatives, because a correspondent stated, jocularly, that Mr. Sawyer, of Ohio, lunched in the House on sausages.   The weak member has since been styled Sausage Sawyer—a name which he will put off only with his mortal coil.   Throughout the Mexican war, the Tribune gave all due honor to the gallantry of the soldiers who fought its battles, on one occasion defending *Gen. Pierce* from the charge of cowardice and boasting.   In 1847, the editor made the tour of the great lake country, going to the uttermost parts of Lake Superior, and writing a series of letters which *revealed* the charms and the capabilities of that region. In the same year it gave a complete exposition of the so-called 'Revelations' of Mr. Andrew Jackson Davis, but without expressing any opinion as to their supernatural origin. War followed, of course. To Mr. Whitney's Pacific Railroad scheme it assigned sufficient space. Agassiz' lectures were admirably reported, with from ten to twenty woodcuts in the report of each lecture. Gen. Taylor's nomination to the presidency it descried in the distance, and opposed vehemently.

The last event of the seventh volume was the dispute with the Herald on the subject of the comparative circulation of the two papers. The Tribune challenged the Herald to an investigation by an impartial committee, whose report each paper should publish, and the losing party to give a hundred dollars to each of the two orphan asylums of the city. The Herald accepted. The report of the committee was as follows:

"The undersigned having been designated by the publishers of the New York Herald and New York Tribune, respectively, to examine jointly and report for publication the actual circulation of these two journals, have made the scrutiny required, and now report, that the average circulation of the two papers during the four weeks preceding the agreement which originated this investigation, was as follows:

New York Herald.		New York Tribune.	
Average Daily circulation	16,711	Average Daily circulation	11,455
" Weekly "	11,455	" Weekly "	15,780
" Presidential "	780	" Semi-Weekly	960
Total	28,946	Total	28,195

"The quantity of paper used by each establishment, during the four weeks above specified, was as follows: By the New York Herald, 975 reams for the Daily; 95¼ reams for the Weekly, and 5 reams for the Presidential. By the New York Tribune, 573 reams for the Daily; 131¼ reams for the Weekly, and 16 reams for the Semi-Weekly.

"We therefore decide that the Herald has the larger average circulation.

"JAMES G. WILSON,
"DANIEL H. MEGIE."

The Tribune paid the money, but protested that the 'Presidential Herald,' and, above all, the Sunday Herald, ought to have been excluded from the comparison.

CHAPTER XXII.

1848!

THE Year of Hope! You have not forgotten, O reader, the thrill, the tumult, the ecstasy of joy with which, on the morning of March 28th, 1848, you read in the morning papers these electric and transporting capitals. Regale your eyes with them once more:

FIFTEEN DAYS LATER FROM EUROPE.

ARRIVAL OF THE CAMBRIA.

HIGHLY IMPORTANT NEWS!

ABDICATION OF LOUIS PHILIPPE!

A REPUBLIC PROCLAIMED.

THE ROYAL FAMILY HAVE LEFT PARIS.

ASSAULT ON THE PALAIS ROYAL.

GREAT LOSS OF LIFE.

COMMUNICATION WITH THE INTERIOR CUT OFF.

RESIGNATION OF MINISTERS.

REVOLT IN AMIENS.—PARIS IN ALARM.

What history is condensed in these few words? Why has not that history been faithfully and minutely recorded, as a warning and a guide to the men of future revolutions? Why has no one deduced from the events of the last eighty years a science of Revolution, laid down the principles upon which success is possible, probable, certain? The attempt, and not the deed confounded Europe, and condemned her to more years of festering stagnation. "As I looked out of the window of my hotel, in Boulogne," says a recent traveler, "it seemed to me that all the men were soldiers, and that women did all the work." How pitiful! How shameful! A million of men under arms! The army, the elite of the nation! One man of every ten to keep the other nine *in order!* O! infinite and dastardly imbecility!

I need not say that the Tribune plunged into the European contests headlong. It chronicled every popular triumph with exultation unbounded. One of the editors of the paper, Mr. Charles A. Dana, went to Europe to procure the most authentic and direct information of events as they transpired, and his letters over the well-known initials, 'C. A. D.,' were a conspicuous and valuable feature of the year. Mr. Greeley wrote incessantly on the subject, blending advice with exhortation, jubilation with warning. In behalf of Ireland, his sympathies were most strongly aroused, and he accepted a place in the "Directory of the Friends of Ireland," to the funds of which he contributed liberally.

It was in August of this year, that the famous "Slievegammon" letters were published. As frequent allusions to this amusing affair are still made in the papers, it may as well be explained here. The country was on the tiptoe of expectation for important news of the Irish rebellion. The steamer arrived. Among the despatches of the Tribune were three letters from Dublin, giving news not contained in the newspapers. The Tribune "without vouching for the accuracy of the statements," made haste to publish the letters, with due glorification. This is one of them:

"DUBLIN, Aug. 3, 1848.

"No newspaper here dare tell the truth concerning the battle of Slievenamon, but from all we can learn, the people have had a great victory. Gen. Macdonald, the commander of the British forces, is killed, and six thousand troops are killed and wounded. The road for three miles is covered with the dead. We also have the inspiring intelligence that Kilkenny and Limerick have been taken by the people. *The people of Dublin have gone in thousands to assist in the country.* Mr. John B. Dillon was wounded in both legs. Mr. Meagher was also wounded in both arms. *It is generally expected that Dublin will rise and attack the jails on Sunday night,* (*Aug.* 6.)

"All the people coming in on the Railroad are cautioned and commanded not to tell the news. When the cars arrive, thousands of the Dublin people are waiting for the intelligence. The police drive away those who are seen asking questions. Why all this care of the government to prevent the spread of intelligence, unless it be that something has happened which they want kept as a secret? If they had obtained a victory they would be very apt to let us know it.

"We are informed that the 3d Bluffs (a regiment of Infantry) *turned and fought with the people*. The 31st regiment, at Athlone, have also declared for the people, and two regiments have been sent to disarm them.

"The mountain of Slievenamon is almost inaccessible. There is but one approach to it. It is said to be well supplied with provisions. It was a glorious place for our noble Smith O'Brien to select. It is said he has sixty thousand men around him, with a considerable supply of arms, ammunition, and cannon. In '98, the rebels could not be taken from Slievenamon until they chose to come out themselves.

"A lady who came to town yesterday, and who had passed the scene of battle, said that for three miles the stench arising from the dead men and horses was almost suffocating.

"Wexford was quite peaceable till recently—but the government in its madness proclaimed it, and now it is in arms to assist the cause. Now that we are fairly and spiritedly at it, are we not worthy of help? What are you doing for us? People of America, Ireland stretches her hand to you for assistance. Do not let us be disappointed.   B."

For a day or two, the Irish and the friends of Ireland exulted; but when the truth became known, their note was sadly changed, and the Tribune was widely accused of having originated a hoax. Whereas, it was only *too* innocent!

The most remarkable feature of the affair was, that the letters were written in good faith. The mind of Dublin was in a delirium of excitement, rumors of the wildest description were readily believed, and the writer of the Slievegammon letters was as completely deceived as any of his readers. It need only be added, that Horace Greeley never saw the letters till he saw them in print in the columns of the Tribune; when they appeared, he was touring in the uttermost parts of Lake Superior.

This was the year, too, of the Taylor and Fillmore 'campaign;' from which, however, the Tribune held obstinately aloof till late in the summer. Mr. Greeley had opposed the nomination of Gen. Taylor from the day it began to be agitated. He opposed it at the nominating convention in Philadelphia, and used all his influence to secure the nomination of Henry Clay. As soon as the final ballot decided the contest in favor of Taylor, he rushed from the hall in disgust, and, on his return to New York, could not sufficiently overcome his repugnance to the ticket, to print it, as the custom then was, at the head of his editorial columns. He ceased to *oppose* the election of Gen. Taylor, but would do nothing to promote it. The list of candidates does not appear, in the usual place in the Tribune, as the regular 'Whig nominations,' till the twenty-ninth of September, and even then, our editor consented to its appearance with great reluctance. Two days before, a whig meeting had been held at Vauxhall Garden, which Mr. Greeley chanced to attend. He was seen by the crowd, and after many, and very vociferous calls, he made a short address, to the following effect :

"I trust, fellow-citizens, I shall never be afraid nor ashamed to meet a Whig assemblage and express my sentiments on the political questions of the day. And although I have had no intimation till now that my presence here was expected or desired, I am the more ready to answer your call since I have heard intimations, even from this stand, that there was some mystery in my course to be cleared up—some astounding revelation with regard to it to be expected. And our eloquent friend from Kentucky even volunteered, in his remarks, to see me personally and get me right. If there be indeed any mystery in the premises, I will do my best to dispel it. But I have, in truth, nothing to reveal. I stated in announcing Gen. Taylor's nomination, the day after it was made, that I would support if I saw no other way to defeat the election of Lewis Cass. That pledge I have ever regarded. I shall faithfully redeem it. And, since there is now no chance remaining that any other than Gen. Taylor or Gen. Cass can be elected, I shall henceforth support the ticket nominated at Philadelphia, and do what I can for its election.

"But I have not changed my opinion of the nomination of Gen. Taylor. I believe it was unwise and unjust. For Gen. Taylor, personally, I have ever spoken with respect ; but I believe a candidate could and should have been chosen more deserving, more capable, more popular. I cannot pretend to support him with enthusiasm, for I do not feel any.

"Yet while I frankly avow that I would do little merely to make Gen. Taylor President, I cannot forget that others stand or fall with him, and that among them are Fillmore and Fish and Patterson, with whom I have battled for the Whig cause ever since I was entitled to vote, and to whom I cannot now be unfaithful. I cannot forget that if Gen. Taylor be elected we shall in all probability have a Whig Congress; if Gen. Cass is elected, a Loco-Foco Congress. Who can ask me to throw away all these because of my objections to Gen. Taylor?

"And then the question of Free Soil, what shall be the fate of that? I presume there are here some Free Soil men ['Yes! Yes! *all* Free Soil!']—I mean those to whom the question of extending or restricting Slavery outweighs all other considerations. I ask these what hope they have of keeping Slavery out of California and New-Mexico with Gen. Cass President, and a Loco-Foco Congress? I have none. And I appeal to every Free Soil Whig to ask himself this question—'How would South Carolina and Texas wish you to vote?' Can you doubt that your bitter adversaries would rejoice to hear that you had resolved to break off from the Whig party and permit Gen Cass to be chosen President, with an obedient Congress? *I* cannot doubt it. And I cannot believe that a wise or worthy course, which my bitterest adversaries would gladly work out for me.

"Of Gen. Taylor's soundness on this question, I feel no assurance, and can give none. But I believe him clearly pledged by his letters to leave legislation to Congress, and not attempt to control by his veto the policy of the country. I believe a Whig Congress will not consent to extend Slavery, and that a Whig President will not go to war with Congress and the general spirit of his party. So believing, I shall support the Whig nominations with a view to the triumph of Free Soil, trusting that the day is not distant when an amendment of the Federal Constitution will give the appointment of Postmasters and other local officers to the People, and strip the President of the enormous and anti-republican patronage which now causes the whole Political action of the country to hinge upon its Presidential Elections. Such are my views; such will be my course. I trust it will no longer be pretended that there is any mystery about them."

This speech was received with particular demonstrations of approval. It was felt that a serious obstacle to Gen. Taylor's success was removed, and that *now* the whig party would march on in an unbroken phalanx to certain victory.

The day which secured its triumph elected Horace Greeley to a seat in the House of Representatives, which the death of a member had made vacant. He was elected for one session only, and that, the short one of three months. How he came to be nominated has been explained by himself in a paragraph on the corruptive machinery of our primary elections: "An editor of the Tribune was once nominated through that machinery. So he was—to serve ninety days in Congress—and he does n't feel a bit proud of it. But let it be considered that the Convention was not chosen to nominate him, and did not (we presume) think of doing any such thing,

until it had unanimously nominated another, who unexpectedly declined, and then one of us was pitched upon to supply his place.
We don't know whether the Primaries were as corrupt then as now
or not; our impression is that they have been growing steadily
worse and worse—but no matter—let us have them reformed."

His nomination introduced great spirit into the contest, and he
was voted for with enthusiasm, particularly by two classes, working-men and thinking-men. His majority over his opponent was
3,177, the whole number of votes being 5,985. His majority considerably exceeded that of Gen. Taylor in the same wards. At
the same election Mr. Brooks, of the Express, was elected to a seat
in the House, and his 'Card' of thanksgiving to those who had
voted for him, elicited or suggested the following from Mr.
Greeley :

"TO THE ELECTORS OF THE VITH CONGRESSIONAL DISTRICT.

"The undersigned, late a candidate for Congress, respectfully returns his
thanks—first, to his political opponents for the uniform kindness and consideration with which he was treated by them throughout the canvass, and the un-
solicited suffrages with which he was honored by many of them ; secondly, to
the great mass of his political brethren, for the ardent, enthusiastic and effective support which they rendered him ; and, lastly, to that small portion of
the Whig electors who saw fit to withhold from him their votes, thereby
nearly or quite neutralizing the support he received from the opposite party.
Claiming for himself the right to vote for or against any candidate of his
party as his own sense of right and duty shall dictate, he very freely accords
to all others the same liberty, without offense or inquisition.

"During the late canvass I have not, according to my best recollection,
spoken of myself, and have not replied in any way to any sort of attack or
imputation. I have in no manner sought to deprecate the objections, nor to
soothe the terrors of that large and most influential class who deem my advocacy of Land Reform and Social Re-organization synonymous with Infidelity and systematic Robbery. To have entered upon explanations or vin-
dications of my views on these subjects in the crisis of a great National
struggle, which taxed every energy, and demanded every thought, comported
neither with my leisure nor my inclination.

"Neither have I seen fit at any time to justify nor allude to my participation in the efforts made here last summer to aid the people of Ireland in their
anticipated struggle for Liberty and Independence. I shall not do so now.
What I did then, in behalf of the Irish millions, I stand ready to do again,

so far as my means will permit, when a similar opportunity, with a like prospect of success, is presented—and not for them only, but for any equally oppressed and suffering people on the face of the earth. If any 'extortion and
plunder' were contrived and perpetrated in the meetings for Ireland at
Vauxhall last season, I am wholly unconscious of it, though I ought to be as
well informed as to the alleged 'extortion and plunder' as most others, whether
my information were obtained in the character of conspirator or that of victim. I feel impelled, however, by the expressions employed in Mr. Brooks's
card, to state that I have found nothing like an inclination to 'extortion and
plunder' in the councils of the leading friends of Ireland in this city, and nothing like a suspicion of such baseness among the thousands who sustained and
cheered them in their efforts. All the suspicions and imputations to which
those have been subjected, who freely gave their money and their exertions in aid of the generous though ineffectual effort for Ireland's liberation,
have originated with those who never gave that cause a prayer or a shilling,
and have not yet traveled beyond them.

"Respectfully,

"HORACE GREELEY.

"New York, Nov. 8, 1848."

CHAPTER XXIII.

THREE MONTHS IN CONGRESS.

His objects as a Member of Congress—His first acts—The Chaplain hypocrisy—The
Land Reform Bill—Distributing the Documents—Offers a novel Resolution—The
Mileage Exposé—Congressional delays—Explosion in the House—Mr. Turner's oration—Mr. Greeley defends himself—The Walker Tariff—Congress in a pet—Speech
at the Printers' Festival—The House in good humor—Traveling dead-head—Personal explanations—A dry haul—The amendment game—Congressional dignity—
Battle of the books—The Recruiting System—The last night of the Session—The
'usual gratuity'—The Inauguration Ball—Farewell to his constituents.

IN the composition of this work, I have, as a rule, abstained from
the impertinence of panegyric, and most of the few sentences of
an applausive nature which escaped my pen were promptly erased
on the first perusal of the passages which they disfigured. Of a
good action, the simplest narrative is the best panegyric; of a bad
action, the best justification is the *whole* truth about it. Therefore,

1.

We publish in another place some original
communications suggesting various means of
avoiding are ... within of the little people
... some of those seem to us of
disaster, some of those circumstances utilized
we were willing to let ... order be made.

though Horace Greeley's career in Congress is that part of his life which I regard with *unmingled* admiration, and though the conduct of his enemies during that period fills me with inexpressible disgust, I shall present here little more than a catalogue of his acts and endeavors while he held a place in the National bear-garden.

He seems to have kept two objects in view, during those three turbulent and exciting months: 1, to do his duty as a Representative of the People; 2, to let the people know exactly and fully what manner of place the House of Representatives is, by what methods their business is kept from being done, and under what pretexts their money is plundered. The first of these objects kept him constantly in his place on the floor of the House. The second he accomplished by daily letters to the Tribune, written, not at his desk in the House, but in his room before and after each day's hubbub. It will be convenient to arrange this chapter in the form of a journal.

Dec. 4th. This was Monday, the first day of the session. Horace Greeley 'took the oaths and his seat.'

Dec. 5th. He gave notice of his intention to bring in a bill to discourage speculation in the public lands, and establish homesteads upon the same.

Dec. 6th. He wrote a letter to the Tribune, in which he gave his first impressions of the House, and used some plain English. He spoke strongly upon the dishonesty of members drawing pay and yet not giving attendance at the early sessions, though the House had a hundred bills ready for conclusive action, and every day lost at the outset insures the defeat of ten bills at the close. As a specimen of plain English take this:

"On the third day, the Senate did not even succeed in forming a quorum; out of fifty-seven or eight members, who are all sure to be in for their pay and mileage, only twenty-nine appeared in their seats; and the annual hypocrisy of electing a chaplain had to go over and waste another day. If either House *had* a chaplain who dare preach to its members what they ought to hear —of their faithlessness, their neglect of duty, their iniquitous waste of time, and robbery of the public by taking from the treasury money which they have not even attempted to earn—then there would be some sense in the chaplain business: but any ill-bred Nathan or Elijah who should undertake such a job

13

would be kicked out in short order. So the chaplaincy remains a thing of grimace and mummery, nicely calculated to help some flockless and complaisant shepherd to a few hundred dollars, and impose on devout simpletons an exalted notion of the piety of Congress. Should not the truth be spoken?

*　*　*　*　*　*　*　*

"But in truth the great sorrow is, that so many of the Members of Congress, as of men in high station elsewhere, are merely dexterous jugglers, or the tools of dexterous jugglers, with the cup and balls of politics, shuffled into responsible places as a reward for past compliances, or in the hope of being there made useful to the inventors and patentees of their intellectual and moral greatness. To such men, the idea of anybody's coming to Congress for anything else than the distinction and the plunder, unless it be in the hope of intriguing their way up to some still lazier and more lucrative post, is so irresistibly comic—such an exhibition of jolly greenness, that they cannot contemplate it without danger of explosion."

Dec. 18th. Mr. Greeley introduced the Land Reform bill, of which he had given notice. It provided:

1. That any citizen, and any alien who had declared his intention of becoming a citizen, may file a pre-emption claim to 160 acres of Public Land, settle upon it, improve it, and have the privilege of buying it at any time within seven years of filing the claim, at the Government price of $1 25 per acre: *provided*, that he is not the owner or claimant of any other real estate.

2. That the Land office where a claim is filed, shall issue a Warrant of Pre-emption, securing the claimant in seven years' possession.

3. That, after five years' occupancy, a warrant-holder who makes oath of his intention to reside on and cultivate his land for life shall become the owner of any forty acres of his claim which he may select; the head of a family eighty acres.

4. That the price of public lands, when not sold to actual settlers, shall be five dollars per acre.

5. That false affidavits, made to procure land under the provisions of this bill, shall be punished by three years' hard labor in a State prison, by a fine not exceeding $1,000, and by the loss of the land fraudulently obtained.

Dec. 16th. The following notice appeared in the Tribune:

"In reference to many requests for copies of the President's Message and accompanying Documents, I desire to state that such Message and Documents are expected to cover twelve to fourteen hundred printed octavo pages, and to include three maps, the engraving of which will probably delay the publication for two or three weeks yet. I shall distribute my share of them as soon as possible, and make them go as far as they will; but I cannot satisfy half the demands upon me. As each Senator will have nearly two hundred copies, while Representatives have but about sixty each, applications to Senators, especially from the smaller States, are obviously the most promising."

Dec. 18th. Mr. Greeley offered the following resolution in the House:

"*Resolved,* That the Secretary of the Navy be requested to inquire into and report upon the expediency and feasibility of temporarily employing the whole or a portion of our national vessels, now on the Pacific station, in the transportation, at moderate rates, of American citizens and their effects from Panama and the Mexican ports on the Pacific to San Francisco in California."

This was the year of the gold fever. The fate of the above resolution may be given in its proposer's own words

"Monday," he wrote, "was expressly a resolution day; and (the order commencing at Ohio) it was about 2 o'clock before New York was called, and I had a chance to offer the foregoing. It was received, but could not be acted on except by unanimous consent (which was refused) until it shall have laid over one day—when of course it will never be reached again. When the States had been called through, I rose and asked the House to consider the above as modified so as to have the inquiry made by its own Naval Committee instead of the Secretary of the Navy—thus bringing its immediate consideration within the rules. No use—two or three on the other side sang out 'Object,' 'Object,' and the resolution went over—as all resolutions which any member indicates a purpose to debate must do. So the resolution cannot be reached again this Session."

Dec. 19th. Mr. Greeley made what the reporters styled 'a plain and forcible speech,' on the tariff, in which he animadverted upon a passage of the Message, wherein the President had alluded to manufacturers as an 'aristocratic class, and one that claimed exclusive privileges.' Mr. Greeley walked into the President.

Dec. 22d. On this day appeared in the Tribune, the famous Congressional Mileage Exposé. The history of this exposé is briefly related by Mr. Greeley, in the Whig Almanac for 1850.

"Early in December, I called on the Sergeant-at-Arms, for some money on account, he being paymaster of the House. The Schedule used by that officer was placed before me, showing the amount of mileage respectively accorded to every member of the House. Many of these amounts struck me as excessive, and I tried to recollect if any publication of all the allowances in a like case had ever been made through the journals, but could not remember any such publicity. On inquiry, I was informed that the amounts *were* regularly published in a certain document entitled 'The Public Accounts,' of which no considerable number was printed, and which was obviously not intended for popular distribution. [It is even omitted in *this* document for the year 1848, printed since I published my exposé, so that I can now find it in *no* public document whatever.] I could not remember that I had ever seen a copy, though one had been obtained and used by my assistant in making up last year's Almanac. It seemed to me, therefore, desirable that the facts should be brought to the knowledge of the public, and I resolved that it should be done.

"But how ? To have picked out a few of what seemed to me the most flagrant cases of overcharge, and print these alone, would be to invite and secure the reputation of partiality, partisanship, and personal animosity. No other course seemed so fair as to print the mileage of each member, with necessary elucidations. I accordingly employed an ex-clerk in one of the departments, and instructed him to make out a tabular exposé as follows :

"1. Name of each member of the House ;

"2. Actual distance from his residence to Washington by the shortest post-route ;

"3. Distance for which he is allowed and paid mileage ;

"4. Amount of mileage received by him ;

"5. Excess of mileage so received over what would have been if the distance had been computed by the shortest or most direct mail-route.

"The exposé was made out accordingly, and promptly forwarded to the Tribune, in which it appeared "

In the remarks which introduced the tabular statement, Mr. Greeley expressly and pointedly laid the blame of the enormous excess to the *law*. "Let no man," he said "jump at the conclusion that this excess has been charged and received contrary to law. The fact is otherwise. The members are all honorable men—if any irreverent infidel should doubt it, we can silence him by referring to the prefix to their names in the newspapers, and we presume each has charged just what the law allows him. That law expressly says that each shall receive eight dollars for every twenty miles traveled in coming to and returning from Congress, 'by the usually traveled route;' and of course if the route usually traveled from California to Washington is around Cape Horn, or the members from that embryo State shall choose to think it is—they will each be entitled to charge some $12,000 mileage per session, accordly. We assume that each has charged precisely what the law allows him, and thereupon we press home the question—*Ought not* THAT LAW *to be amended?*"

It appeared from the statement, that the whole number of " circuitous miles" charged was 183081, which, at forty cents a mile, amounted to $73,492 60. With about twelve exceptions, it showed that every member of the Senate and House had drawn more mileage than he *ought* to have been legally entitled to, the excess varying in amount from less than two dollars to more than a thousand dollars. Viewed merely as a piece of editorship, this mileage exposé was the best hit ever made by a New York paper. The effect of it upon the town was immediate and immense. It flew upon the wings of the country press, and became, in a few days, the talk of the nation. Its effect upon Congress, and upon the subsequent congressional career of its author, we shall see in a moment.

Dec. 23*d.* Mr. Greeley wrote a letter to the Tribune, in which he explained the maneuvering by which Congress, though it cannot legally adjourn over for more than three consecutive days, generally contrives to be idle during the whole of the Christmas holidays; *i. e.* from a day or two before Christmas, to a day or two after New Year's. "I was warned," he wrote, "when going to Baltimore last evening, that I might as well keep on to New York, as nothing would be done till some time in January. But I came back, determined to see at least how it was done." It was 'done' by making two bites at the cherry, adjourning first from Saturday to Wednesday; and, after a little show of work on Wednesday, Thursday and Friday, adjourning again till after New Year's day. Mr. Greeley spoke in opposition to the adjournment, and demanded the yeas and nays; but they were refused, and the first bite was consummated. "The old soldiers" of the House were too much for him, he said; but he took care to print the names of those who voted for the adjournment.

Dec. 27*th.* To-day the pent-up rage of Congress at the Mileage

Exposé, which had been fermenting for three days, burst forth; **and**
the gentleman who knocked out the bung, so to speak, was no other
than Mr. Sawyer, of Ohio, Mr. Sausage Sawyer of the Tribune.
Mr. Sawyer was 'down' in the Exposé for an excess of $281 60,
and he rose to a 'question of privilege.' A long and angry debate ensued, first upon the question whether the Exposé could be
debated at all; and secondly, if it could, what should be done about
it. It was decided, after much struggle and turmoil, that it was a
proper subject of discussion, and Mr. Turner, of Illinois, whose *excess*
amounted to the interesting sum of $998 40, moved a series of
resolutions, of which the following was the most important :

" *Resolved*, That a publication made in the New York Tribune on the
day of December, 1848, in which the mileage of members is set forth and
commented on, be referred to a Committee, with instructions to inquire
into and report whether said publication does not amount, in substance, to an
allegation of fraud against most of the members of this House in this matter
of their mileage; and if, in the judgment of the Committee, it does amount to
an allegation of fraud, then to inquire into it, and report whether that allegation is true or false."

The speech by which Mr. Turner introduced his resolutions was
not conceived in the most amiable spirit, nor delivered with that
'ofty composure which, it is supposed, should characterize the elocution of a legislator. These sentences from it will suffice for a
specimen :

" He now wished to call the attention of the House particularly to these
charges made by the editor of the New York Tribune, most, if not all, of which
charges he intended to show were absolutely false; and that the individual
who made them had either been actuated by the low, groveling, base, and
malignant desire to represent the Congress of the nation in a false and un-
enviable light before the country and the world, or that he had been actuated
by motives still more base—by the desire of acquiring an ephemeral notoriety,
by blazoning forth to the world what the writer attempted to show was fraud.
The whole article abounded in gross errors and willfully false statements, and
was evidently prompted by motives as base, unprincipled and corrupt as ever
actuated an individual in wielding his pen for the public press.

　　*　　*　　*　　*　　*　　*　　*　　*

" Perhaps the gentleman (he begged pardon), or rather the individual, perhaps the *thing*, that penned that article was not aware that his (Mr. T.'s) portion of the country was not cut up by railroads and traveled by stage-coaches

and other direct means of public conveyance, like the omnibuses in the City of New York, between all points; they had no other channel of communication except the mighty lakes or the rivers of the West; he could not get here in any other way. The law on the subject of Mileage authorized the members to charge upon the most direct usually-traveled route. Now, he ventured the assertion that there was not an individual in his District who ever came to this city, or to any of the North-eastern cities, who did not come by the way of the lakes or the rivers.

*　　*　　*　　*　　*　　*　　*　　*　　*

" He did not know but he was engaged in a very small business. A gentleman near him suggested that the writer of this article would not be believed anyhow; that, therefore, it was no slander. But his constituents, living two or three thousand miles distant, might not be aware of the facts, and therefore it was that he had deemed it necessary to repel the slanderous charges and imputations of fraud, so far as they concerned him."

Other honorable gentlemen followed, and discoursed eloquent discord in a similar strain. Mr. Greeley sat with unruffled composure and heard himself vilified for some hours without attempting to reply. At length, in a pause of the storm, he arose and gave notice, that when the resolutions were disposed of he should rise to a privileged question. The following sprightly conversation ensued:

" Mr. Thompson, of Indiana, moved that the resolutions be laid on the table.

" The Yeas and Nays were asked and ordered; and, being taken, were— Yeas 28, Nays 128.

" And the question recurring on the demand for the previous question:

" Mr. Fries inquired of the Speaker whether the question was susceptible of division.

" The Speaker said that the question could be taken separately on each resolution.

" A number of members here requested Mr. Evans to withdraw the demand for the previous question (i. e. permit Mr. Greeley to speak).

" Mr. Evans declined to withdraw the motion, and desired to state the reason why he did so. The reason was, that the gentleman from New York [Mr. Greeley] had spoken to an audience to which the members of this House could not speak. If the gentleman wished to assail any member of this House, let him do so here.

" The Speaker interposed, and was imperfectly heard, but was understood to say that it was out of order to refer personally to gentlemen on this floor.

" Mr. Evans said he would refer to the editor of the Tribune, and he insisted that the gentleman was not entitled to reply.

[" Loud cries from all parts of the House, ' Let him speak,' with mingling dissent.]

"The question was then taken on the demand for the previous question.

"But the House refused to second it.

"Mr. Greeley, after alluding to the comments that had been made upon the article in the Tribune relative to the subject of Mileage, and the abuse which had notoriously been practiced relating to it, said he had heard no gentleman quote one word in that article imputing an illegal charge to any member of this House, imputing anything but a legal, proper charge. The whole ground of the argument was this : Ought not the law to be changed? Ought not the mileage to be settled by the nearest route, instead of what was called the usually-traveled route, which authorized a gentleman coming from the center of Ohio to go around by Sandusky, Albany, New York, Philadelphia, and Baltimore, and to charge mileage upon that route. He did not object to any gentleman's taking that course if he saw fit; but was that the route upon which the mileage ought to be computed?

"Mr. Turner interposed, and inquired if the gentleman wrote that article?

"Mr. Greeley replied that the introduction to the article on mileage was written by himself; the transcript from the books of this House and from the accounts of the Senate was made by a reporter, at his direction. That reporter, who was formerly a clerk in the Post-Office Department, [Mr. Douglass Howard,] had taken the latest book in the Department, which contained the distances of the several post-offices in the country from Washington; and from that book he had got—honestly, he knew, though it might not have been entirely accurate in an instance or two—the official list of the distances of the several post-offices from this city. In every case, the post-office of the member, whether of the Senate or the House, had been looked out, his distance as charged set down, then the post-office book referred to, and the actual, honest distance by the shortest route set down opposite, and then the computation made how much the charge was an excess, not of legal mileage, but of what would be legal, if the mileage was computed by the nearest mail route.

"Mr. King, of Georgia, desired, at this point of the gentleman's remarks, to say a word; the gentleman said that the members charged; now, he (Mr. K.) desired to say, with reference to himself, that from the first, he had always refused to give any information to the Committee on Mileage with respect to the mileage to which he would be entitled. He had told them it was their special duty to settle the matter; that he would have nothing to do with it. He, therefore, had charged nothing.

"Mr. Greeley (continuing) said he thought all this showed the necessity of a new rule on the subject, for here they saw members shirking off, shrinking from the responsibility, and throwing it from one place to another. Nobody made up the account, but somehow an excess of $60,000 or $70,000 was charged in the accounts for mileage, and was paid from the Treasury.

"Mr. King interrupted, and asked if he meant to charge him (Mr. K.) with shirking? Was that the gentleman's remark?

Mr. Greeley replied, that he only said that by some means or other, this excess of mileage was charged, and was paid by the Treasury. This money ought to be saved. The same rule ought to be applied to members of Congress that was applied to other persons.

"Mr. King desired to ask the gentleman from New York if he had correctly understood his language, for he had heard him indistinctly? He (Mr. K.) had made the positive statement that he had never had anything to do with reference to the charge of his mileage, and he had understood the gentleman from New York to speak of shirking from responsibility. He desired to know if the gentleman applied that term to him?

"Mr. Greeley said he had applied it to no member.

"Mr. King asked, why make use of this term, then?

"Mr. Greeley's reply to this interrogatory was lost in the confusion which prevailed in consequence of members leaving their seats and coming forward to the area in the center.

"The Speaker called the House to order, and requested gentlemen to take their seats.

"Mr. Greeley proceeded. There was no intimation in the article that any member had made out his own account, but somehow or other the accounts had been so made up as to make a total excess of some $60,000 or $70,000, chargeable upon the Treasury. The general facts had been stated, to show that the law ought to be different, and there were several cases cited to show how the law worked badly; for instance, from one district in Ohio, the member formerly charged for four hundred miles, when he came on his own horse all the way; but now the member from the same district received mileage for some eight or nine hundred miles. Now, ought that to be so? The whole argument turned on this; now, the distances were traveled much easier than formerly, and yet more, in many cases *much* more, mileage was charged. The gentleman from Ohio who commenced this discussion, had made the point that there was some defect, some miscalculation in the estimate of distances. He could not help it; they had taken the post-office books, and relied on them, and if any member of the press had picked out a few members of this House, and held up their charges for mileage, it would have been considered invidious.

"Mr. Turner called the attention of the member from New York to the fact that the Postmaster General himself had thrown aside that Post Office book, in consequence of its incorrectness. He asked the gentleman if he did not know that fact?

"Mr. Greeley replied that the article itself stated that the Department did not charge mileage upon that book. Every possible excuse and mitigation had been given in the article; but he appealed to the House—they were the masters of the law—why would they not change it, and make it more just and equal?

"Mr. Sawyer wished to be allowed to ask the gentleman from New York a

13*

question. His complaint was that the article had done him injustice, by setting him down as some 300 miles nearer the seat of Government than his colleague [Mr. Schenck], although his colleague had stated before the House that
he [Mr. Sawyer] resided some 60 or 70 miles further.

"Now, he wanted to know why the gentleman had made this calculation
against him, and in favor of his colleague ?

"Mr. Greeley replied that he begged to assure the gentleman from Ohio
that he did not think he had ever been in his thoughts from the day he
had come here until the present day; but he had taken the figures from the
Post Office book, as transcribed by a former Clerk in the Post Office Department."

After much more sparring of the same description, the resolutions were adopted, the Committee was appointed, the House adjourned, and Mr. Greeley went home and wrote a somewhat facetious account of the day's proceedings. The most remarkable sentence in that letter was this:

"*It was but yesterday that a Senator said to me that though he was utterly
opposed to any reduction of Mileage, yet if the House did not stop passing
Retrenchment bills for Buncombe, and then running to the Senate and begging Senators to stop them there, he, for one, would vote to put through the
next Mileage Reduction bill that came to the Senate, just to punish Members
for their hypocrisy.*"

Jan. 2nd. Mr. Greeley offered a resolution calling on the Secretary of the Treasury to communicate to the House the advantages
resulting from the imposition by the Tariff of 1846 of duties of 5
and 10 per cent. on certain manufactures of wool and hemp, more
than was imposed on the raw material, and if they were not advantageous, then to state what action was required.

Jan. 3rd. The resolution came up.

"Mr. Wentworth objected to the Secretary of the Treasury being called
upon for such information. If the gentleman from New York would apply to
him [Mr. W.], he would give him his reasons, but he objected to this reference
to the Secretary of the Treasury. He moved to lay it on the table, but with-
drew it at the request of—

"Mr. Greeley, who said it was well known that the Tariff of 1846 was
prepared by the Secretary; he had been its eulogist and defender, and he
now wished for his views on the particular points specified. He had un-
officially more than thirty times called on the defenders of the Tariff of 1846

to explain these things, but had never been able to get one, and now he wanted to go to headquarters.

"Mr. Wentworth was not satified with this at all, and asked why the gentleman from New York did not call on him. He was ready to give him any information he had.

"Mr. Greeley—That call is not in order. [A laugh.]

"Mr. W.—But he objected to the passage of a resolution imputing that the Secretary of the Treasury had dictated a Tariff bill to the House.

"Mr. Washington Hunt—Does not the gentleman from Illinois know that the Committee of Ways and Means called upon the Secretary for a Tariff, and that he prepared and transmitted this Tariff to them?

"Mr. Wentworth—I do not *know* anything about it.

"Mr. Hunt—Well, the gentleman's ignorance is remarkable, for it was very generally, known.

"Mr. Wentworth renewed his motion to lay the resolution on the table, on which the Ayes and Noes were demanded, and resulted Ayes 86, Noes 87."

Jan. 4th. Congress, to-day, showed its spite at the mileage exposé in a truly extraordinary manner. At the last session of this very Congress the mileage of the Messengers appointed by the Electoral Colleges to bear their respective votes for President and Vice President to Washington, had been reduced to twelve and a half cents per mile each way. But *now* it was perceived by members that either the mileage of the Messengers must be restored or their own reduced. "Accordingly," wrote Mr. Greeley in one of his letters, "a joint resolution was promptly submitted to the Senate, doubling the mileage of Messengers, and it went through that exalted body very quickly and easily. I had not noticed that it had been definitively acted on at all until it made its appearance in the House to-day, and was driven through with indecent rapidity well befitting its character. No Committee was allowed to examine it, no opportunity was afforded to discuss it, but by whip and spur, Previous Question and brute force of numbers, it was rushed through the necessary stages, and sent to the President for his sanction."

The injustice of this impudent measure is apparent from the fact, that on the *reduced* scale of compensation, messengers received from ten to twenty dollars a day during the period of their *necessary* absence from home. "The messenger from Maine, for instance, brings the vote of his State five hundred and ninety-five miles, and need not be more than eight days absent from his business, at an expense certainly not exceeding $60 in all. The reduced compensation was $148 75, paying his expenses and giving him $11 per day over."

Jan. 7th. The Printers' Festival was held this evening at Washington, and Mr. Greeley attended it, and made a speech. His remarks were designed to show, that " the interests of tradesmen generally, but especially of the printing and publishing trade, including authors and editors, were intimately involved in the establishment and maintenance of high rates of compensation for labor in all departments of industry. It is of vital interest to us all that the entire community shall be buyers of books and subscribers to journals, which they cannot be unless their earnings are sufficient to supply generously their physical wants and leave some surplus for intellectual aliment. We ought, therefore, as a class, from regard to our own interests, if from no higher motive, to combine to keep up higher rates of compensation in our own business, and to favor every movement in behalf of such rates in other callings."

He concluded by offering a sentiment:

" *The Lightning of Intelligence*—Now crashing ancient tyrannies and toppling down thrones—May it swiftly irradiate the world."

Jan. 9th. The second debate on the subject of Mileage occurred to-day. It arose thus:

The following item being under consideration, viz.: " For Compensation and Mileage of Senators, Members of the House of Representatives, and Delegates, $768,200," Mr. Embree moved to amend it by adding thereto the following: " *Provided*, That the Mileage of Members of both Houses of Congress shall hereafter be estimated and charged upon the shortest mail-route from their places of residence, respectively, to the city of Washington."

The debate which ensued was long and animated, but wholly different in tone and manner from that of the previous week. Strange to relate, the Exposé found, on this occasion, stanch defenders, and the House was in excellent humor. The reader, if he feels curious to know the secret of this happy change, may find it, I think, in that part of a speech delivered in the course of the debate, where the orator said, that " he had not seen a single newspaper of the country which did not approve of the course which the gentleman from New York had taken ; and he believed there was no instance where the Editor of a paper had spoken out the genuine sentiments of the people, and made any expression of disapprobation in regard to the effort of the gentleman from New York to limit this unjustifiable taxation of Milage."

The debate relapsed, at length, into a merry conversation on the subject of traveling ' *dead-heads.*'

" Mr. Murphy said, when he came on, he left New York at 5 o'clock in the afternoon, and arrived at Philadelphia to.supper ; and then entering the car again, he slept very comfortably, and was here in the morning at 8 o'clock. He lost no time. The mileage was ninety dollars.

" Mr. Root would inquire of the gentleman from New York, whether he took his passage and came on as what the agents sometimes call a ' deadhead ?' [Laughter.]

" Mr. Murphy replied (amid considerable merriment and laughter) that he did not know of more than one member belonging to the New York delegation to whom that application could properly attach.

" Mr. Root said, although his friend from New York was tolerably expert in everything he treated of, yet he might not understand the meaning of the term he had used. He would inform him that the term ' dead-head,' was applied by the steamboat gentlemen to passengers who were allowed to travel without paying their fare. [A great deal of merriment prevailed throughout the hall, upon this allusion, as it manifestly referred to the two editors, the gentleman from Pennsylvania, Mr. Levin, and the gentleman from New York, Mr. Greeley.] But Mr. R. (continuing to speak) said he was opposed to all personalities. He never indulged in any such thing himself, and he never would favor such indulgence on the part of other gentlemen.

" Mr. Levin. I want merely to say—

" Mr. Root. I am afraid—

[" The confusion of voices and merriment which followed, completely drowned the few words of pleasant explanation delivered here by Mr. Levin.]

" Mr. Greeley addressed the chair.

" The Chairman. The gentleman from New York will suspend his remarks till the Committee shall come to order.

" Order being restored—

" Mr. Greeley said he did not pretend to know what the editor of the Philadelphia Sun, the gentleman from Pennsylvania [Mr. Levin], had done. But if any gentleman, anxious about the matter, would inquire at the railroad offices in Philadelphia and Baltimore, he would there be informed that he (Mr. G.) never had passed over any portion of either of those roads free of charge —never in the world. One of the gentlemen interested had once told him he might, but he never had.

" Mr. Embree next obtained the floor, but gave way for
" Mr. Haralson, who moved that the Committee rise.

"Mr. Greeley appealed to the gentleman from Georgia [Mr. Haralson] to withhold his motion, while he might, by the courtesy of the gentleman from Indiana [Mr. Embree], make a brief reply to the allusions which had been made to him and his course upon this subject. He asked only for five minutes But

" Mr. Haralson adhered to his motion, which was agreed to.
" So the Committee rose and reported, ' No conclusion.' "

Jan. 10th. The slave-trade in the District of Columbia was the subject of discussion, and the part which Mr. Greeley took in it, he thus described :

"SLAVE-TRADE IN THE DISTRICT.

MR. GREELEY'S REMARKS

In Defense of Mr. Gott's Resolution, (suppressed.)

["Throughout the whole discussion of Wednesday, Mr. Greeley struggled at every opportunity for the floor, and at first was awarded it, but the speaker, on reflection, decided that it belonged to Mr. Wentworth of Ill., who had made a previous motion. Had Mr. G. obtained the floor at any time, it was his intention to have spoken substantially as follows—the first paragraph being suggested by Mr. Sawyer's speech, and of course only meditated after that speech was delivered."]

Then follows the speech, which was short, eloquent, and convincing.

Jan. 11th. The third debate on the mileage question. Mr. Greeley, who " had been for three days struggling for the floor," obtained it, and spoke in defense of his course. For two highly autobiographical paragraphs of his speech, room must be found in these pages :

" The gentleman saw fit to speak of my vocation as an editor, and to charge me with editing my paper from my seat on this floor. Mr. Chairman, I do not believe there is one member in this Hall who has written less in his seat this session than I have done. I have been too much absorbed in the (to me) novel and exciting scenes around me to write, and have written no editorial here. Time enough for that, Sir, before and after your daily sessions. But the gentleman either directly charged or plainly insinuated that I have neglected my duties as a member of this House to attend to my own private business. I meet this charge with a positive and circumstantial denial. Except a brief sitting one Private Bill day, I have not been absent one hour in all, nor the half of it, from the deliberations of this House. I have never voted for an early adjournment, nor to adjourn over. My name will be found recorded on every call of the yeas and nays. And, as the gentleman insinuated a neglect of my duties as a member of a Committee (Public Lands,) I appeal to its Chairman for proof to any that need it, that I have never been absent from a meeting of that Committee, nor any part of one ; and that I have rather sought than shunned labor upon it. And I am confident that, alike in my seat, and out of it, I shall do as large a share of the work devolving upon this House as the gentleman from Mississippi will deem desirable.

"And now, Mr. Chairman, a word on the main question before us. I know very well—I knew from the first—what a low, contemptible, demagoguing business this of attempting to save public money always is. It is not a task for gentlemen—it is esteemed rather disreputable even for editors. Your gentlemenly work is spending—lavishing—distributing—taking. Savings are always such vulgar, beggarly, two-penny affairs—there is a sorry and stingy look about them most repugnant to all gentlemanly instincts. And beside, they never happen to hit the right place—it is always 'Strike higher !' 'Strike lower !' To be generous with other people's money—generous to self and friends especially, that is the way to be popular and commended. Go ahead, and never care for expense !—if your debts become inconvenient, you can repudiate, and blackguard your creditors as descended from Judas Iscariot !—Ah ! Mr. Chairman, *I* was not rocked in the cradle of gentility !"

Jan. 14th. He wrote out another speech on a noted slave case, which at that time was attracting much attention. This effort was entitled, " My Speech on Pacheco and his Negro." It was humorous, but it was a 'settler'; and it is a pity there is not room for it here.

Jan. 16th. The Mileage Committee made their report, exonerating members, condemning the Exposé, and asking to be excused from further consideration of the subject.

Jan. 17th. A running debate on Mileage—many suggestions made for the alteration of the law—nothing done—the proposed reform substantially defeated. The following conversation occurred upon the subject of Mr. Greeley's own mileage. Mr. Greeley tells the story himself, heading his letter ' A Dry Haul.

" The House having resolved itself again into a Committtee of the Whole, and taken up the Civil and Diplomatic Appropriation Bill, on which Mr. Murphy of New York had the floor, I stepped out to attend to some business, and was rather surprised to learn, on my way back to the Hall, that Mr. M. was making *me* the subject of his remarks. As I went in, Mr. M. continued—

" MURPHY.—As the gentleman is now in his seat, I will repeat what I have stated. I said that the gentleman who started this breeze about Mileage, by his publication in the Tribune, has himself charged and received Mileage by the *usual* instead of the *shortest* Mail Route. He charges me with taking $3 20 too much, yet I live a mile further than he, and charge but the same.

" GREELEY.—The gentleman is entirely mistaken. Finding my Mileage was computed at $184 for two hundred and thirty miles, and seeing that the shortest Mail Route, by the Post-Office Book of 1842, made the distance but two hundred and twenty-five miles, I, about three weeks ago, directed the Sergeant-at-Arms to correct his schedule and make my Mileage $180 for two hundred and twenty-five miles. I have not inquired since, but presume he has done so. So that I do not charge so much as the gentleman from Brooklyn, though, instead of living nearer, I live some two or three miles further from this city than he does, or fully two hundred and twenty-nine miles by the shortest Post Route.

" RICHARDSON of Illinois.—Did not the gentleman make out his own account at two hundred and thirty miles?

" GREELEY.—Yes, sir, I did at first; but, on learning that there was a shorter Post Route than that by which the Mileage from our city had been charged, I stepped at once to the Sergeant's room, informed him of the fact, and desired the proper correction. Living four miles beyond the New York Post Office, I might fairly have let the account stand as it was, but I did not.'

Jan. 18th. Mr. Greeley's own suggestion with regard to Mileage appears in the Tribune:

" 1. Reduce the Mileage to a generous but not extravagant allowance for the time and expense of traveling;

" 2. Reduce the ordinary or minimum pay to $5 per day, or (we prefer) $8 for each day of actual service, deducting Sundays, days of adjournment within two hours from the time of assembling, and all absences not caused by sickness;

" 3. Whenever a Member shall have served six sessions in either House, or both together, let his pay thenceforward be increased fifty per cent., and after he shall have served twelve years as aforesaid, let it be double that of an ordinary or new Member;

" 4. Pay the Chairman of each Committee, and all the Members of the three most important and laborious Committees of each House, fifty per cent above the ordinary rates, and the Chairmen of the three (or more) most responsible and laborious Committees of each House (say Ways and Means, Judiciary and Claims) double the ordinary rates; the Speaker double or treble, as should be deemed just;

"5. Limit the Long Sessions to four months, or half-pay thereafter."

Jan. 20th. Another letter appears to-day, exposing some of the expedients by which the time of Congress is wasted, and the public business delayed. The bill for the appointment of Private Claims' Commissioners was before the House. If it had passed, Congress would have been relieved of one-third of its business, and the claims of individuals against the government would have had a chance of fair adjustment. But no. "Amendment was piled on amendment, half of them merely as excuses for speaking, and so were withdrawn as soon as the Chairman's hammer fell to cut off the five-minute speech in full flow. The first section was finally worried through, and the second (there are sixteen) was mouthed over for half an hour or so. At two o'clock an amendment was ready to be voted on, tellers were ordered, and behold! *no quorum.* The roll was called over; members came running in from the lobbies and lounging-places; a large quorum was found present; the Chairman reported the fact to the Speaker, and the House relapsed into Committee again. The dull, droning business of proposing amendments which were scarcely heeded, making five-minute speeches that were not listened to, and taking votes where not half voted, and half of those who did were ignorant of what they were voting upon, proceeded some fifteen minutes longer, when the patriotic fortitude of the House gave way, and a motion that the Committee rise prevailed." The bill has not yet been passed. Just claims clamor in vain for liquidation, and doubtful ones are bullied or maneuvered through.

Jan. 22d. To-day the House of Representatives covered itself with glory. Mr. Greeley proposed an additional section to the General Appropriation Bill, to the effect, that members should not be paid for attendance when they did not attend, unless their absence was caused by sickness or public business. "At this very session," said Mr. Greeley in his speech on this occasion, "members have been absent for weeks together, attending to their private business, while this Committee is almost daily broken up for want of a quorum in attendance. This is a gross wrong to their constituents, to the country, and to those members who remain in their seats, and endeavor to urge forward the public business."

What followed is thus related by Mr. Greeley in his letter to the Tribune:

" Whereupon, Hon. Henry C. Murphy, of Brooklyn, (it takes him !) rose and moved the following addition to the proposed new section :

" ' And there shall also be deducted for such time from the compensation of members, who shall attend the sittings of *the House*, as they shall be employed in writing for newspapers.' "

" No objection being made, the House, with that exquisite sense of dignity and propriety which has characterized its conduct throughout, adopted this amendment.

" And then the whole section was voted down.

" Mr. Greeley next, with a view of arresting the prodigal habit which has grown up here of voting a bonus of $250 to each of the sub-clerks, messengers, pages, &c., &c., (their name is Legion) of both Houses, moved the following new section :

" ' Sec. 5. *And be it further enacted*, That it shall not henceforth be lawful for either Houses of Congress to appropriate and pay from its Contingent Fund any gratuity or extra compensation to any person whatever ; but every appropriation of public money for gratuities shall be lawful only when expressly approved and passed by both Houses of Congress.'

" This was voted down of course ; and on the last night or last but one of the session, a motion will doubtless be sprung in each house for the ' usual ' gratuity to these already enormously overpaid attendants, and it will probably pass, though I am informed that it is already contrary to law. But what of that ?"

Jan. 23*d.* An HONEST MAN in the House of Representatives of the United States seemed to be a foreign element, a fly in its cup, an ingredient that would not mix, a novelty that disturbed its peace. It struggled hard to find a pretext for the expulsion of the offensive person ; but not finding one, the next best thing was to endeavor to show the country that Horace Greeley was, after all, no better than members of Congress generally. To-day occurred the celebrated, yet pitiful, Battle of the Books. Congress, as every one knows, is accustomed annually to vote each member a small library of books, consisting of public documents, reports, statistics. Mr.

Greeley approved the appropriation for reasons which will appear in a moment, and he knew the measure was *sure* to pass ; yet, unwilling to give certain blackguards of the House a handle against him and against the reforms with which he was identified, he voted formally against the appropriation. It is but fair to all concerned in the Battle, that an account of it, published in the Congressional Globe, should be given here entire, or nearly so. Accordingly, here it is :

"In the House of Representatives on Tuesday, while the General Appropriation Bill was up, Mr. Edwards, of Ohio, offered the following amendment :

"*Be it further enacted,* That the sums of money appropriated in this bill for books be deducted from the pay of those members who voted for the appropriation.

"Mr. Edwards, in explanation, said that he had voted in favor of the appropriation, and was of course willing that the amendment should operate upon himself precisely as it would upon any other member. He had no apology to make for the vote he had given. He would send to the Clerk's table the New York 'Tribune' of January 18th, and would request the Clerk to read the paragraph which he (Mr. E.) had marked.

"The clerk read the following :

"'And yet, Mr. Speaker, it has been hinted if not asserted on this floor that I voted for these Congressional books! I certainly voted *against* them at every opportunity, when I understood the question. I voted against agreeing to that item of the report of the Committee of the Whole in favor of the Deficiency bill, and, the item prevailing, I voted against the whole bill. I tried to be against them at every opportunity. But it seems that on some stand-up vote in Committee of the Whole, when I utterly misunderstood what was the question before the Committee, I voted for this item. Gentlemen say I did, and I must presume they are right. I certainly never meant to do so, and I did all in my power in the House to defeat this appropriation. But it is common with me in incidental and hasty divisions, when I do not clearly understand the point to be decided, to vote with the Chairman of the Committee of Ways and Means, [Mr. Vinton,] who is so generally right and who has special charge of appropriation bills, and of expediting business generally. Thus only can I have voted for these books, as on all other occasions I certainly voted against them.'

"The paragraph having been read :

"Mr. Edwards (addressing Mr. Greeley) said, I wish to inquire of the gentleman from New York, if I am in order, whether that is his editorial ?

"Mr. Greeley rose.

[Hubbub for some minutes. After which ——]

"Mr. Greeley said, every gentleman here must remember that that was but the substance of what he had spoken on this floor. His colleague next him [Mr. Rumsey] had told him, that upon one occasion he (Mr. G.) had voted for the appropriation for books when he did not understand the vote. He (Mr. G.) had voted for tellers when a motion was made to pass the item; but by mistake the Chairman passed over the motion for tellers, and counted him in favor of the item.

"Mr. Edwards. I understand, then, that the gentleman voted without understanding what he was voting upon, and that he would have voted against taking the books had he not been mistaken.

"Mr. Greeley assented.

"Mr. Edwards. I assert that that declaration is unfounded in fact. I have the proof that the gentleman justified his vote both before and after the voting.

"Mr. Greeley called for the proof.

"Mr. Edwards said he held himself responsible, not elsewhere, but here, to prove that the gentleman from New York [Mr. Greeley] had justified his vote in favor of the books both before and after he gave that vote, upon the ground on which they all justified it, and that this editorial was an afterthought, written because he [Mr. G.] had been twitted by certain newspapers with having voted for the books. He held himself ready to name the persons by whom he could prove it.

"[Loud cries of 'Name them; name them.']

"Mr. Edwards (responding to the repeated invitations which were addressed to him) said, Charles Hudson, Dr. Darling, and Mr. Putnam.

"[The excitement was very great, and there was much confusion in all parts of the Hall—many members standing in the aisles, or crowding forward to the area and the vicinity of Mr. Greeley.]

"Mr. Greeley (addressing Mr. Edwards). I say, neither of these gentlemen will say so.

"Mr. Edwards. I hold myself responsible for the proof. (Addressing Mr. Hudson). Mr. Hudson will come to the stand. [General laughter.]

*   *   *   *   *   *   *   *

"Mr. Greeley. Now, if there is any gentleman who will say that he has understood me to say that I voted for it understandingly, I call upon him to come forward.

"Mr. Edwards. The gentleman calls for the testimony. Mr. Hudson is the man—Dr. Darling is the man.

"[Members had again flocked into the area. There were cries of 'Hudson, Hudson,' 'down in front,' and great disorder throughout the House.]

"The Chairman again earnestly called to order; and all proceedings were arrested for the moment, in order to obtain order.

"The House having become partially stilled—

"Mr. Hudson rose and said: I suppose it is not in order for me to address the Committee; but, as I have been called upon, if there is no objection, I have no objection on my part, to state what I have heard the gentleman from New York [Mr. Greeley] say.

"[Cries from all quarters, 'Hear him, hear him.']

"The Chairman. If there is no objection the gentleman can proceed.

"No objection being made—

"Mr. Hudson said, I can say, then, that on a particular day, when this book resolution had been before the House—as it was before the House several times, I cannot designate the day—but one day, when we had been passing upon the question of books, in walking from the Capitol, I fell in with my friend from New York, [Mr. Greeley;] that we conversed from the Capitol down on to the avenue in relation to these books; that he stated,—as I understood him (and I think I could not have been mistaken)—that he was in favor of the purchase of the books; that he either had or should vote for the books, and he stated two reasons: the one was, that some of these publications were of such a character that they would never be published unless there was some public patronage held out to the publishers; and the other reason was, that the other class of these books at least contained important elements of history, which would be lost unless gathered up and published soon, and as the distribution of these books was to diffuse the information over the community, he was in favor of the purchase of these books; and that he himself had suffered from not having access to works of this character. That was the substance of the conversation.

"Mr. Hudson having concluded—

"[There were cries of 'Darling, Darling.']

"Mr. Darling rose and (no objection being made) proceeded to say: On one of the days on which we voted for the books now in question—the day that the appropriation passed the House—I was on my way from the Capitol, and, passing down the steps, I accidentally came alongside the gentleman from New York, [Mr. Greeley,] who was in conversation with another gentleman— a member of the House—whose name I do not recollect. I heard him (Mr. G.) say he justified the appropriation for the books to the members, on the ground of their diffusing general information. He said that in the City of New York he knew of no place where he could go to obtain the information contained in these books; that although it was supposed that in that place the sources of information were much greater than in almost any other portion of the country, he would hardly know where to go in that City to find this information; and upon this ground that he would support the resolution in favor of the books. This conversation, the gentleman will recollect, took place going down from the west door of the Capitol and before we got to the avenue. I do not now recollect the gentleman who was with the gentleman from New York.

"Mr. Putnam rose amid loud cries of invitation, and (no objection being made,) said : As my name has been referred to in relation to this question, it is due perhaps to the gentleman from New York [Mr. Greeley] that I should state this : That some few days since the gentleman from Ohio [Mr. Edwards] called upon me here, and inquired of me whether I had heard my colleague [Mr. Greeley] say anything in relation to his vote as to the books. I that morning had received the paper, and I referred him to the editorial contained therein which has been read by the Clerk ; but I have no recollection of stating to the gentleman from Ohio that I heard my colleague say he justified the vote which he gave ; nor have I any recollection whatever that I ever heard my colleague say anything upon the subject after the vote given by him.

"The gentleman from Ohio must have misunderstood me, and it is due to my colleague that this explanation should be made.

"[Several voices : ' What did he say *before* the vote ?']

"I have no recollection [said Mr. P.] that I ever heard him say anything.

"Mr. Edwards rose, and wished to know if any of his five minutes was left ?

"No reply was heard ; but, after some conversation, (being allowed to proceed,) he said, I have stated that I have no apologies to make for giving this vote. I voted for these books for the very reasons which the gentleman from New York [Mr. Greeley] gave to these witnesses. I stated that I could prove by witnesses that the gentleman has given reasons of this kind, and that that editorial was an afterthought. If the House requires any more testimony. it can be had ; but out of the mouths of two witnesses he is condemned. That is scriptural as well as legal.

"I have not risen to retaliate for anything this editor has said in reference to the subject of mileage. I have been classed among those who have received excessive mileage. I traveled in coming to Washington forty-three miles further than the Committee paid me ; but I stated before the Committee the reasons why I made the change of route. I had been capsized once——

"The Chairman interposed, and said he felt bound to arrest this debate.

"[Cries of ' Greeley ! Greeley !']

"Mr. Greeley rose——

"The Chairman stated that it would not be in order for the gentleman to address the House while there was no question pending.

"[Cries of ' Suspend the rules ; hear him.']

"Mr. Tallmadge rose and inquired if his colleague could not proceed by general consent ?

"The Chairman replied in the affirmative

"No objection was made, and

"Mr. Greeley proceeded. The gentleman from Massachusetts [Mr. Hudson] simply misunderstood only one thing. He states me to have urged the considerations which he urged to me. He urged these considerations—and I think forcibly. I say now, as I did the other day on the floor of this House,

I approve of the appropriation for the books, provided they are honestly disposed of according to the intent of the appropriation.

"Mr. Edwards. Why, then, did you make the denial in the Tribune, and say that you voted against it?

"Mr. Greeley. I did vote against it. I did not vote for it, because I did not choose to have some sort of gentlemen on this floor hawk at me. The gentleman from Massachusetts [Mr. Hudson] submitted considerations to me of which I admitted the force. I admit them now; I admit that the House was justifiable in voting for this appropriation, for the reason ably stated by the Chairman of the Committee of Ways and Means; and I think I was justifiable, as this Hall will show, in not voting for it. In no particular was there collision between what I said on this floor, the editorial, and what I said in conversation. The conversation to which the gentleman from Wisconsin [Mr. Darling] refers is doubtless the same of which the gentleman from Massachusetts [Mr. Hudson] has spoken.

" Mr. G. having concluded—

" On motion of Mr. Vinton, the Committee rose and reported the bill to the House, with sundry amendments."

After the flurry was over, Mr. Greeley went home and wrote an explanation which appeared a day or two after in the Tribune. It began thus:

"The attack upon me by Dr. Edwards of Ohio to-day, was entirely unexpected. I had never heard nor suspected that he cherished ill-will toward me, or took exception to anything I had said or done. I have spoken with him almost daily as a friendly acquaintance, and only this morning had a familiar conference with him respecting his report on the importation of adulterated drugs, which has just been presented. I have endeavored through the Tribune to do justice to his spirited and most useful labors on that subject. Neither in word nor look did he ever intimate that he was offended with me—not even this morning. Conceive, then, my astonishment, when, in Committee of the Whole, after the general appropriation bill had been gone through by items and sections, he rose, and moving a sham amendment in order to obtain the floor, sent to the clerk's desk to be read, a Tribune containing the substance of my remarks on a recent occasion, repelling the charge that I had voted for the Congressional books, and that having been read, he proceeded to pronounce it false, and declare that he had three wit nesses in the House to prove it. I certainly could not have been more surprised had he drawn a pistol and taken aim at me."

*   *   *   *   *   *   *

Jan. 25th. Mr. Greeley (as a member of the Committee on public lands,) reported a bill providing for the reduction of the price of lands bordering on Lake Superior. In Committee of the Whole, he moved to strike from the army appropriation bill the item of $38,000 for the recruiting service, sustaining his amendment by an elaborate speech on the recruiting system. Rejected. Mr. Greeley moved, later in the day, that the mileage of officers be calculated by the shortest route. Rejected. The most striking passage of the speech on the recruiting system was this:

"Mr. Chairman, of all the iniquities and rascalities committed in our country, I think those perpetrated in this business of recruiting are among the most flagrant. I doubt whether this government punishes as many frauds in all as it incites by maintaining this system of recruiting. I have seen something of it, and been by hearsay made acquainted with much more. A simple, poor man, somewhat addicted to drinking, awakes from a drunken revel in which he has disgraced himself by some outrage, or inflicted some injury, or has squandered means essential to the support of his family. He is ashamed to enter his home—ashamed to meet the friends who have known him a respectable and sober man. At this moment of half insanity and utter horror, the tempter besets him, portrays the joys of a soldier's life in the most glowing and seductive colors, and persuades him to enlist. Doubtless men have often been made drunk on purpose to delude them into an enlistment ; for there is (or lately was) a bounty paid to whoever will bring in an acceptable recruit to the station. All manner of false inducements are constantly held out —absurd hopes of promotion and glory are incited, and, when not in his right mind, the dupe is fastened for a term which will probably outlast his life. Very soon he repents and begs to be released—his distracted wife pleads—his famishing children implore—but all in vain. Shylock must have his bond, and the husband and father is torn away from them for years—probably for ever. This whole business of recruiting is a systematic robbery of husbands from their wives, fathers from their children, and sons from their widowed and dependent mothers. It is not possible that a Christian people have any need of such a fabric of iniquity, and I call upon this House to unite in decreeing its abolition."

Jan. 31st. In Committee of the Whole, the naval appropriation bill being under consideration, Mr. Greeley offered an amendment reducing the list of warrant officers.   Rejected.   He also spoke for abolishing the grog system.

Feb. 1*st.*   Mr. Greeley made a motion to the effect, that no officer of the navy should be promoted, as long as there were others of the higher rank unemployed.·   Rejected.

Feb 14*th.*   Mr. Greeley submitted the following resolution .

" *Resolved,* That the Committee on the Judiciary be instructed to inquire whether there be anything in our laws or authoritative Judicial decisions which countenances the British doctrine of ' Once a subject always a subject,' and to report what action of Congress, if any, be necessary to conform the laws and decisions aforesaid, consistently and thoroughly to the American doctrine, affirming the right of every man to migrate from his native land to some other, and, in becoming a citizen of the latter, to renounce all allegiance and responsibility to the former."

Objected to.   The resolution, was therefore, according to the rule, withdrawn.

Feb. 26th.   A proposal having been made that the New Mexico and Texas Boundary Question be referred to the Supreme Court, Mr. Greeley objected, on the ground that the majority of the members of that Court were slaveholders.

Feb. 27th.   The Committee to whom had been referred Mr. Greeley's Land Reform Bill, asked leave to be relieved from the further consideration of the subject.   Mr. Greeley demanded the yeas and nays.   Refused.   A motion was made to lay the bill on the table, which was carried, the yeas and nays being again refused.   In the debates on the organization of the new territories, California, etc., Mr. Greeley took a spirited part.

March 4th.   The last night of the session had arrived.   It was Saturday.   The appropriation bills were not yet passed.   The bill for the organization of the new territories, acquired by the Mexican war, had still to be acted upon.   It was a night of struggle, turmoil, and violence, though the interests of future empires were concerned in its *deliberations.*   A few sentences from Mr. Greeley's own narrative will give an idea of the scene :

14

" The House met after recess at six—the seats soon filled, the lobbies and galleries densely crowded.

*   *   *   *   *

" Members struggled in wild tumult for the floor.

*   *   *   *   *

" A vehement yell of ' Mr. Speaker !' rose from the scores who jumped on the instant for the floor.

*   *   *   *   *   *   *   *

" Here the effect of the Previous Question was exhausted, and the wild rush of half the House for the floor—the universal yell of ' Mr. Speaker !' was renewed.

*   *   *   *   *   *   *   *

" The House, still intensely excited, proceeded very irregularly to other business—mainly because they must await the Senate's action on the Thomson substitute.

*   *   *   *   *   *   *   *

" At length—after weary watching till five o'clock in the morning, when even garrulity had exhausted itself with talking on all manner of frivolous pretexts, and relapsed into grateful silence—when profligacy had been satiated with rascally votes of the public money in gratuities to almost everybody connected with Congress, &c., &c.,—word came that the Senate had receded altogether from its Walker amendment and everything of the sort, agreeing to the bill as an Appropriation Bill simply, and killing the House amendment by surrendering its own. Close on its heels came the Senate's concurrence in the House bill extending the Revenue Laws to California; and a message was sent with both bills to rouse Mr. Polk (still President by sufferance) from his first slumbers at the Irving House (whither he had retired from the Capitol some hours before), and procure his signature to the two bills. In due time—though it seemed *very* long now that it was broad daylight and the excitement was subsiding—word was returned that the President had signed the bills and had nothing further to offer, a message having been sent to the Senate, and the House was ready to adjourn; Mr. Winthrop made an eloquent and affecting address on relinquishing the Chair; and the House, a little before seven o'clock in the bright sunshine of this blessed Sunday morning—twice blessed after a cloudy week of fog and mist, snow and rain without, and of fierce contention and angry discord within the Capitol—adjourned *sine die*.

" The Senate, I understand, has not yet adjourned, but the latter end of it had gathered in a bundle about the Vice-President's chair, and was still passing extra gratuities to everybody—and if the bottom is not out of the Treasury, may be doing so yet for aught I know. Having seen enough of this, I did not go over to their chamber, but came wearily away."

March 5th.   One more glimpse ought to be given at the House during that last night of the session. Mr. Greeley explains the methods, the infamous tricks, by which the ' usual' extra allowance to the employés of the House is maneuvered through.

"Let me," he wrote, "explain the origin of this ' usual' iniquity. I am informed that it commenced at the close of one of the earlier of the Long Sessions now unhappily almost biennial. It was then urged, with some plausibility, that a number (perhaps half) of the sub-officers and employés of the House were paid a fixed sum for the session—that, having now been obliged to labor an unusually long term, they were justly entitled to additional pay. The Treasury was full—the expectants were assiduous and seductive—the Members were generous—(it is so easy for most men to be flush with other people's money)—and the resolution passed. Next session the precedent was pleaded, although the reason for it utterly failed, and the resolution slipped through again—I never saw how till last night. Thenceforward the thing went easier and easier, until the disease has become chronic, and only to be cured by the most determined surgery.

"Late last night—or rather early this morning—while the House was awaiting the final action of the Senate on the Territorial collision—a fresh attempt was made to get in the ' usual extra allowance' again. Being objected to and not in order, a direct attempt was made to suspend the Rules, (I think I cannot be mistaken in my recollection,) and defeated—not two-thirds rising in its favor, although the free liquor and trimmings provided by the expectants of the bounty had for hours stood open to all comers in a convenient side-room, and a great many had already taken too much. In this dilemma the motion was revamped into one to suspend the Rules to admit a resolution to *pay the Chaplain his usual* compensation for the Session's service, and I was personally and urgently entreated not to resist *this*, and thus leave the Chaplain utterly unpaid. I *did* resist it, however, not believing it true that no provision had till this hour been made for paying the Chaplain, and suspecting some swindle lay behind it. The appeal was more successful with others, and the House suspended its Rules to admit this Chaplain-paying resolution, out of order. The moment this was done a motion was made to *amend the resolution* by providing another allowance for somebody or other, and upon this was piled still another amendment—' Monsieur Tonson come again· -to pay ' the usual extra compensation' to the sub-Clerks, Messengers, Pages, etc., etc. As soon as this amendment was reached for consideration—in fact as soon as I could get the floor to do it—I raised the point of order that it could not be in order, when the rules had been suspended for a particular purpose, to let in, under cover of that suspension, an entirely different proposition, for which, by itself, it was notorious that a suspension could not be obtained. This was promptly overruled, the Ayes and Noes on the amendment refused—ditto on e Resolution as amended—and the whole crowded through under the Previous

Question in less than no time. Monroe Edwards would have admired the dexterity and celerity of the performance. All that could be obtained was a vote by Tellers, and ninety-four voted in favor to twenty-two against—a bare quorum in all, a great many being then in the Senate—none, I believe, at that moment in the 'extra' refectory. But had no such refectory been opened in either end of the Capitol, I believe the personal collisions which disgraced the Nation through its Representatives would not have occurred. I shall not speak further of them—I would not mention them at all if they were not unhappily notorious already.''

March 6*th.* Mr. Greeley was one of the three thousand persons who attended the Inauguration ball, which he describes as "a sweaty, seething, sweltering jam, a crowd of duped foregatherers from all creation."

" I went," he says, "to see the new President, who had not before come within my contracted range of vision, and to mark the reception accorded to him by the assembled thousands. I came to gaze on stately heads, not nimble feet, and for an hour have been content to gaze on the flitting phantasmagoria of senatorial brows and epauletted shoulders—of orators and brunettes, office-seekers and beauties. I have had 'something too much of this,' and lo ! 'the hour of hours' has come—the buzz of expectation subsides into a murmur of satisfaction—the new President is descending the grand stairway which terminates in the ball-room, and the human mass forms in two deep columns to receive him. Between these, General Taylor, supported on either hand, walks through the long saloon and back through other like columns, bowing and greeting with kind familiarity those on this side and on that, paying especial attention to the ladies as is fit, and everywhere welcomed in turn with the most cordial good wishes. All wish him well in his new and arduous position, even those who struggled hardest to prevent his reaching it.

"But, as at the Inauguration, there is the least possible enthusiasm. Now and then a cheer is attempted, but the result is so nearly a failure that the daring leader in the exploit is among the first to laugh at the miscarriage. There is not a bit of heart in it.

" ' They don't seem to cheer with much unction,' I remarked to a Taylor original.

" ' Ne-e-o, they don't cheer much,' he as faintly replied ; 'there is a good deal of doubt as to the decorum of cheering at a social ball.'

"True enough : the possibility of indecorum was sufficient to check the impulse to cheer, and very few passed the barrier. The cheers 'stuck in the throat,' like Macbeth's Amen, and the proprieties of the occasion were well cared for.

" But just imagine Old Hal walking down that staircase, the just inaugurated President of the United States, into the midst of three thousand of the *elite* of the beauty and chivalry of the Whig party, and think how the rafters would have quivered with the universal acclamation. Just think of some one stopping to consider whether it might not be indecorous to cheer on such an occasion! What a solitary hermit that considerer would be!

*   *   *   *   *   *   *   *

" Let those who will, flatter the chief dispenser of Executive patronage, discovering in every act and feature some resemblance to Washington—I am content to wait, and watch, and hope. I burn no incense on his altar, attach no flattering epithets to his name. I turn from this imposing pageant, so rich in glitter, so poor in feeling, to think of him who *should* have been the central figure of this grand panorama—the distant, the powerless, the unforgotten—' behind the mountains, but not setting'—the eloquent champion of Liberty in both hemispheres—whose voice thrilled the hearts of the uprising, the long-trampled sons of Leonidas and Xenophon—whose appeals for South American independence were read to the hastily mustered squadrons of Bolivar, and nerved them to sweep from this fair continent the myrmidons of Spanish oppression. My heart is with him in his far southern abiding-place—with him, the early advocate of African Emancipation; the life-long champion of a diversified Home Industry; of Internal Improvement; and not less glorious in his later years as the stern reprover of the fatal spirit of conquest and aggression. Let the exulting thousands quaff their red wines at the revel to the victor of Monterey and Buena Vista, while wit points the sentiment with an epigram, and beauty crowns it with her smiles : more grateful to me the stillness of my lonely chamber, this cup of crystal water in which I honor the cherished memory with the old, familiar aspiration—

' Here 's to you, Harry Clay !' "

March 9th. Mr. Greeley has returned to New York. To-day he took leave of his constituents in a long letter published in the Tribune, in which he reviewed the proceedings of the late session, characterized it as a Failure, and declined to take to himself any part of the blame thereof. These were his concluding words :

"My work as your servant is done—whether well or ill it remains for you to judge. Very likely I gave the wrong vote on some of the difficult and complicated questions to which I was called to respond Ay or No with hardly a moment's warning. If so, you can detect and condemn the error; for my name stands recorded in the divisions by Yeas and Nays on every public and all but one private bill, (which was laid on the table the moment the sitting opened, and on which my name had just been passed as I entered the Hall.) I wish it were the usage among us to publish less of speeches and

more of propositions and votes thereupon—it would give the mass of the people a much clearer insight into the management of their public affairs. My
successor being already chosen and commissioned, I shall hardly be suspected
of seeking your further kindness, and I shall be heartily rejoiced if he
shall be able to combine equal zeal in your service with greater efficiency—
equal fearlessness with greater popularity. That I have been somewhat
annoyed at times by some of the consequences of my Mileage Exposé is
true, but I have never wished to recall it, nor have I felt that I owed an
apology to any, and I am quite confident, that if you had sent to Washington
(as you doubtless might have done) a more sternly honest and fearless Representative, he would have made himself more unpopular with a large portion of the House than I did. I thank you heartily for the glimpse of public
life which your favor has afforded me, and hope to render it useful henceforth not to myself only but to the public. In ceasing to be your agent, and
returning with renewed zest to my private cares and duties, I have a single
additional favor to ask, not of you especially, but of all; and I am sure my
friends at least will grant it without hesitation. It is that you and they will
oblige me henceforth by remembering that my name is simply

"HORACE GREELEY."

And thus ended Horace Greeley's three months in Congress. No
man ever served his country more faithfully. No man ever received
less reward. One would have supposed, that such a manly and
brave endeavor to economize the public money and the public time,
such singular devotion to the public interests in the face of opposition, obloquy, insult, would have elicited from the whole country,
or at least from many parts of it, cordial expressions of approval.
It did not, however. With no applauding shouts was Horace
Greeley welcomed on his return from the Seat of Corruption. No
enthusiastic mass-meetings of his constituents passed a series of
resolutions, approving his course. He has not been named for re-
election. Do the people, then, generally feel that an Honest Man
is out of place in the Congress of the United States?

Only from the little town of North Fairfield, Ohio, came a hearty
cry of WELL DONE! A meeting of the citizens of that place was
held for the purpose of expressing their sense of his gallant and
honorable conduct. He responded to their applauding resolutions
in a characteristic letter. "Let me beg of you," said he, "to think
little of *Persons*, in this connection, and much of *Measures*. Should
any see fit to tell you that I am dishonest, or ambitious, or hollow-

hearted in this matter, don't stop to contradict or confute him, but press on his attention the main question respecting the honesty of these crooked charges. It is with these the public is concerned, and not this or that man's motives. Calling me a hypocrite or demagogue cannot make a charge of $1,664 for coming to Congress from Illinois and going back again an honest one."

CHAPTER XXIV.

ASSOCIATION IN THE TRIBUNE OFFICE.

Accessions to the corps—The course of the Tribune—Horace Greeley in Ohio—The Rochester knockings—The mediums at Mr. Greeley's house—Jenny Lind goes to see them—Her behavior—Woman's Rights Convention—The Tribune Association —The hireling system.

But the Tribune held on its strong, triumphant way. Circula-tion, ever on the increase; advertisements, from twenty to twenty-six columns daily; supplements, three, four, and five times a week; price increased to a shilling a week without loss of subscribers; European reputation extending; correspondence more and more able and various; editorials more and more elaborate and telling; new ink infused into the Tribune's swelling veins. What with the supplements and the thickness of the paper, the volumes of 1849 and 1850 are of dimensions most huge. We must look through them, notwithstanding, turning over the broad black leaves swiftly, pausing seldom, lingering never.

The letter R. attached to the literary notices apprises us that early in 1849, Mr. George Ripley began to lend the Tribune the aid of his various learning and considerate pen. Bayard Taylor, re-turned from viewing Europe a-foot, is now one of the Tribune corps, and this year he goes to California, and 'opens up' the land of gold to the view of all the world, by writing a series of letters, graphic and glowing. Mr. Dana comes home and resumes his place in the office as manager-general and second-in-command. During the disgraceful period of Re-action, William Henry Fry, now the Tribune's sledge-hammer, and the country's sham-demolisher, then an American in Paris, sent across the Atlantic to the Tribune many a letter of savage protest. Mr. G. G. Foster served up New York in savory 'slices' and dainty 'items.' Horace Greeley confined himself less to the office than before; but whether he went on a tour of observation, or of lecturing, or of political agitation, he brought all he saw, heard and thought, to bear in enhancing the interest and value of his paper.

In 1849, the Tribune, true to its instinct of giving hospitality to every new or revived idea, afforded Proudhon a full hearing in reviews, essays and biography. His maxim, PROPERTY IS ROBBERY, a maxim felt to be true, and acted upon by the early Christians who had all things in common, furnished a superior text to the conservative papers and pulpits. As usual, the Tribune was accused of *uttering* those benign words, not of publishing them merely. On the occasion of the Astor-Place riot, the Tribune supported the authorities, and wrote much for law and order. In the Hungarian war, the editors of the Tribune took an intense interest, and Mr. Greeley tried hard to condense some of the prevalent enthusiasm into substantial help for the cause. He thought that embroidered flags and parchment addresses were not exactly the commodities of which Kossuth stood most in need, and he proposed the raising of a patriotic loan for Hungary, in shares of a hundred dollars each. "Let each village, each rural town, each club, make up by collections or otherwise, enough to take one share of scrip, and so up to as many as possible ; let our men of wealth and income be personally solicited to invest generously, and let us resolve at least to raise one million dollars off-hand. Another million will come much easier after the first." But alas ! soon came the news of the catastrophe. For a reformed code, the Tribune contended powerfully during the whole time of the agitation of that subject. It welcomed Father Matthew this year—fought Bishop Hughes—discussed slavery—bewailed the fall of Rome—denounced Louis Napoleon—had Consul Walsh, the American apologist of despotism, recalled from Paris— helped Mrs. Putnam finish Bowen of the North American Review —explained to workmen the advantages of association in labor— assisted Watson G. Haynes in his crusade against flogging in the navy—went dead against the divorce theories of Henry James and others—and did whatsoever else seemed good in its own eyes. Among other things, it did this: Horace Greeley being accused by the Evening Post of a corrupt compliancy with the slave interest, the Tribune began its reply with these words:

"You lie, villain! willfully, wickedly, basely lie!"

This observation called forth much remark at the time.

Thrice the editor of the Tribune visited the Great West this year, and he received many private assurances, though, I believe, no public ones, that his course in Congress was approved by the Great West. In Cincinnati he received marked attention, which he gracefully acknowledged in a letter, published May 21st, 1849:—"I can hardly close this letter without acknowledging the many acts of personal generosity, the uniform and positive kindness, with which I was treated by the citizens of the stately Queen of the West. I would not so far misconstrue and outrage these hospitalities as to drag the names of those who tendered them before the public gaze; but I may express in these general terms my regret that time was not afforded me to testify more expressly my appreciation of regards which could not fail to gratify, even while they embarrassed, one so unfitted for and unambitious of personal attentions. In these, the disappointment caused by the failure of our expected National Temperance Jubilee was quickly forgotten, and only the stern demands of an exacting vocation impelled me to leave so soon a city at once so munificent and so interesting, the majestic outpost of Free Labor and Free Institutions, in whose every street the sound of the builder's hammer and trowel speaks so audibly of a growth and greatness hardly yet begun. Kind friends of Cincinnati and of Southern Ohio! I wave you a grateful farewell!"

In December appeared the first account of the 'Rochester Knockings' in the Tribune, in the form of a letter from that most practical of cities. The letter was received and published quite in the ordinary course of business, and without the slightest suspicion on the part of the editors, that they were doing an act of historical importance. On the contrary, they were disposed to laugh at the mysterious narrative; and, a few days after its publication, in reply to an anxious correspondent, the paper held the following language:—

" For ourselves, we really cannot see that these singular revelations and experiences have, so far, amounted to much.   We have yet to hear of a clairvoyant whose statements concerning facts were reliable, or whose facts were any better than any other person's, or who could discourse rationally without mixing in a proportion of nonsense.   And as for these spirits in Western New York or elsewhere, it strikes us they might be better engaged than in going about to give from one to three knocks on the floor in response to successive letters of the alphabet; and we are confident that ghosts who had anything to communicate worth listening to, would hardly stoop to so uninteresting a business as hammering."

Nor has the Tribune, since, contained one editorial word intimating a belief in the spiritual origin of the ' manifestations.'   The subject, however, attracted much attention, and, when the Rochester ' mediums' came to the city, Horace Greeley, in the hope of elucidating the mystery, invited them to reside at his house, which they did for several weeks.   He did not discover, nor has any one discovered, the cause of the singular phenomena, but he very soon arrived at the conclusion, that, whatever their cause might be, they could be of no practical utility, could throw no light on the tortuous and difficult path of human life, nor cast any trustworthy gleams into the future.   During the stay of the mediums at his house, they were visited by a host of distinguished persons, and, among others, by Jenny Lind, whose behavior on the occasion was not exactly what the devotees of that vocalist would expect.

At the request of her manager, Mr. Greeley called upon the Nightingale at the Union Hotel, and, in the course of his visit, fell into conversation with gentlemen present on the topic of the day, the Spiritual Manifestations.   The Swede approached, listened to the conversation with greedy ears, and expressed a desire to witness some of the marvels which she heard described.   Mr. Greeley invited *her* to his house, and the following Sunday morning was appointed for the visit.   She came, and a crowd came with her, filling up the narrow parlor of the house, and rendering anything in the way of calm investigation impossible.   Mr. Greeley said as much; but the ' mediums' entered, and the rappings struck up with vigor, Jenny sitting on one side of the table and Mr. Greeley on the other.

"Take your hands from under the table," said she to the master of the house, with the air of a new duchess.

It was as though she had said, ' I did n't come here to be hum-bugged, Mr. Pale Face, and you 'd better not try it.' The insulted gentleman raised his hands into the air, and did not request her to leave the house, nor manifest in any other way his evidently acute sense of her impertinent conduct. As long as we worship a woman on account of a slight peculiarity in the formation of part of her throat, the woman so worshiped will give herself airs. The blame is ours, not hers. The rapping continued, and the party retired, after some hours, sufficiently puzzled, but apparently convinced that there was no collusion between the table and the ' mediums.'

The subsequent history of the spiritual movement is well known. It has caused much pain, and harm, and loss. But, like every other Event, its good results, realized and prospective, are greater far than its evil. It has awakened some from the insanity of indiffer-ence, to the insanity of an exclusive devotion to things spiritual. But many spiritualists have stopped short of the latter insanity, and are better men, in every respect, than they were—better, happier, and more hopeful. It has delivered many from the degrading fear of death and the future, a fear more prevalent, perhaps, than is supposed; for men are naturally and justly ashamed of their fears, and do not willingly tell them. Spiritualism, moreover, may be among the means by which the way is to be prepared for that gen-eral, that earnest, that fearless consideration of our religious sys-tems to which they will, one day, be subjected, and from which the truth in them has nothing to fear, but how much to hope!

It was about the same time that the Tribune rendered another service to the country, by publishing a fair and full report of the first Woman's Convention, accompanying the report with respectful and favorable remarks. "It is easy," said the Tribune, "to be smart, to be droll, to be facetious, in opposition to the demands of these Female Reformers; and, in decrying assumptions so novel and opposed to established habits and usages, a little wit will go a great way. But when a sincere republican is asked to say in sober earnest what adequate reason he can give for refusing the demand of women to an equal participation with men in political rights, he must answer, None at all. True, he may say that he believes it unwise in them to make the demand—he may say the great major-ity desire no such thing; that they prefer to devote their time to the discharge of home duties and the enjoyment of home delights, leaving the functions of legislators, sheriffs, jurymen, militia, to their fathers, husbands, brothers; yet if, after all, the question recurs, 'But suppose the women *should* generally prefer a complete political equality with men, what would you say to that demand?'—the answer must be, 'I accede to it. However unwise or mistaken the demand, it is but the assertion of a natural right, and as such must be conceded.'"

The report of this convention excited much discussion and more ridicule. The ridicule has died away, but the discussion of the subject of woman's rights and wrongs will probably continue until every statute which does wrong to woman is expunged from the laws. And if, before voting goes out of fashion, the ladies should generally desire the happiness, such as it is, of taking part in elections, doubtless that happiness will be conceded them also.

Meanwhile, an important movement was going on in the office of the Tribune. Since the time when Mr. Greeley practically gave up Fourierism, he had taken a deep interest in the subject of Associated Labor, and in 1848, 1849, and 1850, the Tribune published countless articles, showing workingmen how to become their own employers, and share among themselves the profits of their work, instead of letting them go to swell the gains of a 'Boss.' It was but natural that workingmen should reply, as they often did,—'If Association is the right principle on which to conduct business, if it is best, safest, and most just to all concerned, why not try it yourself, O Tribune of the People!' That was precisely what the Tribune of the People had long meditated, and, in the year 1849, he and his partner resolved to make the experiment. They were both, at the time, in the enjoyment of incomes superfluously large, and the contemplated change in their business was, therefore, not induced by any business exigency. It was the result of a pure, disinterested attachment to principle; a desire to add practice to preaching.

The establishment was valued by competent judges at a hundred thousand dollars, a low valuation; for its annual profits amounted to more than thirty thousand dollars. But newspaper property differs from all other. It is won with difficulty, but it is precarious. An unlucky paragraph may depreciate it one-half; a perverse editor, destroy it altogether. It is tangible, and yet intangible. It is a body and it is a soul. Horace Greeley might have said, *The Tribune—it is I*, with more truth than the French King could boast, when he made a similar remark touching himself and the State. And Mr. McElrath, glancing round at the types, the subscription books, the iron chest, the mighty heaps of paper, and listening to the thunder of the press in the vaults below, might have been pardoned if he had said, *The Tribune—these are the Tribune*.

The property was divided into a hundred shares of a thousand dollars each, and a few of them were offered for sale to the leading men in each department, the foremen of the composing and press-rooms, the chief clerks and bookkeepers, the most prominent editors. In all, about twenty shares were thus disposed of, each of the original partners selling six. In some cases, the purchasers paid only a part of the price in cash, and were allowed to pay the remainder out of the income of their share. Each share entitled its possessor to one vote in the decisions of the company. In the course of time, further sales of shares took place, until the original proprietors were owners of not more than two-thirds of the concern. Practically, the power, the controlling voice, belonged still to Messrs. Greeley and McElrath; but the dignity and advantage of OWNERSHIP were conferred on all those who exercised authority in the several departments. And this was the great good of the new system.

That there is something in being a hired servant which is naturally and deeply abhorrent to men is shown by the intense desire that every hireling manifests to escape from that condition. Many are the ties by which man has been bound in industry to his fellow man; but, of them all, *that* seems to be one of the most unfraternal, unsafe, unfair, and demoralizing. The slave, degraded and defrauded as he is, is *safe;* the hireling holds his life at the caprice of another man; for, says Shylock, he takes my life who takes from me my means of living. "How is business?" said one employer to another, a few days ago. "Dull," was the reply. "I hold on merely to keep the hands in work." Think of that. *Merely* to keep the hands in work. *Merely!* As if there *could* be a better reason for 'holding on;' as if all other reasons combined were not infinitely inferior in weight to this one of keeping men in work.

keeping men in heart, keeping men in happiness, keeping men in use! But universal hirelingism is quite inevitable at present, when the governments and institutions most admired may be defined as Organized Distrusts. When we are better, and truer, and wiser, we shall labor together on very different terms than are known to Wayland's Political Economy. Till then, we must live in pitiful estrangement from one another, and strive in sorry competition for triumphs which bless not when they are gained.

The experiment of association in the office of the Tribune, has, to all appearance, worked well. The paper has improved steadily and rapidly. It has lost none of its independence, none of its vivacity, and has gained in weight, wisdom, and influence. A vast amount of work of various kinds is done in the office, but it is done harmoniously and easily. And of all the proprietors, there is not one, whether he be editor, printer, or clerk, who does not live in a more stylish house, fare more sumptuously, and dress more expensively, than the Editor in Chief. The experiment, however, is incomplete. Nine-tenths of those who assist in the work of the Tribune are connected with it solely by the tie of wages, which change not, whether the profits of the establishment fall to zero or rise to the highest notch upon the scale.

More of association in the next chapter, where our hero appears, for the first time, in the character of author.

CHAPTER XXV.

ON THE PLATFORM.

HINTS TOWARDS REFORMS.

The Lecture System—Comparative popularity of the leading Lecturers—Horace Greeley at the Tabernacle—His audience—His appearance—His manner of speaking—His occasional addresses—The 'Hints' published—Its one subject, the Emancipation of Labor—The Problems of the Time—The 'successful' man—The duty of the State—The educated class—A narrative for workingmen—The catastrophe.

LECTURING, of late years, has become, in this country, what is facetiously termed 'an institution.' And whether we regard it as a means of public instruction, or as a means of making money, we cannot deny that it is an institution of great importance.

"The bubble reputation," said Shakspeare. Reputation is a bubble no longer. Reputation, it has been discovered, will '*draw*.' Reputation *alone* will draw ! That airy nothing is, through the instrumentality of the new institution, convertible into solid cash, into a large pile of solid cash. Small fortunes have been made by it in a single winter, by a single lecture or course of lectures. Thackeray, by much toil and continuous production, attained an income of seven thousand dollars a year. He crosses the Atlantic, and, in one short season, without producing a line, gains thirteen thousand, and could have gained twice as much if he had been half as much a man of business as he is a man of genius. Ik Marvel writes a book or two which brings him great praise and some cash. Then he writes one lecture, and not a very good one either, and transmutes a little of his glory into plenty of money, with which he buys leisure to produce a work worthy of his powers. Bayard Taylor roams over a great part of the habitable and uninhabitable globe. He writes letters to the Tribune, very long, very fatiguing to write on a journey, and not salable at a high price. He comes home, and sighs, perchance, that there are no more lands to visit. " Lecture !" suggests the Tribune, and he lectures. He carries two or three manuscripts in his carpet-bag, equal to half a dozen of his Tribune letters in bulk. He ranges the country, far and wide, and brings back money enough to carry him ten times round the world. It was his reputation that did the business. He *earned* that money by years of adventure and endurance in strange and exceedingly hot countries ; he *gathered up* his earnings in three months—earnings which, but for the invention of lecturing, he would never have touched a dollar of. Park Benjamin, if he sold his satirical poems to Putnam's Magazine, would get less than hod-carriers' wages ; but, selling them directly to the public, at so much a *hear*, they bring him in, by the time he has supplied all his customers, five thousand dollars apiece. Lecturing has been commended as an antidote to the alleged ' docility' of the press, and the alleged dullness of the pulpit. It may be. *I* praise it because it enables the man of letters to get partial payment from the public for the incalculable services which he renders the public.

Lectures are important, too, as the means by which the public are brought into actual contact and acquaintance with the famous men of the country. What a delight it is to *see* the men whose writings have charmed, and moved, and formed us! And there is something in the presence of a man, in the living voice, in the eye, the face, the gesture, that gives to thought and feeling an expression far more effective than the pen, unassisted by these, can ever attain. Horace Greeley is aware of this, and he seldom omits an opportunity of bringing the influence of his presence to bear in inculcating the doctrines to which he is attached. He has been for many years in the habit of writing one or two lectures in the course of the season, and delivering them as occasion offered. No man, not a professional lecturer, appears oftener on the platform than he. In the winter of 1853–4, he lectured, on an average, twice a week. He has this advantage over the professional lecturer. The professional lecturer stands before the public in the same position as an editor; that is, he is subject to the same necessity to make the banquet palatable to those who pay for it, and who will not come again if they do not like it. But the man whose position is already secure, to whom lecturing is only a subsidiary employment, is free to utter the most unpopular truths.

A statement published last winter, of the proceeds of a course of lectures delivered before the Young Men's Association of Chicago, affords a test, though an imperfect one, of the popularity of some of our lecturers. E. P. Whipple, again to borrow the language of the theater, 'drew' seventy-nine dollars; Horace Mann, ninety-five; Geo. W. Curtis, eighty-seven; Dr. Lord, thirty-three; Horace Greeley, one hundred and ninety-three; Theodore Parker, one hundred and twelve; W. H. Channing, thirty-three; Ralph Waldo Emerson, (did it rain?) thirty-seven; Bishop Potter, forty-five; John G. Saxe, one hundred and thirty-five; W. H. C. Hosmer, twenty-six; Bayard Taylor (lucky fellow!) two hundred and fifty-two.

In large cities, the lecturer has to contend with rival attractions, theater, concert, and opera. His performance is subject to a comparison with the sermons of distinguished clergymen, of which some are of a quality that no lecture surpasses. To know the importance of the popular lecturer, one must reside in a country town the even tenor of whose way is seldom broken by an event of commanding interest. The arrival of the great man is expected with eagerness. A committee of the village magnates meet him at the cars and escort him to his lodging. There has been contention who should be his entertainer, and the owner of the best house has carried off the prize. He is introduced to half the adult population. There is a buzz and an agitation throughout the town. There is talk of the distinguished visitor at all the tea-tables, in the stores, and across the palings of garden-fences. The largest church is generally the scene of his triumph, and it *is* a triumph. The words of the stranger are listened to with attentive admiration, and the impression they make is not obliterated by the recurrence of a new excitement on the morrow.

Not so in the city, the hurrying, tumultuous city, where the reappearance of Solomon in all his glory, preceded by Dodworth's band, would serve as the leading feature of the newspapers for one day, give occasion for a few depreciatory articles on the next, and be swept from remembrance by a new astonishment on the third. Yet, as we are here, let us go to the Tabernacle and hear Horace Greeley lecture.

The Tabernacle, otherwise called 'The Cave,' is a church which looks as little like an ecclesiastical edifice as can be imagined. It is a large, circular building, with a floor slanting towards the platform—pulpit it has none—and galleries that rise, rank above rank, nearly to the ceiling, which is supported by six thick, smooth columns, that stand round what has been impiously styled the 'pit,' like giant spectators of a pigmy show. The platform is so placed, that the speaker stands not far from the center of the building, where he seems engulfed in a sea of audience, that swells and surges all around and far above him. A better place for an oratorical display the city does not afford. It received its cavernous nickname, merely in derision of the economical expenditure of gas that its proprietors venture upon when they let the building for an evening entertainment; and the dismal hue of the walls and columns gives further propriety to the epithet. The Tabernacle will contain an audience of three thousand persons. At present, there are not more than six speakers and speakeresses in the United States who can 'draw' it full; and of these, Horace Greeley is not

one. His number is about twelve hundred. Let us suppose it half
past seven, and the twelve hundred arrived.

The audience, we observe, has decidedly the air of a country audience. Fine ladies and fine gentlemen there are none. Of farmers
who look as if they took the Weekly Tribune and are in town to-
night by accident, there are hundreds. City mechanics are present
in considerable numbers. An ardent-looking young man, with a
spacious forehead and a turn-over shirt-collar, may be seen here and
there. A few ladies in Bloomer costume of surpassing ugliness—
the costume, not the ladies—come down the steep aisles now and
then, with a well-preserved air of unconsciousness. In *that* assembly no one laughs at them. The audience is sturdy, solid-looking,
appreciative and opinionative, ready for broad views and broad
humor, and hard hits. Every third man is reading a newspaper,
for they are men of progress, and must make haste to keep up with
the times, and the times are fast. Men are going about offering
books for sale—perhaps Uncle Tom, perhaps a treatise on Water
Cure, and perhaps Horace Greeley's Hints toward Reforms; but
certainly something which belongs to the Nineteenth Century. A
good many free and independent citizens keep their hats on, and
some 'speak right out in meeting,' as they converse with their
neighbors.

But the lecturer enters at the little door under the gallery on the
right, and when the applause apprizes us of the fact, we catch a
glimpse of his bald head and sweet face as he wags his hasty way
to the platform, escorted by a few special adherents of the " Cause"
he is about to advocate. The newspapers, the hats, the conversation, the book-selling are discontinued, and silent attention is the
order of the night. People with 'causes' at their hearts are full of
business, and on such occasions there are always some preliminary
announcements to be made—of lectures to come, of meetings to be
held, of articles to appear, of days to celebrate, of subscriptions to
be undertaken. These over, the lecturer rises, takes his place at
the desk, and, while the applause, which never fails on any public
occasion to greet this man, continues, he opens his lecture, puts on
his spectacles, and then, looking up at the audience with an expression of inquiring benignity, waits to begin.

Generally, Mr. Greeley's attire is in a condition of the most hopeless, and, as it were, elaborate disorder.   It would be applauded on the stage as an excellent 'make-up.'   His dress, it is true, is never unclean, and seldom unsound; but he usually presents the appear-ance of a man who has been traveling, night and day, for six weeks in a stage-coach, stopping long enough for an occasional hasty ablu-tion, and a hurried throwing on of clean linen.   It must be admit ted, however, that when he is going to deliver a set lecture to a city audience his apparel does bear marks of an attempted adjustment. But it is the attempt of a man who does something to which he is unaccustomed, and the result is sometimes more surprising than the neglect.   On the present occasion, the lecturer, as he stands there waiting for the noise to subside, has the air of a farmer, not in his Sunday clothes, but in that intermediate rig, once his Sunday suit, in which he attends "the meeting of the trustees," announced last Sunday at church, and which he dons to attend court when a cause is coming on that he is interested in.   A most respect-able man; but the tie of his neckerchief was executed in a fit of abstraction, without the aid of a looking-glass; perhaps in the dark, when he dressed himself this morning before day-*light*—to adopt his own emphasis.

Silence is restored, and the lecture begins.   The voice of the speaker is more like a woman's than a man's, high-pitched, small, soft, but heard with ease in the remotest part of the Tabernacle. His first words are apologetic; they are uttered in a deprecatory, slightly-beseeching tone; and their substance is, 'You must n't, my friends, expect fine words from a rough, busy man like me; yet such observations as I have been able hastily to note down, I will now submit, though wishing an abler man stood at this moment in my shoes.'   He proceeds to read his discourse in a plain, utterly unam-bitious, somewhat too rapid manner, pushing on through any mod-erate degree of applause without waiting.   If there is a man in the world who is more un-oratorical than any other—and of course there *is* such a man—and if that man be not Horace Greeley, I know not where he is to be found.   A plain man reading plain sense to plain men; a practical man stating quietly to practical men the results of his thought and observation, stating what he entirely be lieves, what he wants the world to believe, what he knows will not be generally believed in his time, what he is quite sure will one day be universally believed, and what he is perfectly patient with the world for not believing *yet*. There is no gesticulation, no increased animation at important passages, no glow got up for the closing paragraphs; no aiming at any sort of effect whatever; no warmth of personal feeling against opponents. There is a shrewd humor in the man, however, and his hits excite occasional bursts of laughter; but there is no bitterness in his humor, not the faintest approach to it. An impressive or pathetic passage now and then, which loses none of its effect from the simple, plaintive way in which it is uttered, deepens the silence which prevails in the hall, at the end eliciting warm and general applause, which the speaker 'improves' by drinking a little water. The attention of the audience never flags, and the lecture concludes amid the usual tokens of decided approbation.

Horace Greeley is, indeed, no orator. Yet some who value oratory less than any other kind of bodily labor, and whom the tricks of elocution offend, except when they are performed on the stage, and even there they should be concealed, have expressed the opinion that Mr. Greeley is, strictly speaking, one of the *best* speakers this metropolis can boast. A man, they say, never does a weaker, an unworthier, a more self-demoralizing thing than when he speaks for effect; and of this vice Horace is less guilty than any speaker we are in the habit of hearing, except Ralph Waldo Emerson. Not that he does not make exaggerated statements; not that he does not utter sentiments which are only half true; not that he does not sometimes indulge in language which, when *read*, savors of the high-flown. What I mean is, that his public speeches are literally transcripts of the mind whence they emanate.

At public meetings and public dinners Mr. Greeley is a frequent speaker. His name usually comes at the end of the report, introduced with "Horace Greeley being loudly called for, made a few remarks to the following purport." The call is never declined; nor does he ever speak without saying something; and when he has said it he resumes his seat. He has a way, particularly of late years, of coming to a meeting when it is nearly over, delivering one of his short, enlightening addresses, and then embracing the first opportunity that offers of taking an unobserved departure.

A few words with regard to the subjects upon which Horace

Greeley most loves to discourse. In 1850, a volume, containing ten of his lectures and twenty shorter essays, appeared from the press of the Messrs. Harpers, under the title of "Hints toward Reforms." It has had a sale of 2,000 copies. Two or three other lectures have been published in pamphlet form, of which the one entitled "What the Sister Arts teach as to Farming," delivered before the Indiana State Agricultural Society, at its annual fair at Lafayette in October, 1853, is perhaps the best that Mr. Greeley has written. But let us glance for a moment at the 'Hints.' The title-page contains three quotations or mottoes, appropriate to the book, and characteristic of the author. They are these:

> "HASTEN the day, just Heaven!
>   Accomplish thy design,
> And let the blessings Thou hast freely given
>   Freely on all men shine;
> Till Equal Rights be equally enjoyed,
> And human power for human good employed;
> Till Law, and not the Sovereign, rule sustain
> And Peace and Virtue undisputed reign. HENRY WARE."

"LISTEN not to the everlasting Conservative, who pines and whines at every attempt to drive him from the spot where he has so lazily cast his anchor. . . . Every abuse must be abolished. The whole system must be settled on the right basis. Settle it ten times and settle it wrong, you will have the work to begin again. Be satisfied with nothing but the complete enfranchisement of Humanity, and the restoration of man to the image of his God. HENRY WARD BEECHER."

> "ONCE the welcome Light has broken,
>   Who shall say
> What the unimagined glories
>   Of the day?
> What the evil that shall perish
>   In its ray?
> Aid the dawning, Tongue and Pen!
> Aid it, hopes of honest men!
> Aid it, Paper! aid it, Type!
> Aid it, for the hour is ripe!
> And our earnest must not slacken
>   Into play:
> Men of Thought, and Men of Action,
>   CLEAR THE WAY! CHARLES MACKAY."

The dedication is no less characteristic. I copy that also, as throwing light upon the aim and manner of the man:

"To the generous, the hopeful, the loving, who, firmly and joyfully believing in the impartial and boundless goodness of our Father, trust, that the errors, the crimes, and the miseries, which have long rendered earth a hell, shall yet be swallowed up and forgotten, in a far exceeding and unmeasured reign of truth, purity, and bliss, this volume is respectfully and affectionately inscribed by THE AUTHOR."

Earth is *not* 'a hell.' The expression appears very harsh and very unjust. Earth is not a hell. Its sum of happiness is infinitely greater than its sum of misery. It contains scarcely one creature that does not, in the course of its existence, enjoy more than it suffers, that does not do a greater number of right acts than wrong. Yet the world as it *is*, compared with the world as a benevolent heart *wishes* it to be, is hell-like enough; so we may, in this sense, but in this sense alone, accept the language of the dedication.

The preface informs us, that the lectures were prompted by invitations to address Popular Lyceums and Young Men's Associations, 'generally those of the humbler class,' existing in country villages and rural townships. "They were written," says the author, "in the years from 1842 to 1848, inclusive, each in haste, to fulfill some engagement already made, for which preparation had been delayed, under the pressure of seeming necessities, to the latest moment allowable. A calling whose exactions are seldom intermitted for a day, never for a longer period, and whose requirements, already excessive, seem perpetually to expand and increase, may well excuse the distraction of thought and rapidity of composition which it renders inevitable. At no time has it seemed practicable to devote a whole day, seldom a full half day, to the production of any of the essays. Not until months after the last of them was written did the idea of collecting and printing them in this shape suggest itself, and a hurried perusal is all that has since been given them."

The eleven published lectures of Horace Greeley which lie before me, are variously entitled; but their subject is ONE; *his* subject is ever the same; the object of his public life is single. It is the

'EMANCIPATION OF LABOR;' its emancipation from ignorance, vice, servitude, insecurity, poverty. This is his chosen, *only* theme, whether he speaks from the platform, or writes for the Tribune. If slavery is the subject of discourse, the Dishonor which Slavery does to *Labor* is the light in which he prefers to present it. If protection—he demands it in the name and for the good of American *workingmen*, that their minds may be quickened by diversified employment, their position secured by abundant employment, the farmers enriched by markets near at hand. If Learning—he laments the unnatural divorce between Learning and *Labor*, and advocates their re-union in manual-labor schools. If 'Human Life'—he cannot refrain from reminding his hearers, that "the deep want of the time is, that the vast resources and capacities of Mind, the far-stretching powers of Genius and of Science, be brought to bear practically and intimately on Agriculture, the Mechanic Arts, and all the now rude and simple processes of Day-Labor, and not merely that these processes may be perfected and accelerated, but that the benefits of the improvement may accrue in at least equal measure to those whose accustomed means of livelihood—scanty at best—are interfered with and overturned by the change." If the 'Formation of Character'—he calls upon men who aspire to possess characters equal to the demands of the time, to "question with firm speech all institutions, observances, customs, that they may determine by what mischance or illusion thriftless Pretense and Knavery shall seem to batten on a brave Prosperity, while Labor vainly begs employment, Skill lacks recompense, and Worth pines for bread." If Popular Education—he reminds us, that "the narrow, dingy, squalid tenement, calculated to repel any visitor but the cold and the rain, is hardly fitted to foster lofty ideas of Life, its Duties and its Aims. And he who is constrained to ask each morning, 'Where shall I find food for the day?' is at best unlikely often to ask, 'By what good deed shall the day be signalized?'" Or, in a lighter strain, he tells the story of Tom and the Colonel. "Tom," said a Colonel on the Rio Grande to one of his command, "how can so brave and good a soldier as you are so demean himself as to get drunk at every opportunity?"—"Colone'!" replied the private, "how can you expect all the virtues that adorn the human character for seven dollars a month ?" That anecdote well illustrates one side of Horace Greeley's view of life.

The problems which, he says, at present puzzle the knotted brain of Toil all over the world, which incessantly cry out for solution, and can never more be stifled, but will become even more vehement, till they are solved, are these:

" Why should those by whose toil ALL comforts and luxuries are produced, or made available, enjoy so scanty a share of them ? Why should a man able and eager to work, ever stand idle for want of employment in a world where so much needful work impatiently awaits the doing ? Why should a man be required to surrender something of his independence in accepting the employment which will enable him to earn by honest effort the bread of his family ? Why should the man who faithfully labors for another, and receives therefor less than the product of his labor, be currently held the obliged party, rather than he who buys the work and makes a good bargain of it ? In short, Why should Speculation and Scheming ride so jauntily in their carriages, splashing honest Work as it trudges humbly and wearily by on foot ?"

Who is there so estranged from humanity as never to have pondered questions similar to these, whether he ride jauntily in a carriage, or trudge wearily on foot ? They have been proposed in former ages as abstractions. They are discussed now as though the next generation were to answer them, practically and triumphantly.

First of all, the author of Hints toward Reforms admits frankly, and declares emphatically, that *the* obstacle to the workingman's elevation is the workingman's own improvidence, ignorance, and unworthiness. This side of the case is well presented in a sketch of the career of the 'successful' man of business:

"A keen observer," says the lecturer, "could have picked him out from among his schoolfellows, and said, ' Here is the lad who will die a bank-president, owning factories and blocks of stores.' Trace his history closely," he continues, " and you find that, in his boyhood, he was provident and frugal— that he shunned expense and dissipation—that he feasted and quaffed seldom, unless at others' cost—that he was rarely seen at balls or frolics—that he was diligent in study and in business—that he did not hesitate to do an uncomfortable job, if it bade fair to be profitable—that he husbanded his hours and made each count one, either in earning or in preparing to work efficiently. He rarely or never stood idle because the business offered him was esteemed ungenteel or disagreeable—he laid up a few dollars during his minority, which proved a sensible help to him on going into business for himself—he married seasonably, prudently, respectably—he lived frugally and delved steadily until it clearly became him to live better, and until he could employ his time to better advantage than at the plow or over the bench. Thus his first thousand dollars came slowly but surely; the next more easily and readily by the help of the former; the next of course more easily still; until now he adds thousands to his hoard with little apparent effort or care. * * * * Talk to such a man as this of the wants of the poor, and he will answer you, that their sons can afford to smoke and drink freely, which he at their age could not; and that he now meets many of these poor in the market, buying luxuries that he cannot afford. Dwell on the miseries occasioned by a dearth of employment, and he will reply that *he* never encountered any such obstacle when poor; for when he could find nothing better, he cleaned streets or stables, and when he could not command twenty dollars a month, he fell to work as heartily and cheerfully for ten or five. In vain will you seek to explain to him that his rare faculty both of doing and of finding to do—his wise adaptation of means to ends in all circumstances, his frugality and others' improvidence—are a part of your case—that it is precisely because all are not created so handy, so thrifty, so worldly-wise, as himself, that you seek so to modify the laws and usages of Society that a man may still labor, steadily, efficiently, and live comfortably, although his youth was not improved to the utmost, and though his can never be the hand that transmutes all it touches to gold. Failing here, you urge that at least his children should be guaranteed an unfailing opportunity to learn and to earn, and that they, surely, should not suffer nor be stifled in ignorance because of their parent's imperfections. Still you talk in Greek to the man of substance, unless he be one of the few who have, in acquiring wealth, outgrown the idolatry of it, and learned to regard it truly as a means of doing good, and not as an end of earthly effort. If he be a man of wealth merely, still cherishing the spirit which impelled him to his life-long endeavor, the world appears to him a vast battle-field, on which some must win victory and glory, while to others are accorded shattered joints and discomfiture, and the former could not be, or would lose their zest, without the latter."

Such is the 'case' of the conservative. So looks the battle of life to the victor. With equal complacency the hawk may philosophize while he is digesting the chicken. But the chicken was of a

15

different opinion ; and died squeaking it to the waving tree-tops, as
he was borne irresistibly along to where the hawk could most conveniently devour him.

Mr. Greeley does not attempt to refute the argument of the prosperous conservative.   He dwells for a moment upon the fact, that
while life is a battle in which men fight, not *for*, but *against* each
other, the victors must *necessarily* be few and ever fewer, the victims numberless and ever more hopeless.   Resting his argument
upon the evident fact that the majority of mankind are poor, unsafe,
and uninstructed, he endeavors to show how the condition of the
masses can be alleviated by legislation, and how by their own co-
operative exertions.   The State, he contends, should ordain, and the
law should be fundamental, that no man may own more than a certain, very limited extent of land ; that the State should fix a definition to the phrase, ' a day's work ;' that the State should see to it,
that no child grows up in ignorance ; that the State is bound to
prevent the selling of alcoholic beverages.   Those who are interested in such subjects will find them amply and ably treated by
Mr. Greeley in his published writings.

But there are two short passages in the volume of Hints toward
Reforms, which seem to contain the *essence* of Horace Greeley's
teachings as to the means by which the people are to be elevated,
spiritually and materially.   The following is extracted from the lecture on the Relations of Learning to Labor.   It is addressed to the
educated and professional classes.

" Why," asks Horace Greeley, "should not the educated class create an atmosphere, not merely of exemplary morals and refined manners, but of palpable utility and blessing ?   Why should not the clergyman, the doctor, the
lawyer, of a country town be not merely the patrons and commenders of
every generous idea, the teachers and dispensers of all that is novel in science
or noble in philosophy—examplars of integrity, of amenity, and of an all-
pervading humanity to those around them—but even in a more material
sphere regarded and blessed as universal benefactors ?   Why should they not
be universally—as I rejoice to say that some of them are—models of wisdom
and thrift in agriculture—their farms and gardens silent but most effective
preachers of the benefits of forecast, calculation, thorough knowledge and
faithful application ?   Nay, more : Why should not the educated class be
everywhere teachers, through lectures, essays, conversations, as well as practically, of those great and important truths of nature, which chemistry and

other sciences are just revealing to bless the industrial world? Why should they not unobtrusively and freely teach the farmer, the mechanic, the worker in any capacity, how best to summon the blind forces of the elements to his aid, and how most effectually to render them subservient to his needs? All this is clearly within the power of the educated class, if truly educated; all this is clearly within the sphere of duty appointed them by providence. Let them but *do* it, and they will stand where they ought to stand, at the head of the community, the directors of public opinion, and the universally recog nized benefactors of the race.

"I stand before an audience in good part of educated men, and I plead for the essential independence of their class—not for their sakes only or mainly but for the sake of mankind. I see clearly, or I am strangely bewildered, a deep-rooted and wide-spreading evil which is palsying the influence and paralyzing the exertions of intellectual and even moral superiority all over our country. The lawyer, so far at least as his livelihood is concerned, is too generally *but* a lawyer; he must live by law, or he has no means of living at all. So with the doctor; so alas! with the pastor. He, too, often finds himself surrounded by a large, expensive family, few or none of whom have been systematically trained to earn their bread in the sweat of their brows, and who, even if approaching maturity in life, lean on him for a subsistence. This son must be sent to the academy, and that one to college; this daughter to an expensive boarding-school, and that must have a piano—and all to be defrayed from his salary, which, however liberal, is scarcely or barely adequate to meet the demands upon it. How shall this man—for man, after all, he is—with expenses, and cares, and debts pressing upon him—hope to be at all times faithful to the responsibilities of his high calling! He may speak over so fluently and feelingly against sin in the abstract, for that cannot give offense to the most fastidiously sensitive incumbent of the richly furnished hundred-dollar pews. But will he dare to rebuke openly, fearlessly, specially, the darling and decorous vices of his most opulent and liberal parishioners—to say to the honored dispenser of liquid poison, ' *Your* trade is murder, and your wealth the price of perdition!'—To him who amasses wealth by stinting honest labor of its reward and grinding the faces of the poor, ' Do not mock God by putting your reluctant dollar into the missionary box—there is no such heathen in New Zealand as yourself!'—and so to every specious hypocrite around him, who patronizes the church to keep to windward of his conscience and freshen the varnish on his character, ' *Thou* art the man!' I tell you, friends! he will not, for he cannot afford to, be thoroughly faithful! One in a thousand may be, and hardly more. We do not half comprehend the profound significance of that statute of the old church which inflexibly enjoins celibacy on her clergy. The very existence of the church, as a steadfast power above the multitude, giving law to the people and not receiving its law day by day from them, depends on its maintenance. And if we are ever to enjoy a Christian ministry which shall systematically, promptly, fearlessly war upon every shape and disguise of evil—which shall fearlessly grapple with war and slavery, and every loathsome device by which man seeks to glut his appetites at the expense of his brother's well-being, it will be secured to us through the instrumentality of the very reform I advocate—a reform which shall render the clergyman independent of his parishioners, and enable him to say manfully to all, ' You may cease to pay, but I shall not cease to preach, so long as you have sins to reprove, and I have strength to reprove them! I live in good part by the labor of my hands, and can do so wholly whenever that shall become necessary to the fearless discharge of my duty.

" A single illustration more, and I draw this long dissertation to a close. I shall speak now more directly to facts within my own knowledge, and which have made on me a deep and mournful impression. I speak to *your* experience, too, friends of the Phœnix and Union Societies—to your future if not to your past experience—and I entreat you to heed me! Every year sends forth from our Colleges an army of brave youth, who have nearly or quite exhausted their little means in procuring what is termed an education, and must now find some remunerating employment to sustain them while they are more specially fitting themselves for and inducting themselves into a Profession. Some of them find and are perforce contented with some meager clerkship; but the great body of them turn their attention to Literature—to the instruction of their juniors in some school or family, or to the instruction of the world through the Press. Hundreds of them hurry at once to the cities and the journals, seeking employment as essayists or collectors of intelligence—bright visions of Fame in the foreground, and the gaunt wolf Famine hard at their heels. Alas for them! they do not see that the very circumstances under which they seek admission to the calling they have chosen almost forbid the idea of their succeeding in it. They do not approach the public with thoughts struggling for utterance, but with stomachs craving bread. They seek the Press, not that they may proclaim through it what it would cost their lives to repress, but that they may preserve their souls to their bodies, at some rate. Do you not see under what immense disadvantages one of this band enters upon his selected vocation, if he has the rare fortune to find or make a place in it? He is surrounded, elbowed on every side by anxious hundreds, eager to obtain employment on any terms; he must write not what he feels, but what another needs; must ' regret' or 'rejoice' to order, working for the day, and not venturing to utter a thought which the day does not readily approve. And can you fancy *that* is the foundation on which to build a lofty and durable renown—a brave and laudable success of any kind? I tell you no, young friends!—the farthest from it possible. There is scarcely any position more perilous to generous impulses and lofty aims—scarcely any which more eminently threatens to sink the Man in the mere schemer and striver for subsistence and selfish gratification. I say, then, in deep earnestness, to every youth who hopes or desires to become usefu to his Race or in any degree eminent through Literature, Seek first of all things a position of pecuniary independence ; learn to live by the labor of your hands, the sweat of your face, as a necessary step toward the career you contemplate. If you can earn but three shillings a day by rugged yet moderate toil, learn to live contentedly on two shillings, and so preserve your mental faculties fresh and unworn to read, to observe, to think, thus preparing yourself for the ultimate path you have chosen. At length, when a mind crowded with discovered or elaborated truths *will* have utterance, begin to write sparingly and tersely for the nearest suitable periodical—no matter how humble and obscure—if the thought is in you, it will find its way to those who need it. Seek not compensation for this utterance until compensation shall seek you ; then accept it if an object, and not involving too great sacrifices of independence and disregard of more immediate duties. In this way alone can something like the proper dignity of the Literary Character be restored and maintained. But while every man who either is or believes himself capable of enlightening others, appears only anxious to sell his faculty at the earliest moment and for the largest price, I cannot hope that the Public will be induced to regard very profoundly either the lesson or the teacher."

Such is the substance of Horace Greeley's message to the literary and refined.

I turn now to the lecture on the Organization of Labor, and select from it a short narrative, the perusal of which will enable the reader to understand the nature of Mr. Greeley's advice to working-men. The story may *become* historically valuable ; because the principle which it illustrates may be destined to play a great part in the Future of Industry. It may be true, that the despotic principle is *not* essential to permanence and prosperity, though nothing has *yet* attained a condition of permanent prosperity except by virtue of it. But here is the narrative, and it is worthy of profound consideration :

"The first if not most important movement to be made in advance of our present Social position is the ORGANIZATION OF LABOR. This is to be effected by degrees, by steps, by installments. I propose here, in place of setting forth any formal theory or system of Labor Reform, simply to narrate what I saw and heard of the history and state of an experiment now in progress near Cincinnati, and which differs in no material respects from some dozen or score of others already commenced in various parts of the United States, not to speak of twenty times as many established by the Working Men of Paris and other portions of France.

"The business of IRON-MOLDING, casting, or whatever it may be called, is one of the most extensive and thrifty of the manufactures of Cincinnati, and I believe the labor employed therein is quite as well rewarded as Labor generally. It is entirely paid by the piece, according to an established scale of prices, so that each workman, in whatever department of the business, is paid according to his individual skill and industry, not a rough average of what is supposed to be earned by himself and others, as is the case where work is paid for at so much per day, week or month. I know no reason why the Iron-Molders of Cincinnati should not have been as well satisfied with the old ways as anybody else.

"Yet the system did not 'work well,' even for them. Beyond the general unsteadiness of demand for Labor and the ever-increasing pressure of competition, there was a pretty steadily recurring 'dull season,' commencing about the first of January, when the Winter's call for stoves, &c., had been supplied, and holding on for two or three months, or until the Spring business opened. In this hiatus, the prior savings of the Molders were generally consumed—sometimes less, but perhaps oftener more—so that, taking one with another, they did not lay up ten dollars per annum. By-and-by came a collision respecting wages and a 'strike,' wherein the Journeymen tried for months the experiment of running their heads against a stone wall. How they came out of it, no matter whether victors or vanquished, the intelligent reader will readily guess. I never heard of any evils so serious and complicated as those which eat out the heart of Labor being cured by doing nothing.

"At length—but I believe after the strike had somehow terminated—some of the Journeymen Molders said to each other : 'Standing idle is not the true cure for our grievances : why not employ ourselves?' They finally concluded to try it, and, in the dead of the Winter of 1847-8, when a great many of their trade were out of employment, the business being unusually depressed, they formed an association under the General Manufacturing Law of Ohio (which is very similar to that of New York), and undertook to establish the Journeymen Molders' Union Foundry. There were about twenty of them who put their hands to the work, and the whole amount of capital they could scrape together was two thousand one hundred dollars, held in shares of twenty-five dollars each. With this they purchased an eligible piece of ground, directly on the bank of the Ohio, eight miles below Cincinnati, with which 'the Whitewater Canal' also affords the means of ready and cheap communication. With their capital they bought some patterns, flasks, an engine and tools, paid for their ground, and five hundred dollars on their first building, which was erected for them partly on long credit by a firm in Cincinnati, who knew that the property was a perfect security for so much of its cost, and decline taking credit for any benevolence in the matter. Their iron, coal, &c., to commence upon were entirely and necessarily bought on credit.

"Having elected Directors, a Foreman, and a Business Agent (the last to open a store in Cincinnati, buy stock, sell wares, &c.) the Journeymen's Union set to work, in August, 1848. Its accommodations were then meager; they have since been gradually enlarged by additions, until their Foundry is now the most commodious on the river. Their stock of patterns, flasks, &c., has grown to be one of the best; while their arrangements for unloading coal and iron, sending off stoves, coking coal, &c., &c., are almost perfect. They commenced with ten associates actually at work; the number has gradually grown to forty; and there is not a better set of workmen in any foundry in America. I profess to know a little as to the quality of castings, and there are no better than may be seen in the Foundry of 'Industry' and its store at Cincinnati. And there is obvious reason for this in the fact that every workman is a proprietor in the concern, and it is his interest to turn out not only his own work in the best order, but to take care that all the rest is of like quality. All is carefully examined before it is sent away, and any found imperfect is condemned, the loss falling on the causer of it. But there is seldom any deserving condemnation.

" A strict account is kept with every member, who is credited for all he does according to the Cincinnati Scale of Prices, paid so much as he needs of his earnings in money, the balance being devoted to the extension of the concern and the payment of its debts, and new stock issued to him therefor. Whenever the debts shall have been paid off, and an adequate supply of implements, teams, stock, &c., bought or provided for, they expect to pay every man his earnings weekly in cash, as of course they may. I hope, however, they will prefer to buy more land, erect thereon a most substantial and commodious dwelling, surround it with a garden, shade-trees, &c., and resolve to live as well as work like brethren. There are few uses to which a member can put a hundred dollars which might not as well be subserved by seventy-five if the money of the whole were invested together.

" The members were earning when I visited them an average of fifteen dollars per week, and meant to keep doing so. Of course they work hard. Many of them live inside of four dollars per week, none go beyond eight. Their Business Agent is one of themselves, who worked with them in the Foundry for some months after it was started. He has often been obliged to report, 'I can pay you no money this week,' and never heard a murmur in reply. On one occasion he went down to say, 'There are my books; you see what I have received and where most of it has gone: here is one hundred dollars, which is all there is left.' The members consulted, calculated, and made answer: 'We can pay our board so as to get through another week with fifty dollars, and you had better take back the other fifty, for the business may need it before the week is through.' When I was there, there had been an Iron note to pay, ditto a Coal, and a boat-load of coal to lay in for the winter, sweeping off all the money, so that for more than three weeks no man had had a dollar. Yet no one had thought of complaining, for all knew that the delay was dictated, not by another's interest, but their own. They knew, too, that the assurance of their payment did not depend on the frugality or extravagance of some employer, who might swamp the proceeds of his business and their labor in an unlucky speculation, or a sumptuous dwelling, leaving them to whistle for their money. There were their year's earnings visibly around them in stoves and hollow ware, for which they had abundant and eager demand in Cincinnati, but which a break in the canal had temporarily kept back; in iron and coal for the winter's work; in the building over their heads and the implements in their hands. And while other molders have had work 'off and on,' according to the state of the business, no member of the Journeymen's Union has stood idle a day for want of work since their Foundry was first started. Of course, as their capital increases, the danger of being compelled to suspend work at any future day grows less and less continually.

"The ultimate capital of the Journeymen's Union Foundry (on the presumption that the Foundry is to stand by itself, leaving every member to provide his own home, &c.) is to be eighteen thousand dollars, of which seven thousand dollars has already been paid in, most of it in labor. The remainder is all subscribed by the several associates, and is to be paid in labor as fast as possible. That done, every man may be paid in cash weekly for his work, and a dividend on his stock at the close of each business year. The workers have saved and invested from three hundred dollars to six hundred dollars each since their commencement in August of last year, though those who have joined since the start have of course earned less. Few or none had laid by so much in five to ten years' working for others as they have in one year working for themselves. The total value of their products up to the time of my visit is thirty thousand dollars, and they were then making at the rate of five thousand dollars' worth per month, which they do not mean to diminish. All the profits of the business, above the cost of doing the work at journeymen's wages, will be distributed among the stockholders in dividends. The officers of the Union are a Managing Agent, Foreman of the Foundry, and five Directors, chosen annually, but who can be changed meantime in case of necessity. A Reading-Room and Library were to be started directly; a spacious boarding-house (though probably not owned by the Union) will go up this season. No liquor is sold within a long distance of the Union, and there is little or no demand for any. Those original members of the Union who were least favorable to Temperance have seen fit to sell out and go away.

"Now is it reasonable that the million or so of hireling laborers throughout our country who have work when it suits others' convenience to employ them, and must stand idle perforce when it does not, can read the above simple narration—which I have tried to render as lucid as possible—and not be moved to action thereby? Suppose they receive all they earn when employed—which of course they generally do not, or how could employers grow rich by merely buying their labor and selling it again?—should not the simple fact that these Associated Workers never lack employment when they desire it, and never ask any master's leave to refrain from working when they see fit, arrest public attention? Who is such a slave in soul that he would not rather be an equal member of a commonwealth than the subject of a despotism? Who would not like to taste the sweets of Liberty on work-days as well as holidays? Is there a creature so abject that he considers all this mere poetry and moonshine, which a little hard experience will dissipate? Suppose the Cincinnati Iron-Molders' Association should break down, either through some defect in its organization or some dishonesty or other misconduct on the part of one or more of its members—what would that prove? Would it any more prove the impracticability of Industrial Associations than the shipwreck and death of Columbus, had such a disaster occurred on his second or third voyage to America, would have disproved the existence of the New World?

The story is incomplete; the catastrophe is wanting. It can be told in one word, and that word is *failure!* The Union existed about two years. It then broke up, not, as I am very positively assured, from any defect in the system upon which it was conducted; but from a total stagnation in the market, which not only ruined the co-operators, but others engaged in the same business. They made castings on the co-operative principle, made them well, made them as long as anybody would buy them; then—stopped.

The reader of the volume from which I have quoted will find in it much that does less honor to the author's head than his heart. But I defy any one to read it, and not respect the man that wrote it. The kernel of the book is sound. The root of the matter is there. It shows Horace Greeley to be a man whose interest in human welfare is sincere, habitual, innate, and indestructible. We all know what is the usual course of a person who—as the stupid phrase is—'*rises*' from the condition of a manual laborer to a position of influence and wealth. If our own observation were not sufficient, Thackeray and Curtis have told the whole world the sorry history of the modern snob; how he ignores his origin, and bends all his little soul to the task of cutting a figure in the circles to which he has gained admittance.

Twenty men are suffocating in a dungeon—one man, by climbing upon the shoulders of some of his companions, and assisted up still higher by the strength of others, *escapes*, breathes the pure air of heaven, exults in freedom! Does he not, instantly and with all

15*

his might, strive for the rescue of his late companions, still suffering ? Is he not prompt with rope, and pole, and ladder, and food, and cheering words ? No—the caitiff wanders off to seek his pleasure, and makes haste to remove from his person, and his memory too, every trace of his recent misery. *This* it is to be a snob. No treason like this clings to the skirts of Horace Greeley. He has stood by his Order. The landless, the hireling, the uninstructed—he was their Companion once—he is their Champion now.

CHAPTER XXVI.

THREE MONTHS IN EUROPE.

" THE *thing* called Crystal Palace !" This was the language which the intense and spiritual Carlyle thought proper to employ on the only occasion when he alluded to the World's Fair of 1851. And Horace Greeley appears, at first, to have thought little of Prince Albert's scheme, or at least to have taken little interest in it. " We mean," he said, " to attend the World's Fair at London, with very little interest in the show generally, or the people whom it will collect, but with special reference to a subject which seems to us of great and general importance—namely, the improvements recently made, or now being made, in the modes of dressing flax and hemp and preparing them to be spun and woven by steam or water-power." " Only adequate knowledge," he thought, was necessary to give a new and profitable direction to Free Labor, both agricultural and manufacturing."

Accordingly, Horace Greeley was one of the two thousand Americans who crossed the Atlantic for the purpose of attending the World's Fair, and, like many others, he seized the opportunity to make a hurried tour of the most accessible parts of the European Continent. It was the longest holiday of his life. Holiday is not the word, however. His sky was changed, but not the man; and his labors in Europe were as incessant and arduous as they had been in America, nor unlike them in kind. A strange apparition he among the elegant and leisurely Europeans. Since Franklin's day, no American had appeared in Europe whose 'style' had in it so little of the European as his, nor one who so well and so consistently represented some of the best sides of the American character. He proved to be one of the Americans who can calmly contemplate a duke, and value him neither the less nor the more on account of his dukeship. Swiftly he traveled. Swiftly we pursue him.

At noon on Saturday, the sixteenth of April, 1851, the steamship Baltic moved from the wharf at the foot of Canal-street, with Horace Greeley on board as one of her two hundred passengers. It was a chilly, dismal day, with a storm brewing and lowering in the north-east. The wharf was covered with people, as usual on sailing days; and when the huge vessel was seen to be in motion, and the inevitable White Coat was observed among the crowd on her deck, a hearty cheer broke from a group of Mr. Greeley's personal friends, and was caught up by the rest of the spectators. He took off his hat and waved response and farewell, while the steamer rolled away like a black cloud, and settled down upon the river.

The passage was exceedingly disagreeable, though not tempestuous. The north-easter that hung over the city when the steamer sailed 'clung to her like a brother' all the way over, varying a point or two now and then, but not changing to a fair wind for more than six hours. Before four o'clock on the first day—before the steamer had gone five miles from the Hook, the pangs of sea-sickness came over the soul of Horace Greeley, and laid him prostrate. At six o'clock in the evening, a friend, who found him in the smoker's room, helpless, hopeless, and recumbent, persuaded and assisted him to go below, where he had strength only to un-boot

and sway into his berth. There he remained for twenty-four hours.
He then managed to crawl upon deck; but a perpetual head-wind
and cross-sea were too much for so delicate a system as his, and he
enjoyed not one hour of health and happiness during the passage.
His opinion of the sea, therefore, is unfavorable. He thought, that
a sea-voyage of twelve days was about equal, in the amount of
misery it inflicts, to two months' hard labor in the State Prison,
or to the average agony of five years of life on shore. It was a
consolation to him, however, even when most sick and impatient,
to think that the gales which were so adverse to the pleasure-
seekers of the Baltic, were wafting the emigrant ships, which it
hourly passed, all the more swiftly to the land of opportunity and
hope. His were ' light afflictions' compared with those of the mul-
titudes crowded into *their* stifling steerages.

At seven o'clock on the evening of Thursday, the twenty-eighth
of April, under sullen skies and a dripping rain, the passengers of
the Baltic were taken ashore at Liverpool in a steam-tug, which in
New York, thought Mr. Greeley, would be deemed unworthy to
convey market-garbage. With regard to the weather, he tells us,
in his first letter from England, that he had become reconciled to
sullen skies and dripping rains: he wanted *to see the thing out*, and
would have taken amiss any deceitful smiles of fortune, now that
he had learned to dispense with her favors. He advised Americans, on the day of their departure for Europe, to take a long, earnest gaze at the sun, that they might know him again on their return; for the thing called Sun in England was only shown occasionally, and bore a nearer resemblance to a boiled turnip than to its
American namesake.

Liverpool the traveler scarcely saw, and it impressed him un-
favorably. The working-class seemed " exceedingly ill-dressed,
stolid, abject, and hopeless." Extortion and beggary appeared very
prevalent. In a day or two he was off to London by the Trent
Valley Railroad, which passes through one of the finest agricultural
districts in England.

To most men their first ride in a foreign country is a thrilling
and memorable delight. Whatever Horace Greeley may have *felt*
on his journey from Liverpool to London, his remarks upon what
he saw are the opposite of rapturous; yet, as they are character-

istic, they are interesting.　The mind of that man is a 'study,' who, when he has passed through two hundred miles of the enchanting rural scenery of England, and sits down to write a letter about it, begins by describing the construction of the railroad, continues by telling us that much of the *land* he saw is held at .five hundred dollars per acre, that two-thirds of it was 'in grass,' that there are fewer fruit-trees on the two hundred miles of railroad between Liverpool and London, than on the forty miles of the Harlem railroad north of White Plains, that the wooded grounds looked meager and scanty, and that the western towns of America ought to take warning from this fact and preserve some portions of the primeval forest, which, once destroyed, can never be renewed by cultivation in their original grandeur.　'The eye sees what it brought with it the means of seeing,' and these practical observations are infinitely more welcome than affected sentiment, or even than genuine sentiment inadequately expressed.　Besides, the suggestion with regard to the primeval forests is good and valuable. On his arrival in London, Mr. Greeley drove to the house of Mr. John Chapman, the well-known publisher, with whom he resided during his stay in the metropolis.

On the first of May the Great Exhibition was opened, and our traveler saw the show both within and without the Crystal Palace. The day was a fine one—for England.　He thought the London sunshine a little superior in brilliancy to American moonlight; and wondered how the government could have the conscience to tax *such* light.　The royal procession, he says, was not much; a parade of the New York Firemen or Odd Fellows could beat it; but then it was a new thing to see a Queen, a court, and an aristocracy doing honor to industry.　He was glad to see the queen in the pageant, though he could not but feel that her *vocation* was behind the intelligence of the age, and likely to go out of fashion at no distant day; but not through *her* fault.　He could not see, however, what the Master of the Buck-hounds, the Groom of the Stole, the Mistress of the Robes, and 'such uncouth fossils,' had to do with a grand exhibition of the fruits of industry.　The Mistress of the Robes *made* no robes; the Ladies of the Bed-chamber did nothing with beds but sleep on them.　The posts of honor nearest the Queen's person ought to have been confided to the descendants of Watt and Arkwright,

'Napoleon's *real* conquerors;' while the foreign ambassadors should have been the sons of Fitch, Fulton, Whitney, Daguerre and Morse; and the places less conspicuous should have been assigned, not to Gold-stick, Silver-stick, and 'kindred absurdities,' but to the Queen's gardeners, horticulturists, carpenters, upholsterers and milliners! (Fancy Gold-stick reading this passage!) The traveler, however, even at such a moment is not unmindful of similar nuisances across the ocean, and pauses to express the hope that we may be able, before the century is out, to elect 'something else' than Generals to the Presidency.

Before the arrival of Mr. Greeley in London, he had been named by the American Commissioner as a member of the Jury on Hardware, etc. There were so few Americans in London at the time, who were not exhibitors, that he did not feel at liberty to decline the duties of the proffered post, and accordingly devoted nearly every day, from ten o'clock to three, for a month, to an examination of the articles upon whose comparative merits the jury were to decide. Few men would have spent their first month in Europe in the discharge of a duty so onerous, so tedious, and so likely to be thankless. His reward, however, was, that his official position opened to him sources of information, gave him facilities for observation, and enabled him to form acquaintances, that would not have been within the compass of a mere spectator of the Exhibition. Among other advantages, it procured him a seat at the banquet given at Richmond by the London Commissioners to the Commissioners from foreign countries, a feast presided over by Lord Ashburton, and attended by an ample representation of the science, talent, worth and rank of both hemispheres. It was the particular desire of Lord Ashburton that the health of Mr. Paxton, the Architect of the Palace, should be proposed by an American, and Mr. Riddle, the American Commissioner, designated Horace Greeley for that service. The speech delivered by him on that occasion, since it is short, appropriate, and characteristic, may properly have a place here. Mr. Greeley, being called upon by the Chairman, spoke as follows:

" In my own land, my lords and gentlemen, where Nature is still so rugged and unconquered, where Population is yet so scanty and the demands for human exertion are so various and urgent, it is but natural that we should render marked honor to Labor, and especially to those who by invention or discovery contribute to shorten the processes and increase the efficiency of Industry. It is but natural, therefore, that this grand conception of a comparison of the state of Industry in all Nations, by means of a World's Exhibition, should there have been received and canvassed with a lively and general interest,—an interest which is not measured by the extent of our contributions. Ours is still one of the youngest of Nations, with few large accumulations of the fruits of manufacturing activity or artistic skill, and these so generally needed for use that we were not likely to send them three thousand miles away, merely for show. It is none the less certain that the progress of this great Exhibition, from its original conception to that perfect realization which we here commemorate, has been watched and discussed not more earnestly throughout the saloons of Europe, than by the smith's forge and the mechanic's bench in America. Especially the hopes and fears alternately predominant on this side with respect to the edifice required for the Exhibition—the doubts as to the practicability of erecting one sufficiently capacious and commodious to contain and display the contributions of the whole world—the apprehension that it could not be rendered impervious to water—the confident assertions that it could not be completed in season for opening the Exhibition on the first of May as promised—all found an echo on our shores; and now the tidings that all these doubts have been dispelled, these difficulties removed, will have been hailed there with unmingled satisfaction.

"I trust, gentlemen, that among the ultimate fruits of this Exhibition we are to reckon a wider and deeper appreciation of the worth of Labor, and especially of those 'Captains of Industry' by whose conceptions and achievements our Race is so rapidly borne onward in its progress to a loftier and more benignant destiny. We shall not be likely to appreciate less fully the merits of the wise Statesmen, by whose measures a People's thrift and happiness are promoted—of the brave Soldier, who joyfully pours out his blood in defense of the rights or in vindication of the honor of his Country—of the Sacred Teacher, by whose precepts and example our steps are guided in the pathway to heaven—if we render fit honor also to those 'Captains of Industry' whose fearless victories redden no river and whose conquering march is unmarked by the tears of the widow and the cries of the orphan. I give you, therefore,

" *The Health of Joseph Paxton, Esq., Designer of the Crystal Palace—* Honor to him whose genius does honor to Industry and to Man !'"

This speech was not published in the newspaper report of the banquet, nor was the name of the speaker even mentioned. The omission gave him an opportunity to retort upon the London Times its assertion, that with the *English* press, 'fidelity in reporting is a religion.' The speech was written out by Mr. Greeley himself, and

published in the Tribune. It must be confessed, that the grad *e*
of a Vermont printing-office made a creditable appearance before
the 'lords and gentlemen.'

The sights in and about London seem to have made no great impression on the mind of Horace Greeley. He spent a day at Hamp-
ton Court, which he oddly describes as larger than the Astor House,
but less lofty and containing fewer rooms. Westminster Abbey
appeared to him a mere barbaric profusion of lofty ceilings, stained
windows, carving, groining, and all manner of contrivances for
absorbing labor and money—' waste, not taste ; the contortions of the
sybil without her inspiration.' The part of the building devoted to
public worship he thought less adapted to that purpose than a fifty-
thousand dollar church in New York. The new fashion of 'intoun-
ing' the service sounded to his ear, as though a Friar Tuck had
wormed himself into the desk and was trying, under pretense of
reading the service, to caricature, as broadly as possible, the alleged
peculiarity of the methodistic pulpit super-imposed upon the regular
Yankee drawl. The Epsom races he declined to attend for three
reasons; he had much to do at home, he did not care a button
which of thirty colts could run fastest, and he preferred that his
delight and that of swindlers, robbers, and gamblers, should not
'exactly coincide.' He found time, however, to visit the Model
Lodging houses, the People's Bathing establishments, and a Ragged
School. The spectacle of want and woe presented at the Ragged
School touched him nearly. It made him feel, to quote his own
language, that "he had hitherto said too little, done too little, dared
too little, sacrificed too little, to awaken attention to the infernal
wrongs and abuses, which are inherent in the very structure and
constitution, the nature and essence of civilized society, as it now
exists throughout Christendom." He was in haste to be gone from
a scene, to look upon which, as a mere visitor, seemed an insult
heaped on injury, an unjustifiable prying into the saddest secrets of
the prison-house of human woe ; but he apologized for the fancied
impertinence by a gift of money.

While in London, Mr. Greeley attended the anniversary of the
British and Foreign Anti-Slavery Society, and made a speech of a
somewhat novel and unexpected nature. The question that was
under discussion was, ' What can we Britons do to hasten the over-

throw of Slavery?' Three colored gentlemen and an M. P. had extolled Britain as the land of *true* freedom and equality, had urged Britons to refuse recognition to 'pro-slavery clergymen,' to avoid using the products of slave-labor, and to assist the free-colored people to educate their children. One of the colored orators had observed the entrance of Horace Greeley, and named him commendingly to the audience; whereupon he was invited to take a seat upon the platform, and afterwards to address the meeting; both of which invitations were promptly accepted. He spoke fifteen minutes. He began by stating the fact, that American Slavery justifies itself mainly on the ground, that the class who live by manual toil are everywhere, but *particularly in England*, degraded and ill-requited. Therefore, he urged upon English Abolitionists, first, to use systematic exertions to increase the reward of Labor and the comfort and consideration of the depressed Laboring Class *at home;* and to diffuse and cherish respect for Man as Man, without regard to class, color or vocation. Secondly, to put forth determined efforts for the eradication of those Social evils and miseries *in England* which are appealed to and relied on by slaveholders and their champions everywhere as justifying the continuance of Slavery; and thirdly, to colonize our Slave States by thousands of intelligent, moral, industrious Free Laborers, who will silently and practically dispel the wide-spread delusion which affirms that the Southern States must be cultivated and their great staples produced by Slave Labor, or not at all.

These suggestions were listened to with respectful attention; but they did not elicit the 'thunder of applause' which had greeted the 'Stand-aside-for-I-am-holier-than-thou' oratory of the preceding speakers.

Our traveler witnessed the second performance at the Devonshire House, of Bulwer's play, 'Not so Bad as we Seem,' for the benefit of the Literary Guild, the characters by Charles Dickens, Douglas Jerrold, and other literary notabilities. Not that he hoped much for the success of the project; but it was, at least, an *attempt* to mend the fortunes of unlucky British authors, whose works 'we Americans habitually steal,' and to whom he, as an individual, felt himself indebted. The price of the tickets for the first performance was twenty-five dollars. He applied for one too late, and was therefore obliged to content himself with purchasing a ten-dollar ticket for the second. The play, however, he found rather dull than otherwise, the performance being indebted, he thought, for its main interest to the personal character of the actors, who played respectably for amateurs, but not well. Dickens was not at home in the leading part, as 'stateliness sits ill upon him;' but he shone in the scene where, as a bookseller in disguise, he tempts the virtue of a poor author. In the afterpiece, however, in which the novelist personated in rapid succession a lawyer, a servant, a gentleman and an invalid, the acting seemed 'perfect,' and the play was heartily enjoyed throughout. Mr. Greeley thought, that the "raw material of a capital comedian was put to a better use when Charles Dickens took to authorship." It was half-past twelve when the curtain fell, and the audience repaired to a supper room, where the munificence of the Duke of Devonshire had provided a superb and profuse entertainment. "I did not venture, at that hour," says the traveler, "to partake; but those who did would be quite unlikely to repent of it —till morning." He left the ducal mansion at one, just as 'the violins began to give note of coming melody, to which nimble feet were eager to respond.'

The eightieth birthday of Robert Owen was celebrated on the fourteenth of May, by a dinner at the Colbourne hotel, attended by a few of Mr. Owen's personal friends, among whom Horace Greeley was one. "I cannot," wrote Mr. Greeley, "see many things as he does; it seems to me that he is stone-blind on the side of Faith in the invisible, and exaggerates the truths he perceives until they almost become falsehoods; but I love his sunny, benevolent nature, I admire his unwearied exertions for what he deems the good of humanity; and, believing with the great apostle to the Gentiles, that 'Now abide faith, hope, charity; these three; but the greatest of these is charity,' I consider him practically a better Christian than half those who, professing to be such, believe more and do less." The only other banquet at which Mr. Greeley was a guest in London during his first visit, was the dinner of the Fishmonger's Company. There he heard a harangue from from Sir James Brooke, the Rajah of Borneo. From reading, he had formed the opinion that the Rajah was doing a good work for civilization and humanity in Borneo, but this impression was not confirmed by the ornate and fluent speech delivered by him on this occasion.

During Mr. Greeley's stay in London, the repeal of the 'taxes on knowledge' was agitated in and out of parliament. Those taxes were a duty on advertisements, and a stamp-duty of one penny per copy on every periodical containing news. A parliamentary committee, consisting of eight members of the House of Commons, the Rt. Hon. T. Milnor Gibson, Messrs. Tufnell, Ewart, Cobden, Rich, Adair, Hamilton, and Sir J. Walmsey, had the subject under consideration, and Mr. Greeley, as the representative of the only untrammeled press in the world, was invited to give the committee the benefit of his experience. Mr. Greeley's evidence, given in two sessions of the committee, no doubt had influence upon the subsequent action of parliament. The advertisement duty was entirely removed. The penny stamp was retained for revenue reasons only, but must finally yield to the demands of the nation.

The chief part of Mr. Greeley's evidence claims a place in this work, both because of its interesting character, and because it really influenced legislation on a subject of singular importance. He told England what England did not understand before he told her—*why* the Times newspaper was devouring its contemporaries; and he assisted in preparing the way for that coming penny-press which is destined to play so great a part in the future of 'Great England.'

In reply to a question by the chairman of the committee with regard to the effect of the duty upon the advertising business, Mr. Greeley replied substantially as follows:

"Your duty is the same on the advertisements in a journal with fifty thousand circulation, as in a journal with one thousand, although the *value* of the article is twenty times as much in the one case as in the other. The duty operates precisely as though you were to lay a tax of one shilling a day on every day's labor that a man were to do; to a man whose labor is worth two shillings a day, it would be destructive; while by a man who earns twenty shillings a day, it would be very lightly felt. An advertisement is worth but a certain amount, and the public soon get to know what it is worth; you put a duty on advertisements and you destroy the value of those coming to new establishments. People who advertise in your well-established journals, could afford to pay a price to include the duty; but in a new paper, the advertisements would not be worth the amount of the duty *alone;* and consequently the new concern would have no chance   Now, the advertisements are one main source of the income of daily papers, and thousands of business men take them mainly for those advertisements.   For instance, at the time when our auctioneers were appointed by law (they were, of course, party politicians), one journal, which was high in the confidence of ,he party in power, obtained not a law, but an *understanding*, that all the auctioneers appointed should advertise in that journal.   Now, though the journal referred to has ceased to be of that party, and the auctioneers are no longer appointed by the State, yet that journal has almost the monopoly of the auctioneers' business to this day.   Auctioneers *must* advertise in it because they know that purchasers are looking there ; and purchasers must take the paper, because they know that it contains just the advertisements they want to see; and this, without regard to the goodness or the principles of the paper.   I know men in this town who take one journal mainly for its advertisements, and they *must* take the Times, because everything is advertised in it ; for the same reason, advertisers *must* advertise in the Times.   If we had a duty on advertisements, I will not say it would be impossible to build a new concern up in New York against the competition of the older ones ; but I do say, it would be impossible to preserve the weaker papers from being swallowed up by the stronger."

Mr. Cobden. "Do you then consider the fact, that the Times newspaper for the last fifteen years has been increasing so largely in circulation, is to be accounted for mainly by the existence of the advertisement duty ?"

Mr. Greeley. "Yes; much more than the stamp. By the operation of the advertisement duty, an advertisement is charged ten times as much in one paper as in another. An advertisement in the Times may be worth five pounds, while in another paper it is only worth one pound; but the duty is the same."

Mr. Rich. "The greater the number of small advertisements in papers, the greater the advantage to their proprietors ?"

Mr. Greeley. "Yes. Suppose the cost of a small advertisement to be five shillings, the usual charge in the Times ; if you have to pay a shilling or eighteen pence duty, that advertisement is worth *nothing* in a journal with a fourth part of the circulation of the Times."

Chairman. "Does it not appear to you that the taxes on the press are hostile to one another ; in the first place, lessening the circulation of papers by means of the stamp duty, we diminish the consumption of paper, and therefore lessen the amount of paper duty ; secondly, by diminishing the sale of papers through the stamp, we lessen the number of advertisements, and therefore the receipts of the advertisement duty ?"

Mr. Greeley. "I should say that if the government were, simply as a matter of revenue, to fix a duty, say of half a penny per pound, on paper, it would be easily collected, and produce more money ; and then, a law which is equal

In its operation does not require any considerable number of officers to collect the duty, and it would require no particular vigilance ; and the duty on paper alone would be most equal and most efficient as a revenue duty."

CHAIRMAN. " It is clear, then, that the effect of the stamp and advertisement duty is to lessen the amount of the receipt from the duty on paper."

Mr. GREELEY. " Enormously. I see that the circulation of daily papers in London is but sixty thousand, against a hundred thousand in New York ; while the tendency is more to concentrate on London than on New York. Not a tenth part of our daily papers are printed in New York."

Mr. COBDEN. " Do you consider, that there are upwards of a million papers issued daily from the press in the United States ?"

Mr. GREELEY. " I should say about a million : I cannot say upwards. I think there are about two hundred and fifty daily journals published in the United States."

Mr. COBDEN. " At what amount of population does a town in the United States begin to have a daily paper ? They first of all begin with a weekly paper, do they not ?"

Mr. GREELEY. " Yes. The general rule is, that each county will have one weekly newspaper. In all the Free States, if a county have a population of twenty thousand, it has two papers, one for each party. The general average in the agricultural counties is one local journal to every ten thousand inhabitants. When a town grows to have fifteen thousand inhabitants in and about it, then it has a daily paper ; but sometimes that is the case when it has as few as ten thousand : it depends more on the business of a place than its population. But fifteen thousand may be stated as the average at which a daily paper commences ; at twenty thousand they have two, and so on. In central towns, like Buffalo, Rochester, Troy, they have from three to five daily journals, each of which prints a semi-weekly or a weekly journal."

Mr. RICH. " Have your papers much circulation outside the towns in which they are published ?"

Mr. GREELEY. " The county is the general limit ; though some have a judicial district of five or six counties."

Mr. RICH. " Would the New York paper, for instance, have much circulation in Charleston ?"

Mr. GREELEY. " The New York Herald, I think, which is considered the journal most friendly to Southern interests, has a considerable circulation there."

CHAIRMAN. " When a person proposes to publish a paper in New York, he is not required to go to any office to register himself, or to give security that he will not insert libels or seditious matter ? A newspaper publisher is not subject to any liability more than other persons ?"

Mr. GREELEY. " No ; no more than a man that starts a blacksmith's shop."

CHAIRMAN. "They do not presume in the United States, that because a man is going to print news in a paper, he is going to libel?"

Mr. GREELEY. "No; nor do they presume that his libeling would be worth much, unless he is a responsible character."

Mr. COBDEN. "From what you have stated with regard to the circulation of the daily papers in New York, it appears that a very large proportion of the adult population must be customers for them?"

Mr. GREELEY. "Yes; I think three-fourths of all the families take a daily paper of some kind."

Mr. COBDEN. "The purchasers of the daily papers must consist of a different class from those in England; mechanics must purchase them?"

Mr. GREELEY. "Every mechanic takes a paper, or nearly every one."

Mr. COBDEN. "Do those people generally get them before they leave home for their work?"

Mr. GREELEY. "Yes; and you are complained of if you do not furnish a man with his newspaper at his breakfast; he wants to read it between six or seven usually."

Mr. COBDEN. "Then a ship-builder, or a cooper, or a joiner, needs his daily paper at his breakfast-time?"

Mr. GREELEY. "Yes; and he may take it with him to read at his dinner, between twelve and one; but the rule is, that he wants his paper at his breakfast."

Mr. COBDEN. "After he has finished his breakfast or his dinner, he may be found reading the daily newspaper, just as the people of the upper classes do in England?"

Mr. GREELEY. "Yes; if they do."

Mr. COBDEN. "And that is quite common, is it not?"

Mr. GREELEY. "Almost universal, I think. There is a very low class, a good many foreigners, who do not know how to read; but no native, I think."

Mr. EWART. "Do the agricultural laborers read much?"

Mr. GREELEY. "Yes; they take our weekly papers, which they receive through the post generally."

Mr. COBDEN. "The working people in New York are not in the habit of resorting to public-houses to read the newspapers, are they?"

Mr. GREELEY. "They go to public-houses, but not to read the papers. It is not the general practice; but, still, we have quite a class who do so."

Mr. COBDEN. "The newspapers, then, is not the attraction to the public-house?"

Mr. GREELEY. "No. I think a very small proportion of our reading class go there at all; those that I have seen there are mainly the foreign population, those who do not read."

CHAIRMAN. "Are there any papers published in New York, or in other parts, which may be said to be of an obscene or immoral character?"

Mr. Greeley. "We call the New York Herald a very bad paper—those who do not like it; but that is not the cheapest."

Chairman. "Have you heard of a paper called the 'The Town,' published in this country, with pictures of a certain character in it? Have you any publications in the United States of that character?"

Mr. Greeley. "Not daily papers. There are weekly papers got up from time to time called the 'Scorpion,' the 'Flash,' and so on, whose purpose is to extort money from parties who can be threatened with exposure of immoral practices, or for visiting infamous houses."

Mr. Ewart. "They do not last, do they?"

Mr Greeley. "I do not know of any one being continued for any considerable time. If one dies, another is got up, and that goes down. Our cheap daily papers, the very cheapest, are, as a class, quite as discreet in their conduct and conversation as other journals. They do not embody the same amount of talent; they devote themselves mainly to news. They are not party journals; they are nominally independent; they are not given to harsh language with regard to public men: they are very moderate.

Mr. Ewart. "Is scurility or personality common in the publications of the United States?"

Mr. Greeley. "It is not common; it is much less frequent than it was; but it is not absolutely unknown."

Mr. Cobden. "What is the circulation of the New York Herald?"

Mr. Greeley. "Twenty-five thousand, I believe."

Mr. Cobden. "Is that an influential paper in America?"

Mr. Greeley. "I think not."

Mr. Cobden. "It has a higher reputation in Europe probably than at home.'

Mr. Greeley. "A certain class of journals in this country find it their interest or pleasure to quote it a good deal."

Chairman. "As the demand is extensive, is the remuneration for the services of the literary men who are employed on the press, good?"

Mr. Greeley. "The prices of literary labor are more moderate than in this country. The highest salary, I think, that would be commanded by any one connected with the press would be five thousand dollars—the highest that could be thought of. I have not heard of higher than three thousand."

Mr. Rich. "What would be about the ordinary remuneration?"

Mr. Greeley. "In our own concern it is, besides the principal editor, from fifteen hundred dollars down to five hundred. I think that is the usual range."

Chairman. "Are your leading men in America, in point of literary ability, employed from time to time upon the press as an occupation?"

Mr. Greeley. "It is beginning to be so, but it has not been the custom. There have been leading men connected with the press; but the press has not been usually conducted by the most powerful men. With a few exceptions, the leading political journals are conducted ably, and they are becoming more so; and, with a wider diffusion of the circulation, the press is more able to pay for it."

Mr. RICH. "Is it a profession apart?"

Mr. GREELEY. "No; usually the men have been brought up to the bar, to the pulpit, and so on; they are literary men."

CHAIRMAN. "I presume that the non-reading class in the United States is a very limited one?"

Mr. GREELEY. "Yes; except in the Slave States."

CHAIRMAN. "Do not you consider that newspaper reading is calculated to keep up a habit of reading?"

Mr. GREELEY. "I think it is worth all the schools in the country. I think it creates a taste for reading in every child's mind, and it increases his interest in his lessons; he is attracted from always seeing a newspaper and hearing it read, I think."

CHAIRMAN. "Supposing that you had your schools as now, but that your newspaper press were reduced within the limits of the press in England, do you not think that the habit of reading acquired at school would be frequently laid aside?"

Mr. GREELEY. "I think that the habit would not be acquired, and that paper reading would fall into disuse."

Mr. EWART. "Having observed both countries, can you state whether the press has greater influence on public opinion in the United States than in England, or the reverse?"

Mr. GREELEY. "I think it has more influence with us. I do not know that any class is despotically governed by the press, but its influence is more universal; every one reads and talks about it with us, and more weight is laid upon intelligence than on editorials; the paper which brings the quickest news is the thing looked to."

Mr. EWART. "The leading article has not so much influence as in England?"

Mr. GREELEY. "No; the telegraphic dispatch is the great point."

Mr. COBDEN. "Observing our newspapers and comparing them with the American papers, do you find that we make much less use of the electric telegraph for transmitting news than in America?"

Mr. GREELEY. "Not a hundredth part as much as we do."

Mr. COBDEN. "An impression prevails in this country that our newspaper press incurs a great deal more expense to expedite news than you do in New York. Are you of that opinion?"

Mr. GREELEY. "I do not know what your expense is. I should say that a hundred thousand dollars a year is paid by our association of the six leading daily papers, besides what each gets separately for itself."

Mr. COBDEN. "Twenty thousand pounds a year is paid by your association, consisting of six papers, for what you get in common?"

Mr. GREELEY. "Yes; we telegraph a great deal in the United States. Assuming that a scientific meeting was held at Cincinnati this year, we should telegraph the reports from that place, and I presume other journals would have special reporters to report the proceedings at length. We have a report every day, fifteen hundred miles, from New Orleans daily; from St. Louis too, and other places."

"The Committee then adjourned."

On Saturday morning, the seventh of June, after a residence of seven busy weeks in London, our traveler left that 'magnificent Babel,' for Paris, selecting the dearest and, of course, the quickest route. Dover, quaint and curious Dover, he thought a 'mean old town;' and the steamboat which conveyed him from Dover to Calais was 'one of those long, black, narrow scow-contrivances, about equal to a buttonwood dug-out, which England appears to delight in.' Two hours of deadly sea-sickness, and he stood on the shores of France. At Calais, which he styles 'a queer old town,' he was detained a long hour, obtained an execrable dinner for thirty-seven and a half cents, and changed some sovereigns for French money, 'at a shave which was not atrocious.' Then away to Paris by the swiftest train, arriving at half-past two on Sunday morning, four hours after the time promised in the enticing advertisement of the route. The ordeal of the custom-house he passed with little delay. "I did not," he says, "at first comprehend, that the number on my trunk, standing out fair before me in honest, unequivocal Arabic figures, could possibly mean anything but 'fifty-two;' but a friend cautioned me in season that those figures spelled 'cinquante-deux,' or phonetically 'sank-on-du' to the officer, and I made my first attempt at mouthing French accordingly, and succeeded in making myself intelligible."

About daylight on Sunday morning, he reached the Hotel Choiseul, Rue St. Honore, where he found shelter, but not bed. After breakfast, however, he sallied forth and saw his first sight in Paris, high mass at the Church of the Madeleine; which he thought a gorgeous, but 'inexplicable dumb show.'

Eight days were all that the indefatigable man could afford to a stay in the gay capital; but he improved the time. The obelisk of Luxor, brought from the banks of the Nile, and covered with mysterious inscriptions, that had braved the winds and rains of four thousand years, impressed him more deeply than any object he had seen in Europe. The Tuileries were to his eye only an irregular mass of buildings with little architectural beauty, and remarkable chiefly for their magnitude. At the French Opera, he saw the musical spectacle of Azael the Prodigal, or rather, three acts of it; for his patience gave way at the end of the third act. "Such a medley of drinking, praying, dancing, idol-worship, and Delilah-craft he had never before encountered." To comprehend an Englishman, he says, follow him to the fireside; a Frenchman, join him at the opera, and contemplate him during the performance of the ballet, of which France is the cradle and the home. "Though no *practitioner*," he adds, "I am yet a lover of the dance;" but the attitudes and contortions of the ballet are disagreeable and tasteless, and the tendency of such a performance as he that night beheld, was earthy, sensual, devilish. Notre Dame he thought not only the finest church, but the most imposing edifice in Paris, infinitely superior, as a place of worship, to the damp, gloomy, dungeon-like Westminster Abbey. The Hotel de Ville, like the New York City Hall, ' lacks another story.' In the Palace of Versailles, he saw fresh proofs of the selfishness of king-craft, the long-suffering patience of nations, and the necessary servility of Art when patronized by royalty. He wandered for hours through its innumerable halls, encrusted with splendor, till the intervention of a naked ante-room was a relief to the eye; and the ruling idea in picture and statue and carving was military glory. "Carriages shattered and overturned, animals transfixed by spear-thrusts and writhing in speechless agony, men riddled by cannon-shot or pierced by musket-balls, and ghastly with coming death; such are the spectacles which the more favored and fortunate of the Gallic youth have been called for generations to admire and enjoy. The whole collection is, in its general effect, delusive and mischievous, the purpose being to exhibit War as always glorious, and France as uniformly triumphant. It is by means like these that the business of shattering knee-joints and multiplying orphans is kept in countenance."

At the Louvre, however, the traveler spent the greater part of two days in rapturous contemplation of its wonderful collection of paintings. Two days out of eight --the fact is significant.

Let no man who has spent but three days in a foreign country, venture on prophecy with regard to its future. France, at the time of Horace Greeley's brief visit, went by the name of Republic, and Louis Napoleon was called President. For a sturdy republican like Mr. Greeley, it was but natural that one of his first inquiries should be, 'Will the Republic stand?' It is amusing, *now*, to read in a letter of his, written on the third day of his residence in Paris, the most confident predictions of its stability. "Alike," he says, "by its own strength and by its enemies' divisions, the safety of the Republic is assured;" and again, "Time is on the popular side, and every hour's endurance adds strength to the Republic." And yet again, "An open attack by the Autocrat would certainly consolidate it; a prolongation of Louis Napoleon's power (*no longer probable*) would have the same effect." "No longer probable." The striking events of history have seldom seemed 'probable' a year before they occurred.

Other impressions made upon the mind of the traveler were more correct. France, which the English press was daily representing as a nation inhabited equally by felons, bankrupts, paupers and lunatics, he found as tranquil and prosperous as England herself. He saw there less plate upon the sideboards of her landlords and bankers, but he observed evidences on all hands of general though unostentatious thrift. The French he thought intelligent, vivacious, courteous, obliging, generous and humane, eager to enjoy, but willing that all the world should enjoy with them; but at the same time, they are impulsive, fickle, sensual and irreverent. Paris, the 'paradise of the senses,' contained tens of thousands who could die fighting for liberty, but no class who could even comprehend the *idea* of the temperance pledge ! ! The poor of Paris seemed to suffer less than the poor of London; but in London there were ten philanthropic enterprises for one in Paris. In Paris he saw none of that abject servility in the bearing of the poor to the rich which had excited his disgust and commiseration in London. A hundred princes and dukes attract less attention in Paris than one in London; for 'Democracy triumphed in the drawing-rooms of Paris before it had erected its first barricade in the streets;' and once more the traveler "marvels at the *obliquity of vision*, whereby any one is enabled, standing in this metropolis, to anticipate the subversion of the Republic." "And if," he adds, "passing over the mob of generals and politicians-by-trade, the choice of candidates for the next presidential term should fall on some modest and unambitious citizen, who has earned a character by quiet probity and his bread by honest labor, I shall hope to see his name at the head of the poll in spite of the unconstitutional overthrow of Uni versal Suffrage." Thus he thought that France, fickle, glory-loving France, would do in 1852, what he only hoped America would be capable of some time before the year 1900; that is, ' elect something else than Generals to the presidency.'

Away to Lyons on the sixteenth of June. To an impetuous traveler like Horace Greeley, the tedious formalities of the European railroads were sufficiently irritating; but the "passport nuisance" was disgusting almost beyond endurance. One of the very few anecdotes which he found time to tell in his letters to the Tribune, occurs in connection with his remarks upon this subject. "Every one in Paris who lodges a stranger must see forthwith that he has a passport in good condition, in default of which said host is liable to a penalty. Now, two Americans, when applied to, produced passports in due form, but the professions set forth therein were not transparent to the landlord's apprehension. One of them was duly designated in his passport as a ' *loafer*,' the other as a ' *rowdy*,' and they informed him, on application, that though these · professions were highly popular in America and extensively followed, they knew no French synonyms into which they could be translated. The landlord, not content with the sign manual of Daniel Webster, affirming that all was right, applied to an American friend for a translation of the inexplicable professions, but I am not sure that he has even yet been fully enlightened with regard to them." He thought that three days' endurance of the passport system as it exists on the continent of Europe would send any American citizen home with his love of liberty and country kindled to a blaze of enthusiasm.

On the long railroad ride to Lyons, the traveler was half stifled with the tobacco smoke in the cars. His companions were all Frenchmen and all smokers, who " kept puff-puffing, through the day; first all of them, then three, two, and at all events one, till they all got out at Dijon near nightfall; when, before I had time to congratulate myself on the atmospheric improvement, another Frenchman got in, lit his cigar, and went at it. All this was in direct and flagrant violation of the rules posted up in the car;

but when did a smoker ever care for law or decency?" However, he flattened his nose diligently against the car windows, and spied what he could of the crops, the culture, the houses and the people of the country. He discovered that a Yankee could mow twice as much grass in a day as a Frenchman, but not get as much from each acre; that the women did more than half the work of the farms; that the agricultural implements were primitive and rude, the hay-carts "wretchedly small;" that the farm-houses were low small, steep-roofed, huddled together, and not worth a hundred dollars each; that fruit-trees were deplorably scarce; and that the stalls and stables for the cattle were 'visible only to the eye of faith.' He reached Chalons on the Saone, at nine in the evening; and Lyons per steamboat in the afternoon of the next day. Lyons, the capital of the silk-trade, furnished him, as might have been anticipated, with an excellent text for a letter on Protection, in which he endeavored to prove that it is not best for mankind that one hundred thousand silk-workers should be clustered on any square mile or two of earth.

The traveler's next ride was across the Alps to Turin. The letter which describes it contains, besides the usual remarks upon wheat, grass, fruit-trees and bad farming, one slight addition to our stock of personal anecdotes. The diligence had stopped at Chambery, the capital of Savoy, for breakfast.

"There was enough," he writes, "and good enough to eat, wine in abundance without charge, but tea, coffee, or chocolate, must be ordered and paid for extra. Yet I was unable to obtain a cup of chocolate, the excuse being that there was not time to make it. I did not understand, therefore, why I was charged more than others for breakfast; but to talk English against French or Italian is to get a mile behind in no time, so I pocketed the change offered me and came away. On the coach, however, with an Englishman near me who had traveled this way before and spoke French and Italian, I ventured to expose my ignorance as follows:

"'Neighbor, why was I charged three francs for breakfast, and the rest of you but two and a half?'

"'Don't know—perhaps you had tea or coffee.'

"'No, sir—don't drink either.'

"'Then perhaps you washed your face and hands.'

"'Well, it would be just like me.'

"'O, then, that's it! The half franc was for the basin and towel.'

"'Ah oui, oui.' So the milk in that cocoanut was accounted for."

Anecdotes are precious for biographical purposes. This is a little story, but the reader may infer from it something respecting Horace Greeley's manners, habits, and character. The morning of June the twentieth found the diligence rumbling over the beautiful plain of Piedmont towards Turin. Horace Greeley was in Italy. One of the first observations which he made in that enchanting country was, that he had never seen a region where *a few sub-soil plows*, with men qualified to use and explain them, were so much wanted! Refreshing remark! The sky of Italy had been overdone. At length, a traveler crossed the Alps who had an eye for the necessities of the soil.

Mr. Greeley spent twenty-one days in Italy, paying flying visits to Turin, Genoa, Pisa, Florence, Padua, Bologna, Venice, Milan, and passing about a week in Rome. At Genoa, he remarked that the kingdom of Sardinia, which contains a population of only four millions, maintains sixty thousand priests, but not five thousand teachers of elementary knowledge ; and that, while the churches of Genoa are worth four millions of dollars, the school-houses would not bring fifty thousand. " The black-coated gentry fairly overshadow the land with their shovel-hats, so that corn has no chance of sunshine." Pisa, too, could afford to spend a hundred thousand dollars in fireworks to celebrate the anniversary of its patron saint; but can spare nothing for popular education. At Florence, the traveler passed some agreeable hours with Hiram Powers, felt that his Greek Slave and Fisher Boy were not the loftiest achievements of that artist, defied antiquity to surpass his Proserpine and Psyche, and predicted that Powers, unlike Alexander, has realms still to conquer, and will fulfill his destiny. At Bologna the most notable thing he saw was an awning spread over the center of the main street for a distance of half a mile, and he thought the idea might be worth borrowing. On entering Venice his carpet-bags were searched for tobacco ; and he remarks, that when any tide-waiter finds more of that noxious weed about him than the chronic ill-breeding of smokers compels him to carry in his clothes, he is welcome to confiscate all his worldly possessions. Before reaching Venice, another diligence-incident occurred, which the traveler may be permitted himself to relate

"As midnight drew on," he writes, "I grew weary of gazing at the same endless diversity of grain-fields, vineyards, rows of trees, &c., though the bright moon was now shining; and, shutting out the chill night-air, I disposed myself on my old great-coat and softest carpet-bag for a drowse, having ample room at my command if I could but have brought it into a straight line. But the road was hard, the coach a little the uneasiest I ever hardened my bones upon, and my slumber was of a disturbed and dubious character, a dim sense of physical discomfort shaping and coloring my incoherent and fitful visions. For a time I fancied myself held down on my back while some malevolent wretch drenched the floor (and me) with filthy water; then I was in a rude scuffle, and came out third or fourth best, with my clothes badly torn; anon I had lost my hat in a strange place, and could not begin to find it; and at last my clothes were full of grasshoppers and spiders, who were beguiling their leisure by biting and stinging me. The misery at last became unbearable and I awoke. But where? I was plainly in a tight, dark box that needed more air; I soon recollected that it was a stage-coach, wherein I had been making my way from Ferrara to Padua. I threw open the door and looked out. Horses, postilions, and guard were all gone; the moon, the fields, the road were gone: I was in a close court-yard, alone with Night and Silence; but where? A church clock struck three; but it was only promised that we should reach Padua by four, and I, making the usual discount on such promises, had set down five as the probable hour of our arrival. I got out to take a more deliberate survey, and the tall form and bright bayonet of an Austrian sentinel, standing guard over the egress of the court-yard, were before me. To talk German was beyond the sweep of my dizziest ambition, but an Italian runner or porter instantly presented himself. From him I made out that I was in Padua of ancient and learned renown (Italian *Padova*), and that the first train for Venice would not start for three hours yet. I followed him into a convenient *café*, which was all open and well lighted, where I ordered a cup of chocolate, and proceeded leisurely to discuss it. When I had finished, the other guests had all gone out, but daylight was coming in, and I began to feel more at home. The *café* tender was asleep in his chair; the porter had gone off; the sentinel alone kept awake on his post. Soon the welcome face of the coach-guard, whom I had borne company from Bologna, appeared; I hailed him, obtained my baggage, hired a porter, and, having nothing more to wait for, started at a little past four for the Railroad station, nearly a mile distant; taking observations as I went. Arrived at the dépôt, I discharged my porter, sat down and waited for the place to open, with ample leisure for reflection. At six o'clock I felt once more the welcome motion of a railroad car, and at eight was in Venice."

At Venice, amid a thousand signs of decay, he saw one, and only one, indication of progress. It was a gondola with the word OM-

NIBUS written upon it; and the omnibus, he remarks, typifies Asso-CIATION, the simple but grandly fruitful idea which is destined to renovate the world of industry and production, substituting abundance and comfort for penury and misery. For Man, he thought, this quickening word is yet seasonable; for Venice, it is too late.

Rome our hurrying traveler reached through much tribulation. Even *his* patience gave way when the petty and numberless exactions of passport officials, hotel runners, postilions, and porters, had wrung the last copper from his pocket. After he and his fellow-passengers had paid every conceivable demand, when they supposed they had bought off every enemy, and had nothing to do but drive quietly into the city, "our postilion," says the indignant traveler, "came down upon us for more money for taking us to a hotel; and as we could do no better, we agreed to give him four francs to set down four of us (all the Americans and English he had) at one hotel. He drove by the Diligence Office, however, and there three or four rough customers jumped unbidden on the vehicle, and, when we reached our hotel, made themselves busy with our little luggage, which we would have thanked them to let alone. Having obtained it, we settled with the postilion, who grumbled and scolded, though we paid him more than his four francs. Then came the leader of our volunteer aids, to be paid for taking down the luggage. I had not a penny of change left, but others of our company scraped their pockets of a handful of coppers, which the '*facchini*' rejected with scorn, throwing them after us up stairs (I hope they did not pick them up afterwards), and I heard their imprecations until I had reached my room, but a blessed ignorance of Italian shielded me from any insult in the premises. Soon my two light carpet-bags, which I was not allowed to carry, came up with a fresh demand for porterage. 'Don't you belong to the hotel?' 'Yes.' 'Then vanish instantly!' I shut the door in his face, and let him growl to his heart's content; and thus closed my first day in the more especial dominions of His Holiness Pius IX."

But he was in Rome, and Rome impressed him deeply; for, in the nature of Horace Greeley, the poetical element exists as undeniably as the practical. He has an eye for a picture and a prospect, as well as for a potato-field and a sub-soil plough.

The greater part of his week in Rome was spent in the galleries of art; and while feasting his eyes with their manifold glories, practical suggestions for the *diffusion* of all that wealth of beauty occur to his mind.   It is well, he thought, that there should be somewhere in the world an Emporium of the Fine Arts; but not well that the heart should absorb all the blood and leave the limbs destitute; and, "if Rome would but consider herself under a mora responsibility to impart as well as receive, and would liberally dispose of so many of her master-pieces as would not at all impoverish her, buying in return such as could be spared her from abroad, and would thus enrich her collections by diversifying them, she would render the cause of Art a signal service, and earn the gratitude of mankind, without the least prejudice to her own permanent well-being."

Among the Sights of Rome, the Coliseum seems to have made the most lasting impression upon the mind of the traveler.   He was fortunate in the hour of his visit.   As he slowly made the circuit of the gigantic ruin, a body of French cavalry were exercising their horses along the eastern side, while in a neighboring grove the rattle of the kettle-drum revealed the presence of infantry.   At length the horsemen rode slowly away, and the attention of the visitors was attracted to some groups of Italians in the interior, who were slowly marching and chanting.

"We entered," says Mr. Greeley, "and were witnesses of a strange, impressive ceremony.   It is among the traditions of Rome that a great number of the early Christians were compelled by their heathen persecutors to fight and die here as gladiators, as a punishment for their contumacious, treasonable resistance to the 'lower law' then in the ascendant, which the high priests and circuit judges of that day were wont in their sermons and charges to demonstrate that every one was bound as a law-abiding citizen to obey, no matter what might be his private, personal convictions with regard to it.   Since the Coliseum has been cleared of rubbish, fourteen little oratories or places of prayer have been cheaply constructed around its inner circumference, and here at certain seasons prayers are offered for the eternal bliss of the martyred Christians of the Coliseum.   These prayers were being offered on this occasion.   Twenty or thirty men (priests or monks I inferred), partly bareheaded, but as many with their heads completely covered by hooded cloaks, which left only two small holes for the eyes, accompanied by a large number of women, marched slowly and sadly to one oratory, chanting a prayer by the way, setting up their lighted tapers by its semblance of an altar, kneeling and praying for some minutes, then rising and proceeding to the next oratory, and so on until they had repeated the service before every one.   They all seemed to be of the poorer class, and I presume the ceremony is often repeated or the participators would have been much more numerous.   The praying was fervent and I trust excellent,—as the music decidedly was not ; but the whole scene, with the setting sun shining redly through the shattered arches and upon the ruined wall, with a few French soldiers standing heedlessly by, was strangely picturesque, and to me affecting.   I came away before it concluded, to avoid the damp night-air ; but many checkered years and scenes of stirring interest must intervene to efface from my memory that sun-set and those strange prayers in the Coliseum."

St. Peter's, he styles the Niagara of edifices; and, like Niagara, the first view of it is disappointing.   In the Sistine chapel, he observed a picture of the Death of Admiral Coligny at the Massacre of St. Bartholomew, and if the placing of that picture there was not intended to express approbation of the Massacre, he wanted to know what it *was* intended to express.

The tenth of July was the traveler's last day in Italy.   A swift journey through Switzerland, Germany, Belgium, and North Eastern France brought him once more to England.   In Switzerland, he saw everywhere the signs of frugal thrift and homely content. He was assailed by no beggar, cheated by no official ; though, as he truly remarks, he was ' *very palpably* a stranger.'   A more ' upright, kindly, truly religious people ' than the Catholic Swiss, he had never seen ; and he thought their superiority to the Italians attributable to their republican institutions ! !   He liked the Germans.   Their good humor, their kind-heartedness, their deference to each other's wishes, their quiet, unostentatious manner, their self-respect, won his particular regard.   In the main cabins of German steamboats, he was gratified to see " well-dressed young ladies take out their home-prepared dinner and eat it at their own good time without seeking the company and countenance of others, or troubling themselves to see who was observing.   A Lowell factory girl would consider this entirely out of character, and a New York milliner would be shocked at the idea of it."

Nowhere, he here remarks, had he found Aristocracy a chronic disease, except in England.

" Your Paris boot-black will make you a low bow in acknowledgment of a franc, but he has not a trace of the abjectness of a

London waiter, and would evidently decline the honor of being kicked by a Duke. In Italy, there is little manhood but no class-worship; her millions of beggars will not abase themselves one whit lower before a Prince than before any one else from whom they hope to worm a copper. The Swiss are freemen, and wear the fact unconsciously but palpably on their brows and beaming from their eyes. The Germans submit passively to arbitrary power which they see not how successfully to resist, but they render to rank or dignity no more homage than is necessary—their souls are still free, and their manners evince a simplicity and frankness which might shame, or at least instruct America."

On the twenty-first of July, Horace Greeley was again in London. One incident of his journey from the court to the metropolis was sufficiently ludicrous. There were three Frenchmen and two French women in the car, going up to see the Exhibition. " *London Stout*,' displayed in tall letters across the front of a tavern, attracted the attention of the party. ' *Stoot? Stoot?*' queried one of them; but the rest were as much in the dark as he, and the American was as deficient in French as they in English. The befogged one pulled out his dictionary and read over and over all the French synonyms of ' Stout,' but this only increased his perplexity. ' Stout ' signified ' robust,' ' hearty,' ' vigorous,' ' resolute,' &c., but what then could ' *London* Stout ' be? He closed his book at length in despair and resumed his observations."

The remaining sixteen days of Mr. Greeley's three months in Europe were busy ones indeed. The great Peace Convention was in session in London; but, as he was not a delegate, he took no part in its proceedings. If he *had* been a delegate, he tells us, that he should have offered a resolution which would have *affirmed*, not denied, the right of a nation, wantonly invaded by a foreign army or intolerably oppressed by its own rulers, to resist force by force; a proposition which he thought might perhaps have marred the ' harmony and happiness ' of the Convention.

A few days after his return to London, he had the very great gratification of witnessing the triumph of M'Cormick's Reaping Machine, which, as it stood in the Crystal Palace, had excited general derision, and been styled ' a cross between an Astley chariot, a flying machine, and a tread-mill.' It came into the field, therefore, to confront a tribunal prepared for its condemnation. "Before it stood John Bull, burly, dogged, and determined not to be humbugged—his judgment made up and his sentence ready to be recorded. Nothing disconcerted, the brown, rough, homespun Yankee in charge jumped on the box, starting the team at a smart walk, setting the blades of the machine in lively operation, and commenced raking off the grain in sheaf-piles ready for binding,—cutting a breadth of nine or ten feet cleanly and carefully as fast as a span of horses could comfortably step. There was a moment, and but a moment of suspense; human prejudice could hold out no longer; and burst after burst of involuntary cheers from the whole crowd proclaimed the triumph of the Yankee 'treadmill.'"

A rapid tour through the north of England, Scotland, and Ireland absorbed the last week of Mr. Greeley's stay in Europe. The grand old town of Edinburgh 'surpassed his expectations,' and he was amused at the passion of the Edinburghers for erecting public monuments to eminent men. Glasgow looked to him more like an American city than any other he had seen in Europe; it was half Pittsburgh, half Philadelphia. Ireland seemed more desolate, more wretched, even in its best parts, than he had expected to find it. As an additional proof of his instinctive sense of means and ends, take this suggestion for Ireland's deliverance from the pall of ignorance that overspreads it:—"Let the Catholic Bishops unite in an earnest and potential call for teachers, and they can summon thousands and tens of thousands of capable and qualified persons from convents, from seminaries, from cloisters, from drawing-rooms, even from foreign lands if need be, to devote their time and efforts to the work without earthly recompense or any stipulation save for a bare subsistence, which the less needy Catholics, or even the more liberal Protestants, in every parish, would gladly proffer them."

Perfectly practicable—perfectly impossible! The following is the only incident of his Irish tour that space can be found for here:—" Walking with a friend through one of the back streets of Galway beside the outlet of the Lakes, I came where a girl of ten years old was breaking up hard brook pebbles into suitable fragments to mend roads with. We halted, and M. asked her how much she received for that labor. She answered, 'Sixpence a car-load.' 'How long will it take you to break a car-load?' '*About a fortnight.*'"

He concluded his brief sketch of this country with the words, "Alas! unhappy Ireland." Yet, on a calmer and fuller survey of Ireland's case, and after an enumeration of the various measures for her relief and regeneration which were slowly but surely operating, he exclaims, "There shall yet be an Ireland to which her sons in distant lands may turn their eyes with a pride unmingled with sadness; but who can say how soon!"

Mr. Greeley, though he did not 'wholly like those grave and stately English,' appreciated highly and commends frankly their many good qualities. He praised their industry, their method, their economy, their sense of the practical; sparing not, however, their conceit and arrogance. An English duchess, he remarks, does not hesitate to say, 'I cannot afford' a proposed outlay—an avowal rarely and reluctantly made by an American, even in moderate circumstances. The English he thought a most *un-ideal* people, even in their 'obstreperous loyalty'; and when the portly and well-to-do Briton exclaims, 'God save the Queen,' with intense enthusiasm, he means, 'God save my estates, my rents, my shares, my consols, my expectations.' He liked the amiable women of England, so excellent at the fireside, so tame in the drawing-room; but he doubted whether they could so much as *comprehend* the 'ideas which underlie the woman's-rights movement.' The English have a sharp eye to business, he thought; particularly the Free Traders. Our champion of Protection on this subject remarks :—"The French widow who appended to the high-wrought eulogium engraved on her husband's tombstone, that 'His disconsolate widow still keeps the shop No. 16 Rue St. Denis,' had not a keener eye to business than these apostles of the Economic faith. No consideration of time or place is regarded; in festive meetings, peace conventions, or gatherings of any kind, where men of various lands and views are notoriously congregated, and where no reply could be made without disturbing the harmony and distracting the attention of the assemblage, the disciples of Cobden are sure to interlard their harangues with advice to foreigners substantially thus—'N. B. Protection is a great humbug and a great waste. Better abolish your tariffs, stop your factories, and buy at our shops. We're the boys to give you thirteen pence for every shilling.' I cannot say how this affected others, but to me it seemed hardly more ill-mannered than impolitic."

Yet, the better qualities of the British decidedly preponderate; and he adds, that the quiet comfort and heartfelt warmth of an English fireside must be felt to be appreciated.

On Wednesday, the sixth of August, Horace Greeley was once more on board the steamship Baltic, homeward bound.

"I rejoice," he wrote on the morning of his departure, "I rejoice to feel that every hour, henceforth, must lessen the distance which divides me from my country, whose advantages and blessings this four months' absence has taught me to appreciate more dearly and to prize more deeply than before. With a glow of unwonted rapture I see our stately vessel's prow turned toward the setting sun, and strive to realize that only some ten days separate me from those I know and love best on earth. Hark! the last gun announces that the mail-boat has left us, and that we are fairly afloat on our ocean journey; the shores of Europe recede from our vision; the watery waste is all around us; and now, with God above and Death below, our gallant bark and her clustered company together brave the dangers of the mighty deep. May Infinite Mercy watch over our onward path and bring us safely to our several homes; for to die away from home and kindred seems one of the saddest calamities that could befall me. This mortal tenement would rest uneasily in an ocean shroud; this spirit reluctantly resign that tenement to the chill and pitiless brine: these eyes close regretfully on the stranger skies and bleak inhospitality of the sullen and stormy main. No! let me see once more the scenes so well remembered and beloved; let me grasp, if but once again, the hand of Friendship, and hear the thrilling accents of proved Affection, and when sooner or later the hour of mortal agony shall come, let my last gaze be fixed on eyes that will not forget me when I am gone, and let my ashes repose in that congenial soil which, however I may there be esteemed or hated, is still 'My own green land forever!'"

Neptune was more gracious to the voyager on his homeward than he had been on his outward passage. The skies were clearer, the winds more favorable and gentler. A few days, not intolerably disagreeable, landed him on the shores of Manhattan. The ship reached the wharf about six o'clock in the morning, cheating the expectant morning papers of their foreign news, which the editor of the Tribune had already 'made up' for publication on board the steamer. However, he had no sooner got on shore than he rushed away to the office, bent on getting out an 'extra' in advance of all contemporaries. The compositors were all absent, of course; but boys were forthwith dispatched to summon them from bed and breakfast. Meanwhile, the impetuous Editor-in-Chief proceeded *with his own hands* to set the matter in type, and continued to assist till the form was ready to be lowered away to the press-room in the basement. In an hour or two the streets resounded with the cry, "Extra Try-bune; 'yival of the Bal*tic*." *Then*, but not till then, Horace Greeley might have been seen in a corner of an omnibus, going slowly up town, towards his residence in Nineteenth street.

CHAPTER XXVII.

RECENTLY.

Deliverance from Party—A Private Platform—Last Interview with Henry Clay—Horace Greeley a Farmer—He irrigates and drains—His Advice to a Young Man—The Daily Times—A costly Mistake—The Isms of the Tribune—The Tribune gets Glory—The Tribune in Parliament—Proposed Nomination for Governor—His Life written—A Judge's Daughter for Sale.

DURING the first eight or nine volumes of the Tribune, the history of that newspaper and the life of Horace Greeley were one and the same thing. But the time has passed, and passed forever, when a New York morning paper can be the vehicle of a single mind. Since the year 1850, when the Tribune came upon the town as a double sheet nearly twice its original size, its affairs have had a metropolitan complexity and extensiveness, and Horace Greeley has run through it only as the original stream courses its way through a river swollen and expanded by many tributaries. The quaffing traveler cannot tell, as he rises from the shore refreshed, whether he has been drinking Hudson, or Mohawk, or Moodna, or two of them mingled, or one of the hundred rivulets that trickle into the ample stream upon which fleets and ' palaces' securely ride. Some wayfarers *think* they can, but they cannot; and their erroneous guesses are among the amusements of the tributary corps. Occasionally, however, the original Greeley flavor is recognizable to the dullest palate.

The most important recent event in the history of the Tribune occurred in November, 1852, when, on the defeat of General Scott and the annihilation of the Whig party, it ceased to be a party paper, and its editor ceased to be a party man. And this blessed emancipation, with its effect upon the press of the country, was worth that disaster. We never had great newspapers in this country while our leading papers gave allegiance to party, and never could have had. A great newspaper must be above everything and everybody. Its independence must be absolute, and then its power will be as nearly so as it ought to be.

It was fit that the last triumph of party should be its greatest, and that triumph was secured when it enlisted such a man as Horace Greeley as the special and head champion of a man like General Scott. But as a *partisan*, what other choice had he? To use his own language, he supported Scott and Graham, because,

" 1. They can be *elected*, and the others *can't*.

" 2. They are openly and thoroughly for PROTECTION TO HOME INDUSTRY, while the others, (judged by their supporters,) lean to Free Trade.

" 3. Scott and Graham are backed by the general support of those who hold with us, that government may and should do much *positive good*."

At the same time he 'spat upon the (Baltimore compromise, profugitive law) platform,' and in its place, gave one of his own. As this private platform is the most condensed and characteristic statement of Horace Greeley's political opinions that I have seen, it may properly be printed here.

OUR PLATFORM.

" I. As to *the Tariff*:—Duties on Imports—specific so far as practicable, affording ample protection to undeveloped or peculiarly exposed branches of our National Industry, and adequate revenue for the support of the government and the payment of its debts. Low duties, as a general rule, on rude, bulky staples, whereof the cost of transportation is of itself equivalent to a heavy impost, and high duties on such fabrics, wares, &c., as come into depressing competition with our own depressed infantile or endangered pursuits.

" II. As to *National Works*:—Liberal appropriations yearly for the improvement of rivers and harbors, and such eminently national enterprises as the Saut St. Marie canal and the Pacific railroad from the Mississippi. Cut down the expenditures for forts, ships, troops and warlike enginery of all kinds, and aid largely to those for works which do not ' perish in the using,' but will re

main for ages to benefit our people, strengthen the Union, and contribute far
more to the national defense than the costly machinery of war ever could.

"III. As to *Foreign Policy* :—' Do unto others [the weak and oppressed
as well as the powerful and mighty] as we would have them do unto us.'
No shuffling, no evasion of duties nor shirking responsibilities, but a firm
front to despots, a prompt rebuke to every outrage on the law of Nations, and
a generous, active sympathy with the victims of tyranny and usurpation.

"IV. As to *Slavery* :—No interference by Congress with its existence in any
slave State, but a firm and vigilant resistance to its legalization in any national
Territory, or the acquisition of any foreign Territory wherein slavery may exist. A perpetual protest against the hunting of fugitive slaves in free States
as an irresistible cause of agitation, ill feeling and alienation between the
North and the South. A firm, earnest, inflexible testimony, in common with
the whole non-slaveholding Christian world, that human slavery, though legally protected, is morally wrong, and ought to be speedily terminated.

"V. As to *State rights* :—More regard for and less cant about them.

"VI. One Presidential Term, and no man a candidate for any office while
wielding the vast patronage of the national executive.

"VII. Reform in Congress :—Payment by the session, with a rigorous de-
duction for each day's absence, and a reduction and straightening of mileage.
We would suggest $2,000 compensation for the first (or long), and $1,000 for
the second (or short) session ; with ten cents per mile for traveling (by a bee-
line) to and from Washington."

The Tribune fought gallantly for Scott, and made no wry faces at
the ' brogue,' or any other of the peculiarities of the candidate's
stump efforts. When the sorry fight was over, the Tribune submitted with its usual good humor, spoke jocularly of the ' *late* whig
party,' declared its independence of party organizations for the future, and avowed its continued adhesion to all the principles which
it had hoped to promote by battling with the whigs. It would still
war with the aggressions of the slave power, still strive for free
homesteads, still denounce the fillibusters, and still argue for the
Maine Law.

" ' Doctor," said a querulous, suffering invalid who had paid a good deal of
money for physic to little apparent purpose, " you don't seem to reach the
seat of my disease. Why don't you strike at the seat of my disorder ?"

" ' Well, I will," was the prompt reply, " if you insist on it ;" and, lifting
his cane, he smashed the brandy bottle on the sideboard.' "

And thus ended the long connection of the New York Tribune
with the whig party

In the summer of 1852, Horace Greeley performed the melancholy duty of finishing Sargent's Life of Henry Clay. He added little, however, to Mr. Sargent's narrative, except the proceedings of Congress on the occasion of Mr. Clay's death and funeral. One paragraph, descriptive of the last interview between the dying statesman and the editor of the Tribune, claims insertion:

"Learning from others," says Mr. Greeley, "how ill and feeble he was, I had not intended to call upon him, and remained two days under the same roof without asking permission to do so. Meantime, however, he was casually informed of my being in Washington, and sent me a request to call at his room. I did so, and enjoyed a half hour's free and friendly conversation with him, the saddest and the last! His state was even worse than I feared; he was already emaciated, a prey to a severe and distressing cough, and complained of spells of difficult breathing. I think no physician could have judged him likely to live two months longer. Yet his mind was unclouded and brilliant as ever, his aspirations for his country's welfare as ardent; and, though all personal ambition had long been banished, his interest in the events and impulses of the day was nowise diminished. He listened attentively to all I had to say of the repulsive aspects and revolting features of the Fugitive Slave Law and the necessary tendency of its operation to excite hostility and alienation on the part of our Northern people, unaccustomed to Slavery, and seeing it exemplified only in the brutal arrest and imprisonment of some humble and inoffensive negro whom they had learned to regard as a neighbor. I think I may without impropriety say that Mr. Clay regretted that more care had not been taken in its passage to divest this act of features needlessly repulsive to Northern sentiment, though he did not deem any change in its provisions now practicable."

A strange, but not inexplicable, fondness existed in the bosom of Horace Greeley for the aspiring chieftain of the Whig party. Very masculine men, men of complete physical development, the gallant, the graceful, the daring, often enjoy the sincere homage of souls superior to their own; because such are apt to place an extravagant value upon the shining qualities which they do not possess. From Webster, the great over-Praised, the false god of cold New England, Horace Greeley seems ever to have shrunk with an instinctive aversion.

As he lost his interest in party politics, his mind reverted to the soil. He yearned for the repose and the calm delights of country life.

"As for me," he said, at the conclusion of an address before the Indiana State Agricultural Society, delivered in October, 1853, " as for me, long-tossed on the stormiest waves of doubtful conflict and arduous endeavor, I have begun to feel, since the shades of forty years fell upon me, the weary, tempest-driven voyager's longing for land, the wanderer's yearning for the hamlet where in childhood he nestled by his mother's knee, and was soothed to sleep on her breast. The sober down-hill of life dispels many illusions, while it develops or strengthens within us the attachment, perhaps long smothered or overlaid, for 'that dear hut, our home.' And so I, in the sober afternoon of life, when its sun, if not high, is still warm, have bought a few acres of land in the broad, still country, and, bearing thither my household treasures, have resolved to steal from the City's labors and anxieties at least one day in each week, wherein to revive as a farmer the memories of my childhood's humble home. And already I realize that the experiment cannot cost so much as it is worth. Already I find in that day's quiet an antidote and a solace for the feverish, festering cares of the weeks which environ it. Already my brook murmurs a soothing even-song to my burning, throbbing brain; and my trees, gently stirred by the fresh breezes, whisper to my spirit something of their own quiet strength and patient trust in God. And thus do I faintly realize, though but for a brief and flitting day, the serene joy which shall irradiate the Farmer's vocation, when a fuller and truer Education shall have refined and chastened his animal cravings, and when Science shall have endowed him with her treasures, redeeming Labor from drudgery while quadrupling its efficiency, and crowning with beauty and plenty our bounteous, beneficent Earth."

The portion of the 'broad, still country' alluded to in this eloquent passage, is a farm of fifty acres in Westchester county, near Newcastle, close to the Harlem railroad, thirty-four miles from the city of New York. Thither the tired editor repairs every Saturday morning by an early train, and there he remains directing and assisting in the labors of the farm for that single day only, returning early enough on Sunday to hear the flowing rhetoric of Mr. Chapin's morning sermon. From church—to the office and to work.

This farm has seen marvelous things done on it during the three years of Mr. Greeley's ownership. What it was when he bought it may be partly inferred from another passage of the same address : " I once went to look at a farm of fifty acres that I thought of buying for a summer home, some forty miles from the city of New York. The owner had been born on it, as I believe had his father before him ; but it yielded only a meager subsistence for his family, and he thought of selling and going West. I went over it with him late in June, passing through a well-filled barn-yard which had not been disturbed that season, and stepping thence into a corn-field of five acres, with a like field of potatoes just beyond it. 'Why, neighbor !' asked I, in astonishment, 'how *could* you leave all this manure so handy to your plowed land, and plant ten acres without any ?' 'O, I was sick a good part of the spring, and so hurried that I could not find time to haul it out.' 'Why, suppose you had planted but five acres in all, and emptied your barn-yard on those five, leaving the residue untouched, don't you think you would have harvested a larger crop ?' 'Well, perhaps I should,' was the poor farmer's response. It seemed never before to have occurred to him that he *could* let alone a part of his land. Had he progressed so far, he might have ventured thence to the conclusion that it is less expensive and more profitable to raise a full crop on five acres than half a crop on ten. I am sorry to say we have a good many such farmers still left at the East." But, he might have added, Horace Greeley is not one of them. He did not, however, and the deficiency shall here be supplied.

The farm is at present a practical commentary upon the oft-repeated recommendations of the Tribune with regard to 'high farming.' It consisted, three years ago, of grove, bog, and exhausted upland, in nearly equal proportions. In the grove, which is a fine growth of hickory, hemlock, iron-wood and oak, a small white cottage is concealed, built by Mr. Greeley, at a cost of a few hundred dollars. The farm-buildings, far more costly and expensive, are at the foot of the hill on which the house stands, and around them are the gardens. The marshy land, which was formerly very wet, very boggy, and quite useless, has been drained by a system of ditches and tiles ; the bogs have been pared off and burnt, the land plowed and planted, and made exceedingly productive. The upland has been prepared for irrigation, the water being supplied by a brook, which tumbled down the hill through a deep glen. Its course was arrested by a dam, and from the reservoir thus formed, pipes are laid to the different fields, which can be inundated by the turning of a cock. The experiment of irrigation, however, has been suspended. Last spring the brook, swollen with rage at the loss of its ancient liberty, burst through the dam, and scattered four thousand dollars' worth of solid masonry in the space of a minute and a half. This year a new attempt will be made to reduce it to submission, and conduct its waters in peaceful and fertilizing rivulets down the rows of corn and potatoes. Then Mr. Greeley can take down his weather-cock, and smile in the midst of drought, water his crops with less trouble than he can water his horses, and sow turnips in July, regardless of the clouds. If a crop is well put in the ground, and well cared for as it progresses, its perfect success depends upon two things, water and sunshine. Science has enabled the farmer partly to regulate the supply of the latter, and perfectly to regulate the supply of the former. The slant of the hills, the reflection of walls, glass covers, trees, awnings, and other contrivances, may be made to concentrate or ward off the rays of the sun. Irrigation and drainage go far to complete the farmer's independence of the wayward weather. In all the operations of his little farm, Mr. Greeley takes the liveliest interest, and he means to astonish his neighbors with some wonderful crops, by-and-by, when he has everything in training. Indeed, he may have done so already ; as, in the list of prizes awarded at our last Agricultural State Fair, held in New York, October, 1854, we read, under the head of ' vegetables,' these two items:—"Turnips, H. Greeley, Chappaqua, Westchester Co., Two Dollars," (the second prize); "Twelve second-best ears of White Seed Corn, H. Greeley, Two Dollars." Looking down over the reclaimed swamp, all bright now with waving flax, he said one day, " All else that I have done may be of no avail ; but what I have done here is *done ;* it will last."

A private letter, written about this time, appeared in the country papers, and still emerges occasionally. A young man wrote to Mr.

Greeley, requesting his advice upon a project of going to college and studying law. The reply was as follows:

"MY DEAR SIR,—Had you asked me whether I would advise you to desert agriculture for law, I should have answered no! very decidedly. There is already a superabundance of lawyers, coupled with a great scarcity of good farmers. Why carry your coals to Newcastle?

"As to a collegiate education, my own lack of it probably disqualifies me to appreciate it fully; but I think you might better be learning to fiddle. And if you are without means, I would advise you to hire ten acres of good land, work ten hours a day on it, for five days each week, and devote all your spare hours to reading and study, especially to the study of agricultural science, and thus 'owe no man anything,' while you receive a thorough practical education. Such is not the advice you seek; nevertheless, I remain yours,   HORACE GREELEY."

This letter may serve as a specimen of hundreds of similar ones. Probably there never lived a man to whom so many perplexed individuals applied for advice and aid, as to Horace Greeley. He might with great advantage have taken a hint from the practice of Field Marshal the Duke of Wellington, who, it is said, had forms of reply printed, which he filled up and dispatched to anxious correspondents, with commendable promptitude. From facts which I have observed, and from others of which I have heard, I think it safe to say, that Horace Greeley receives, on an average, five applications daily for advice and assistance. His advice he gives very freely, but the wealth of Astor would not suffice to answer all his begging letters in the way the writers of them desire.

In the fall of 1852, the Daily Times was started by Mr. H. J. Raymond, an event which gave an impetus to the daily press of the city. The success of the Times was signal and immediate, for three reasons: 1, it was conducted with tact, industry and prudence; 2, it was not the Herald; 8, it was not the Tribune. Before the Times appeared, the Tribune and Herald shared the cream of the daily paper business between them; but there was a large class who disliked the Tribune's principles and the Herald's want of principle. The majority of people take a daily paper solely to ascertain what is going on in the world. They are averse to profligacy and time-serving, and yet are offended at the independent avowal of ideas in advance of their own. And though Horace

Greeley is not the least conservative of men, yet, from his practice of giving every new thought and every new man a hearing in the columns of his paper, unthinking persons received the impression that he was an *advocate* of every new idea, and a *champion* of every new man. They thought the Tribune was an unsafe, disorganizing paper. "An excellent paper," said they, "and honest, but then it's so full of *isms !*" The Times stepped in with a complaisant bow, and won over twenty thousand of the ism-hating class in a single year, and yet without reducing the circulation of either of its elder rivals. Where those twenty thousand subscribers came from is one of the mysteries of journalism.

In the spring of 1853 the Tribune signalized its 'entrance into its teens' by making a very costly mistake. It enlarged its borders to such an extent that the price of subscription did not quite cover the cost of the white paper upon which it was printed, thus throwing the burden of its support upon the advertiser. And this, too, in the face of the fact that the Tribune, though the best vehicle of advertising then in existence, was in least favor among the class whose advertising is the most profitable. Yet it was natural for Horace Greeley to commit an error of this kind. Years ago he had written, "Better a dinner of herbs with a large circulation than a stalled ox with a small one." And, in announcing the enlargement, he said, "We are confessedly ambitious to make the Tribune the leading journal of America, and have dared and done somewhat to that end."

How much he 'dared' in the case of this enlargement may be inferred from the fact that it involved an addition of $1,044 to the weekly, $54,329 to the annual, expenses of the concern. Yet he 'dared' not add a cent to the price of the paper, which it is thought he might have done with perfect safety, because those who like the Tribune like it very much, and will have it at any price. Men have been heard to talk of their Bible, their Shakspeare, and their Tribune, as the three necessities of their spiritual life; while those who dislike it, dislike it excessively, and are wont to protest that they should deem their houses defiled by its presence. The Tribune, however, stepped bravely out under its self-imposed load of white paper. In one year the circulation of the Daily increased from 17,040 to 26,880, the Semi-Weekly from 3.120 to 11,400, the Week-

ly from 51,000 to 103,680, the California Tribune from 2,800 to
8,500, and the receipts of the office increased $70,900. The profits,
however, were inadequate to reward suitably the exertions of
its proprietors, and recently the paper was slightly reduced in
size.

The enlargement called public attention to the career and the
merits of the Tribune in a remarkable manner. The press generally applauded its spirit, ability and courage, but deplored its isms,
which gave rise to a set article in the Tribune on the subject of isms.
This is the substance of the Tribune's opinions of isms and ismists.
It is worth considering:

"A very natural division of mankind is that which contemplates them in
two classes—those who think for themselves, and those who have their thinking done by others, dead or living. With the former class, the paramount
consideration is—'What is *right?*' With the latter, the first inquiry is—
'What do the majority, or the great, or the pious, or the fashionable think
about it?   How did our fathers regard it?   What will Mrs. Grundy say?'

     *   *   *   *   *   *   *   *

"And truly, if the life were *not* more than meat—if its chief ends were
wealth, station and luxury—then the smooth and plausible gentlemen who assent to whatever is popular without inquiring or caring whether it is essentially true or false, are the Solomons of their generation.

"Yet in a world so full as this is of wrong and suffering, of oppression and
degradation, there must be radical causes for so many and so vast practical
evils. It cannot be that the ideas, beliefs, institutions, usages, prejudices,
whereof such gigantic miseries are born—wherewith at least they co-exist—
transcend criticism and rightfully refuse scrutiny. It cannot be that the
springs are pure whence flow such turbid and poisonous currents.

"Now the Reformer—the man who thinks for himself and acts as his own
judgment and conscience dictate—is very likely to form erroneous opinions.
* * *   But Time will confirm and establish his good works and gently
amend his mistakes. The detected error dies; the misconceived and rejected
truth is but temporarily obscured and soon vindicates its claim to general acceptance and regard.

"'The world *does* move,' and its motive power, under God, is the fearless
thought and speech of those who dare be in advance of their time—who are
sneered at and shunned through their days of struggle and of trial as lunatics, dreamers, impracticables and visionaries—men of crotchets, of vagaries,
or of 'isms.' These are the masts and sails of the ship, to which Conservatism answers as ballast. The ballast is important—at times indispensable
—but it would be of no account if the ship were not bound to go ahead."

Many papers, however, gave the Tribune its full due of appreciation and praise. Two notices which appeared at the time are worth copying, at least in part. The Newark Mercury gave it this unequaled and deserved commendation :—" *We never knew a man of illiberal sentiments, one unjust to his workmen, and groveling in his aspirations, who liked the Tribune;* and it is rare to find one with liberal views who does not admit its claims upon the public regard."

The St. Joseph Valley Register, a paper published at South Bend, Indiana, held the following language :

" The influence of the Tribune upon public opinion is greater even than its conductors claim for it. Its Isms, with scarce an exception, though the people may reject them at first, yet ripen into strength insensibly. A few years since the Tribune commenced the advocacy of the principle of Free Lands for the Landless. The first bill upon that subject, presented by Mr. Greeley to Congress, was hooted out of that body. But who doubts what the result would be, if the people of the whole nation had the right to vote upon the question to-day ? It struck the first blow in earnest at the corruptions of the Mileage system, and in return, Congressmen of all parties heaped opprobrium upon it, and calumny upon its Editor. A corrupt Congress may postpone its Reform, but is there any doubt of what nine-tenths of the whole people would accomplish on this subject if direct legislation were in their hands ? It has inveighed in severe language against the flimsy penalties which the American legislatures have imposed for offenses upon female virtue. And how many States, our own among the number, have tightened up their legislation upon that subject within the last half-dozen years. The blows that it directs against Intemperance have more power than the combined attacks of half the distinctive Temperance Journals in the land. It has contended for some plan by which the people should choose their Presidents rather than National Conventions ; and he must be a careless observer of the progress of events who does not see that the Election of 1856 is more likely to be won by a Western Statesman, pledged solely to the Pacific Railroad and Honest Government, than by any political nominee ? And, to conclude, the numerous Industrial Associations of Workers to manufacture Iron, Boots and Shoes, Hats, &c., on their own account, with the Joint Stock Family Blocks of Buildings, so popular now in New York, Model Wash-houses, &c., &c., seem like a faint recognition at least of the main principles of Fourierism (whose *details* we like as little as any one), Opportunity for Work for all, and Economy in the Expenses and Labor of the Family."

From across the Atlantic, also, came compliments for the Tribune. In one of the debates in the House of Commons upon the

17

abolition of the advertisement duty, Mr. Bright used a copy of the Tribune, as Burke once did a French Republican dagger, for the purposes of his argument. Mr. Bright said:

" He had a newspaper there (the New York Tribune), which he was bound to say, was as good as any published in England this week. [The Hon. Member here opened out a copy of the New York Tribune, and exhibited it to the House.] It was printed with a finer type than any London daily paper. It was exceedingly good as a journal, quite sufficient for all the purposes of a newspaper. [Spreading it out before the House, the honorable gentleman detailed its contents, commencing with very numerous advertisements.] It contained various articles, amongst others, one against public dinners, in which he thought honorable members would fully agree—one criticising our Chancellor of the Exchequer's budget, in part justly—and one upon the Manchester school; but he must say, as far as the Manchester school went, it did not do them justice at all. [Laughter.] He ventured to say that there was not a better paper than this in London. Moreover, it especially wrote in favor of Temperance and Anti-Slavery, and though honorable members were not all members of the Temperance Society perhaps, they yet, he was sure, all admitted the advantages of Temperance, while not a voice could be lifted there in favor of Slavery. Here, then, was a newspaper advocating great principles, and conducted in all respects with the greatest propriety—a newspaper in which he found not a syllable that he might not put on his table and allow his wife and daughter to read with satisfaction. And this was placed on the table every morning for 1d. [Hear, hear.] What he wanted, then, to ask the Government, was this—How comes it, and for what good end, and by what contrivance of fiscal oppression—for it can be nothing else—was it, that while the workman of New York could have such a paper on his breakfast table every morning for 1d., the workman of London must go without or pay five-pence for the accommodation ? [Hear, hear.] How was it possible that the latter could keep up with his transatlantic competitor in the race, if one had daily intelligence of everything that was stirring in the world, while the other was kept completely in ignorance ? [Hear, hear.] Were they not running a race, in the face of the world, with the people of America ? Were not the Collins and Cunard lines calculating their voyages to within sixteen minutes of time ? And if, while such a race was going on, the one artisan paid five-pence for the daily intelligence which the other obtained for a penny, how was it possible that the former could keep his place in the international rivalry ? [Hear, hear.]"

This visible, tangible, and unanswerable argument had its effect. The advertisement duty has been abolished, and now only the stamp duty intervenes between the English workingman and his penny paper—the future Tribune of the English people, which is to expound their duties and defend their rights.

In the summer of 1854, Mr. Greeley was frequently spoken of in the papers in connection with the office of Governor of the State of New York. A very little of the usual maneuvering on his part would have secured his nominatir n, and if he had been nominated, he would have been elected by a majority that would have surprised politicians by trade.

In 1854, his life was written by a young and unknown scribbler for the press, who had observed his career with much interest, and who knew enough of the story of his life to be aware, that, if simply told, that story would be read with pleasure and do good. This volume is the result of his labors.

Here, this chapter had ended, and it was about to be consigned to the hands of the printer. But an event transpires which, it is urgently suggested, ought to have notice. It is nothing more than a new and peculiarly characteristic editorial repartee, or rather, a public reply by Mr. Greeley to a private letter. And though the force of the reply was greatly, and quite unnecessarily, diminished by the publication of the correspondent's name and address, contrary to his request, yet the correspondence seems too interesting to be omitted:

THE LETTER.

"———— COUNTY, Miss., Sept. 1854.

"HON. HORACE GREELEY, New York City:

"My object in addressing you these lines is this: I own a negro girl named Catharine, a bright mulatto, aged between twenty-eight and thirty years, who is intelligent and beautiful. The girl wishes to obtain her freedom, and reside in either Ohio or New York State; and, to gratify her desire, I am willing to take the sum of $1,000, which the friends of liberty will no doubt make up. Catharine, as she tells me, was born near Savannah, Ga., and was a daughter of a Judge Hopkins, and, at the age of seven years, accompanied her young mistress (who was a legitimate daughter of the Judge's) on a visit to New Orleans, where she (the legitimate) died. Catharine was then seized and sold by the Sheriff of New Orleans, under attachment, to pay the debts contracted in the city by her young mistress, and was purchased by a Dutchman named Shinoski. Shinoski, being pleased with the young girl's looks, placed her in a quadroon school, and gave her a good education. The girl can read and write as well or better than myself, and speaks the Dutch and French languages almost to perfection. When the girl attained the age of eighteen, Shinoski died, and she was again sold, and fell into a trader's hands, by the name of John Valentine, a native of your State. Valentine brought her up to ————, where I purchased her in 1844, for the sum of $1,150. Catharine is considered the best seamstress and cook in this county, and I could to-morrow sell her for $1,600, but I prefer letting her go for $1,000, so that she may obtain her freedom. She has had opportunities to get to a free State, and obtain her freedom; but she says that she will never run away to do it. Her father, she says, promised to free her, and so did Shinoski. If I was able, I would free her without any compensation, but losing $15,000 on the last presidential election has taken very near my all.

"Mr. Geo. D. Prentice, editor of the Louisville (Ky.) Journal, knows me very well by character, to whom (if you wish to make any inquiries regarding this matter) you are at liberty to refer.

"If you should make any publication in your paper in relation to this matter, you will please not mention my name in connection with it, nor the place whence this letter was written. Catharine is honest; and, for the ten years that I have owned her, I never struck her a lick, about her work or anything else.

"If it was not that I intend to emigrate to California, money could not buy her.

"I have given you a complete and accurate statement concerning this girl, and am willing that she shall be examined here, or in Louisville, Ky., before the bargain is closed.

"Very respectfully.

[Name in full.]

REPLY.

"Mr. ————, I have carried your letter of the 28th ult. in my hat for several days, awaiting an opportunity to answer it. I now seize the first opportune moment, and, as yours is one of a class with which I am frequently favored, I will send you my reply through the Tribune, wishing it regarded as a general answer to all such applications.

"Let me begin by frankly stating that I am not engaged in the slave trade, and do not now contemplate embarking in that business; but no man can say confidently what he may or may not become; and, if I ever *should* engage in the traffic you suggest, it will be but fair to remember you as among my prompters to undertake it. Yet even then I must decline any such examination as you proffer of the property you wish to dispose of. Your biography is so full and precise, so frank and straight-forward, that I prefer to rest satisfied with your assurance in the premises.

"You will see that I have disregarded your request that your name and residence should be suppressed by me. That request seems to me inspired by a modesty and self-sacrifice unsuited to the Age of Brass we live in. Are you not seeking to do a humane and generous act? Are you not proposing to tax yourself $600 in order to raise an intelligent, capable, deserving woman from slavery to freedom? Are you not proposing to do this in a manner perfectly lawful and unobjectionable, involving no surrender or compromise of 'Southern Rights'? My dear sir! such virtue must not be allowed to 'blush unseen.' Our age needs the inspiration of heroic examples, and those who would 'do good by stealth, and blush to find it Fame,' must—by gentle violence, if need be—stand revealed to an amazed, admiring world. True, it might (and might not) have been still more astounding but for your unlucky gambling on the late presidential election, wherein it is hard to tell whether you who lost your money or those who won their president were most unfortunate. I affectionately advise you both never to do so again.

"And now as to this daughter of the late Judge Hopkins of Savannah, Georgia, whom you propose to sell me:

"I cannot now remember that I have ever heard Slavery justified on any ground which did not assert or imply that *it is the best condition for the negro.* The blacks, we are daily told, cannot take care of themselves, but sink into idleness, debauchery, squalid poverty and utter brutality, the moment the master's sustaining rule and care are withdrawn. If this is true, how dare you turn this poor dependent, for whose well-being you are responsible, over to me, who neither would nor could exert a master's control over her? If this slave ought not to be set at liberty, why do you ask me to bribe you with $1,000 to do her that wrong? If she ought to be, why should I pay you $1,000 for doing your duty in the premises? *You* hold a peculiar and responsible relation to her, through your own voluntary act, but *I* am only related to her through Adam, the same as to every Esquimaux, Patagonian, or New-Zealander. Whatever may be *your* duty in the premises, why should I be called on to help you discharge it?

"Full as your account of this girl is, you say nothing of her children, though such she undoubtedly has, whether they be also those of her several masters, as she was, or their fathers were her fellow-slaves. If she is liberated and comes North, what is to become of them? How is she to be reconciled to leaving them in slavery? How can we be assured that the masters who own or to whom you will sell them before leaving for California, will prove as humane and liberal as you are?

"You inform me that 'the friends of Liberty' in New York or hereabout, 'will no doubt make up' the $1,000 you demand, in order to give this daughter of a Georgia Judge her freedom. I think and trust you misapprehend them. For though they have, to my certain knowledge, under the impulse of special appeals to their sympathies, and in view of peculiar dangers or hardships, paid a great deal more money than they could comfortably spare (few of them being rich) to buy individual slaves out of bondage, yet their judgment has never approved such payment of tribute to man-thieves, and every day's *earnest* consideration causes it to be regarded with less and less favor. For it is not the snatching of here and there a person from Slavery, at the possible rate of one for every thousand increase of our slave population, that they desire, but the overthrow and extermination of *the slave-holding system;* and this end, they realize, is rather hindered than helped by their buying here and there a slave into freedom. If by so buying ten thousand a year, at a cost of Ten Millions of Dollars, they should confirm you and other slave-holders in the misconception that Slavery is regarded without abhorrence by intelligent Christian freemen at the North, they would be doing great harm to their cause and injury to their fellow-Christians in bondage. You may have heard, perhaps, of the sentiment proclaimed by Decatur to the slave-holders of the Barbary Coast—' Millions for defense—not a cent for tribute !' —and perhaps also of its counterpart in the Scotch ballad—

> Instead of broad pieces, we 'll pay them broadswords ;'—

but ' the friends of Liberty ' in this quarter will fight her battle neither with lead nor steel—much less with gold. Their trust is in the might of Opinion— in the resistless power of Truth where Discussion is untrammeled and Commercial Intercourse constant—in the growing Humanity of our age—in the deepening sense of Common Brotherhood—in the swelling hiss of Christendom and the just benignity of God. In the earnest faith that these must soon eradicate a wrong so gigantic and so palpable as Christian Slavery, they serenely await the auspicious hour which must surely come.

"Requesting you, Mr. ———, *not* to suppress my name in case you see fit to reply to this, and to be assured that I write no letter that I am ashamed of, I remain,   Yours, so-so,

                                            "HORACE GREELEY."

And here, closing the last volume of the Tribune, the reader is invited to a survey of the place whence it was issued, to glance at the routine of the daily press, to witness the scene in which our hero has labored so long. The Tribune building remains to be exhibited.

CHAPTER XXVIII.

DAY AND NIGHT IN THE TRIBUNE OFFICE.

WE are in the streets, walking from the regions where money is spent towards those narrow and crooked places wherein it is earned. The day is about to dawn, but the street lights are still burning, and the greater part of the million people who live within sight of the City Hall's illuminated dial, are lying horizontal and unconscious, in the morning's last slumber. The streets are neither silent nor deserted—the streets of New York never are. The earliest milkmen have begun their morning crow, squeak, whoop, and yell. The first omnibus has not yet come down town, but the butcher's carts, heaped with horrid flesh, with men sitting upon it reeking with a night's carnage, are rattling along Broadway at the furious pace for which the butcher's carts of all nations are noted. The earliest workmen are abroad, dinner-kettle in hand; carriers with their bundles of newspapers slung across their backs by a strap, are emerging from Nassau street, and making their way across the Park—towards all the ferries—up Broadway—up Chatham street— to wherever their district of distribution begins. The hotels have just opened their doors and lighted up their offices; and drowsy waiters are perambulating the interminable passages, knocking up passengers for the early trains, and waking up everybody else. In unnumbered kitchens the breakfast fire is kindling, but not yet, in any except the market restaurants, is a cup of coffee attainable. The very groggeries—strange to see—are closed. Apparently, the

last drunkard has toppled home, and the last debauchee has skulked
like a thieving hound to his own bed; for the wickedness of the
night has been done, and the work of the day is beginning.
There is something in the aspect of the city at this hour—the stars
glittering over-head—the long lines of gas-lights that stretch away
in every direction—the few wayfarers stealing in and out among
them in silence, like spirits—the myriad sign-boards so staring now,
and useless—the houses all magnified in the imperfect light—so
many evidences of intense life around, and yet so little of life visibly present—which, to one who sees it for the first time (and few
of us have ever seen it), is strangely impressive.

The Tribune building is before us. It looks as we never saw it
look before. The office is closed, and a gas-light dimly burning
shows that no one is in it. The dismal inky aperture in Spruce
street by which the upper regions of the Tribune den are usually
reached is shut, and the door is locked. That glare of light which
on all previous nocturnal walks we have seen illuminating the
windows of the third and fourth stories, revealing the bobbing compositor in his paper cap, and the bustling night-editor making up
his news, shines not at this hour; and those windows are undistin-
guished from the lustreless ones of the houses adjacent. Coiled up
on the steps, stretched out on the pavement, are half a dozen
sleeping newsboys. Two or three others are awake and up, of
whom one is devising and putting into practice various modes of
suddenly waking the sleepers. He rolls one off the step to the
pavement, the shock of which is very effectual. He deals another
who lies temptingly exposed, a 'loud-resounding' slap, which
brings the slumberer to his feet, and to his fists, in an instant. Into
the ear of a third he yells the magic word *Fire*, a word which
the New York newsboy never hears with indifference; the sleeper
starts up, but perceiving the trick, growls a curse or two, and addresses himself again to sleep. In a few minutes all the boys are
awake, and taking their morning exercise of scuffling. The basement of the building, we observe, is all a-glow with light, though
the clanking of the press is silent. The carrier's entrance is open,
and we descend into the fiery bowels of the street.

We are in the Tribune's press-room. It is a large, low, cellar-like
apartment, unceiled, white-washed, inky, and unclean, with a vast

folding table in the middle, tall heaps of dampened paper all about, a quietly-running steam engine of nine-horse power on one side, twenty-five inky men and boys variously employed, and the whole brilliantly lighted up by jets of gas, numerous and flaring. On one side is a kind of desk or pulpit, with a table before it, and the whole separated from the rest of the apartment by a rail. In the pulpit, the night-clerk stands, counts and serves out the papers, with a nonchalant and graceful rapidity, that must be seen to be appreciated. The regular carriers were all served an hour ago; they have folded their papers and gone their several ways; and early risers, two miles off, have already read the news of the day. The later newsboys, now, keep dropping in, singly, or in squads of three or four, each with his money ready in his hand. Usually, no words pass between them and the clerk; he either knows how many papers they have come for, or they show him by exhibiting their money; and in three seconds after his eye lights upon a newly-arrived dirty face, he has counted the requisite number of papers, counted the money for them, and thrown the papers in a heap into the boy's arms, who slings them over his shoulder and hurries off for his supply of *Times* and *Heralds*. Occasionally a woman comes in for a few papers, or a little girl, or a boy so small that he cannot see over the low rail in front of the clerk, and is obliged to announce his presence and his desires by holding above it his little cash capital in his little black paw. In another part of the press-room, a dozen or fifteen boys are folding papers for the early mails, and folding them at the average rate of thirty a minute. A boy *has* folded sixty papers a minute in that press-room. Each paper has to be folded six times, and then laid evenly on the pile; and the velocity of movement required for the performance of such a minute's work, the reader can have no idea of till he sees it done. As a feat, nothing known to the sporting world approaches it. The huge presses, that shed six printed leaves at a stroke, are in deep vaults adjoining the press-room. They are motionless now, but the gas that has lighted them during their morning's work still spurts out in flame all over them, and men with blue shirts and black faces are hoisting out the 'forms' that have stamped their story on thirty thousand sheets. The vaults are oily, inky, and warm. Let us ascend.

17*

The day has dawned. As we approach the stairs that lead to the upper stories, we get a peep into a small, paved yard, where a group of pressmen, blue-overalled, ink-smeared, and pale, are washing themselves and the ink-rollers; and looking, in the dim light of the morning, like writhing devils. The stairs of the Tribune building are supposed to be the dirtiest in the world. By their assistance, however, we wind our upward way, past the editorial rooms in the third story, which are locked, to the composing-room in the fourth, which are open, and in which the labor of transposing the news of the morning to the form of the weekly paper is in progress. Only two men are present, the foreman, Mr. Rooker, and one of his assistants. Neither of them wish to be spoken to, as their minds are occupied with a task that requires care; but we are at liberty to look around.

The composing-room of the Tribune is, I believe, the most convenient, complete, and agreeable one in the country. It is very spacious, nearly square, lighted by windows on two sides, and by sky-lights from above. It presents an ample expanse of type-fonts, gas-jets with large brown-paper shades above them, long tables covered with columns of bright, copper-faced type, either 'dead' or waiting its turn for publication; and whatever else appertains to the printing of a newspaper. Stuffed into corners and interstices are aprons and slippers in curious variety. Pasted on the walls, lamp-shades, and doors, we observe a number of printed notices, from the perusal of which, aided by an occasional word from the obliging foreman, we are enabled to penetrate the mystery, and comprehend the routine, of the place.

Here, for example, near the middle of the apartment, are a row of hooks, labeled respectively, 'Leaded Brevier;' 'Solid Brevier;' 'Minion;' 'Proofs to revise;' 'Compositors' Proofs—let no profane hand touch them except Smith's;' 'Bogus minion—when there is no other copy to be given out, then take from this hook.' Upon these hooks, the foreman hangs the 'copy' as he receives it from below, and the men take it in turn, requiring no further direction as to the kind of type into which it is to be set. The 'bogus-minion' hook contains matter not intended to be used; it is designed merely to keep the men constantly employed, so as to obviate the necessity of their making petty charges for lost time, and thus complicating their accounts. Below the 'bogus-book,' there appears this 'Particular Notice:' 'This copy must be set, and the Takes emptied, with the same care as the rest.' From which we may in-fer, that a man is inclined to slight work that he knows to be use-less, even though it be paid for at the usual price per thousand.

Another printed paper lets us into another secret. It is a list of the compositors employed in the office, divided into four "Phalanxes" of about ten men each, a highly advantageous arrangement, devised by Mr. Rooker. At night, when the copy begins to "slack up," *i. e.* when the work of the night approaches completion, one phalanx is dismissed; then another; then another; then the last; and the phalanx which leaves first at night comes first in the morning, and so on. The men who left work at eleven o'clock at night must be again in the office at nine, to distribute type and set up news for the evening edition of the paper. The second phalanx begins work at two, the third at five; and at seven the whole company must be at their posts; for, at seven, the business of the night begins in earnest. Printers *will* have their joke—as appears from this list. It is set in double columns, and as the number of men happened to be an un-even one, one name was obliged to occupy a line by itself, and it appears thus—"Baker, (the teat-pig.)"

The following notice deserves attention from the *word* with which it begins : " Gentlemen desiring to wash and soak their distributing matter will please use hereafter the metal galleys I had cast for the purpose, as it is ruinous to galleys having wooden sides to keep wet type in them locked up. Thos. N. Rooker." It took the world an unknown number of thousand years to arrive at that word 'GEN-TLEMEN.' Indeed, the *world* has not arrived at it; but there it is, in the composing-room of the New York Tribune, legible to all visitors.

Passing by other notices, such as "Attend to the gas-meter on Wednesdays and Saturdays, and to the clock on Monday morning," we may spend a minute or two in looking over a long printed cata-logue, posted on the door, entitled, " Tribune Directory. Corrected May 10, 1854. A list of Editors, Reporters, Publishers, Clerks, Compositors, Proof-Readers, Pressmen, &c., employed on the New York Tribune."

From this Directory one may learn that the Editor of the Tribune is Horace Greeley, the Managing-Editor Charles A. Dana, the Associate-Editors, James S. Pike, William H. Fry, George Ripley, George M. Snow, Bayard Taylor, F. J. Ottarson, William Newman, B. Brookway, Solon Robinson, and Donald C. Henderson.   We perceive also that Mr. Ottarson is the City Editor, and that his assistants are in number fourteen.   One of these keeps an eye on the Police, chronicles arrests, walks the hospitals in search of dreadful accidents, and keeps the public advised of the state of its health.   Three report lectures and speeches.   Another gathers items of intelligence in Jersey City, Newark, and parts adjacent.   Others do the same in Brooklyn and Williamsburgh.   One gentleman devotes himself to the reporting of fires, and the movements of the military.   Two examine and translate from the New York papers which are published in the German, French, Italian and Spanish languages.   Then, there is a Law Reporter, a Police Court Reporter, and a Collector of Marine Intelligence.   Proceeding down the formidable catalogue, we discover that the 'Marine Bureau' (in common with the Associated Press) is under the charge of Commodore John T. Hall, who is assisted by twelve agents and reporters.   Besides these, the Tribune has a special 'Ship News Editor.'   The 'Telegraphic Bureau' (also in common with the Associated Press) employs one general agent and two subordinates, (one at Liverpool and one at Halifax,) and fifty reporters in various parts of the country.   The number of regular and paid correspondents is thirty-eight—eighteen foreign, twenty home.   The remaining force of the Tribune, as we are informed by the Directory, is, Thos. M'Elrath, chief of the department of publication, assisted by eight clerks; Thos. N. Rooker, foreman of the composing-room, with eight assistant-foremen (three by day, five by night), thirty-eight regular compositors, and twenty-five substitutes; George Hall, foreman of the press-room, with three assistants, sixteen feeders, twenty-five folders, three wrapper-writers, and three boys.   Besides these, there are four proof-readers, and a number of miscellaneous individuals.   It thus appears that the whole number of persons employed upon the paper is about two hundred and twenty, of whom about one hundred and thirty devote to it their whole time.   The Directory further informs us that the proprietors of the establishment are sixteen in number—namely, seven editors, the publisher, four clerks, the foreman of the composing-room, the foreman of the press-room, one compositor and one press-man.

Except for a few hours on Saturday afternoon and Sunday morning, the work of a daily paper never entirely ceases; but, at this hour of the day, between six and seven o'clock, it does nearly cease. The editors are still, it is to be hoped, asleep. The compositors have been in bed for two hours or more. The pressmen of the night are going home, and those of the day have not arrived. The carriers have gone their rounds. The youngest clerks have not yet appeared in the office. All but the slowest of the newsboys have got their supply of papers, and are making the streets and ferries vocal, or vociferous, with their well-known names. There is a general lull; and while that lull continues, we shall lose nothing by going to breakfast.

Part of which is the New York Tribune; and we may linger over it a little longer than usual this morning.

It does not look like it, but it is a fact, as any one moderately endowed with arithmetic can easily ascertain, that one number of the Tribune, if it were printed in the form of a book, with liberal type and spacing, would make a duodecimo volume of four hundred pages—a volume, in fact, not much less in magnitude than the one which the reader has, at this moment, the singular happiness of perusing. Each number is the result of, at least, two hundred days' work, or the work of two hundred men for one day; and it is sold (to carriers and newsboys) for one cent and a half. Lucifer matches, at forty-four cents for a hundred and forty-four boxes, are supposed, and justly, to be a miracle of cheapness. Pins are cheap, considering; and so are steel pens. But the cheapest thing yet realized under the sun is the New York Tribune.

The number for this morning contains six hundred and forty-one separate articles—from two-line advertisements to two-column essays—of which five hundred and ten are advertisements, the remainder, one hundred and thirty-one, belonging to the various departments of reading matter. The reading matter, however, occupies about one half of the whole space—nearly four of the eight broad pages, nearly twenty-four of the forty-eight columns. The articles and paragraphs which must have been written for this number, yesterday, or very recently, in the office or at the editors' residences, fill thirteen columns, equal to a hundred pages of foolscap, or eighty such pages as this. There are five columns of telegraphic intelligence, which is, perhaps, two columns above the average. There are twelve letters from 'our own' and voluntary correspondents, of which five are from foreign countries. There have been as many as thirty letters in one number of the Tribune; there are seldom less than ten.

What has the Tribune of this morning to say to us? Let us see.

It is often asked, who reads advertisements? and the question is often inconsiderately answered, 'Nobody.' But, idle reader, if you were in search of a boarding-house this morning, these two columns of advertisements, headed 'Board and Rooms,' would be read by you with the liveliest interest; and so, in other circumstances, would those which reveal a hundred and fifty ' Wants,' twenty-two places of amusement, twenty-seven new publications, forty-two schools, and thirteen establishments where the best pianos in existence are made. If you had come into the possession of a fortune yesterday, this column of bank-dividend announcements would not be passed by with indifference. And if *you* were the middle-aged gentleman who advertises his desire to open a correspondence with a young lady (all communications post-paid and the strictest secresy observed), you might peruse with anxiety these seven advertisements of hair-dye, each of which is either infallible, unapproachable, or the acknowledged best. And the eye of the 'young lady' who addresses you a post-paid communication in reply, informing you where an interview may be had, would perhaps rest for a moment upon the description of the new Baby-Walker, with some complacency. If the negotiation were successful, it were difficult to say what column of advertisements would *not*, in its turn, become of the highest interest to one or the other, or both of you. In truth, every one reads the advertisements which concern them.

The wonders of the telegraph are not novel, and, therefore, they seem wonderful no longer. We glance up and down the columns of telegraphic intelligence, and read without the slightest emotion, dispatches from Michigan, Halifax, Washington, Baltimore, Cincinnati, Boston, Cleveland, St. Louis, New Orleans, and a dozen places nearer the city, some of which give us news of events that had not occurred when we went to bed last night. The telegraphic news of this morning has run along four thousand seven hundred and fifty miles of wire, and its transmission, at the published rates, must have cost between two and three hundred dollars. On one occasion, recently, the steamer arrived at Halifax at half-past eleven in the evening, and the substance of her news was contained in the New York papers the next morning, and probably in the papers of New Orleans. A debate which concludes in Washington at midnight, is read in Fiftieth street, New York, six hours after. But these are stale marvels, and they are received by us entirely as a matter of course.

The City department of the paper, conducted with uncommon efficiency by Mr. Ottarson, gives us this morning, in sufficient detail, the proceedings of a 'Demonstration' at Tammany Hall—of a meeting of the Bible Union—a session of the committee investigating the affairs of Columbia college—a meeting to devise measures for the improvement of the colored population—a temperance 'Demonstration'—a session of the Board of Aldermen—a meeting of the commissioners of emigration—and one of the commissioners of excise. A trial for murder is reported; the particulars of seven fires are stated; the performance of the opera is noticed; the progress of the 'State Fair' is chronicled, and there are thirteen 'city items.' And what is most surprising is, that seven-tenths of the city matter must have been prepared in the evening, for most of the events narrated did not occur till after dark.

The Law Intelligence includes brief notices of the transactions of five courts. The Commercial Intelligence gives minute information respecting the demand for, the supply of, the price, and the recent sales, of twenty-one leading articles of trade. The Marine Journal takes note of the sailing and arrival of two hundred and seven vessels, with the name of the captain, owners and consignees. This is, in truth, the most astonishing department of a daily paper. Arranged under the heads of "Cleared," "Arrived," "Disasters," "To mariners," "Spoken," "Whalers," "Foreign Ports," "Domestic Ports," "Passengers sailed," "Passengers arrived," it presents daily a mass and a variety of facts, which do not astound us, only because we see the wonder daily repeated. Nor is the shipping intelligence a mere catalogue of names, places and figures. Witness these sentences cut almost at random from the dense columns of small type in which the affairs of the sea are printed:

"Bark Gen. Jones, (of Boston,) Hodgden, London 47 days, chalk to E. S. Belknap & Sons. Aug. 14, lat. 50° 11', lon. 9° 20', spoke ship Merensa, of Boston, 19 days from Eastport for London. Aug. 19, signalized a ship showing Nos. 55, 31, steering E. Aug. 20, signalized ship Isaac Allerton, of New York. Sept. 1, spoke Br. Emerald, and supplied her with some provisions. Sept. 13, lat. 43° 36', lon. 49° 54', passed a number of empty barrels and broken pieces of oars. Sept. 13, lat 43°, long 50° 40', while lying to in a gale, passed a vessel's spars and broken pieces of bulwarks, painted black and white; supposed the spars to be a ship's topmasts. Sept. 19, lat. 41° 14', lon. 56°, signalized a bark showing a red signal with a white spot in center."

As no one not interested in marine affairs ever bestows a glance upon this part of his daily paper, these condensed tragedies of the sea will be novel to the general reader. To compile the ship-news of this single morning, the log-books of twenty-seven vessels must have been examined, and information obtained by letter, telegraph, or exchange papers, from ninety-three sea-port towns, of which thirty-one are in foreign countries. Copied here, it would fill thirty-five pages, and every line of it was procured yesterday.

The money article of the Tribune, to those who have any money, is highly interesting. It chronicles, to-day, the sales of stocks, the price of exchange and freight, the arrivals and departures of gold, the condition of the sub-treasury, the state of the coal-trade and other mining interests, and ends with gossip and argument about the Schuyler frauds. There is a vast amount of labor condensed in the two columns which the money article usually occupies.

The Tribune, from the beginning of its career, has kept a vigilant eye upon passing literature. Its judgments have great weight with the reading public. They are always pronounced with, at least, an air of deliberation. They are always able, generally just, occasionally cruel, more frequently too kind. In this department, taking into account the quantity of information given—both of home and foreign literature, of books published and of books to be published—and the talent and knowledge displayed in its notices and reviews, the superiority of the Tribune to any existing daily paper is simply undeniable. Articles occasionally appear in the London journals, written *after* every other paper has expressed its judgment, written at ample leisure and by men pre-eminent in the one branch of letters to which the reviewed book belongs, which are superior to the reviews of the Tribune. It is the literary *department* of the paper.

for which superiority is here asserted. To-day, it happens, that the paper contains nothing literary. In a daily paper, news has the precedence of everything, and a review of an epic greater than Paradise Lost might be crowded out by the report of an election brawl in the Sixth Ward. Thus, a poor author is often kept in trembling suspense for days, or even weeks, waiting for the review which he erroneously thinks will make or mar him.

Like People, like Priest, says the old maxim; which we may amend by saying, Like Editor, like Correspondent. From these 'Letters from the People,' we infer, that when a man has something to say to the public, of a reformatory or humanitary nature, he is prone to indite an epistle 'to the Editor of the New York Tribune,' who, on his part, in tenderness to the public, is exceedingly prone to consign it to the basket of oblivion. A good many of these letters, however, escape into print—to-day, four, on some days a dozen. The London letters of the Tribune are written in London, the Paris letters in Paris, the Timbuctoo letters in Timbuctoo. This is strange, but true.

In its editorial department, the Tribune has two advantages over most of its contemporaries. In the first place, it has an object of attack, the slave power; and secondly, by a long course of warfare, it has won the conceded privilege of being sincere. Any one who has had to do with the press, is aware, that articles in newspapers are of two kinds, namely, those which are written *for a purpose* not avowed, and those which are written spontaneously, from the impulse and convictions of the writer's own mind. And any one who has written articles of both descriptions is aware, further, that a man who is writing with perfect sincerity, writing with a pure desire to move, interest, or convince, writes *better*, than when the necessities of his vocation compel him to *grind the axe* for a party, or an individual. There is more or less of axe-grinding done in every newspaper office in the world; and a perfectly independent newspaper never existed. Take, for example, the London Times, which is claimed to be the most incorruptible of journals. The writers for the Times are trammeled, first, by the immense *position* of the paper, which gives to its leading articles a possible influence upon the affairs of the world. The aim of the writer is to express, not himself, but ENGLAND; as the Times is, in other countries, the

recognized voice of the British Empire; and it is this which renders much of the writing in the Times as safe, as vague, and as
pointless, as a diplomatist's dispatch. The Times is further train
meled by the business necessity of keeping on terms with those
who have it in their power to give and withhold important intelligence. And, still further, by the fact, that *general England*, whom
it addresses, is not up to the liberality of the age—in which the
leading minds alone fully participate. Thus, it happens, that the
articles in a paper like The Leader, which reaches only the liberal
class, are often more pointed, more vigorous, more interesting, than
those of the Times, though the resources of the Leader are extremely
limited, and the Times can have its pick of the wit, talent, and learning of the empire. When a man writes with perfect freedom, then,
and only then, he writes his *best*. Without claiming for the Tribune a perfect innocence of axe-grinding, it may with truth be said,
that the power of its leading editorial articles is vastly increased by
the fact, that those who write them, do so with as near an approach
to perfect freedom, *i. e.* sincerity, as the nature of newspaper-writ-
ing, at present, admits of. What it gains, too, in spirit and interest
by having the preposterous inaptitude of the Southern press to ridicule, and the horrors of Southern brutality to denounce, is sufficiently known.

But it is time we returned to the office. It is ten o'clock in the
morning. The clerks in the office are at their posts, receiving advertisements, recording them, entering the names of new subscribers received by the morning's mail, of which on some mornings of
the year there are hundreds. It is a busy scene.

Up the dismal stairs to a dingy door in the third story, upon
which we read, "Editorial Rooms of the New York Tribune. H.
Greeley." We ought not to be allowed to enter, but we are, and
we do; no one hinders us, or even notices our entrance. First, a
narrow passage, with two small rooms on the left, whence, later in
the day, the rapid hum of proof-reading issues unceasingly, one man
reading the 'copy' aloud, another having his eyes fixed upon the slip
of proof. One may insert his visage into the square aperture in the
doors of these minute apartments, and gaze upon the performance
with persistent impertinence; but the proof-reading goes on, like a
machine. At this hour, however, these rooms contain no one. A

few steps, and the principal Editorial Room is before us. It is a long, narrow apartment, with desks for the principal editors along the sides, with shelves well-loaded with books and manuscripts, a great heap of exchange papers in the midst, and a file of the Tribune on a broad desk, slanting from the wall. Everything is in real order, but apparent confusion, and the whole is ' blended in a common element of dust.' Nothing particular appears to be going on. Two or three gentlemen are looking over the papers ; but the desks are all vacant, and each has upon its lid a pile of letters and papers awaiting the arrival of him to whose department they belong. One desk presents an array of new publications that might well appal the most industrious critic—twenty-four new books, seven magazines, nine pamphlets, and two new papers, all expecting a ' first-rate notice.' At the right, we observe another and smaller room, with a green carpet, two desks, a sofa, and a large book-case, filled with books of reference. This is the sanctum sanctorum. The desk near the window, that looks out upon the green Park, the white City Hall in the midst thereof, and the lines of moving life that bound the same, is the desk of the Editor-in-Chief. It presents confusion merely. The shelves are heaped with manuscripts, books, and pamphlets ; its lid is covered with clippings from newspapers, each containing something supposed by the assiduous exchange-reader to be of special interest to the Editor ; and over all, on the highest shelf, near the ceiling, stands a large bronze bust of Henry Clay, wearing a crown of dust. The other desk, near the door, belongs to the second in command. It is in perfect order. A heap of foreign letters, covered with stamps and post-marks, awaits his coming. The row of huge, musty volumes along the floor against one of the walls of the room, is a complete file of the Tribune, with some odd volumes of the New Yorker and Log Cabin.

An hour later. One by one the editors arrive. Solon Robinson, looking, with his flowing white beard and healthy countenance, like a good-humored Prophet Isaiah, or a High Priest in undress, has dropped into his corner, and is compiling, from letters and newspapers, a column of paragraphs touching the effect of the drouth upon the potato crop. Bayard Taylor is reading a paper in the American attitude. His countenance has quite lost the Nubian bronze with which it darkened on the banks of the White Nile, as well as the Japanning which his last excursion gave it. Pale, delicate-featured, with a curling beard and subdued moustache, slight in figure, and dressed with care, he has as little the aspect of an adventurous traveler, and as much the air of a nice young gentleman, as can be imagined. He may read in peace, for he is not now one of the 'hack-horses' of the daily press. The tall, pale, intense-looking gentleman who is slowly pacing the carpet of the inner sanctum is Mr. William H. Fry, the composer of Leonora. At this moment he is thinking out thunder for to-morrow's Tribune. William Henry Fry is one of the noblest fellows alive—a hater of meanness and wrong, a lover of man and right, with a power of expression equal to the intensity of his hate and the enthusiasm of his love. There is more merit in his little finger than in a whole mass-meeting of Douglass-senators; and from any but a grog-ruled city he would have been sent to Congress long ago; but perhaps, as Othello remarks, 'it is better as it is.' Mr. Ripley, who came in a few minutes ago, and sat down before that marshaled array of books and magazines, might be described in the language of Mr. Weller the elder, as 'a stout gentleman of eight and forty.' He is in for a long day's work apparently, and has taken off his coat. Luckily for authors, Mr. Ripley is a gentleman of sound digestion and indomitable good humor, who enjoys life and helps others enjoy it, and believes that anger and hatred are seldom proper, and never 'pay.' He examines each book, we observe, with care. Without ever being in a hurry, he gets through an amazing quantity of work; and all he does shows the touch and finish of the practical hand. Mr. Dana enters with a quick, decided step, goes straight to his desk in the green-carpeted sanctum sanctorum, and is soon lost in the perusal of 'Karl Marx,' or 'An American Woman in Paris.' In figure, face, and flowing beard, he looks enough like Louis Kossuth to be his cousin, if not his brother. Mr. Dana, as befits his place, is a gentleman of peremptory habits. It is his office to *decide ;* and, as he is called upon to perform the act of decision a hundred times a day, he has acquired the power both of deciding with despatch and of announcing his decision with civil brevity. If you desire a plain answer to a plain question, Charles A. Dana is the gentleman who can accommodate you. He is an able and, in description, a brilliant writer ; a good speaker ; fond and proud of his profession ; indefatigable in the discharge of its duties ; when out of harness, agreeable as a companion ; in harness, a man not to be interrupted. Mr. Ottarson, the city editor, has not yet made h's appearance ; he did not leave the office last night till three hours after midnight. Before he left, however, he prepared a list of things to be reported and described to-day, writing opposite each expected occurrence the name of the man whom he wished to attend to it. The reporters come to the office in the morning, and from this list ascertain what special duty is expected of them. Mr. Ottarson rose from the ranks. He has been everything in a newspaper office, from devil to editor. He is one of the busiest of men, and fills the most difficult post in the establishment with great ability. That elegant and rather *distingué* gentleman with the small, black, Albert moustache, who is writing at the desk over there in the corner, is the commercial editor, the writer of the money article—Mr. George M. Snow. We should have taken him for anything but a commercial gentlemen. Mr. Pike, the 'J. S. P.' of former Washington correspondence, now a writer on political subjects, is not present ; nor are other members of the corps.

Between twelve and one, Mr. Greeley comes in, with his pockets full of papers, and a bundle under his arm. His first act is to dispatch his special aid-de-sanctum on various errands, such as to deliver notes, letters and messages, to procure seeds or implements for the farm, et cetera. Then, perhaps, he will comment on the morning's paper, dwelling with pertinacious emphasis upon its defects, hard to be convinced that an alleged fault was unavoidable. After two or three amusing colloquies of this nature, he makes his way to the sanctum, where, usually, several people are waiting to see him. He takes his seat at his desk and begins to examine the heap of notes, letters, newspapers and clippings, with which it is covered, while one after another of his visitors states his business. One is an exile who wants advice, or a loan, or an advertisement inserted gratis ; he does not get the loan, for Mr. Greeley long ago shut down the door upon miscellaneous borrowers and beggars. Another visitor has an invention which he wishes paragraphed into celebrity. Another is one of the lecture-committee of a country Lyceum, and wants our editor to 'come out and give

us a lecture this winter.' Another is a country clergyman who has
called to say how much he likes the semi-weekly Tribune, and to
gratify his curiosity by speaking with the editor face to face. Gradually the throng diminishes and the pile of papers is reduced. By
three or four o'clock, this preliminary botheration is disposed of,
and Mr. Greeley goes to dinner.

Meanwhile, all the departments of the establishment have been
in a state of activity. It is Thursday, the day of the Weekly Tri
bune, the inside of which began to be printed at seven in the morning. Before the day closes, the whole edition, one hundred and
sixteen thousand, forty-eight cart-loads, will have been printed,
folded, wrapped, bundled, bagged, and carried to the post-office.
The press-room on Thursdays does its utmost, and presents a scene
of bustle and movement 'easier imagined than described.' No
small amount of work, too, is done in the office of publication.
To-day, as we ascertain, two hundred and thirteen business letters
were received, containing, among other things less interesting,
eleven hundred and seventy-two dollars, and four hundred and ten
new or renewed subscriptions, each of which has been recorded
and placed upon the wrapper-writer's books. The largest sum
ever received by one mail was eighteen hundred dollars. The
weekly expenditures of the concern average about six thousand
two hundred dollars, of which sum four thousand is for paper.
During the six dull months of the year, the receipts and expenditures are about equal; in the active months the receipts exceed
the expenditures.

It is nine o'clock in the evening. Gas has resumed. The clank
of the press has ceased, and the basement is dimly lighted. The
clerks, who have been so busy all day, have gone home, and the
night-clerk, whom we saw this morning in his press-room pulpit, is
now behind the counter of the office receiving advertisements.
Night-work agrees with him, apparently, for he is robust, ruddy
and smiling. Aloft in the composing room, thirty-eight men are
setting type, silently and fast. No sound is heard but the click of
the type, or the voice, now and then, of a foreman, or the noise of
of the copy-box rattling up the wooden pipe from the editor's room
below, or a muffled grunt from the tin tube by which the different
rooms hold converse with one another, or the bell which calls for

the application of an ear to the mouth of that tube. The place is warm, close, light, and still. Whether it is *necessarily* detrimental to a compositor's health to work from eight to ten hours every night in such an atmosphere, in such a light, is still, it appears, a question. Mr. Greeley thinks it is not. The compositors think it is, and seldom feel able to work more than four nights a week, filling their places on the other nights from the list of substitutes, or in printer's language 'subs.' Compositors say, that sleep in the day time is a very different thing from sleep at night, particularly in summer, when to create an artificial night is to exclude the needful air. They say that they never get perfectly used to the reversion of nature's order; and often, after a night of drowsiness so extreme that they would give the world if they could sink down upon the floor and sleep, they go to bed at length, and find that offended Morpheus has taken his flight, and left their eye-lids glued to their brows; and they cannot close them before the inexorable hour arrives that summons them to work again. In the middle of the room the principal night-foreman is already 'making up' the outside forms of to-morrow's paper, four in number, each a section of a cylinder, with rims of polished iron, and type of copper face. It is slow work, and a moment's inattention might produce results more ridiculous than cross-readings.

The editorial rooms, too, have become intense. Seven desks are occupied with silent writers, most of them in the Tribune uniform—shirt-sleeves and moustache. The night-reader is looking over the papers last arrived, with scissors ready for any paragraph of news that catches his eye. An editor occasionally goes to the copy-box, places in it a page or two of the article he is writing, and rings the bell; the box slides up to the composing-room, and the pages are in type and corrected before the article is finished. Such articles are those which are prompted by the event of the hour; others are more deliberately written; some are weeks in preparation; and of some the keel is laid months before they are launched upon the public mind. The Editor-in-Chief is at his desk writing in a singular attitude, the desk on a level with his nose, and the writer sitting bolt upright. He writes rapidly, with scarcely a pause for thought, and not once in a page makes an erasure. The foolscap leaves fly from under his pen at the rate of one in fifteen minutes. He does most of the *thinking* before he begins to write, and produces matter about as fast as a swift copyist can copy.   Yet he leaves nothing for the compositor to guess at, and if he makes an alteration in the proof, he is careful to do it in such a way that the printer loses no time in 'overrunning;' that is, he inserts as many words as he erases.   Not unfrequently he bounds up into the composing-room, and makes a correction or adds a sentence with his own hand.   He is not patient under the infliction of an error; and he expects men to understand his wishes by intuition; and when they do *not*, but interpret his half-expressed orders in a way exactly contrary to his intention, a scene is likely to ensue.

And so they write and read in the editorial rooms of the Tribune for some hours.   Occasionally a City Reporter comes in with his budget of intelligence, or his short-hand notes, and sits down at a desk to arrange or write them out.   Telegraphic messages arrive from the agent of the Associated Press, or from 'our own correspondent.'   Mr. Dana glances over them, sends them aloft, and, if they are important, indites a paragraph calling attention to the fact.   That omnipresent creature, the down-town apple-woman, whom no labyrinth puzzles, no extent of stairs fatigues, no presence overawes, enters, and thrusts her basket in deliberate succession under each editorial nose.   Some of the corps, deep in the affairs of the nation, pause in their writing, gaze at the woman in utter abstraction, slowly come to a sense of her errand, shake their heads, and resume their work.   Others hurriedly buy an apple, and taking one prodigious bite, lay it aside and forget it.   A band of music is heard in the street; it is a target-excursion returning late from Hoboken; it passes the office and gives it three cheers; the city men go to the windows; the rest write on unconscious of the honor that has been done them; the Tribune returns the salute by a paragraph.

Midnight.   The strain is off.   Mr. Greeley finished his work about eleven, chatted a while with Mr. Dana, and went home.   Mr. Dana has received from the foreman the list of the articles in type, the articles now in hand, and the articles expected; he has designated those which *must* go in; those which it is highly desirable *should* go in, and those which will 'keep.'   He has also marked the order in which the articles are to appear; and, having performed this last duty, he returns the list to the compositor, puts on his coat and departs. Mr. Fry is on the last page of his critique of this evening's Grisi, which he executes with steam-engine rapidity, and sends up without reading. He lingers awhile, and then strolls off up town. Mr. Ottarson is still busy, as reporters continually arrive with items of news, which he hastily examines, and consigns either to the basket under his desk, or to the copy-box. The first phalanx of compositors is dismissed, and they come thundering down the dark stairs, putting on their coats as they descend. The foreman is absorbed in making up the inside forms, as he has just sent those of the outside below, and the distant clanking of the press announces that they have begun to be printed. We descend, and find the sheets coming off the press at the rate of a hundred and sixty a minute. The engine-man is commodiously seated on an inverted basket, under a gas-jet, reading the outside of the morning's paper, and the chief of the press-room is scanning a sheet to see if the impression is perfect. The gigantic press has six mouths, and six men are feeding him with white paper, slipping in the sheets with the easy knack acquired by long practice. It looks a simple matter, this 'feeding;' but if a new hand were to attempt it, the iron maw of the monster would be instantly choked, and his whole system disarranged. For he is as delicate as he is strong; the little finger of a child can start and stop him, moderate his pace, or quicken it to the snapping of his sinews.

Three o'clock in the morning. Mr. Ottarson is in trouble. The outside of the paper is printed, the inside forms are ready to be lowered away to the basement, and the press-men are impatiently waiting the signal to receive it. The pulpit of the night clerk is ready for his reception, the spacious folding-table is cleared, and two carriers have already arrived. All the compositors except the last phalanx have gone home; and they have corrected the last proof, and desire nothing so much as to be allowed to depart. But an English steamer is overdue, and a telegraphic dispatch from the agent of the Associated Press at Sandy Hook, who has been all night in his yacht cruising for the news, is anxiously expected. It does not come. The steamer (as we afterwards ascertain) has arrived, but the captain churlishly refused to throw on board the yacht the customary newspaper. Mr. Ottarson fancies he hears a gun. A moment after he is positive he hears another. He has five men of

18

his corps within call, and he sends them flying! One goes to the Astor House to see if *they* have heard of the steamer's arrival; another to the offices of the Times and Herald, on the same errand; others to Jersey City, to be ready in case the steamer reaches her wharf in time. It is ascertained, about half-past three, that the steamer is coming up the bay, and that her news cannot possibly be procured before five; and so, Mr. Ottarson, having first ascertained that the other morning papers have given up the hope of the news for their first editions, goes to press in despair, and home in ill humor. In a few minutes, the forms are lowered to the basement, wheeled to the side of the press, and hoisted to their places on the press by a crank. The feeders take their stands, the foreman causes the press to make one revolution, examines a sheet, pronounces it all right, sets the press in motion at a rattling rate, and nothing remains to be done except to print off thirty thousand copies and distribute them.

The last scene of all is a busy one indeed. The press-room is all alive with carriers, news-men and folding-boys, each of whom is in a fever of hurry. Four or five boys are carrying the papers in backloads from the press to the clerk, and to the mailing tables. The carriers receive their papers in the order of the comparative distance of their districts from the office. No money passes between them and the clerk. They come to the office every afternoon, examine the book of subscribers, note the changes ordered in their respective routes, pay for the number of papers they will require on the following morning, and receive a ticket entitling them to receive the designated number. The number of papers distributed by one carrier varies from two hundred and fifty to five hundred. Some of the carriers, however, are assisted by boys As a carrier gains a weekly profit of three cents on each subscriber, one who delivers five hundred papers has an income of fifteen dollars a week; and it is well earned. Most of the small news-men in town, country, and railroad-car, are supplied with their papers by a wholesale firm, who deliver them at a slight increase of price over the first cost. The firm alluded to purchases from four to five thousand copies of the Tribune every morning.

By five o'clock, usually, the morning edition has been printed off, the carriers supplied, the early mail dispatched, and the bundles

for adjacent towns made up. Again there is a lull in the activity
of the Tribune building, and, sleepily, we bend our steps homeward.

There is something extremely pleasing in the spectacle afforded
by a large number of strong men co-operating in cheerful activity,
by which they at once secure their own career, and render an important service to the public. Such a spectacle the Tribune building presents. At present men show to best advantage when they
are at work; we have not yet learned to sport with grace and un-
mixed benefit; and still further are we from that stage of development where work and play become one. But the Tribune building
is a very cheerful place. No one is oppressed or degraded ; and,
by the minute subdivision of labor in all departments, there is seldom any occasion for hurry or excessive exertion. The distinctions
which there exist between one man and another, are not artificial,
but natural and necessary; foreman and editor, office-boy and head
clerk, if they converse together at all, converse as friends and
equals; and the posts of honor *are* posts of honor, only because they
are posts of difficulty. In a word, the republicanism of the Continent has come to a focus at the corner of Nassau and Spruce-
streets. There it has its nearest approach to practical realization;
thence proceeds its strongest expression.

CHAPTER XXIX.

POSITION AND INFLUENCE OF HORACE GREELEY.

At the head of his Profession—Extent of his Influence—Nature of his Influence—A
Conservative-Radical — His Practical Suggestions—To Aspiring Young Men —
Have a Home of your own—To Young Mechanics—Coming to the City—A Labor
Exchange—Pay as you go—To the Lovers of Knowledge—To Young Orators—The
Colored People—To young Lawyers and Doctors—To an inquiring Slaveholder—
To Country Editors—In Peace, prepare for War—To Country Merchants—Tene-
ment Houses.

A SATIRIST observes, that the difference, in modern days, between
a distinguished and a common man is, that the name of a distin-

guished man is frequently printed in newspapers, the name of a common man never or seldom.   If the remark is correct, then Horace Greeley is by far the most distinguished person, out of office, in the United States.   The click of the types that set up his name is seldom hushed.   Probably, more than half of our three thousand newspapers published this week, contain something about him or by him, something at least which but for him they would not contain.   And who has seen, for the last few years, a political caricature in which the man with the white coat, and long locks, and hat on the back of his head, does not figure conspicuously?   In England, it is a maxim, that the politician who is not caricatured is a failure.   What an immense success, then, would the English accord to Horace Greeley!

It is rare indeed for a man to attain precisely that position in life, which, in his youthful days, he coveted and aimed at.   This happiness, this success, our hero enjoys.   He tells us, that in his boyhood, he had ' no other ambition than that of attaining usefulness and position as an editor, and to this end all the studies and efforts of his life have tended.'   As editor of the New York Tribune, Horace Greeley, at this moment, stands at the head of the editorial profession in this country.   The Tribune, with all its faults and deficiencies, is incomparably the ablest paper that we have yet realized. He who denies this convicts himself, not of error, but of ignorance or defective understanding.   Yet many will deny it; but few who are at all acquainted with the country, will dispute the following assertion :

During the last ten years or more, Horace Greeley has influenced a greater amount of thought and a greater number of characters, than any other individual who has lived in this land.

At a rough calculation, he has written and published, during his editorial career, matter enough to fill one hundred and fifty volumes like this; and his writings, whatever other merit they possess or lack, have the peculiarity of being *readable*, and they *are read.*   He has, moreover, addressed a larger number of persons than any other editor or man ; and the majority of his readers live in these northern States, where the Intelligence, the Virtue, and (therefore) the Wealth, of this confederacy chiefly reside.   He edits a paper to which many able men contribute, who write under the unavoidable condition of not expressing an opinion to which the editor-in-chief is opposed; and who owe their connection with the paper to the fact of their general concordance with him on subjects of the first importance. To these means of influence, add his continual lecturing and public speaking, add the Whig Almanac, add the scores of *Tribunes* that have been started all over the northern States, Tribunes similar in spirit and intent to their great original, and then doubt, if you can, that Horace Greeley has long been the most influential man among all the millions of his countrymen!

What is the nature of his influence? What has he tried to effect?

Any man who is not entirely a fool is better acquainted with himself than any one else is acquainted with him. In the preface to the Hints toward Reforms, Horace Greeley states what, he conceives, has been his aim as a politician. He has 'aspired to be a mediator, an interpreter, a reconciler, between Conservatism and Radicalism—to bring the two into such connection and relation, that the good in each may obey the law of chemical affinity, and abandon whatever portion of either is false, mistaken or out-worn, to sink down and perish.' And again, he has 'endeavored so to elucidate what is just and practical in the demands of our time for a social Renovation, that the humane and philanthropic can no longer misrepresent and malign them as destructive or infidel in their tendencies; but must joyfully recognize in them the fruits of past, and the seeds of future, progress in the history of our race.' Thus, with all his radical and progressive tendencies, he was for many arduous years a leading champion of our conservative party. That a position like this, between two opposing forces, is more apt to excite the hostility of both than the confidence of either, has been frequently shown in the career of Horace Greeley. Party, like the heart of a woman, demands all, or refuses any.

On this point, however,—the nature of Horace Greeley's influence in this country,—we may properly and profitably be more particular. His opinions on such subjects as religion and politics, which include all others, the reader is acquainted with. The *forte* of the man lies in making *practical suggestions* for the better conduct of the material life of the American people. He knows the American people—he is, emphatically, one of them—and he knows what they need and what they wish. Passing by, without further statement, what may be called, in a technical sense, Horace Greeley's Opinions, I will append a few of the suggestions he has made, from time to time, designed to reform or improve:

TO ASPIRING YOUNG MEN.

" 'I want to go into business,' is the aspiration of our young men: 'can't you find me a place in the city?' their constant inquiry. 'Friend,' we answer to many, 'the best business you can go into you will find on your father's farm or in his workshop. If you have no family or friends to aid you, and no prospect opened to you there, turn your face to the Great West, and there build up a home and fortune. But dream not of getting suddenly rich by speculation, rapidly by trade, or any how by a profession: all these avenues are choked by eager, struggling aspirants, and ten must be trodden down in the press where one can vault upon his neighbor's shoulders to honor or wealth. Above all, be neither afraid nor ashamed of honest industry; and if you catch yourself fancying anything more *respectable* than this, be ashamed of it to the last day of your life. Or, if you find yourself shaking more cordially the hand of your cousin the Congressman than of your uncle the blacksmith, *as such*, write yourself down an enemy to the principles of our institutions, and a traitor to the dignity of Humanity.' "

THE WORLD OWES ME A LIVING.

" How owes? Have you earned it by good service? If you have, whether on the anvil or in the pulpit, as a toiler or a teacher, you have acquired a just right to a livelihood. But if you have eaten as much as you have earned, or—worse still—have done little or no good, the world owes you nothing. You may be worth millions, and able to enjoy every imaginary luxury without care or effort; but if you have done nothing to increase the sum of human comforts, instead of the world owing you anything, as fools have babbled, you are morally bankrupt and a beggar."

TO FARMERS.

" 'I can't afford to cultivate my land so nicely; I am not able.' Then, sir, sell all you are unable to use properly, and obtain means to cultivate thoroughly what you retain. If you have a hundred acres sell fifty, keep twenty acres of arable, and thirty of rocky woodland, and bring *this* to perfection."

A HOME OF YOUR OWN.

" We wish it were possible to imbue every man, but especially every young man, with the desire of having a HOME of his own—a home to be adhered to through life. Next to the home itself, an earnest, overruling *desire* for one, would be a great blessing. A man who owns the roof that shelters him, and the soil from which he draws his subsistence—and few acres are requisite for *that*—need not envy any Nabob's great fortune."

TO YOUNG MECHANICS.

"'It is the first step that costs.' The main obstacle to saving is the lack of the habit. He who at twenty-two has saved a hundred dollars, earned by honest, useful effort during the first year of his self-control, will be very unlikely ever to be destitute thereafter. On the other hand, he who has saved nothing at the end of his first year of independence, will be pretty certain to carry a poor man's head on his shoulders while he lives.

"Our young mechanics are not thrifty, because of the evil habits they have formed during their minority. * * * By-and-by he marries, and retrenches some of his worst expenses, but too late—the increased demands of a growing family absorb every cent he can earn ; and at fifty or sixty years of age you will see him emerging, seedy and sickly, from the groggery, whither he has repaired for his bitters or his eleven o'clock, enfeebled in body, and discouraged in spirit, out of humor with everything and everybody, and cursing the banks, or the landlords, the capitalists, or the speculators, as plunderers and enslavers of the poor."

COMING TO THE CITY.

"The young man fit to come to a city does not begin by importuning some relative or friend to find or make a place for him. Having first qualified himself, so far as he may, for usefulness here, he comes understanding that he must begin at the foot of the class, and work his way up. Having found a place to stop, he makes himself acquainted with those places where work in his line may be found, sees the advertisements of ' Wants' in the leading journals at an early hour each morning, notes those which hold out some prospect for him, and accepts the first place offered him which he can take honorably and fill acceptably. He who commences in this way is quite likely to get on."

A LABOR-EXCHANGE.

" What I would suggest would be the Union and Organization of all workers for their mutual improvement and benefit, leading to the erection of a spacious edifice at some central point in our city to form a Laborers' Exchange, just as Commerce now has its Exchange, very properly. Let the new Exchange be erected and owned as a joint-stock property, paying a fair dividend to those whose money erected it ; let it contain the best spacious hall for general meetings to be found in our city, with smaller lecture-rooms for the meetings of particular sections or callings—all to be leased or rented at fair prices to all who may choose to hire them, when not needed for the primary purpose of discussing and advancing the interests of labor. Let us have here books opened, wherein any one wanting work may inscribe his name, residence, capacities and terms, while any one wishing to hire may do likewise, as well as meet personally those seeking employment."

PAY AS YOU GO.

" ' Mr. President,' said John Randolph once, *apropos* to nothing in one of his rambling Congressional harangues, ' I have found the philosopher's stone! It consists of four short English words—' Pay as you go.' "

TO THE LOVERS OF KNOWLEDGE.

" Avoid the pernicious error that you must have a profession—must be a clergyman, lawyer, doctor, or something of the sort—in order to be influential, useful, respected; or, to state the case in its best aspect, that you may lead an intellectual life. Nothing of the kind is necessary—very far from it. If your tendencies are intellectual—if you love knowledge, wisdom, virtue for themselves, you will grow in them, whether you earn your bread by a profession, a trade, or by tilling the ground. Nay, it may be doubted whether the farmer or mechanic, who devotes his leisure hours to intellectual pursuits from a pure love of them, has not some advantages therein over the professional man. *He* comes to his book at evening with his head clear and his mental appetite sharpened by the manual labors, taxing lightly the spirit or brain; while the lawyer, who has been running over dry books for precedents, the doctor, who has been racking his wits for a remedy adapted to some new modification of disease, or the divine, who, immured in his closet, has been busy preparing his next sermon, may well approach the evening volume with faculties jaded and palled."

TO YOUNG ORATORS.

" A young Whig inquires how are young men who *can* speak to be distinguished from the many who only *think* they can, and brought into the field. We answer—Step out into any neighborhood where you are acquainted, and if there is no Clay Club there now, aid in getting one up. You will there naturally be called on to speak at its opening, and be sure you have a thorough acquaintance with the *facts* material to the great issue, and the documents under your elbow to sustain them. After that, if you speak to the purpose, you will be called on quite as often as you will choose to speak. But *choose* small gatherings, until you know that you are master of the questions in issue."

A WASHINGTON MONUMENT.

" We have not much faith in monument-building; yet it strikes us that a monument to Washington, so planned as to minister at every point to purposes of great public utility, would be a good thing. Let it contain apartments corsecrated to art and knowledge—let its summit be an observatory, telegraph station, &c., and the common and forcible objection to monuments will be obviated."

THE COLORED PEOPLE.

"What the colored people need is not so much Power as Self-Elevation—not so much better manners and greater consideration from the whites as greater respect for and confidence in themselves, based on substantial grounds. So ong as they remain pretty generally boot-blacks, tavern-waiters, clothes-scourers, &c., from seeming choice, the Right to Vote will be of precious little account to them. But let them as a class step aside from those who insult and degrade them, like a small band of them in Ohio, buy a tract of land which shall be all their own, and go to work upon it, clearing, building, farming, manufacturing, &c., and they will no longer care much that those who are of baser spirit, though with whiter skins, refuse to consider them men and admit them to the common privileges of manhood. We see no plan of elevating them half so certain or so feasible as this."

TO YOUNG LAWYERS AND DOCTORS.

"*Qualify yourselves at College to enlighten the farmers and mechanics among whom you settle in the scientific principles and facts which underlie their several vocations.* The great truths of Geology, Chemistry, &c., &c., ought to be well known to you when your education is completed, and these, if you have the ability to impart and elucidate them, will make you honorably known to the inhabitants of any county wherein you may pitch your tent, and will thus insure you a subsistence from the start, and ultimately professional employment and competence. Qualify yourself to lecture accurately and fluently on the more practical and important principles of Natural Science, and you will soon find opportunities, auditors, customers, friends. Show the farmer how to fertilize his fields more cheaply and effectively than he has hitherto done—teach the builder the principles and more expedient methods of heating and ventilation—tell the mason how to correct, by understanding and obeying Nature's laws, the defect which makes a chimney smoke at the wrong end—and you need never stand idle, nor long await remunerating employment."

TO AN INQUIRING SLAVEHOLDER.

"It seems to us that a conscientious man, convinced of the *wrong* of slaveholding, should *begin* the work of redressing that wrong at once. And if we were in our correspondent's place, and the laws of that State forbade emancipation on her soil and the teaching of slaves, we should remove with them at once to some convenient locality where no such tyrannical statutes existed. Then (or on our old plantation, if the laws did not forbid) we should say to

18*

those slaves : ' You are free, and may leave if you choose ; but I advise you to stay with me till I shall have taught you how to use and enjoy your freedom. I will either myself teach you two hours daily, or I will employ some competent person to do so ; and I will share fairly with you the proceeds of my land and *your* labor. At the year's end, I will settle fairly with you, and any one who chooses may then take his portion and leave, while I with those who remain will endeavor to raise a better crop next year. I think you can all earn more, live better, and save more, by staying with me than by going off ; if you don't think so, go ; or, if you stay now, go whenever you shall come to think so. But while you stay here, I must be obeyed ; and any one who don't obey me and behave himself will have to leave.'

"Now we feel confident that a slaveholder who should adopt this course and firmly pursue it, would soon have the finest plantation and the best crops in his county—keeping all his good blacks and getting rid of the bad ones, and with all his laborers working under the stimulus of personal interest, and impelled by pride to make as good a show as possible in the settlement at the end of the year. We believe the great majority of any planter's slaves might thus be quietly educated into fitness for freedom and self-direction, as well as into a competent knowledge of letters and the elemental arts, while the planter would find himself, at ten years' end, not only wiser but actually richer than if he had continued to hold his laborers in hopeless slavery. Rely on it, friend ! it can never be dangerous nor impolitic to do right ; and what Washington, John Randolph, and many other eminent Southrons saw fit to do on their death-beds you may safely and wisely do while you live."

TO COUNTRY EDITORS.

"We fear there are some Country editors who do not clearly perceive and improve the advantages of their position. If they would only make their papers the vigilant gleaners of all local intelligence, the fosterers of local interests, local institutes for promoting knowledge, &c., &c.,—above all, if they would stop publishing so many frivolous stories and other mere transcripts from the City Magazines and Journals, filling their columns instead with accounts of the latest and most valuable discoveries and improvements in Agriculture, the Arts and all branches of practical Science, they would have an abundance of subscribers, and could not be 'destroyed' even though City Editors were so 'unprincipled' as to give their papers away and pay the postage. Only make your papers what they should be, and the people of your vicinity cannot afford to do without them.

"Do these remarks offend any ? They surely ought not, for they are dictated by a sincere desire to benefit. We learned what little we know of our business mainly in 'sticking type,' &c., for various Country papers, and ought to know something about them. We have an earnest desire that they should deserve a generous support and receive it, for we know how essential a good Country Press is."

ADVERTISING AND CASH.

"Extensive Advertising of itself is morally certain to work a revolution in trade, by driving thousands of the easy-going out of it, and concentrating business in the hands of the few who know how to obtain and keep it. Unite with this the substitution of cash for credit, and one-fifth of those now engaged in trade will amply suffice to do the whole—and will soon have it to do. The revolution is already begun."

IN PEACE, PREPARE FOR WAR.

"It is not true that *our* best security for peace is keeping up an army at a cost of $15,000,000 a year to the people. All that we need are iron, lead, men, good schools, and good roads. There is more of military capability for defense in one *railroad* than in all the fortifications from Boston to Charleston. No; we want the legislation that will make the country independent and prosperous; we want the money-changers driven from the temple; in each State, if you will, a school for the diffusion of the science of *civil* engineering and military science, to convert our people in case of need into 'disciplined soldiers.' It does indeed behoove us in peace to prepare for war; but this is all the preparation we want."

TO COUNTRY MERCHANTS.

"The merchant's virtue should be not merely negative and obstructive—it should be actively beneficent. He should use opportunities afforded by his vocation to foster agricultural and mechanical improvement, to advance the cause of education and diffuse the principles not only of virtue but of refinement and correct taste. He should be continually on the watch for whatever seems calculated to instruct, ennoble, refine, dignify and benefit the community in which he lives. He should be an early and generous patron of useful inventions and discoveries, so far as his position and means will permit. He should be a regular purchaser of new and rare books, such as the majority will not buy, yet ought to read, with a view to the widest dissemination of the truths they unfold. If located in the country, he should never visit the city to replenish his stock without endeavoring to bring back something that will afford valuable suggestions to his customers and neighbors. If these are in good part farmers, and no store in the vicinity is devoted especially to this department, he should be careful to keep a supply of the best plows and other implements of farming, as well as the choicest seeds, cuttings, &c., and those fertilizing substances best adapted to the soil of his township, or most advantageously transported thither; and those he should be very willing to sell at cost, especially to the poor or the penurious, in order to encourage their gen

eral acceptance and use.   Though he make no profit directly on the sale of
these, he is indirectly but substantially benefited by whatsoever shall increase
the annual production of his township, and thus the ability of his customers
to purchase and consume his goods.   The merchant whose customers and
neighbors are enabled to turn off three, five, seven or nine hundred dollars'
worth of produce per annum from farms which formerly yielded but one or
two hundred dollars' worth, beyond the direct consumption of their occupants,
is in the true and safe road to competence and wealth if he knows how to
manage his business.   Every wild wood or waste morass rendered arable and
fruitful, every field made to grow fifty bushels of grain per acre, where but
fifteen or twenty were formally realized, is a new tributary to the stream of his
trade, and so clearly conducive to his prosperity."

TENEMENT HOUSES.

"The wretched, tumble-down rookeries now largely inhabited by the poor
of our city are horribly wasteful in every way—wasteful of space, of property, of health, of life.   Sweep away all these kennels on a block—say about
Elizabeth or Stanton street, and build up in their stead a substantial structure, six to eight stories high, with basement and sub-cellar, the whole divided
into rooms and suites of rooms for families and single persons, with baths,
wash-houses, refectories, &c., in the basement, and public and private parlors,
library, reading-room, &c., on the second floors.   Let the first floor for stores
or shops, and a part of the second for offices if required ; put the whole building in charge of some responsible person disqualified for rugged labor, to be
let at reasonable rates, payable monthly in advance—the highest story not
more than fifty cents per bed-room.   Such an edifice (economizing the space
now required for cooking, washing, yard-room, &c.) might afford accommodations to families at $100 to $200, according to size and location ; while two
seamstresses might have an attic in common for one dollar each per month.
As each family could hire a parlor or bed-room (retained for this purpose) whenever it had company, no one need hire regularly any more room than it absolutely needed, while a large square in the center of the block should be embel-
lished with trees and shrubbery, gravel-walks, grass-plat and fountain.   One
such edifice, filled with tenants and paying ten per cent. to its owners, with a
liberal margin for repairs, would very soon be imitated and improved upon,
until our whole laboring population would be far better lodged than they now
are, at half the expense, while room would be made on our Island for thrice
the population it can stow away under the present architectural anarchy.   Pes-
tilence would be all but rendered impossible by this building reform."

These paragraphs, selected from more than a hundred of similar
tendency, will show better than ever so much statement by another

hand, what the nature of Horace Greeley's influence is upon the affairs of his time, and upon the conduct of those who value his opinion. That his practice and his preaching correspond, the reader is aware. He *knows* whereof he affirms, and his message is *exactly suited to our case;* hence, its power.

CHAPTER XXX.

APPEARANCE—MANNERS—HABITS.

His person and countenance—Phrenological developments—His rustic manners—Town eccentricities—Horace Greeley in Broadway—'Horatius' at church—Horace Greeley at home.

HORACE GREELEY stands five feet ten and a half inches, in his stockings. He weighs one hundred and forty-five pounds. Since his return from Europe in 1851, he has increased in weight, and promises to attain, in due time, something of the dignity which belongs to amplitude of person. He stoops considerably, not from age, but from a constitutional pliancy of the back-bone, aided by his early habit of incessant reading. In walking, he swings or sways from side to side. Seen from behind, he looks, as he walks with head depressed, bended back, and swaying gait, like an old man; an illusion which is heightened, if a stray lock of white hair escapes from under his hat. But the expression of his face is singularly and engagingly youthful. His complexion is extremely fair, and a smile plays ever upon his countenance. His head, measured round the organs of Individuality and Philoprogenitiveness, is twenty-three and a half inches in circumference, which is considerably larger than the average. His forehead is round and full, and rises into a high and ample dome. The hair is white, inclining to red at the ends, and thinly scattered over the head. Seated in company, with his hat off, he looks not unlike the 'Philosopher' he is often called; no one could take him for a common man.

According to the Phrenological Journal, his brain is *very* large, in the right place, well balanced, and of the best form, long, narrow, and high. It indicates, says the same authority, small animality and selfishness, extreme benevolence, natural nobleness, and loftiness of aim. His controlling organs are, Adhesiveness, Benevolence, Firmness, and Conscientiousness. Reverence is small; Destructiveness and Acquisitiveness less. Amativeness and Philoprogenitiveness are fully developed. The Love of Approbation is prominent; Self-Esteem not so. Resistance and Moral Courage are very full; Secretiveness full; Cautiousness large; Continuity small; Ideality fair; Taste *very* small; Imitation small; Mirthfulness very large; Eventuality and Comparison large; Language good; Reasoning better; Agreeableness deficient; Intuition great; Temperament active. His body, adds the Phrenologist, is not enough for his head. Time, as I have just remarked, is remedying that.

In manner, Horace Greeley is still a rustic. The Metropolis has not been able to make much impression upon him He lives amidst the million of his fellow-citizens, in their various uniforms, an unassimilated man.

Great, very great, as we all perceive, is the assimilating power of great cities. A youth comes here to New York, awkward, ill-dressed, bashful, and capable of being surprised. He visits his country home, after only a few years' residence in the city, a changed being; his clothes, his manners, his accent, and his affectations, are 'town-made.' His hair is shorter and more elaborately brushed; his words are fewer and he utters them in a lower tone; his collar is higher; he wears strange things fastened in a curious way; he gets up late in the morning, and takes his sustenance with a fork. The country people, the younger ones at least, are rather overawed by him, and secretly resolve to have their next coat made like his. What he calls his opinions, too, are not what they were. His talk is a languid echo of the undertone of conservative indifference which prevails in the counting-rooms where he has plied the assiduous pen, or wagged the wheedling tongue. He is, in a word, another man. He is a stranger in his father's house. He comes back to town, and, as years roll on, he hardens and sharpens into the finished citizen.

It is so with most, but not with all. Some men there are—very few, yet some—who resist effectually, and to the last, the assimilating influence of cities. These are the oddities, the stared-at, the

men of whom anecdotes are told. They are generally either much
wiser, or else much more nearly mad than their fellow-citizens.
Girard, the tough, sensible, benevolent banker of Philadelphia was
an oddity; and so was that other Philadelphian who placed all his
hopes of distinction upon his persistence in the practice of not
wearing a hat. Franklin was an oddity; and so was he who,
says popular tradition, took his nightly repose in a lime-kiln, and
never used a clothes-brush. It is best, perhaps, not to be odd; and,
certainly, the wisest man *need* not be. The saying of Goethe on
this subject seems good and commendable, that people who are
compelled to differ from the world in important things should take
all the more pains to conform to it in things unimportant. Yet all
large towns contain one or more—always one—of the eccentric
sort. It is a *way* large towns have.

I have seen Horace Greeley in Broadway on Sunday morning
with a hole in his elbow and straws clinging to his hat. I have
seen him asleep while Alboni was singing her grandest. When he
is asked respecting his health, he answers sometimes by the single
word 'stout,' and there the subject drops. He is a man who could
save a Nation, but never learn to tie a cravat; no, not if Brummell
gave him a thousand lessons.

The manner and style of the man, however, can best be shown
by printing here two short pieces of narrative, which I chance to
have in my possession. An enthusiastic youth, fresh from school
and the country, came a few years ago to the city to see the lions.
The following is a part of one of his letters home. He describes
'Horatius' at church, and does it well:

"I have seen Horace Greeley, sister mine, and I am going to tell
you all about it.

"It is Sunday morning. The weather is fine. The bells are
ringing. People are going to church. Broadway, from Grace
Church to the Battery, is fringed on both sides with a procession of
bright-colored fellow-creatures moving with less than their usual
languor, in the hope of not being too late at church. The steps of
the crowd, I observe, for the first time, are *audible*; for, no profane vehicle, no omnibus, cart, hack, or wagon, drowns all other
noises in their ceaseless thunder. Only a private carriage rolls
along occasionally, laden with a family of the uppermost thousand,

bound for Trinity or St. George's, or the Brick Chapel, where Dr.
Spring discourses of 'First Things' *to* First Things. It is possible
now, and safe, for the admiring stranger, your affectionate brother,
to stand in the middle of the street, and to discover that it is perfectly straight, from the rising ground above the Park to where the
tall, white spire of Grace Church, so strikingly terminates the beautiful promenade—a feat which no man hath been able to accomplish on a week-day these thirty years. The sun upon this cloud-
less morning brilliantly lights up the scene, and covers all things
with glory.

"I am among the church-goers, and I saunter down-town-wards.
I make my observations on the passing throng, and marvel chiefly
that, among so many countenances, so few should wear an expression of intelligence, so few even of bodily health, and wonder if,
after all, the nineteenth century is really and truly so great a century as it thinks it is. But there is walking just before me a man
whose contour, walk and attire, are strikingly different from those of
every other person in the crowd,—a tall man, slightly made, with a
stoop and shamble. I know not why it is, but I immediately
take that man to be *somebody*, a Western member of Congress, perhaps, and I am not at all surprised when I hear it whispered,
'That's Horace Greeley.' I prick up my ears, and resolve to follow him wherever he goes.

"Horatius, let me assure you, is a person in whose mind there
lingers none of childhood's reverence for the institution of Sunday
clothes. Do not conclude from this circumstance that he is one of
those superfine gentlemen who, in their magnanimous endeavor to
differ from the profane vulgar, contrive to be as shabbily dressed on
Sundays, when others dress in their best, as they are elegantly attired on Saturdays, when people in general are shabbiest. Horatius is no such person. No fine gentleman could be brought on any
terms to appear in Broadway in the rig he wore on this occasion.
My eye was first caught by his boots, which were coarse, large and
heavy, such as dangle from the ceiling of a country store, such as
'stalk a-field' when ploughmen go forth to plough. This particular
pair can *never*, in the whole course of their existence, have added
one farthing to the colossal fortune of Day and Martin. They were
spattered with mud, and so were the trowsers that, curtailed of

fair proportions, hung over their tops. His hat is a large, black beaver, and it certainly has known no touch of the brush since its maker gave it the finishing twirl, and pronounced it good. It differs from the hats of mankind in general, as an enraged porcupine differs from a porcupine whose evil passions slumber. It appears to have been thrown on his head, and has chanced to fall rather behind, like Sam Slick's. Fragments of straw adhere to the nap, as though the owner had been taking morning exercise in a stable. In truth, I hear that he *has* little faith in 'Orange County,' and keeps a cow. A very long, very loose, well-worn, white over-coat, with the collar standing up, and the long skirts flying behind, envelops the singular figure. This coat is long, apparently, because it was made a long time ago, before any Parisian or London tailor had from his back-shop issued to Christendom the mandate, 'LET THE OVER-COATS OF MANKIND BE WORN SHORT TILL FURTHER NOTICE.' There is, indeed, so little of the citizen in the appearance of the individual I am describing, that, if it were not Sunday, he would be taken, often must be taken, for a farmer just come to town upon a load of produce, who is now hurrying about the streets on errands for the good wife at home.

"On he goes, and I at his heels. At the door of the building known as the Stuyvesant Institute, he enters. A slight change, I perceive, has taken place in the exterior of this edifice since I passed it yesterday. The Daguerreotype-cases and exhibition transparencies have been removed, and over the door a signboard, similar in style and cost to those which tell a hungry public where Family Baking is done at ten and two, announces, that here the Independent Christian Society holds its meetings, and that the seats are Free. Other sign-boards about the door set forth the same facts. Fired by curiosity, and emboldened by the promised freedom of the seats, I enter, and find my way to the lecture room.

"It is a semi-circular apartment of six hundred medical student capacity, slanting steeply downward to the lecturer's platform. It is early, and only a few of the Independent Christians have arrived. Horatius, I see, has taken the seat nearest the door, and is already absorbed in the perusal of a newspaper, the London Times. With his hat off and his coat thrown open, he looks quite a different per

son. True, the newly-revealed garments are no more ornamental
than those I had already seen. It is clear that Beman's artistic
hand bore no part in the production of that crumpled shirt, nor in
the getting-up of that overlapping collar, nor in the frantic tie of
that disconsolate neckerchief. But the eye of the stranger rests not
upon these things; they are remembered afterwards; the stranger
is taken up in the contemplation of that countenance, upon which
Benignity's self has alighted, and sits enthroned on whitest ivory.
Such a face, so fair, so good! No picture has caught its expression,
at once youthful and venerable, at once feminine and manly. A
smile, like that which plays over a baby's face when it dreams,
rests ever on his countenance, and lends to it an indescribable
charm. It is expressive of inward serenity, kindliness of nature,
and blamelessness of life.

"The congregation assembles, and the room becomes half full.
The gentleman in the white coat continues to read. The preacher
arrives, the 'Rev. T. L. Harris,' a slender, pale, dark-haired, black-
eyed man, with the youthful look of seventeen. He glances at the
extremely Independent Christian with the newspaper, as he brushes
by, but receives no nod of recognition in return. He gains his place
on the platform, stands up to begin, the people fumbling for their
hymn-books. Horatius gives no sign; the Times possesses him
wholly. Will he read all through the service, and disconcert the
young minister? No. At the first word from the preacher's lips,
he drops the paper upon the bench, and addresses himself to—what
do you think? Meditation? Finding the hymn? Looking about
at the congregation? None of these. Leaning his white head upon
his fair, slender hand, and his elbow upon the back of the pew, he
closes his eyes, and instantaneously goes to sleep! Not Wellington,
nor Napoleon, nor Ney, nor Julius Cæsar, ever, after the longest
fight, was sooner in the land of dreams. To all appearance—
mind, I do not say it *was* so, but to all appearance—he was asleep
before the hymn had been read to the end. Overtasked nature will
assert and have her rights, and the weary wanderer find repose at
last. Horatius neither stands at the singing, nor during the prayer
does he assume any of the singular attitudes which are said to be
those of devotion, nor does he pay the slightest attention to the sermon, though it was a truly extraordinary performance, displaying a

mighty sweep of intelligence, an amazing fervency of hero-worship, and an unequaled splendor of illustration. It was delivered with a vehemence of affection that made the speaker's frail frame tremble, as though the spirit it encased were struggling to escape its tenement. And still the editor slept. Not a word of the sermon did he *seem* to hear, unless it was the last word; for, at the very last, he roused his drowsy powers, and as Mr. Harris sat down, Horace Greeley woke up. Refreshed by his slumbers, he looks about him, and, hearing the premonitory tinkle of the collection, he thrusts his hand into his pocket, draws forth a small silver coin, which he drops into the box, where it shines among the copper like a 'good deed in a naughty world.' The service over, he lingers not a moment, and I catch my last glimpse of him as he posts down Broadway toward the Tribune office, the white coat-tails streaming behind him, his head thrust forward into the FUTURE, his body borne along by the force of to-morrow's leading article. His appearance is decidedly that of a man of progress, and of progress against the wind, for his hat cannot quite keep up with his head. As he threads his way through the well-dressed throng, gentlemen tell ladies who he is, and both turn and gaze after him, till the ghostly garment is lost behind the many-colored clouds of silk and cashmere."

Thus wrote the enthusiastic, lion-loving youth. The scene now changes, and the time is put four or five years forward. Mr. Greeley, in the winter season, is " at home" on Saturday evenings to all callers. A gentleman attended one of the Saturday evenings last winter, took notes of what he saw and heard, which he has since kindly written out for insertion here :

" In point of pretension, Horace Greeley's house in Nineteenth street is about midway between the palaces of the Fifth Avenue and the hovels of the Five Points. It is one of a row of rather small houses, two and a half stories high, built of brick, and painted brown; the rent of which, I was told, is likely to be about seven hundred dollars a year. It was a chilly, disagreeable evening. I went early, hoping to have a little talk with the editor before other company should arrive. I rang the bell, and looked through the pane at the side of the door. The white coat was not upon its accustomed peg, and the old hat stuffed with newspapers was not in its usual place at the bottom of the hat-stand. Therefore 1 knew that the wearer of these articles was not at home, before the 'girl' told me so; but, upon her informing me that he was expected in a few minutes, I concluded to go in and wait. The entrance-hall is exceedingly narrow, and the stairs, narrower still, begin at a few feet from the door, affording room only for the hat-stand and a chair. The carpet on the stairs and hall was common in pattern, coarse in texture. A lady, the very picture of a prosperous farmer's wife, with her clean delaine dress and long, wide, white apron, stood at the head of the stairs, and came down to meet me. She lighted the gas in the parlors, and then, summoned by the crying of a child up stairs, left me to my observations.

"Neither I nor anybody else ever saw parlors so curiously furnished. There are three of them, and the inventory of the furniture would read thus:—One small mahogany table at the head of the front parlor; one lounge in ditto; eleven light cane-chairs in front and back parlors; one book-case of carved black-walnut in the small apartment behind the back parlor; and, except the carpets, not another article of furniture in either room. But the walls were almost covered with paintings; the mantel pieces were densely peopled with statuettes, busts, and medallions; in a corner on a pedestal stood a beautiful copy of (I believe) Powers' Proserpine in marble; and various other works of art were disposed about the floor or leaned against the walls. Of the quality of the pictures I could not, in that light, form an opinion. The subjects of more than half of them were religious, such as, the Virgin rapt; Peter, lovest thou me? Christ crowned with thorns; Mary, Joseph, and Child; Virgin and Child; a woman praying before an image in a cathedral; Mary praying; Hermit and Skull; and others. There were some books upon the table, among them a few annuals containing contributions by Horace Greeley, volumes of Burns, Byron, and Hawthorne, Downing's Rural Essays, West's complete Analysis of the Holy Bible, and Ballou's Voice of Universalism.

"I waited an hour. There came a double and decided ring at the bell. No one answered the summons. Another and most tremendous ring brought the servant to the door, and in a moment, the face of the master of the house beamed into the room. He apologized thus:—' I ought to have been here sooner, but I could n't.

He flung off his overcoat, hung it up in the hall, and looking into the parlor, said : ' Just let me run up and see my babies *one* minute ; I have n't seen 'em all day, you know ;' and he sprung up the stairs two steps at a time. I heard him talk in high glee to the children in the room above, for just ' one minute,' and then he re·joined me. He began to talk something in this style :

" ' Sit down. I have had a rough day of it—eaten nothing since breakfast—just got in from my farm—been up the country lecturing —started from Goshen this morning at five—broke down—crossed the river on the ice—had a hard time of it—ice a good deal broken and quite dangerous—lost the cars on this side—went *dogging* around to hire a conveyance—got to Sing Sing—went over to my farm and transacted my business there as well as I could in the time—started for the city, and as luck would have it, they had taken off the four o'clock train—did n't know that I should get down at all—harnessed up my own team, and pushed over to Sing Sing again—had n't gone far before snap went the whippletree—got another though— and reached Sing Sing just two minutes before the cars came along —I 've just got in—my feet are cold—let 's go to the fire.'

" With these words, he rose quickly and went into the back room, not to the fire-place, but to a corner near the folding door, where hot air gushed up from a cheerless round hole in the floor. His dress, as I now observed, amply corroborated his account of the day's adventures—shirt all crumpled, cravat all awry, coat all wrinkles, stockings about his heels, and general dilapidation.

" I said it was not usual at the West to go into a corner to warm one's feet ; to which he replied by quoting some verses of Holmes which I did not catch. I entreated him to go to tea, as he must be hungry, but he refused ' pine blank.' The conversation fell upon poetry. He said there was one more book he should like to make before he died, and that was a *Song-Book for the People.* There was no collection of songs in existence which satisfied his idea of what a popular song-book ought to be. He should *like* to compile one, or help do it. He said he had written verses himself, but was no poet ; and bursting into a prolonged peal of laughter, he added, that when he and Park Benjamin were editing the New Yorker, he wrote some verses for insertion in that paper, and showed them to ' Park,' and ' Park ' roared out, ' Thunder and lightning, Greeley, do you call *that* poetry?' Speaking of a certain well-known versifier, he said : 'He's a good fellow enough, but he can't write poetry, and if ——— had remained in Boston he would have killed him, he takes criticism so hard. As for me, I like a little opposition, I enjoy it, I can't understand the feeling of those thin-skinned people.'

"I said I had been looking to see what books he preferred should lie on his table. 'I don't prefer,' he said, 'I read no books. I have been trying for years to get a chance to read Wilhelm Meister, and other books. *Was* Goethe a dissolute man?' To which I replied with a sweeping negative. This led the conversation to biography, and he remarked, 'How many *wooden* biographies there are about. They are of no use. There are not half a dozen good biographies in our language. You know what Carlyle says : 'I want to know what a man eats, what time he gets up, what color his stockings are?' (His, on this occasion, were white, with a hole in each heel.) 'There's no use in any man's writing a biography unless he can tell what no one else can tell.' Seeing me glance at his pictures, he said he had brought them from Italy, but there was only one or two of them that he boasted of.

"A talk upon politics ensued. He said he had had enough of party politics. He would speak for temperance, and labor, and agriculture, and some other objects, but he was not going to stump the country any more to promote the interest of party or candidates. In alluding to political persons he used the utmost freedom of vituperation, but there was such an evident absence of anger and bitterness on his part, that if the vituperated individuals had overheard the conversation, they would not have been offended, but amused. Speaking of association, he said : 'Ah! our workingmen must be better educated : we must have better schools; they must learn to confide in one another more; then they will associate.' Then, laughing, he added : 'If you know anybody afflicted with democracy, tell him to join an association; *that* will cure him if anything will; still, association will triumph in its day, and in its own way.' In reply to G———'s definition of Webster as 'a petty man, with petty objects, sought by petty means,' he said : 'I call him a ——— ———; but his last reply to Hayne was the biggest speech yet made; it's only so long,' pointing to a place on his arm, 'but it's very great.' Another remark on another subject elicited from him the energetic assertion that the 'invention of the key was the devil's masterpiece.' Alluding to a recent paragraph of his, I said I thought it the best piece of English he had ever written. 'No,' he replied, ' there 's a bad repetition in it of the word *sober* in the same sentence; I can write better English than that.' I told him of the project of getting half a dozen of the best men and women of the country to join in preparing a series of school reading books. He said, ' They would be in danger of shooting over the heads of the children.' To which I replied: 'No; it is common men who do that; great men are simple, and akin to children.'

" A little child, four years old, with long flaxen hair and ruddy cheeks, came in and said, 'mother wants you up stairs.' He caught it up in his arms with every manifestation of excessive fondness, saying, 'No, you rogue, it 's *you* that want him ;' and the child wriggled out of his arms and ran away.

" As I was going, some ladies came in, and I remained a moment longer, at his request. He made a languid and quite indescribable attempt at introduction, merely mentioning the names of the ladies with a faint *bob* at each. One of them asked a question about Spiritualism. He said, 'I have paid no attention to that subject for two years. I became satisfied it would lead to no good. In fact, I am so taken up with the things of this world, that I have too little time to spend on the affairs of the other.' She said, ' a distinction ought to be made between those who investigate the phenomena *as* phenomena, and those who embrace them fanatically.' ' Yes,' said he, 'I have no objection to their being investigated by those who have more time than I have.' 'Have you heard,' asked the lady, ' of the young man who personates Shakspeare?' 'No,' he replied, ' but I am satisfied there is *no* folly it will *not* run into. Then he rose, and said, 'Take off your things and go up stairs. must get some supper, for I have to go to that meeting at the Tabernacle, to-night,' (anti-Nebraska.)

" As I passed the hat-stand in the hall, I said, 'Here is that immortal white coat.' He smiled and said, ' People suppose it 's the same old coat, but it is n't.' I looked questioningly, and he continued, 'The original white coat came from Ireland. An emigrant brought it out; he wanted money and I wanted a coat; so I bought it of him for twenty dollars, and it was the best coat I ever had. They do work *well,* in the old countries; not in such a hurry as we do.'

" The door closed, and I was alone with the lamp-post. In another hour, Horace Greeley, after such a day of hunger and fatigue, was speaking to an audience of three thousand people in the Tabernacle."

These narratives, with other glimpses previously afforded, will perhaps give the reader a sufficient insight into Horace Greeley's hurried, tumultuous way of life.

Not every day, however, is as hurried and tumultuous as this. Usually, he rises at seven o'clock, having returned from the office about midnight. He takes but two meals a day, breakfast at eight, dinner when he can get it, generally about four. Tea and coffee he drinks never; cocoa is his usual beverage. To depart from his usual routine of diet, or to partake of any viand which experience has shown to be injurious, he justly denominates a 'sin,' and 'groans' over it with very sincere repentance. A public dinner is one of his peculiar aversions; and, indeed, it may be questioned whether human nature ever presents itself in a light more despicable than at a public dinner, particularly towards the close of the entertainment. Mr. Greeley is a regular subscriber to the New York Tribune, and pays for it at the usual rate of one shilling a week. As soon as it arrives in the morning, he begins the perusal of that interesting paper, and examines every department of it with great care, bestowing upon each typographical error a heart-felt anathema. His letters arrive. They vary in number from twenty to fifty a day; every letter requiring an answer, is answered forthwith; and, not unfrequently, twenty replies are written and dispatched by him in one morning. In the intervals of work, there is much romping with the children. But two are left to him out of six. Toward noon, or soon after, the editor is on his way to his office.

Mr. Greeley has few intimate friends and no cronies. He gives no parties, attends few; has no pleasures, so called; and suffers little pain. In some respects, he is exceedingly frank; in others, no man is more reserved. For example—his pecuniary affairs, around which most men throw an awful mystery, he has no scruples about revealing to any passing stranger, or even to the public; and that in the fullest detail. But he can keep a secret with any man living, and he seldom talks about what interests him most. Margaret Fuller had a passion for looking at the naked souls of her friends; and she often tried to get a peep into the inner bosom of Horace Greeley; but he kept it buttoned close against her observation. Indeed, the kind of revelation in which she delighted, he entirely detests; as, probably, every healthy mind does.

He loves a joke, and tells a comic story with great glee. His cheerfulness is habitual, and probably he never knew two consecutive hours of melancholy in his life. His manner is sometimes ex ceedingly ungracious; he is not apt to suppress a yawn in the presence of a conceited bore; but if the bore is a bore innocently, he submits to the infliction with a surprising patience. He has a singular hatred of bungling, and rates a bungler sometimes with extraordinary vehemence. But he

> "Carries anger, as the flint bears fire;
> Who, much enforced, shows a hasty spark,
> And straight is cold again."

He clings to an opinion, however, or a prejudice, with the tenacity of his race; and has rarely been brought to own himself in the wrong. If he changes his opinion, which sometimes he does, he may show it by altered conduct, seldom by a confession in words.

His peculiarities of dress arise from two causes: 1. He is at all times deeply absorbed in the duties of his vocation, and cannot think of his dress without an effort: 2. He has (I think) the correct republican feeling, that no man should submit to have menial offices of a personal nature performed for him by another man. I mean, such offices as blacking boots, brushing clothes, etc.

19

CHAPTER XXXI.

CONCLUSION.

IF Horace Greeley were a flower, botanists would call him 'single,' and examine him with interest. Botanists find small pleasure in those plants, the pride of the garden, which have all gone to flower. They call them 'monsters.' Such are not beautiful to the eye of science, because they are not harmonious, culture having destroyed the natural proportion of their parts. Passing by, with indifference or disgust, the perfumed dandies and painted belles of the flower-garden, the botanist hangs with delight over the simple denizens of the wood-side and the wood-path. Horace Greeley is 'single.' He is what the Germans sometimes style 'a nature.' He is not complicated nor many-sided. He is the way he grew. Other men are like the walking-sticks in a bazaar. *He* was cut from the woods. The bark is on him, the knots are not pared smooth, the crooks have not been bent out, and all the polish he shows is derived from use, not varnish. He could say the first part of the catechism without telling a lie: Who made you? *God.* Walking-sticks often make the same reply, but not with truth. To say of most men in civilized countries that God made them, is rank flattery.

The character of a man is derived, 1, from his breed; 2, from his breeding; 8, from his country; 4, from his time. Horace Greeley's poetry, his humanity, his tenderness, all that makes him lovable and pleasing, his mother gave him, as her ancestors had given them her, with her Scottish blood. His nice sense of honor, his perseverance, his anxious honesty, his tenacity, all that renders him effective and reliable, he derived from his father, to whose English blood such qualities belong. He passed his childhood in republican, puritan New England, in a secluded rural region. Thence came his habits of reflection, his readiness, his independence, his rustic toughness and roughness. He is of this generation, and therefore he shares in the humanitary spirit which yearns in the bosom of every true

Saxon man that lives. He escaped the schools, and so passed through childhood uncorrupt, 'his own man,' not formed upon a pattern. He was not trained up—he grew up. Like a tree, he was left to seek the nourishment he needed and could appropriate. His breeding was unspeakably fortunate. It helped him much, hindered him little; and the result was, a man, not perfect indeed, very imperfect, as all men are, but a man, natural, peculiar, original, interesting; a man dear to other men, a man to whom other men are dear.

Of the countless gifts which God bestows upon man, the rarest, the divinest, is an ability to take supreme interest in human welfare. This has been called Genius; but what is here meant is more than genius; it *includes* genius; it is the parent and inspirer of genius; it is above genius. If any pious soul will accurately ascertain *what it is* in the character of the Man Christ Jesus, the contemplation of which fills his heart with rapture and his eyes with tears, that pious soul will know what is here intended by the expression 'supreme interest in human welfare.' The concurrent instinct of mankind, in all ages, in every clime, proclaims, that *this*, whatever it be named, is the divinest quality known to human nature. It is that which man supremely honors; and well he may. Most of us, alarmed at the dangers that beset our lives, distracted with cares, blinded with desire to secure our own safety, are absorbed in schemes of personal advantage. A few men go apart, ascend a height, survey the scene with serene, unselfish eye, and make discoveries which those in the heat of the struggle could never arrive at. But for such, the race of men would long ago have extirpated itself in its mad, blind strife. But for such, it would never have been discovered that what is not good for the whole swarm is not good for a single bee, that no individual can be safe in welfare, while any other individual is not.

Genius? No. That is not the word. Dr. Arnold was not a man of genius. Carlyle is not a man of genius. But Great Britain owes more to them than to all the men of genius that have lived since Cromwell's time. Such men differ from the poets and authors of their day, precisely in the same way, though not, perhaps, in the same degree, as the Apostles differed from Cicero, Seneca, and Virgil. Between the Clays and Websters of this country and Horace

Greeley, the difference is similar in *kind*. Horace Greeley, Thomas Carlyle, and Dr. Arnold, have each uttered much which, perhaps, the world will not finally accept. Such men seem particularly liable to a certain class of mistakes. But, says Goethe's immortal maxim, "The *Spirit* in which we act is the highest matter"—and it is the contagious, the influencing matter. "See how these Christians love one another." *That* was what made converts !

A young man of liberal soul, ardent mind, small experience, :mited knowledge, no capital, and few friends, is likely to be exceedingly perplexed on his entrance upon the stage of life. The difficulties in his own path, if he has a path, and the horrors that overshadow his soul, if he has not, call his attention in the most forcible manner to the general condition of mankind.

How unjust, how unnecessary, how inexplicable, it seems to his innocent mind, that a human being should be denied an opportunity to do the work for which he is fitted, to attain the blessed ness of which he is capable ! Surely, he thinks, a man is at least entitled to a FAIR START in the race of life, and to a course free from all obstructions except such as belong to the very nature of life. What a mockery, he thinks, is this Freedom which is said to be our birthright, while the Freedom which results from assured plenty, right education, and suitable employment, is attainable only by an inconsiderable few ? He is told, and he is glad to hear it, that the Prince of Wales and a few other boys, here and there in the world, are severely trained, scientifically taught, conveniently lodged, and bountifully provided for in every respect. And he learns with pleasure, that the Duke of Devonshire, and sundry other nobles, princes and millionaires, live in the midst of the means of delight and improvement, surrounded by every beautiful object known to art, at convenient access to all the sources of instruction. Free and far, over wide, enchanting domains, they range at their good pleasure, and wander when they will through groves, gardens, and conservatories. And far above all this, it is in their power deliberately to choose *what they will do* in their day and generation, and to bestow upon their offspring the same priceless freedom of choice. The rest of mankind are 'born thralls,' who toil from youth to hoary age, *apparently* for no other end than t › keep aloft on the splendid summit of affairs a few mortals of average merit.

Yet it is clear to our young friend, that whatever of essential dignity and substantial good is possessed by a few individuals, like those just named, it is within the compass of human talent and the Creator's bounty, to afford to all the family of man! In the contemplation of their possibility, and comparing it with the actual state of things, some of the finest spirits have gone distracted. Others have devoted themselves to impracticable schemes. Others have turned misanthropic, and others, philanthropic. Others have arrived, by degrees, at a variety of conclusions, of which the following are a few; that man is rather a weak creature, and it is doubtful whether it is worth while to take much interest in him; that, as a rule, man enjoys exactly as much freedom as he becomes fit for, and no more; that, except a man have not the necessaries of life, poverty is no evil; that to most men increase of possessions is not of the slightest advantage; that the progress of mankind in wisdom and self-command is so slow, that after two thousand years of Christianity, it is not self-evident that any true advance has been made, though the fact of an advance is probably susceptible of proof; that whatever *is*, is the best that *can* be in the circumstances; and finally, that a man may mind his own business, and let the world alone.

Others, on the contrary, come to very different conclusions. They perceive that man is so great, and wondrous, and divine a creature, that it is irrational, in fact *impossible*, to take a real and deep interest in anything not connected with his welfare. They believe in the *hourly* progress of the species. They discover that the fruits of a good life, a good deed, a good word, can no more be lost than the leaves are lost when they wither and disappear. They long for the time, and confidently expect it, and would fain do something to hasten it, when Man will come forth from his dismal den of selfishness, awake to the truth that the interest of each individual and the interest of the community are identical, strive *with* his fellow for the *general* good, and so cease to be a Prince in exile, in disguise, in sackcloth, and ascend the throne that is rightfully his, and sway, with magnificence and dignity worthy of him, his great inheritance. From the general tenor of Horace Greeley's words and actions, during the last twenty years, I infer that this is something like his habitual view of life and its duties. Shall he be praised for this? Let us envy him rather. Only such a man knows anything of the luxury of being alive. "Horace Greeley," said an old friend of his, "is the only happy man I have ever known."

The great object of Horace Greeley's personal ambition has been to make the Tribune the best newspaper that ever existed, and the leading newspaper of the United States. To a man inflamed with an ambition like this, the temptation to prefer the Popular to the Right, the Expedient to the Just, comes with peculiar, with un-equaled force. No pursuit is so fascinating, none so absorbing, none so difficult. The competition is keen, the struggle intense, the labor continuous, the reward doubtful and distant. And yet, it is a fact, that on nearly every one of its special subjects, the Tribune has stood opposed to the general feeling of the country. Its course on Slavery has excluded it from the Slave States; and if that had not, its elevated tone of thought would; for the southern mind is inferior to the northern. When the whole nation was in a blaze of enthusiasm about the triumphs of the Mexican war, it was not easy even for a private person to refrain from joining in the general huzza. But not for one day was the Tribune forgetful of the un-worthiness of those triumphs, and the essential meanness of the conflict. There were clergymen who illuminated their houses on the occasion of those disgraceful victories—one, I am told, who had preached a sermon on the *unchristian* character of the Tribune.

Mr. Greeley wrote, the other day:

"We are every day greeted by some sage friend with a caution against the certain wreck of our influence and prosperity which we defy by opposing the secret political cabal commonly known as 'the Know-Nothings.' One writes us that he procured one hundred of our present subscribers, and will prevent the renewal of their subscriptions in case we persist in our present course; another wonders why we *will* destroy our influence by resisting the popular current, when we might do so much good by falling in with it and guiding it and so on.

"To the first of these gentlemen we say—'Sir, we give our time and labor to the production of The Tribune, because we believe that to be our sphere of usefulness; but we shall be most happy to abandon journalism for a less anx-ious, exacting, exhausting vocation, whenever we are fairly and honorably released from this. You do not frighten us, therefore, by any such base ap-peals to our presumed selfishness and avarice; for if you could induce not merely your hundred but every one of our subscribers to desert us, we should cheerfully accept such a release from our present duties and try to earn a livelihood in some easier way. So please go ahead!'

"And now to our would-be friend who suggests that we are wrecking our influence by breasting the popular current: 'Good Sir! do you forget that whatever influence or consideration The Tribune has attained has been won, not by sailing with the stream, but *against* it? On what topic has it ever swam with the current, except in a few instances wherein it has aided to *change* the current? Would any one who conducted a journal for Popularity's or Pelf's sake be likely to have taken the side of Liquor Prohibition, or Anti-Slavery, or Woman's Rights, or Suffrage regardless of color, when we did? Would such a one have ventured to speak as we did in behalf of the Anti-Renters, when everybody hereabouts was banded to hunt them down unheard? Can you think it probable that, after what we have dared and endured, we are likely to be silenced now by the cry that we are periling our influence?'

    *   *   *   *   *   *   *   *   *

"And now, if any would prefer to discontinue The Tribune because it is and must remain opposed to every measure or scheme of proscription for opinion's sake, we beg them not to delay one minute on our account. We shall all live till it is our turn to die, whether we earn a living by making newspapers or by doing something else."

Every race has its own idea respecting what is best in the character of a man. The English admire 'pluck;' the French, adroitness; the Germans, perseverance; the Italians, craft. But when a Yankee would bestow his most special commendation upon another, he says, 'That is a man, sir, who generally *succeeds* in what he undertakes.' Properly interpreted, this is high, perhaps the highest, praise; for a man who succeeds in doing what he tries to do, must have the sense to choose enterprises suited to his abilities and circumstances. This praise, it is true, is frequently given to men whose objects are extremely petty—making a fortune, for example; but if those objects were such as they could attain, if enterprises of a higher nature were really beyond their abilities, how much wiser is it in them to attempt petty objects only! But whatever may be the value of the American eulogy—and a Yankee is an American, only more so—it may most justly be bestowed upon Horace Greeley. Whatever he has attempted, he has done as well as, or better than, any one else had done it before him. A piously generous son, a perfect pupil, an apprentice of ideal excellence, a journeyman of unexampled regularity, perseverance, and effectiveness. His New Yorker was the best paper of its class that had been published. The Jeffersonian and Log Cabin excelled all previous and all subsequent 'campaign papers.' The Tribune is our best daily paper. As a member of Congress, he was truer to himself, and dared more in behalf of his constituents, than any man who ever sat for one session only in the House of Representatives. In Europe, he retained possession of all his faculties! In the presence of nobles, he was thoroughly himself, and he spoke eloquently for the toiling million. Emphatically, Horace Greeley is a man, sir, who has generally succeeded in what he has undertaken.

But not always. He tried hard to get Henry Clay elected president. He tried long to wield the whig party for purposes of general beneficence. Neither of these objects could he accomplish.

Of Horace Greeley's talents as a writer little need be said. A man whose vocation obliges him frequently to write at the rate of a column an hour, and who must always write with dispatch, can rarely produce literature. Nor can any man write with faultless accuracy who is acquainted with no language but that in which he writes. But Horace Greeley writes well enough for his purpose, and has given proof, in many a glowing passage and telling argument, of a native talent for composition, which, in other circumstances, might have manifested itself in brilliant and lasting works.

His power as a writer arises from his earnestness of conviction, from his intimate acquaintance with the circumstances and feelings of his readers, from his Scotch-Irish fertility in illustration, and from the limited range of his subjects. He says not many things, but much.

His forte is, as I have said, in making practical suggestions for the better conduct of life and affairs. Like Franklin, he confines himself chiefly to the improvement of man's condition in material things; but he is a better man than Franklin; he is Franklin liberalized and enlightened; he is the Franklin of this generation. Like Franklin, too, and like most of the influencing men of this age, he is more pious than religious, more humane than devout.

The reader need not be detained here by remarks upon Horace Greeley's errors of opinion. A man's opinions are the result, the entirely inevitable result of his character and circumstances. *Sin-*

cerity, therefore, is our only just demand when we solicit an expression of opinion. Every man thinks erroneously. God alone knows *all* about anything. The smallest defect in our knowledge, the slightest bias of desire, or fear, or habit, is sufficient to mislead us. And in truth, the errors of a true man are not discreditable to him; for his errors spring from the same source as his excellences. It was said of Charles Lamb, that he liked his friends, not in spite of their faults, *but faults and all!* and I think the gentle Charles was no less right than kind. The crook, the knot, and the great humpy excrescences are as essential features of the oak tree's beauty, as its waving crown of foliage. Let Horace Greeley's errors of opinion be what they may, he has done something in his day to clarify the truth, that no error of opinion is a hundredth part as detrimental to the interest of men as the forcible suppression of opinion, either by the European modes of suppression, or the American. He has made it easier than it was to take the unpopular side. He has helped us onward towards that perfect freedom of thought and speech which it is fondly hoped the people of this country are destined in some distant age to enjoy. Moreover, a critic, to be competent, must be the superior of the person criticised. The critic is a judge, and a judge is the highest person in the court, or should be. This book is a chronicle, not an opinion.

And to conclude, the glory of Horace Greeley is this: He began life as a workingman. As a workingman, he found out, and he experienced the disadvantages of the workingman's condition. He rose from the ranks to a position of commanding influence. But he ceased to be a workingman *with* workingmen, only to become a workingman *for* workingmen. In the editor's chair, on the lecturer's platform, on the floor of Congress, at ducal banquets, in good report and in ill report, in the darkest days of his cause as in its brightest, against his own interest, his own honor, his own safety, he has been ever true, in heart and aim, to his order, *i. e.* his countrymen. In other lands, less happy than ours, the people are a class; here we are all people; all together we must rise in the scale of humanity, or all together sink.

A great man? No. A great man has not recently trod this continent—some think not since Columbus left it. A model man? No. Let no man be upheld as a model. Horace Greeley has tried

to be his 'own man.' Be you yours. "I rejoice," says Miss Bre-
mer, "that there *is* such a person as Fanny Kemble; but I should
be sorry if there were two." The spirit of goodness is ever the
same; but the modes of its manifestation are numberless, and every
sterling man is original.

Reader, if you like Horace Greeley, do as well in your place, as
ne has in his. If you like him not, do better. And, to end with a
good word, often repeated, but not too often: "THE SPIRIT IN
WHICH WE ACT IS THE HIGHEST MATTER."

DUE

DUE

6/7/83

3/20/84

9/12/84

10/23/86

4-8-87

1·19·89

1/15/96

UX 000 503 635

UX 000 503 635

Check Out More Titles From HardPress Classics Series In this collection we are offering thousands of classic and hard to find books. This series spans a vast array of subjects – so you are bound to find something of interest to enjoy reading and learning about.

Subjects:
Architecture
Art
Biography & Autobiography
Body, Mind &Spirit
Children & Young Adult
Dramas
Education
Fiction
History
Language Arts & Disciplines
Law
Literary Collections
Music
Poetry
Psychology
Science
…and many more.

Visit us at www.hardpress.net